BUY
or
RUN

October 2013

Cover by: St. Jacobs Printery, Ontario Canada

Formatting and Layout by: St. Jacobs Printery, Ontario Canada

Printed by: Edwards Brothers Malloy, Michigan USA

Contact www.BuyorRunBook.com for;

• E-Book & Canadian retail sales

• For educational purposes

• Requests for speaking engagements

• Other information

Canada ISBN 978-0-9920990-0-8

Published by:

The Inspectors International Press Inc

www.TheInspectorsInternationalPress.com

BUY
or
RUN

I'm a Real Home Inspector
Not a TV Celebrity!

by
Bruce McClure
RHI, ACI

Table of Contents

Dedication 1

About The Author 3

CHAPTER ONE: **Introduction** 7

CHAPTER TWO: **Industry Overview** 11

  Home Inspections: Where Do You Get Your Information?.... 11

    Story #1: Electrical Inspector's 40 Stops............................14

    Story #2: Talk Soft Write Hard / Leaking Oil Tank..................17

    Story #3: Wrong Listing Information 17

    Story #4: Is This A Finished Basement ? 18

    Story #5: TV Sensationalism 19

  National Associations 22

CHAPTER THREE: **Real Estate Industry**...........................23

  Statistics And Real Estate Market Overview.......................... 23

  Do They Really Make That Much Money? 24

  About The Real Estate Transaction 27

    Story #6: Seller Provides Furnace Servicing.........................31

    Story #7: Seller To Provide Basement Kitchen 31

    Story #8: Seller To Shingle Roof And Vent Attic......................32

    Story #9: Seller Agreed To Repair Foundation Crack 32

    Story #10: Seller Contracted To Finish Major Renovations.......32

The Home Inspection Clause 33

Multiple Offers... 35

Realtor-Bashing Aside... 35

    Story #11: We'll Call This One Realtor "A" 36

    Story #12: We'll Call This One Realtor "B" 37

More About Realtors 38

Home Renovations... 38

CHAPTER FOUR: **New Homes And Condominiums** 41

New Homes 41

    Story #13: New Home Pre-Delivery Inspection 44

    Story #14: Two Identical Houses / Same Builder 45

Condominiums 46

    Story #15: Jumping Fish...48

    Story #16: Retirement Community Reserve Fund 48

    Story #17: Condo Electrical Panel 50

    Story #18: Three X $10K Special Assessments 50

    Story #19: "We Know Everything; We Watch TV" 51

CHAPTER FIVE: **Who's Setting The Standards?** 53

Inspection History In The USA... 56

Inspection History In Canada.. 57

Why An Association?... 59

A Word About Licensing 61

It's Not Just Education, Qualifications And Licensing.......... 64

CHAPTER SIX: **What's A Real Home Inspection All About?** 67

    Story #20: Older Gentleman, Get Me Out Of This.............68

Standards Of Practice 68

Standards Of Care, Duty Of Care And Code Of Conduct.... 70

Limitations... 71

Risk Management... 73

Story #21: On The Job Knee Infection 75
Story #22: Mold And Lawyer's Letter 75
Story #23: Inspector Next Door At Same Time 76
Story #24: Hurricane Destroys House 76
Inspection Report 77
Inspection Tools 79
Story #25: First Day With Moisture Meter 80
Story #26: Carbon Monoxide Meter 80
The Inspection 81
So What Makes A Good Home Inspector? 85
Story #27: I'll Judge You By Your Web-Site 86

CHAPTER SEVEN: Myths About Home Inspection 89
New Homes & Condominiums Don't Need A Home Inspection ...90
The Inspector's Insurance Will Pay For That 91
Story #28: Missing Heating Ducts 92
Infrared, The Latest Myth In Home Inspection 92
Story #29: Home Inspector Showing Off 97
Story #30: Good Use Of A High-Priced Moisture Meter 98
Story #31: Thermography: Flat Roof, Three Visits 98
Story #32: Thermography And The Shower Leak 98

CHAPTER EIGHT: About The Seller/Homeowner 101
Tips For The Homeowner/Seller 101
Story #33: Impressed Homeowner 103
Cover-Ups 104
Story #34: Plumbing Cover-Up 104
Story #35: No Septic / Realtor Says, "Don't Tell Anyone" 106

CHAPTER NINE: Hiring A Home Inspector 109
Questions You Should Be Asking 110
The Inspection Contract 113

Franchises..114

Errors And Omissions Insurance: 115

Title Insurance 116

Story #36: Old Furnace And Lawyer's Letters 117

CHAPTER TEN: **Other Types Of Inspections** 119

Pre-Purchase Inspection....................................120

Pre-Offer Inspection 120

New Home Or Pre-Delivery Inspection..............120

New Construction Inspection By Municipal Building Officials...121

Rural, Well & Septic Inspection 122

Story #37 Septic Pumping..................................125

Walk-Through Inspection 125

Pre-Listing Inspection.......................................126

Maintenance Inspection 127

Limited/Partial Inspection 128

Callback Inspection 128

Pre-Renovation Inspection.................................129

Story #38: Renovation Quotes 129

Indoor Air Quality Inspection And Sick Homes 130

Mold And Mold Inspections..............................133

Story #39: Open House Mold 135

Story #40: Mold Inspection................................136

Radon Inspection 137

Heat Loss Analysis/Energy Audit 140

Insurance Inspections 140

Appraisal 141

Infrared (Thermography) Inspection 142

Wood-Burning Appliances WETT Inspection: 143

Pest Control Inspections 143

Other Inspection Services Provided By Home Inspectors 144

CHAPTER ELEVEN: When Things Don't Work Out 145

   Story #41: My Plumbing Doesn't Work! 146

Unhappy Seller And Unhappy Realtors 147

   Story #42: Re-Build Roof, Mold, Aluminum Wiring 148

   Story #43: Sump Pump Not Connected To Weepers 149

   Story #44: I'll Buy You A Can Of Tar 150

   Story #45: Wait And Watch The Shingles 150

   Story #46: Carbon Monoxide Detector 151

   Story #47: I Don't Want This House / The Peach 152

Electricity Supply Issue, Another Surprise 152

   Story #48: Surprise Electrical Bills 157

CHAPTER TWELVE: The Future 159

Who's In Charge? 160

The Public's Perceived Value And Willingness To Pay 160

Price / Pie Chart 163

My Dream List 165

Untapped Opportunity / North America's Used
   Housing Inventory 167

Final Comments 169

Appendix 171

Dedication

To the forerunners of the home inspection industry who saw the need for rules and regulation and devoted their volunteer time and efforts to building ASHI (American Society of Home Inspectors) and CAHPI (Canadian Association of Home & Property Inspectors) and their chapters.

To those that helped me learn my skill as a home inspector, encouraged my efforts and on occasion corrected me and gave a push when needed.

To my peer reviewers in both the USA & Canada;
Steve Gladstone ACI, Blaine Swan RHI, ACI, Pam Sayne RHI, Peter Weeks RHI

To the support team at St. Jacobs Printery for their patience and dedication. May they survive a second 100 years in the industry;

To my research assistant for his all around general support and continued encouragement; Stephen Duncan.

To all, a sincere *"Thank You"*

Bruce McClure RHI, ACI

About The Author

- The authors first major construction project involved building a foundation, picking up an existing building and moving it to the foundation before renovating it.

- In addition to renovations and commercial construction, today he as has both designed and been the general contractor for a number of custom homes.

- Since 1998 he's been in the front lines as a practicing home inspector and received his RHI (Registered Home Inspector) designation from OAHI/CAHPI Ont. (Ontario Association of Home Inspectors / Canadian Association of Home and Property Inspectors Ontario) the following year.

- Since 2003 he's been the coordinator of the Home Inspection Program at Conestoga College in Kitchener, Ontario where he also serves as a facilitator (teacher) for the program.

- In 2010 he became an ACI (ASHI Certified Inspector / member of the American Society of Home Inspectors)

- He is a past board member of the OAHI, (Ontario Association of Home Inspectors) the group that since 1994 has had the directive from the Ontario government to maintain the RHI standard for home inspectors.

- He served as the CAHPI President (The Canadian Association of Home and Property Inspectors) during the winter of 2001/2)

- To round out his background, in 2008 he took a three-year sabbatical from inspections and acquired his real estate license in order to better understand the other side of the real estate transaction. To avoid conflict of interest he has since given up that license.

- In 2010, having been involved in property management for a number of years, he incorporated a property management company, CondoEase Your Home Canada, Inc.

CHAPTER ONE: Introduction

"It's 8 a.m., I'm just about to step out of my van as I feel a dark cloud fall over me. Pausing slightly I look up to see a realtor step out of her black Mercedes scowling at me, ready to do battle, ready to protect her sale because the client had picked me, a noted "Deal Killer", and not one of her favored "Blind Eyed Home Inspectors". And that's how my day all too often starts."

As the subtitle states, I'm a real home inspector and not a manufactured TV celebrity or one with made-up credentials behind my name. I'm not one that turns a blind eye to issues in order to help a realtor close the deal. In the big picture I see myself as an advocate for the house, while at the same time protecting the best interests of my client. Writing this book is my way of saying that I'm fed up with self-serving television sensationalism and with realtors who are more interested in promoting less-than-reputable or unqualified inspectors. Inspectors that daily play down and turn a blind eye to serious issues and defects in order to save the realtors sale and commission. I'm fed up with television and realtors trying to run my industry. In this book I'm shooting straight from the hip to set the record straight and to expose some of the facts about who is really working for you and who is pretending to work for you while in reality are only looking out for their own personal best interests, at your expense!

Although I'm a real home inspector from the front lines of the home inspection industry, I'm not here to defend home inspectors. Although I'm opinionated (as most inspectors are), my ego doesn't require attention and I don't claim to be a hero. This book is simply based on facts as I know them and personal experience. Whereas we're all familiar with the phrase "Truth is stranger than fiction," I'm often quoted as saying, "Just when you think you've seen it all, there's always tomorrow...!" You should find that the first few chapters serve as an overview; many of the topics touched on there will be elaborated on in later chapters.

Unlike television celebrities or news broadcasters who's job it is to entertain, I don't have an international stage with script writers or thousands of emails from disenfranchised homebuyers with stories to capitalize on. Instead, I've actually been trained and practiced as a home inspector for 15 years. Combining this experience with having designed and built custom homes, been a practicing realtor, taught dozens of new inspectors, performed a few thousand real inspections and having been actively involved with our professional associations, I feel that I'm qualified to comment on the state of the industry. *(see About the Author for details)*. Although I practice in Ontario, Canada, my professional association involvement keeps me abreast of the national picture in both Canada and the United States. Although we have major geographical differences we are united regarding the majority of our industry problems. Where the USA have been both the industry forerunner and leader, it's this little guy from the north who's prepared to stand up and, although politically incorrect, discuss the missing links that others only talk about behind closed doors!

Besides moving a building at age 16, I acquired my introduction to property management and maintenance when my parents decided to purchase an investment property. Dad was always the organizer, Mom was appointed the decorator and I the handyman. Since then I have owned and managed a significant number of different houses, large, small, city and country, as well as vacation properties and office buildings.

From scratch I've designed and been the general contractor for three custom homes, dug wells, laid septic beds, designed and poured footings and foundations by hand. Most recently I was trained and have personally installed two geothermal heating systems. As a divorce survivor, I understand what it's like to start over by purchasing and fixing up a duplex where my downstairs tenants paid the mortgage and I lived upstairs before moving on and holding it as an investment property. I've worked on commercial projects in malls, government buildings, schools and hospitals.

In the world of home inspection, there are many inspectors who know more than I do and others who know less. The one thing that I feel confident in saying is, the list of inspectors who know less than I do is far longer than the list of those who know more. But no matter where any of us stand in such a grand list, seasoned or new, we all bring some special knowledge to the table. Those of us involved in professional associations are required to annually upgrade our education and, simply by associating with fellow inspectors, are continuously learning from each other.

I stress that I'm only writing about things I know through personal first hand experience. All the "stories" and "picture stories" are from my personal files. Where as there are days that I think I'm just getting old and crotchety, it's my hope that this book will help inform readers while righting some of the wrongs and misunderstandings that have been perpetrated by the media, realtors and blind eyed inspectors, towards the home inspection industry.

I'm sure that you'll find a number of my stories as disturbing as they are entertaining, but again they are true. Like most of you, I'm just another little guy in a world of little guys who are dominated by big guys and corporations that hide behind money, bureaucracy, lawyers, legislation and media campaigns which, for the most part, simply piss me off! In the following pages I'm going to unmask a number of those so called respectable institutions and individuals who have involved themselves in our industry and are hiding behind regulation, media glitz and questionable qualifications in order to pull the wool over your eyes.

Again, I'm not here to defend or paint a rosy picture of home inspectors. I'm here to explain what you should know and who you can trust regarding home inspections. In a number of cases I'll expose what is really going on in the industry along with things that are not beneficial to you. At the end of the day it's safe to say that I've always considered myself a bit of an activist and champion of the little guy. As those around me often referred to me as being "passionate" about my beliefs, I, along with many other professional home inspectors, consider ourselves as "advocates of the house" and do our best to speak to our clients on behalf of the house. In the pages to follow, it's my objective to supply you with insight and information in order to help you protect yourself when making decisions about buying or selling property, choosing a home inspector, realtor or even entering the industry as a home inspector or realtor.

For any law makers or legislators I'm also going to be explaining why some of your assumptions may be misguided. I'll explain a number of the missing links as to why your rules and systems do not work as well as they could.

welcome to my world...

CHAPTER TWO: Industry Overview

Home Inspections:
Where Do You Get Your Information?

Whether you are shopping for a home, have had a home inspection and wonder how it stacks up, or are thinking of becoming a home inspector or even a realtor, I'm sure that many of you already have a number of preconceived ideas as to what a home inspector is or should be. Am I right? So, what I'm going to ask you to do right now is set aside those opinions and read on with an open mind. Then, once you've read and digested the information that I'm sharing with you, look back and see how close you were. Have I challenged you? Great! Now we'll move ahead as I try to be objective, informative and, by adding a few war stories, keep things entertaining as well …

During my sabbatical as a realtor I had the privilege of working for a particularly talented individual who provided me with many opportunities and a continual flow of quality advice. During the 2008–2010 economic slump when every television newscast and newspaper headline in the country wanted to talk about how bad things were and about the decline in the residential real estate market, his business flourished and continued to grow. Getting frustrated with clients and potential clients continually trying to tell him how bad it was, he finally coined one of the best phrases I've learned over the years. He simply looked the person straight in the eye and asked, "Where are you getting your information from?" followed by the statement, "My sales have continued to grow by X% (and trust me, he had the percentage numbers memorized) and month after month we're setting sales records!" *(Please note, you folks south of the border; don't jump to conclusions; this had nothing to do with defaults and/or selling short. His success was based on good old-fashioned hard work and honest salesmanship!)* So borrowing his line and applying it to the home inspections I have to ask, "Where are you getting your information about home inspections and home inspectors?"

As the home inspection industry grows, it's difficult, even for inspectors, to keep up with the changes. Although ASHI (American Society of Home Inspectors) in the USA and CAHPI (Canadian Association of Home and Property Inspectors) in Canada are the longstanding formal associations, membership remains optional. Home buyers and sellers are often surprised to find that a number of states and the majority of provinces do not have legislation regarding home inspectors, what their qualifications should be and what they should be doing. In states and provinces that do have regulation and licensing, the qualifications vary dramatically. If you're in an area where there are no regulations or licensing virtually anyone can print a business card and declare themselves a Home Inspector.

Most people have read news headlines or watched reality television programming regarding unsuspecting homebuyers who have hired a home inspector only to end up with a house full of horrors! In this book we're going to talk about why that happens more often than it should – and you may be surprised at the answer. To get started I'm going to pose three questions and follow with answers/discussion on each:

1. Q-1 Were the homebuyer's/seller's expectations realistic?

2. Q-2 Were the issues really due to the inspector's lack of knowledge and skill or did the inspector have a different agenda?

3. Q-3 Who hired the inspector and who was the inspector really working for?

■ ANSWER 1 – Were the homebuyer's/seller's expectations realistic?

Since in many areas home inspection remains unregulated, potential clients don't know where to turn for accurate information. Cruising the internet for legitimate associations and standards of practice is as confusing as trying to sort out the qualifications and claims from individual inspectors who lead people into believing that they have cameras that can see through walls and see things like mold. I've actually had clients who thought I was going to lift every carpet and move every piece of furniture in the house—all in a couple of hours!

Sensationalistic news reporting often blows things out of proportion, frightens people and raises their expectations. So-called reality TV has created a lot of unrealistic expectations by exposing, after the fact, what it considers to be bad inspections. It's easy in any line of work whether it be home inspection, contracting or even proof reading that email you wrote yesterday, for someone to come along and have a second look (especially with no time restrictions on their investigation) and say, "Well, they should have seen that!"

Further, we have one major television celebrity, who for years built his persona around the theme of "Hire a professional and not a DIY" an old acronym for the Do It Yourselfer that he promulgated. Then out of the blue he declared himself, with no formal training or experience in pre-purchase home inspections, the industry expert on home inspections (a true DIY). He implies that most home inspectors are incompetent and that he's the hero because, after the fact with no restrictions or time limitations, he can say the inspector was wrong and again imply that he could have done better because he's the industry expert. No wonder people are often confused by entertainment vs facts and have unrealistic expectations.

We will be discussing the inspector's limitations later in the book, but the basic fact that people must realize is that the home inspector is a guest in another person's house and is limited to a visual inspection and testing of standard operating controls only. Further, there is the public perception that a home inspection has a very low dollar value and should be performed in an unrealistically short time. When I introduce myself to homeowners at the door prior to an inspection, I'm continually told, "Well, the realtor said you'd only be here for 20 minutes!" Early in my career I heard of a court judge who made a very poignant statement along the line of "Nowhere else is someone expected to do so much for so little in such a short period of time," when describing a home inspection. Also it has to be realized that it's not uncommon that prior to the inspection, the homeowner/seller has gone to great lengths to temporarily hide major and expensive defects from the inspector.

Contrary to what is thought by many, a home inspection is not a building code inspection and a home inspector does not "pass" or "fail" a house. Generally a code inspection can be performed only at the time of and during the various stages of construction. Typically, a qualified home inspector will spend more time in a home than municipal building officials did during its original construction.

STORY #1: Electrical Inspector's 40 Stops
One day at lunch my electrician friend told me about an electrical inspector who had shown up at his job site that week to inspect the electrical work. The inspector was rushed and explained that he had 40 job sites to inspect that day. In an 8-hour day, that works out to 12 minutes per inspection without any allowance for travel time!

In my final comment regarding expectations, this is one of the few times in the book that I'll step up on my soapbox and share a couple of frustrating observations in the defense of inspectors.

The Home Inspector:

- Is allowed an unrealistically short period of time to perform his work and is expected to give instant answers.

- Is expected to work under the most limiting of conditions.

- Is just about the lowest paid individual in the real estate transaction, but carries the largest liability!

■ **ANSWER 2 – Were the issues really due to the inspector's lack of knowledge and skill or did the inspector have a different agenda?**
The reality is, for the most part, the home inspection industry is driven by the real estate community simply because the realtor has first contact and the most influence over the potential home inspection client. Although we have many high quality realtors there are a large number that don't want to risk their potential sale/paycheck with a thorough home inspection and often push for an inspector who's going to soft sell and turn a blind eye to issues in order to avoid "blowing the deal." Often realtors refer to home inspectors such as myself and my peers as "deal killers"! As a home inspector I am simply advising on the home's condition. The decision to *buy or run* rests solely with the prospective buyer. In my community, many of the most qualified professional inspectors have been (unofficially, of course) "blacklisted" by the real estate community and clients are simply told that they are not allowed to use us as inspectors. Other realtors are even bold enough to say to their client, "If he does your home inspection, you won't buy the house!"

My personal record is, in one single week, I had three separate clients phone me, after booking an inspection, explaining that they had to cancel because their realtor would not allow me to do their home inspection! In my files I have the original copy of an offer where I witnessed the realtor hand-write, on the offer to purchase, that a particular home inspector (one of the most qualified in the industry) was not allowed to do the home inspection and then demand that the client sign it. I've also had a real estate broker inform me that the same thing has happened, naming myself as the inspector that's not allowed. In other cases, I've seen situations where the real estate company has their own inspector and provides the inspector as part of their real estate package. Is this not a blatant conflict of interest?

Because of the above statements, we have a large number of what I call BEIs' (blind-eyed inspectors). To assure future business and realtor referrals, this caliber of inspector simply turns a blind eye and either doesn't report on issues, or soft-sells them in order to protect the realtor's sale and not be a "deal killer." Obviously this group is not working for their client (the buyer). Their actions contribute to a lack of trust towards home inspectors and add fuel to the media horror stories. In far too many cases, it's not the inspector's skills that are an issue. It's too often more about what the inspector's real objective is and who they are really working for.

When taking my sabbatical and setting up my real estate business, like all other good realtors, I went to work accumulating a database. Now in the grand scheme of things as a home inspector, I typically never really knew if my clients had proceeded to purchase the house that I had inspected or not. Based on the number of repeat inspections that I'd performed, I had a good idea that a fair number of them had not completed the transaction. Actually, a few had not bought a house at all because they were so disillusioned with what was available in their price range.

Going through my files to form a mailing list and re-contact previous clients, I was amazed to discover by the volume of returned mail that between 20-25% had declined to purchase the house that I'd inspected for them. No wonder so many realtors hated me!

The Catch-22 (as us old guys say) of this is that in practice a home inspector's best and most cost effective way of advertising is through the real estate community. For those of us labeled "Deal Killers", the real estate community can also be the kiss of death for our businesses.

It's always frustrating when a realtor doesn't want something pointed out during the inspection, but once their client moves in and there's a problem, the realtors are the first to say, "Well, the inspector should have seen that!" I was quite disturbed by the following experience which best explains where I'm going with this.

STORY #2: Talk Soft Write Hard / Leaking Oil Tank

I was at a study group where an inspector who works for a high-profile franchise shared a story about discovering a leaking oil tank that was sitting on a dirt floor in the basement of a house he'd recently inspected. When asked by one of the others in the room how he reported this to his client, he replied (although not his exact words), "Well, I didn't want to upset anyone, so I didn't say anything. I just wrote it in my report!" (Industry experience shows that typical clients do not read the inspection report until after they've purchased the house, moved in and found a problem) For those of you who don't understand the consequences of leaking oil tanks, they can be more costly than the price of the property to remediate (clean up). It's obvious why this inspector gets a lot of referral business from realtors.

STORY #3: Wrong Listing Information

House # A

This house was listed as having a forced air heating system and 200-amp electrical service. It was a four-level side split in Ontario that had only two decorative gas fireplaces, one in each end of the house—no furnace, no forced air, simply no heating system. The 200-amp electrical service was 60-amps. When I reported this the realtor went crazy on me, as if somehow this was all my fault!

House # B

This was a very large house with a complicated roofing system. As I was coming off my ladder, the realtor made a comment about it being a new roof. I responded with, "New, yes—about 25 years ago!" Everyone was very upset. The amazing part was that night we had six inches of snow, our very first of the season. If the inspection had been the next day, I'd have seen nothing.

House # C

Listed as upgraded electrical with a new 200-amp service, the electrical panel itself was nailed to a single 2x4 loosely propped up in the middle of the basement. It was quite simple to follow the wires and discover that the new 200-amp panel was being fed by an antique 40-amp main meaning it was only a 40-amp electrical service.

STORY #4: Is This A Finished Basement ?

Outside, the garage was literally falling over. The overhead car door was stuck part way up and the man-door was jammed half way open as well. When I explained to my client that the garage was unsafe—it could collapse onto the neighbor's property with one good wind or snowstorm—she broke down and started crying. Inside the house the basement was open with a fully exposed stone foundation, but at one point the floor had been painted. My client came over to me and whispered so the realtor couldn't hear, "Is this a finished basement? The realtor told me it was a finished basement." Again my client was in tears. At that point I called a time out and phoned her boyfriend, who had dropped her off earlier for the inspection, to come back and give her some support. When I told them that the furnace was over 12 years old, again she answered that the listing said it was new (anticipated life span for an average furnace is 20 years). My client did not buy the house, changed realtors and, a couple weeks later, I inspected a beautiful little house that met her real needs.

A few months later I showed up to another inspection and was greeted by the same realtor. She immediately started by yelling at me for a full half hour about costing her the sale and the client and that I'd better not blow this deal!

STORY #5: TV Sensationalism

It always frustrates me how information about my industry is presented by self-serving individuals and organizations for their personal gain in the race to elevated TV ratings. After a very negative television documentary regarding home inspectors was aired on national television I was at a seminar where the speaker, a long-term associate of mine, talked about his involvement in the program. He had been hired as the proclaimed "expert" to make comments during the documentary. He explained how the program was staged. First, the television people hired a number of inspectors who they felt would be the less qualified. Then they set up a house and, without the inspectors' knowledge, recorded the inspections. (I'm not a lawyer but I call that "entrapment.") Then, in order to create their documentary, they edited and manipulated the information to create the most sensationalism possible for their viewing audience. The real kicker was that they also edited the expert's comments (interchanging their questions and his answers) in order to make him look like a fool as well! Don't believe everything you see or hear on television.

■ ANSWERS 3 – Who hired the inspector and who is the inspector really working for?

Putting aside the "morality" question of "Who is the inspector working for?" as discussed previously, here we will briefly touch on the legal contract. Often there is confusion as to whom the home inspector is working for and where their contractual obligations lie. Although a few judges have chosen to decide differently, it is broadly accepted that the home inspector is contracted to and working for the person who is paying the fee and has signed the inspection contract. It is recommended that these should be one and the same.

It is important to consider the above information when a realtor offers to provide and/or pay for the inspection. Although not routine, it's becoming more popular for proactive realtors to recommend or provide a pre-listing inspection which we'll talk about later in the book.

Further, it must be understood that a home inspection represents a particular moment in time and that any obligation or liability by the inspector is not transferable without the consent of both the client that it was performed for and the inspector who provided the service.

Overall, I can say that one of the common reasons my clients (as far as I'm aware) don't purchase a house isn't because I found something spectacularly wrong; it's been because they were pressured or more often misinformed (frankly, lied to) during the real estate transaction about the house.

As a licensed realtor, I had the experience of sitting at the negotiating table (representing my buyer) presenting an offer to the seller and their realtor. When the subject of home inspection came up, the other realtor took off on a half-hour rant slandering and degrading one particular inspector. Twice I told her that her behavior was inappropriate in front of a client, but there was nothing stopping her until she had her say.

The point that I'm making here is that if the home inspector does good work for his clients, he will more than likely be shunned by a large percentage of the real estate community; clearly inspectors have a real dilemma if they want to work. Even for the best of inspectors and realtors there is a very fine line to be walked. Many realtors admitted that they only include a home inspection clause in their offers only as a means of deflecting liabilities from themselves (the realtor) to the home inspector.

Recently a student told me that the reason he was going to be an inspector was the demand for inspectors. He explained that he'd just purchased a house and it took his realtor a full week and a half to find him an inspector in a market that I know is saturated with inspectors. As I asked him more questions, it appeared obvious, from my experience, that the realtor was stalling and making things difficult in an attempt to have him drop the inspection clause.

So the bottom line is when you are purchasing and your realtor is recommending an inspector, do your own homework. Many will offer the home buyer three choices, but remember that in most markets there's no problem finding three BEI's (blind-eyed inspectors). Now don't get me totally wrong, although they appear to be in the minority, there are realtors that do recommend people like myself and my peers. Again, do your own research. You might even consider asking your realtor, "Who should I not use?" and make that person your first call. In a previous career I used this technique often and it was amazing how many times it sent me directly to the person I needed to be dealing with! If you're not getting the answers that you want or are not feeling comfortable with your realtor or the home inspector, simply find another one.

National Associations

I refer to the home inspection industry as still being in the process of "coming of age." Although growing at times rapidly, home inspectors are a relatively small group of individuals that in too many cases are dominated over by the real estate industry.

Due to size and population, the structure of the home inspection industry in the United States is more formally developed than in Canada. ASHI (American Society of Home Inspectors) is the main association with a well-established track record and formalized standards of practice, training, and membership categories depicting the inspectors' level of experience. A volunteer board of directors and committees are supported by a full-time executive staff.

In Canada, CAHPI (Canadian Association of Home and Property Inspectors) also provides most of the same; however, it continues to struggle in its coming-of-age simply because, for the most part, it is run by volunteers. Both organizations have state/provincial and local chapters. At the time of this writing, approximately 35 states in the USA have regulation and licensing. Two provinces in Canada currently have regulation and licensing with two more currently moving towards it.

Both ASHI and CAHPI are challenged by upstart groups, alternative associations (or groups perceived to be associations) and high-profile franchises that all feel they have a better product to offer inspectors. These will be addressed in greater detail later in the book.

CHAPTER THREE: Real Estate Industry

<u>Note:</u> *Although generally similar state to state and province to province, specific references stated regarding the real estate transaction are based on practices in Ontario, Canada.*

There are many aspects to the real estate transaction. Except for some general background, in this book we are going to stay focused mainly on the topics related to the home inspection. Throughout the book, I'll be referring to "the deal." In real estate terms, the word "deal" or "the deal" means that an offer to purchase has been made by a buyer and has been accepted by a seller. The term "ends" refers to the two sides of the deal; the seller represents one end and the buyer is the other end. When a realtor acts for both the buyer and seller (regarding the same house) it is referred to as "double ending." Based on a 5% commission, each end represents 2.5% of the commission.

Statistics And Real Estate Market Overview

When talking about buying and selling homes, it's important that one understands a little more about the inside of the real estate industry. When talking about realtors and their services, the number one thing that many people seem to have a problem with is the amount of commission that realtors supposedly make. In recent years, the response to this has been a major growth in discount or zero commission real estate brokerages and/or sell-it-yourself companies. Yet, as in many other parts of our lives, "The grass always looks greener on the other side," and at the end of the day one typically "gets what they pay for."

As I work into this topic, I want to set the mood with some facts. Anyone who has been to a business seminar or read any of the traditional business self-help books will be familiar with the 80/20 rule, i.e., 80% of your clients use up your time while 20% pay your bills. It's amazing how accurate this formula is and how it can be successfully applied to a shocking number of business scenarios. In real estate, the precise data is well documented and provides a variation on the old 80/20 rule. The fact is that in the North American real estate industry (the United States and Canada) the data shows that approximately 90% of the properties are sold by 10% of the realtors. Others in the front lines feel that those numbers are getting closer to 95% by 5%. Based on the offices that I've worked in, I would say the 90/10 is almost dead on! So where does that leave the 90% of realtors who end up splitting the leftover 10% of the business? In many communities the average realtor sells fewer than 10 ends per year.

Do They Really Make That Much Money?

Over the years, real estate has had its own challenges and growing pains. Although today a growing number of homeowners are protesting the traditional real estate commission by dealing with the sell-it-yourself companies, it's a common fact that many of those homes end up being sold by realtors anyway. Today, professional real estate sales has become a very formalized and developed industry, and the cost of doing business is high. During my time as a realtor, I was amazed at just how many houses got listed but not sold.

Because I've walked both sides of the street, I've developed two presentations: one for realtors entitled "Working with Your Home

Inspector" and another for home inspectors entitled "Understanding the Realtor and the Real Estate Transaction." I'm often surprised by the reactions, when presenting to these groups, just how little understanding each side has of the other's profession.

Here we're going to focus on one of the highlights of the second presentation that revolves around the real estate commission. In this case, we're going to "push numbers" with a house that sells for $400,000 at 5% commission—a high-priced house for some smaller or depressed communities but a very low-priced house for major cities. Although there are many different ways of doing the math and every real estate office has their own way of presenting it, just about all compensation packages work out very similarly at the end of the day. Most realtors are self-employed contractors. In Ontario, real estate salespeople are required to work under a broker and can be paid only by a broker, because all income has to be paid to the broker first. In order to become a broker, a salesperson must complete further education and have practiced as a salesperson for two years. In addition to local real estate board, state, provincial and national licensing fees, residential realtors have to pay all their own expenses, including advertising and signage. Additionally, they pay monthly fees, referred to as "desk fees," to their broker. Yes, that's right: realtors have to pay to go to work and be associated with their broker. "Desk fees" can range from $200 - $2,000 per month depending on the particular brokerage and/or office space and services that are contracted from the brokerage. Even in a no-sale month, as like any other self-employed businessperson, the expense is still there.

Now that we've talked about fees and expenses, what about that big commission? Once the realtor makes a sale and the deal closes, the commission is paid. Sometimes it's a quick sale with a quick close, but more often, if representing the seller, the realtor has been investing his or her time and carrying the cost of promoting the property for months. So, what happens to that 5% commission?

Before we can talk about how the commission is broken up or shared, we need to understand the term "the split." The split is an annual agreement between the salesperson and the broker. It is usually a one-year contract that starts over, from the beginning, every twelve months. A typical split starts with 30% of the commission going to the broker, another 2-5% going towards franchise fees and office advertising, and the balance going to the realtor. Then, based on a predetermined net dollar amount that the realtor pays the broker in any twelve-month period, the broker's 30% shrinks as low as 5%. Now based on the fact that 90% of the realtors are sharing 10% of the business, a large majority don't ever reach the split point (the point at which the broker's portion drops below 30%).

So, let's put that into an example (for the sake of being able to calculate other expenses, we'll base this on a salesperson who's doing 12 ends a year, in order that we can put in other monthly expenses):

Sample Commission Annual Income

Total sale	$400,000.00
Total commission	$20,000.00
Selling broker's commission	<u>$10,000.00</u>
Seller's commission	$10,000.00
Broker's split	-$3,000.00
Miscellaneous royalties, office promotion	-$350.00
Desk fees	-$500.00
Promotion cost of listing	-$1,500.00
Phone	-$125.00
Board fees, errors and omissions insurance	-$125.00
Miscellaneous expenses	-$300.00
Net Before taxes*	$4,100.00
Take-home based on 30% gov't deductions	<u>$2,870.00</u>

* Did you notice that I didn't even factor in the Mercedes payment?

The above is simply a hypothetical example, but for most part should paint a very different picture than what is commonly perceived. Now that you are feeling sorry for the average realtor, don't forget about that 10% on the other side of the fence. It's often difficult for the average person who collects a regular paycheck to relate to those in business for themselves.

About The Real Estate Transaction

Occasionally I receive phone calls from potential clients who are still in the process of house-shopping and are doing their research regarding choosing a home inspector. But the majority of the calls revolve around "I've just put in an offer and need a home inspection". As we start to discuss the inspection and time frame, I find too often that my clients don't understand the process of what they are doing. I'm not going to provide all the details regarding the flow of the real estate transaction, as that's not the purpose of this book. However, in this section I'm going to jump back and forth wearing both my home inspector and realtor hats to cover some basic information regarding how our services affect and interact with each other. Again this is the sequence in Ontario and may vary in your area.

Step 1)   The number one step in purchasing a new home is arranging financing, which for most individuals means getting pre-approved for a mortgage. Pre-approval means that the purchaser's credit has been approved and a maximum dollar amount for a mortgage has been established. Final approval is discussed in Step 6. *(Note: In many areas a realtor will not take a potential client seriously and/or commit much time to them unless the buyer has already been pre-approved. Also, depending on the market and the size of offer deposits required, the realtor may ask for proof of the client's ability to provide an adequate deposit.)*

Step 2) It's all about house hunting.

Step 3) You have found a house and an offer is going to be made. Although getting more common, and as practical as this may seem, it's a safe estimate that fewer than 5% of the inspections occur at this stage, i.e., before the offer is actually made. At this point, the buyer may also be presented with a SPIS (seller's property information sheet or similar type form). On this form, the seller has answered a number of questions regarding the property. Although it's a good concept, I've learned to put little trust in it.

Step 4) On behalf of the client, the realtor prepares the offer to purchase, the client signs and provides the deposit check. Ideally the offer document includes a "condition clause" which stipulates the right to have a home inspection. The clause also stipulates the time frame (typically 3 – 7 days) in which the inspection has to be performed, referred to as the "waiver date." This must not be confused with the closing date, which is when the purchaser actually acquires possession of the house. (I get a number of phone calls from clients who do not understand this and think they have until the closing date to have their inspection). Although an inspection is always recommended, in a hot real estate market with multiple offers (more than one person is making an offer on the same house at the same time), a lot of realtors will warn that an inspection clause may lessen the chances of an offer being accepted. Although this may be a good bargaining tool, dropping the rights for a home inspection should be taken very seriously as there are a lot of people who regret not having had a home inspection. If home inspections were mandatory for all purchases this would not happen and buyers would be much better protected in such situations.

Step 5) Your realtor presents the offer. Sometimes the negotiation goes back and forth a number of times before there is an accepted offer and the deal is struck. At this stage the purchaser has not yet bought a house, but has agreed with the seller to a set of "conditions" that, if met, will lead to a final sale.

Step 6) Following step 5, there are critical timelines to get things done, all pretty much at the same time.

* *Finalize The Mortgage:*
Before proceeding with the inspection, it's critical to follow through with the second half of the mortgage application and make sure that the house also qualifies for the mortgage. It's silly to spend money on an inspection if there's a chance of the mortgage not being approved.

* *Confirm Insurance:*
House insurance will be a condition of the mortgage lender, so sourcing insurance needs to done immediately. Some of the information required by the insurance company may not be available until the home inspection.

* *Home Inspection:*
Although it's important to make sure that the mortgage is finalized before spending money on an inspection, it's now time to book the inspector. You should find that most inspectors are quite used to this and are prepared to adjust or hold an inspection time pending mortgage approval.

Step 7) The inspection. Make sure that you attend!

Step 8) Now that you've had the inspection, it's time to make the decision: buy or run! However, if your inspector has found problems that require further investigation or immediate attention, this can complicate the situation. Perhaps there is a furnace or air conditioning problem needing a heating contractor's evaluation and price for replacement, or a quote for new shingles is required. These are expensive items and may affect what the client is really prepared to pay for the house. If the inspection has been left to the last minute (before the time when conditions have to be met) the realtor may have to ask for an extension of the conditions clause. This requires another set of documents that must be agreed upon and signed by both the buyer and the seller in order to extend the conditions for a longer period of time. I caution that asking for an extension legally reopens the offer, allowing the seller to refuse the request and accept someone else's offer. In an attempt to avoid this situation, I always advise that the inspection be done as soon as possible and not left to the last day of the conditions.

Now if there was no major problem with the furnace and the buyer had already budgeted for new shingles when making their original offer, they now sign the waiver which removes the conditions and the deal is considered "firm" (all negotiation is finished and the paperwork goes off to the lawyers).

Then if it's decided that a new furnace is required and that the cost to replace the shingles is more than expected, the realtor may again go back to the seller, this time asking for reduction in price. Again this opens the offer and the seller can agree or disagree. At this point, a new agreement is struck between the buyer and seller or the deal falls apart because of the home inspection.

Once the deal falls apart a mutual release form (which says everybody's happy about not proceeding with the sale) has to be signed by all parties before the real estate brokerage can return the buyer's deposit money.

STORY #6: Seller Provides Furnace Servicing

During an inspection, I found the furnace full of crusted water stains and slime. I actually put on rubber gloves during that portion of the inspection. As I proceeded through the inspection it was apparent that a bathtub leak had been draining down and through the furnace and more specifically, the heat exchanger. Feeling that it was unsafe to operate the furnace, I recommended further investigation by a qualified heating contractor. Based on the extreme damage to the unit, I also explained to my buyers not to be surprised if a new furnace was required.

The following day I received a very frank and rude phone call from the realtor stating that the heating contractor had been in, found absolutely nothing wrong, that I didn't have a clue what I was doing and that I'd better be prepared to pay for the contractor's service call (note: these kinds of phone calls are not uncommon in the life of an inspector). Remaining calm and collected, I asked the realtor to please fax me a copy of the service report and invoice. Upon receipt of the fax, I phoned the contractor's office and talked to the service technician involved. I introduced myself and requested some details regarding the condition of the furnace. The technician replied, "I was never asked to look at the furnace. I was asked to look at some duct work in a back bedroom that a home inspector said there was a problem with."

STORY #7: Seller To Provide Basement Kitchen

In this case my client explained that, in the terms of the deal, the seller was required to finish the basement apartment and install a kitchen. Although possibly outside my scope as a home inspector I cautioned that this was not a good idea because there were no specifications agreed to regarding the renovation. At closing, the buyer expecting a nice little traditional kitchen found that the seller provided one of those stainless steel sink/hot-plate/fridge combination units with no counters or cabinets, arguing that he'd met the terms of the contract.

STORY #8: Seller To Shingle Roof And Vent Attic

Here the seller agreed to shingle the roof and vent the attic before closing and I was asked to go back to confirm the work. When I arrived, I found that the seller had picked the most inappropriately colored shingles along with flashings that didn't match. The seller was quite surprised when I knocked on the door and asked to be let into the house to check the attic regarding the ventilation work they'd agreed to provide. As you guessed, there was no ventilation work done and when I came down from my ladder the seller had left in his car.

STORY #9: Seller Agreed To Repair Foundation Crack

In this case the seller agreed to have a serious foundation crack professionally repaired, which called for a series of injections covering two large cracks. When I was asked to take a look at the repair on the day of closing, I found that the homeowner had only slopped black tar on the above-ground exterior portion of the two cracks.

STORY #10: Seller Contracted To Finish Major Renovations

One of my most frustrating situations involved an out-of-province client. We had done the inspection and against my advice (I'd recommended that they request a price reduction and hire their own professional contractor), they negotiated with the seller to complete a major renovation that was in progress at the time of the inspection. The day before closing I was re-hired by my client to re-inspect the renovation and report my findings to the lawyer. The renovation was both substandard and incomplete. My buyer's lawyer told the seller's lawyer that he was holding back money so the work could be completed. Hearing this, the seller refused to cooperate and my clients couldn't be reached because they were in transit with the moving van. The closing became a nightmare for all and I don't recall that anyone ended up happy.

The Home Inspection Clause

An important point to keep in mind here is that as the one buying the house, it's your deal. Yes, your realtor will be the one preparing the paperwork and providing advice; however, that advice should be for your protection as the buyer, not their gain. If they start telling you what you cannot do and it doesn't sound right to you, don't be intimidated. Ask questions or get a second opinion. Realtors have a lot of legal hoops and mandatory forms that may not make sense to the buyer or seller, but they are all important so please pay attention and don't be afraid to ask questions.

Here we're going to focus on the home inspection clause. Each province and state has standard real estate forms for the "offer to purchase." In Ontario for example, Appendix A comes after all the formalized print and is where the individual buyer's specific conditions are written in, stating things like, "the seller will include all window coverings" or "the purchaser has the right to a home inspection." Because these are common requests, the realtor's database will have stock clauses that they can cut and paste. There are a number of variations regarding the home inspection clause, a couple of which I totally disagree with. Hence I want you to understand that the wording of this clause/condition is critical and is totally at the buyer's discretion. The buyer is the one purchasing the house and it is their terms and conditions, not the realtor's or the seller's, though the seller will have to agree with them!

In the following paragraphs, we'll discuss some phrases for the inspection clause/condition. Today realtors are learning to accept the inspection clause as part of their business and using open wording along the lines of,

"Pending a <u>satisfactory</u> home inspection…"

This style of wording is totally open to the buyer's definition of "satisfactory" and allows them the right to walk away from the deal, after the inspection, with no obligation to proceed with the purchase or explain their reasoning to anyone. It's unfortunate that sometimes buyers simply change their mind about the house and use such escape clauses to get out of the deal. Being frustrated by this "drive-a-truck-through-it wording" other realtors will tighten the wording to the point that's there's little chance of a buyer declining the deal. Although other variations similar to the following are also used I would not recommend them:

**"The buyer must provide the seller with a copy
of the inspection report"
or "Any defects found must be over $1,000 to repair"
or "The homeowner has the right to make all repairs"**

Supplying the seller with a copy of the inspection report can often get emotional. It may lead to arguments with the seller and their realtor claiming that they've got an inspector or contractor who says the buyer's inspector is wrong. The other two clauses regarding defects and repairs can become very ambiguous and create additional complications. When I was a practicing realtor I favored a clause along the lines of,

"Pending a satisfactory home inspection by an RHI ("Registered Home Inspector") (In the USA one would use the designation ACI / ASHI Certified Inspector)

It's my opinion that such wording protects the buyer while giving the seller the confidence that the buyer is using a qualified inspector and not simply some friend or relative.

I've also found that it is common for realtors to put an inspection clause in the offer to purchase document, then turn around and persuade the client to stroke out the clause and initial it as evidence that they had recommended an inspection but the buyer turned it down. Other times I've seen the realtor and seller stall or create conditions regarding the availability of the house hoping that the purchaser would get frustrated and waive their right for an inspection.

Multiple Offers

In hot markets when things are selling fast, multiple offers (more than one person placing an offer on same house at the same time) are commonplace. In these situations the purchaser is forfeiting their ability to negotiate and must start by making their best possible offer. In many cases people will eliminate the inspection clause to assure the seller they won't be backing out of the deal because of a home inspection. As a realtor, I found it very frustrating when phoning a listing realtor to make an appointment to present my client's offer and they'd say, "Oh I just had another call as well and you will be in a competing offer situation," but when I showed up there was no second offer. It had been a ploy to trick my client into making a better offer and possibly eliminating the inspection clause. This only had to happen to me once before I started carrying two offers in my briefcase. I pulled out the higher one only after I'd physically confirmed that there really was a competing offer. If you are in doubt, don't be afraid to speak up and request proof that your offer was or is legitimately part of a multiple offer situation. As a home inspector, the only time that I ever had to testify before a discipline committee was regarding action being taken against a realtor because of the way he'd handled dropping the inspection clause in a multiple offer situation.

Realtor-Bashing Aside...

Of all the realtors that I've worked with and have been referred by, there are a handful that stand out in my eyes as understanding the big picture in running a successful business. They understand that it's not just about closing the deal, it's about the long-term. They understand the fact that happy clients are not only the best advertising a businesses can have, but they are also the least expensive advertising. Whereas big fancy print ads that often cost thousands of dollars last only a few days or weeks, happy clients keep on working for years. Unfortunately my experience shows that a large percentage of realtors are only concerned about closing the deal. However, there are individuals who continually seek accurate information and put their client's best interest first and foremost and I'd definitely be negligent if I didn't include a couple of their stories here as well! The interesting part of the two following examples is that both individuals are what the industry refers to as "top producers."

STORY #11: We'll Call This One Realtor "A"

This story is about one the highest producing (by ends) residential realtors that I've ever met. If I went through my records I suspect that I'd find over 150 even maybe 200 inspections that he referred to me over a period of three years. What's even more interesting, to the best of my knowledge, he never lost a single sale because of my inspections. So for you realtors reading, let's take a look at why he never lost a sale.

- Did I cut corners or not report on issues? *Not a chance!* And I have to say I looked at some real "bulldozer specials" for his clients.

- Bottom line is, he understood houses and never misinformed his clients. Typically, when recommending me, he would have already identified and pointed out the major issues and would simply say to his clients, "Let's get Bruce in to make sure." In other cases, he'd say, "I'm not sure on that one. Let's get Bruce in, but don't be surprised if he finds something wrong with it and it's an issue." He always prepared his clients in advance so that they showed up at the inspection with both eyes open.

- Also, he always made sure that the sellers understood what we'd be doing and needed access to.

- He always showed up at the inspection and took an active role, but he never tried to control the situation; that was my business. He never tried to create conflict with or undermine me.

I've always considered his passing as a great loss to both his industry and the clients that he served.

STORY #12: We'll Call This One Realtor "B"

A number of this realtor's clients have reported to me that he told them, "Bruce can't tell you not to buy the house, but if he doesn't like it, you'll know, and I don't want you to buy it." This story revolves around one of our mutual clients. It's not simply an interesting story because I went through two pair of shoes (from stepping in dog s***) while inside the house or because when I stated that the electrical system required updating, the client turned to her fiancé and said, "Well, we will be getting some money as wedding gifts…"

From the outside I suspected that we were dealing with a multiple-family dwelling and two undersized 60-amp electrical services. At the rear exterior the two-story porch/mudroom with a sunroom above was dramatically separating away from the house. Once inside, we confirmed that the electrical was outdated as was the furnace. The house went downhill from there.

Totally bewildered after sleeping on it, I finally phoned the realtor and asked him, "Why did you bother putting that deal together? You knew about your client's finances and what kind of condition that house was in."

He explained, "They were in love with it and even had me take parents and friends through as well. All were excited and encouraging them to go ahead and buy it. Based on this I knew that if I refused to put the deal together, they'd simply go to another realtor who would. So, I put the deal together and gave them the money for the home inspection recommending that they call you. I knew that you would bring them around to reality."

Yes, this is an extreme case, but this is also an extremely successful realtor who made it at a very young age simply because, as they say today, he "gets it" and treats others as he'd like to be treated.

More About Realtors

As a seasoned home inspector, educator, previously licensed realtor and career entrepreneur, I feel it's important to point out a few things regarding realtor licensing. In Ontario, one must pass a very formal process of education, exams and internship in order to acquire a real estate license. There are seven courses (approximately 48 hours each) which require a passing grade of 75%. Back in my teens when I started my first business, my father, a career businessman/ salesman, taught me the three basic rules of sales:

1. Know your product!

2. Know your product!

3. If ever in doubt refer back to Rules #1 and #2

Now back to the seven real estate courses. They have very little to do with houses. From what I saw back in 2008 when I took them, I challenge that I or my peers could teach more in one class than these courses covered in total regarding houses, their systems, construction techniques, maintenance and home inspection. Is it hard to see why so many realtors are continuously in conflict with inspectors from a technical point of view? Or is it more a question of, "they don't want to know?"

Home Renovations

Home renovations can have a serious impact on the real estate transaction, and it is pretty difficult to find a house that hasn't had some kind of a renovation. Older homes get updated. New homeowners are always anxious to add their own personal touch, build a deck or finish the basement. Then there is the "flip house". Such renovations range from the "beyond spectacular" to the "disaster" held together by duct tape, lamp cord or less. While beauty lies in the eyes of the beholder, it's the home inspector's challenge to look through the cosmetics and evaluate the technical side of the project.

Although in most areas of the USA and Canada home owners are allowed to renovate and make alterations to their personal house, every state, province and municipality has codes and requirements for permits. An example: I can do electrical work in my own home, but I cannot legally do electrical work in my rental property. Shortly after moving into my latest house and planning the first round of renovations I dropped into the township office to inquire about regulations and permits. The municipal inspector summed it up in one statement, "You can move dirt without a permit and that's about it."

With the wealth of do-it-yourself books, do-it-yourself television programs and big-box stores with aisles full of stuff and staff willing to give advice, it all looks so easy. I'm adamant that people get permits for their work and follow through with the stipulated inspection schedules. On a side note, always be skeptical if a contractor asks you, the homeowner, to pick up the permit and have it in your own name. If you do that, you're the person responsible—not the contractor. Although people will ask "Did you get a permit for the work?" I've learned that it's very important to ask the other half of the question, "Did you get the final inspection required by the permit?" I see permits and inspections as a very small price to pay in order to have someone objectively check my work and insure that it's done correctly to protect the health and safety of both my family as well as future families who will be living in the house.

As home inspectors one of the most frightening issues that we continue to see in abundance is unsafe electrical systems. Sometimes the work has been done by the homeowner, while other times it is an unqualified contractor or a handyman. It's a rare home inspection where I'm not reporting on something electrical. Although many things may be subjective, the basic rule with electrical is that it's either right or it's wrong. If it's wrong, it's dangerous. My electrician friend often comments, "It's interesting how many people play with electricity, but not very many touch the gas lines." People simply don't understand how dangerous electricity can be.

Another side note: Experience has caused me to put tradespeople who do renovations to their own home into two categories;

1. The first group know their trade and respect the skills of their fellow trades. When doing work at home, outside their own trade, they bring in the other tradespeople to make sure that portion of the work is done correctly.

2. The second group, because they work on the job site all day, think they know everything and at home attempt to do everything themselves. Again, experience has taught me that these renovations are usually worse than the typical inexperienced do-it-yourself homeowner. When my client or the realtor says "The homeowner works in construction and did all the work by himself" I always get a shiver down my spine. On the other hand I have enjoyed a few very pleasant surprises with excellent workmanship.

While I'm on the topic I want to quickly comment on "flip houses". Again although sensationalized on television it's very difficult for an investor to purchase a house, do major renovations and sell it for a profit, especially in what is referred to as a mature or developed real estate market. Typically these houses are full of cosmetically pleasing features, but lack quality workmanship in areas that the layperson can't see.

CHAPTER FOUR: New Homes & Condominiums

I can't count the number of times that both realtors and potential clients have commented, "But it's a new home" or "But it's a condominium. Why would it need an inspection?" My replies have traditionally been, "New homes bring some of the biggest surprises that I see." Or I ask, "Why would you think a condominium doesn't need an inspection?" and they simply answer, "But it's a condo…" They never seem to have a qualified answer for that one. First we'll talk about new homes.

New Homes

One of the things that I have to compliment the housing market on is that, in the past 3 – 5 years, I've seen a marked improvement in new home construction. Yet with every new subdivision that I go through, I find it frustrating that cosmetics and toys appear to be more important than the practicality or function of required systems.

Inspecting a new home being delivered directly from the builder is different than inspecting a home that's been lived in; there's typically very little that can be based on "performance" as everything is new. Because the walls are closed in and finished, it can't be a "code inspection" since we can't see the construction materials.

Although it may sound limited, I'm continually surprised at what we discover in new or newer homes. Understanding that the average homeowner knows very little about their house, many inspectors will also focus on teaching the new home owner how the house and its components work. The new homeowner is then off to a good start, understanding some of the do's and don'ts of home maintenance.

In Ontario we have a government backed New Home Warranty Program which most inspectors are critical of. When at seminars or speaking to groups of people, I routinely poll my audience with two basic questions regarding this warranty program:

1. Has anyone in the room ever put in a claim to the New Home Warranty Program? (It was called HUDAC back when I started asking this question; today it is referred to as the Tarion Warranty (Tarion Warranty Corporation)

2. If someone had put in a claim, I always go to the next level and ask in front of the group, "Did you get any satisfaction?"

Over the past 20-plus years and the dozens of times I've posed these questions, only a handful of people have confirmed that they actually got past the denial stage and had a claim processed. To date, none of that group have reported being happy with their claim and the majority said that it hadn't been worth their time or effort. Of the few who eventually had success, all stated that they had to fight for it. All this said, I recently talked to a contractor that was hired to fix a major soils settlement problem (sinking ground) where the warranty program did pay for the repair. He added that it was his opinion that the warranty program only stepped in to protect the builder from going bankrupt. All pretty damning statements for people who actually have the "New Home Warranty" added to the price of their new homes as a mandatory "option." Many inspectors will explain the formalities and procedures of dealing with the New Home Warranty if there is one in your area.

Now back to the inspection. Based on the limitations previously noted, a new home inspection is more one of "best practices." Is everything there and have all the visible components been put together properly? I recall one special day that I was so excited, while standing on the roof of a newer home, I called a fellow inspector and said, "Bob! mark this day on your calendar. I'm standing on the lower roof of a new home looking at the detailing of the wall finish and have just found the first EIFS (Exterior Insulation Finishing System, today's version of a stucco-type siding material) that I've seen properly flashed!"

About four years later, I was on another a roof with a seasoned contractor but this time the discussion wasn't so positive. I'd been hired by the homeowner because of the numerous roof and wall leaks that had developed since the contractor completed major renovations. Although I was armed with the manufacturer's specifications as to how the EIFS was to be installed and flashed, the contractor insisted that the specifications were irrelevant because this was the way he'd been installing it for years.

Anyone who's attended my classes or heard me speak has heard these lines many times:

- "Just because they do it that way doesn't make it right."

- "Yes, that sounds like a great idea or a great new product! How about you come back in 10-15 years and tell me if it worked?" Remember urea formaldehyde, asbestos ceiling tiles, radiant heating in ceilings, aluminum wiring and the first generations of plastic water lines?

Yes, there are building codes and we do have municipal building inspectors but their workloads are high and few go on ladders or roofs. Their not having a ladder can be a good explanation as to why I've found the occasional newer home without insulation in the attic. Also, with the volume of new subdivisions and again, the workload, not every house is even inspected, instead only a random sampling of the individual builder's work is looked at.

Often new homebuilders are reluctant to have home inspectors look at their houses and many of us, although hired by the buyer, have been kicked off the property. Reality is that the builder owns the property up until closing and in most cases has full control over who enters it. Eventually here, the Home Builders Association did take action requesting builders to allow private home inspectors on site. In 2011, CAHPI developed the NCI (New Construction Inspection) training program to assist inspectors with an inspection protocol more suited towards new home inspections.

STORY #13: New Home Pre-Delivery Inspection

In this case, I was inspecting a new higher-end house being delivered from the builder. I inspected on the day before closing. The following are a number of major issues that I found:

- A large number of shingles had been blown up and bent over backwards. This is a common problem when there are high winds or cold weather before new shingles have set in and sealed. However, there was such a high percentage of damaged shingles the builder, based on my inspection, agreed to strip the roof and re-shingle.

- The furnace had been installed and wired incorrectly. It was cycling incorrectly, not distributing heat properly and would have had a very short life span had the problems not been detected during the inspection.

- Improper window installation resulted in water leakage building up in pockets behind the vapor barrier and in the insulation. I estimated that one pocket had more than a quart of water in it.

STORY #14: Two Identical Houses / Same Builder

Oftentimes people will talk about this-is-a-good-builder or that's-a-poor-builder. But I don't find that a good rule. This story started when I received a phone call from a gentleman who had purchased a new subdivision home directly from the builder but hadn't had a home inspection. He had now been living in the house a few months and was starting to have some concerns. He was angry. When I drove up to his house and noticed an eight-foot high banner on the house across the street that read, "Don't buy a house from this builder," I figured that I was in for a treat. The following are a number of the issues that I found in this higher-end house which we'll call house #1:

- There was a standard-height, six-foot sliding patio door. However, the space had been framed for a patio door with a palladium window above. Instead of re-framing the space where the palladium window should have been and making it a proper exterior wall, the builder simply put vinyl siding over the exterior hole in the wall and drywall on the interior. This left a one-foot high by six-foot wide cavity in the wall with no insulation, vapor barrier or proper structural support for the sliding door or siding material.

- On one side of the great room floor, the hardwood floorboards had been installed too close together and were buckling, while on the opposite side of the room they were too far apart with open spaces between.

- In the great room where the walls met the ceiling it appeared that upper sections of the drywall had not been securely fastened to the wall, or foreign material had been left behind the drywall. This problem was not fixed before the plasterers troweled the decorative border on the ceiling, hence the border wasn't just uneven, in places it waved back and forth almost an inch.

- During construction, often a second-story window is left loose so that it can be easily removed for the drywall to be loaded into the house through that space. In this case the builder had gone ahead and finished both the exterior siding and inside window trim without fastening the window to the building or sealing around it.

- The vinyl siding had gaps over two inches wide around exterior wall penetrations such as gas lines and dryer vents.

About six months later I was hired to inspect house #2, which was right next door to house #1. Both were built at the same time by the same builder. House #2 was as close to textbook perfect as a building could be. It's experiences like this that cause me to evaluate each house on its own merit and not make blanket comments regarding individual builders.

Condominiums

There's a great illusion surrounding condominiums and the perception that they don't need an inspection. Far too often I hear realtors and clients comment, "Well, the condominium corporation will look after that." To which I respond by asking, "And who is the condominium corporation?" and they typically respond with a blank stare. From there I explain that the typical condominium board has no requirement that members know anything about buildings, construction or maintenance. The only requirement is that the individual is a good volunteer.

I find that it's important for potential buyers to understand what the "reserve fund" is, how it works and what a "special assessment" is. The reserve fund is the money put aside by the condominium corporation for future repairs. If the fund runs short, the condominium owners are given a special assessment: the cost of repairs divided by the number of owners in the building. Each pays their share. Condominiums were new in Canada in the '70s and by the '90s it was realized that many of the reserve funds were not adequate. Many condominium owners faced special assessments that they couldn't afford.

Originally most condominium corporations maintained and were responsible for everything structural along with anything outside the interior walls of the living unit. But that's no longer the case. We now have properties where the only thing covered or maintained by the condominium corporation is the parking lot and snow removal. When purchasing a condominium, buyers see a clause in the contract that allows for the purchaser's lawyer to review the "status certificate." Typically there is a fee for the certificate and it will take the property management company anywhere from a few days to weeks to produce it. The status certificate will contain the rules and regulations of the condominium corporation along with up-to-date details regarding the reserve fund and overall financial status of the corporation. This is not one of those documents that you simply want your lawyer to review on your behalf and forget about. As a unit owner you are now a responsible partner in the condominium corporation, so it's important that you understand this document. This pro-active exercise may just save a lot of unnecessary grief down the road.

I also recommend to clients that they make a point of attending a few condominium corporation meetings to get the feel of things and understand the personalities and politics of the board. Remember, as an owner you are now a part of the condominium corporation and it's your money that they're dealing with and spending. It's extremely important for members of a condo board to understand their long-term commitment to the building and the need for preventive maintenance. Unfortunately, as an inspector I've seen a number of condominium complexes where very little preventive maintenance has been done and things are not fixed until it's too late. This typically results in higher costs and greater inconvenience to the owners later.

Sorting through the information for this chapter I discovered that I've likely got enough material for a book on just condominiums. But let's get back to home inspections and talk about some of the condominiums that I've inspected.

STORY #15: Jumping Fish

I was inspecting an individual condo unit in a four-plex multiple-story building for a business associate. When the realtor arrived, I had my ladder up and was preparing to inspect the roof of the units. He appeared quite taken aback at this and made a series of comments such as, "Why would a home inspector ever look at the roof of a condominium?" And.... "I've never seen an inspector do such a thing before!" Once inside the unit, he kept making negative comments towards me and, in a very derogatory way was continually asking, "What are you doing now?" followed by more comments along the line of "That's not how other inspectors do it." What the realtor didn't know was that I was unfortunately used to dealing with people like him and that my client knew me well and had hired me for my skill and knowledge. In this particular instance, my client was impressed that I knew the reputation of the particular condominium board and their policy of zero maintenance, low-quality repairs, not fixing things until broken and then doing the work the cheapest way possible. While on the roof, I'd already established that the shingles had outlived their useful lives and had been poorly patched. Regardless of the other issues, we found water stains on the ceilings of almost every room of the unit, both upstairs and down, which typically means some pretty serious leakage. My client finally lost it when the realtor insisted that the water stains were from the homeowners' tropical fish jumping out of their aquariums. Needless to say, the inspection went downhill from there.

STORY #16: Retirement Community Reserve Fund

The following is not an uncommon situation. In this case, the board members were all seniors in a retirement community. Work on the sea-wall had been a heavy burden on the reserve fund and other major repairs were imminent within the next three to five years. The annual meeting of the condominium corporation was coming up and again there was a motion on the agenda (by the property management company) to increase the condo fees in order to top up the reserve fund so that there would be money available for the future repair work. The board members, all looking out for their own interests (realizing that in three to five years they would more than likely be in care homes and not owners) as they had in the past, solicited all the other senior owners and encouraged them to vote down the increase. Typically in this situation (and it had happened with this board before), when major expenses came along there wasn't enough money in the reserve fund and the owners were hit with a special assessment to pay for the work.

Now let's take a look at the pros and cons of this scenario:

Advantages:

1. Condominium fees remain low as long as nothing serious happens

2. If a major assessment comes along and is too high, the unit owner can sell and move out

Disadvantages:

1. Potential buyers for the property will shy away because they are concerned about unpredictable increases in condominium fees or further special assessments

2. As with point #2 under advantages, the property is devalued because of the outstanding assessment which will have to be assumed by the buyer or deducted from the proceeds of the sale

3. The property is more than likely devalued compared to similar properties because it hasn't been well-maintained

STORY #17: Condo Electrical Panel

In this case, the condo board was very upset that a prospective buyer had asked to have a home inspection before buying one of their units. In response, the board stipulated that their condo president be allowed to attend the inspection with me. I must add that the condo president, although respectful, was very skeptical that I would be finding anything of value to my clients. But when I opened the electrical panel (in many areas, home inspectors are not allowed to do this), he was shocked as I pointed out the melted electrical wires and explained the potential for fire. Instantly he was on my side and after the inspection we adjourned to his unit for coffee and an inspection of his electrical panel where we found more melted electrical wires! The condo board took immediate action and had an electrician in before the end of the week to go through the entire complex. There's a good chance that we saved lives that day.

STORY #18: Three x $10,000. Special Assessments

When I arrive for a condo inspection, I always start by taking a good look at the common areas which generally gives me a feel for how the condominium corporation looks after things. In this specific case, I noticed a gentleman giving a very quizzical look toward my truck and, as we made eye contact, he asked what I was up to. It ended up that he was the ex- (voted out), condominium corporation president with a story of his own to tell. He had been trying to deal with a major issue for which the unit owners didn't want to take responsibility. In the end, the work was done and a special assessment of $30,000 was levied against each owner. The first $20,000 had been paid by everyone and the final $10,000 installment would be due and payable a couple of days after my client was to take possession. Although outside the scope of a home inspector, when my client arrived and I explained the situation, it was news to him and apparently to the realtor as well. The information was later confirmed in the status certificate report. Further, as part of my inspection, I pointed out a second major issue that could equal the first special assessment and recommended that my client have their lawyer follow up on it as well.

STORY #19: "We Know Everything; We Watch TV"

It was one of those warm sunny northern days when the snow was melting and the water dripping. I rang the doorbell to introduce myself to the condominium owner, who immediately greeted me with, "Both our realtor and us think this is ridiculous, doing a home inspection on a condominium, especially when it's so new! Besides," he added, with his wife standing behind him, "we watch Mike Holmes on television and we know everything!" – his exact words. I provided my usual smile (expecting that I was going to be in for an interesting day), asked if they'd be leaving and started on the exterior portion of my inspection.

It was an end unit, and because of the specific weather conditions of the day, I was not only able to see the evidence of a potentially serious siding installation issue but was able to establish the likely cause (a common problem regarding the siding detail). At this stage, a relatively minor repair, but five years down the road it could quite easily be a $5,000 repair involving both interior and exterior damage.

Once inside and after removing the homeowner's boxes (beyond the standards of a home inspection) from around the furnace I established that the humidifier (seldom recommended for houses built after the late '80s; this house was built after 2005) had been improperly installed. It was leaking water that was draining across the floor under the stored items. The air conditioning coil had also been leaking down through the interior and possibly into the heat exchanger, of the furnace. In the next room (a large living space which made up the bulk of the lower level) what appeared to be the supply heat register was actually a cold air return. The room was large enough to require two heat registers but had none at all. The ductwork for the upper living level wasn't designed properly for air conditioning and, although it was winter, explained to my clients why the air conditioning in this area of the house would not likely be effective on hot summer days. Once in the attic, I found that the firewall between this unit and the next had been compromised. It was interesting to see the shocked look on the owners' faces when they arrived home four hours later and I was still out front in my van writing a lengthy report.

CHAPTER FIVE: Who's Setting The Standards?

In my role as co-ordinator for the home inspection program at Conestoga College, I continually get calls from individuals wanting to be home inspectors. Often, as I'm listening to their stories and expectations, my mind drifts back many years to all those ads in the back pages of *Popular Mechanics* magazine and a sketch from TV's *Happy Days* about *How to Get Rich at Home in Your Spare Time!*

Unfortunately, there are a lot of so-called home inspectors out there who have no formal training. Even the major franchise operations send out inspectors with only two to three weeks' training. Many feel that government regulations will solve a lot of these problems, yet regulation comes with its own set of problems which we'll discuss later in this section. When talking about home inspections, I'm often heard saying, "A home inspection is 75% communication skills and 25% technical knowledge, but you damn well have to know the technical stuff!"

In many ways, watching a good inspector is like going to a good concert. The successful performers, knowing their craft and material, can make the most difficult performance look easy on stage. What the audience typically forgets is that this didn't come naturally but represents years of practice. For every scene they play or song they perform, they know dozens more.

In the same vein, a good inspector can make his or her job look very easy, and yes, we have a "Greatest Hits List" which I'll call "The Most Typically Found." This list includes such all-time favorites as "Extend Your Downspouts," "Improve the Grading" and of course everyone's favorite "Improve Attic Insulation and Ventilation." But remember, for every old standard we've got hundreds of other issues that we have to be on the watch for and piece together instantly, while making it look like it's second nature to us.

For those who have a family handyman, or a buddy who renovated his basement last year offer to perform an inspection, may I suggest caution. A home inspection is a "systematic procedure based on science." A professional inspector is always looking for signs of non-performance, a cover-up or unsuccessful repairs. A career contractor may have a lifetime of construction knowledge and putting things together, but if he doesn't know how to properly apply and communicate that knowledge into the art of inspection, it could mean very little. Another misconception is that an engineer is automatically qualified to perform home inspections. Whereas engineers have the "systematic design process" ingrained into almost everything that they do, there are many different disciplines of engineering. Their training, their focus is on what's behind the walls and how it's put together as opposed to inspection of or non-performance of residential systems.

Most importantly, the qualified home inspector is most likely the only person who will look at "the house as a system." Roofers look only at roofing, electricians look at electrical components and plumbers look at plumbing. In new construction, after the framers have put all the structural framing (wood or steel) together, the plumbers and heating contractors come in and cut holes and remove material, often compromising structural components of a building. Looking at the house as a system, the home inspector examines how all the systems of the house perform, work together and affect each other. Unfortunately one of the biggest problems with housing is the lack of knowledge by homeowners who don't understand how their house works and/or how to look after it. This is not their fault. It has more to do with our houses getting more complex all the time. Things (like the humidifier) that may have been good practice years ago are now potentially harmful. When it comes to repairs and renovations, I often use the phrase "They know just enough to be dangerous." Too many times I've seen homeowners spend thousands of dollars, along with endless nights and weekends working on renovations that only devalued their house.

I often ask myself, if an inspector has never designed and built a house from scratch, how can they really understand its components in order to inspect one? If inspectors haven't done extensive renovations, demolition, and repairs, how can they understand what that surface stain or patch of mold might look like behind the wall? There's nothing like tracing out a problem and getting your hands dirty on a job site to understand what's really going on. Having the ability to combine the code-related skills and knowledge of new construction (which are typically black or white) with the investigative process of home inspection (which is typically more a shade of gray) can be very advantageous. Take all this knowledge and add professional inspection training and we're starting to put together a serious set of skills for becoming a home inspector.

Unfortunately, in many states and provinces, anyone can print a business card and declare themselves a home inspector. Further, there are others who have declared themselves as training and educating facilities, making up elaborate logos and seals to look official. Then, at the next level there are others, in both countries starting up new Associations. There is one individual who has been very successful by starting what some call an "international marketing company" yet has acquired "not for profit status" representing itself as an official association. Franchises we'll talk about later.

Inspection History In The USA

It was about 1972 a group of like-minded home inspectors started getting together to share ideas and in 1976 ASHI (American Society of Home Inspectors Inc.) formed as the first professional association of home inspectors in North America. Today ASHI remains the oldest not-for-profit professional association for home inspectors and sets the standard by which others are judged. ASHI is the national body *(note; when using the term ASHI, I'm always referring to ASHI national).* with offices and full-time staff located in Des Plaines, Illinois, and has over 80 chapters throughout the USA and Canada. Each chapter is chartered by the national body but enjoys its own autonomy. Chapter members must first be members of ASHI who defines requirements for membership and membership categories. Today the initials ACI (ASHI Certified Inspector) denote the highest qualification level for ASHI inspectors.

Combined with annual conventions, seminars and the ASHI School, ASHI provides an extensive list of continuing education material and learning options, including on-line training.

ASHI has actively worked with legislators to enact regulations that protect the interests of consumers and qualified home inspectors alike. In 2007 ASHI formulated a policy statement outlining the critical elements required in home inspector regulation. Currently there are about 35 states that have regulations and legislation regarding home inspectors. Through the dedicated efforts of both ASHI volunteers and staff, ASHI's standards of practice, which cover all of a home's major systems, are incorporated in many pieces of state legislation and are recognized by consumers as the authoritative standard for professional home inspections.

Inspection History In Canada

Formal home inspections in Canada started during the 1970s and early 1980s. In 1982 CAHI (Canadian Association of Home Inspectors) was formed as a national body, and OAHI (Ontario Association of Home Inspectors) was formalized in Ontario. With the support of ASHI, they both adopted the ASHI standards of practice. In 2002, the name was changed from CAHI to CAHPI (Canadian Association of Home and Property Inspectors). With the encouragement of CMHC (Canada Mortgage and Housing Corporation, a department of the federal government) the model of CAHPI as one national association with the potential for 10 members, (one association from each of the 10 provinces) was adopted. The various provincial associations became CAHPI British Columbia, CAHPI Alberta, etc. Because of the limited population and geographical separation the Maritime provinces (New Brunswick, Nova Scotia, Prince Edward Island and Newfoundland and Labrador) formed as one association, CAHPI Atlantic. Although linked by name and membership in CAHPI, each provincial association operates independently. *Note, In Quebec CAHPI is represented by the AIBQ (Association Des Inspecteurs En Batiments Du Quebec).*

At the time there were two active associations in Ontario, PACHI (Provincial Association of Certified Home Inspectors) and OAHI. In 2001, PACHI merged with OAHI in order to support the national CAHPI model. In Ontario, however, there was another complication. The OAHI had already, in 1994, received official recognition by the Government of Ontario, with the passing of Bill Pr158, which gave them the right to regulate the designation RHI (Registered Home Inspector) in the province. Out of concern that a name change might jeopardize that authority, it was decided to continue using the name OAHI and also allow members to promote that they were members of CAHPI Ontario as well. Today it's safe to consider the OAHI and CAHPI Ontario as one and the same.

In 2009 Bill Pr158 was again recognized by the Ontario Labour Mobility Act. In which OAHI is named as a Non-Governmental Regulatory Authority.

In 2006, as an attempt to further a national qualification standard for home inspectors, CAHPI initiated a program in which qualifying inspectors earned the title National Certificate Holder. Unfortunately, with the advent of separate licensing in British Columbia, complicated by other political issues, the program disappeared in 2010. Since then, a number of the individuals that had been involved with CAHPI formed the NHICC (National Home Inspector Certification Council). They in turn became an accredited testing body for licensing in British Columbia and Alberta and are attempting to establish a new national qualification standards program promoting the designation of NHI (National Home Inspector). Today the requirements may differ slightly, but the initials RHI (Registered Home Inspector) denote the highest level of qualification for inspectors in each of the provinces.

Although this might be considered a very condensed version by those who have been involved, let's call that our Canadian history lesson and take a look at the state of affairs today. At the time of writing, British Columbia and Alberta have government regulation and licensing for home inspectors. In Quebec, governed under their real estate act, there is a standard 8-page inspector/client buyer contract and the seller is required to complete a 6-page disclosure form. Although I've heard it said for more than 10 years that it's only months away in Ontario, in 2012 the government did get some press regarding the fact that they are looking into regulating home inspectors.

It breaks my heart in a time of financial restraint to witness 4 separate provincial governments (with 6 more to follow) invest their time, manpower and *our tax dollars* to come up with 10 different ways of doing the same thing. What's wrong with this picture? Unfortunately in Ontario it looks like we're going to be in for a rough ride as one of the first places our government turned for advice was a shock-television celebrity who has little or no training or field experience in pre-purchase home inspections. Again I have to ask the question, "What's wrong with this picture?"

(A copy of the Standards of Practice for ASHI & CAHPI are included in the Appendix.)

Why An Association?

Throughout history, groups of people who shared similar values, interests or skills have traditionally come together in formal groups, clubs and associations. The first official group that I belonged to was Boy Scouts; the first club was a tropical fish club and the first association was my local Board of Trade. Early in my working career, I was the general manager of a small-town Chamber of Commerce before advancing to assistant general manager of the Ottawa Board of Trade where I also worked directly with the national Canadian Chamber of Commerce. *(I just wanted to share some of that background for credibility's sake when talking about associations.)*

Throughout the book, I've focused on ASHI and CAHPI because they are true not-for-profit member-driven and member-governed associations conducting their affairs under a set of bylaws decided by the membership, for the membership. Today we refer to this as governance. For over 30 years, ASHI and CAHPI have followed a model whereby a volunteer board of directors is supported by dedicated volunteer committees who follow a set of bylaws to provide standards of practice, continuing education, discipline procedures, major conventions and conferences to help keep members up-to-date in an ever-changing marketplace.

In the last decade, a couple of questionable associations have come to the forefront. Although some have not-for-profit status they appear more like proprietor-run businesses focused on capitalizing, for the founders' personal gain, on the work that has been done by thousands of volunteers over the past 30 years to build an industry and set standards. In the inner circles these have been referred to as "Virtual Associations" or "Marketing Companies" A good example of this is NACHI, which later changed their name to Inter-NACHI, followed by Can-NACHI. NACHI's original business model allowed free memberships and, in the early 2000s, anyone could become a NACHI certified home inspector in less than an hour on-line. ABC News presented a very interesting report in which they interviewed a 12-year-old boy from Utah who explained how he went on-line, answered a few questions and became a "NACHI Certified Home Inspector" complete with an official diploma that followed later in the mail. However, today these businesses have morphed their way into credibility by pretty much plagiarizing ASHI and CAHPI membership qualifications and standards. Based on these facts, I choose not to put them in the same league with the true member-driven not-for-profit associations.

I will make no apologies for my passion and dedication toward ASHI and CAHPI and give my thanks to the thousands of volunteers who have dedicated their time and efforts to building our industry while loathing the others noted above. Naturally, I can't agree with all the decisions that have been made over the years by ASHI and CAHPI and they may not necessarily agree with some of mine, but that's part of what makes our two countries so great. Further I don't believe that membership alone in these associations makes an individual a good inspector, however it does make the statement that they agree to work to a standard of practice, code of ethics and to be held accountable by their peers through a formalized disciplinary process and not just by their clients. This is a much bigger value than might be perceived by the general public who feel licensing provides their best means for protection.

Although we'll talk more about licensing shortly, it has to be understood that licensing, in many cases, only sets a base level of qualifications in order to practice and often does not deal with the actual issues related to performing inspections. Also, there are a number of inspectors out there who are not members of ASHI and CAHPI but claim that their inspections are performed in accordance with ASHI or CAHPI standards. This is completely misleading, bordering on deception, because if they aren't an up-to-date member of ASHI or CAHPI, they can't be held accountable by ASHI or CAHPI. An inspector's membership qualifications can always be confirmed on ASHI or CAHPI websites, which are noted in the appendix.

As I've said before, ASHI has been the forerunner of organized home inspectors in the USA and, with their support and blessing, CAHPI along with the provincial chapters has followed closely in their footsteps in Canada. One of things that I've found interesting while researching for this book is that no matter who else has tried to start up or compete with them, not-for-profit or for-profit, they've routinely merged with or replicated ASHI or CAHPI's standards of practice, code of ethics and membership qualifications. If these two independent associations have proven their ability to work together, nationwide, in two countries and be the model that others emulate, why can't our 60 governments recognize that the wheel has already been invented and that it just needs the tire pressure adjusted for the various terrains that it needs to be driven on?

A Word About Licensing

At this point we've made a number of references regarding government regulation and licensing. Yet with everything that has been done to date in both the USA and Canada, I still consider the home inspection industry as being in the process of "coming of age." In the majority of the provinces and in many of the states, home inspectors are self-regulated, which means there is no direct government involvement. Anyone can print a business card and call themselves a home inspector. If your state or province licenses inspectors, you may still be surprised to find out just how much or how little it takes to become licensed.

Because each province (currently two) and each state (currently 35) has its own set of requirements for licensing, we now have 37 different sets of rules for being a home inspector. Further, of those 37, a number deal only with what an individual inspector's qualifications are to become licensed, which is only one of what I see as the four major issues/topics affecting the home inspection industry. To date, although a few have tried, no one has yet dared to officially speak out and cross the line to address the number-one problem plaguing home inspectors and the best interests of the general public today.

In the following paragraphs I'll highlight what I see as the four major areas of concern affecting licensing in the home inspection industry:

1. Inspector's Qualifications / Experience
Although there are disparities among the 37 different governments which have implemented licensing, they've at least set minimum baselines and made positive starts. Unfortunately, in a number of cases, as governments implement regulation, they have to be extremely sensitive not to exclude anyone currently working in a particular field (in this case home inspectors) and initially grandfather in individuals with less than desirable qualifications. But we must remember that they have drawn a line in the sand and things are getting started.

2: Inspection Guidelines/Report Writing/Standards Of Practice And Discipline
Establishing an inspector's initial qualifications may be a start, but it does little to insure the quality of an actual home inspection unless it also includes inspection procedure guidelines, report-writing requirements, a standard of practice, code of ethics and a disciplinary system. Without these missing components, licensing can create a false sense

of security to the trusting public. Simply stating that inspectors follow the ASHI or CAHPI Standards of Practice is a total deception unless they also stipulate membership in ASHI or CAHPI.

3: Uniformity

Based on today's transient society where the average home owner moves every 3 – 5 years, it's always confusing to see different rules and regulations for the same things in the different states and provinces. For more than 30 years, ASHI and CAHPI have proven that the industry can co-operate internationally at all constituency levels. With this model already in place and working, why does every government want to start over from scratch, instead of building on what's already been started?

4. Independence From The Real Estate Community

Now I'll step out directly into the firing lines and open up with what all home inspectors talk about behind closed doors but are afraid to say in an open forum. Here I'll discuss the number-one problem facing the home inspection industry today. Based on a combination of my front-line field experience and 15 years of talking with hundreds of other home inspectors, the major problem with our industry revolves around the lack of independence or arm's-length relationship between home inspectors and realtors. It's my stance that, until the public can be assured of a truly independent home inspection that's 100% out of the realtors' control or field of influence, there's little chance of public confidence in the home inspection industry. After all, do realtors tell the lawyers or mortgage brokers how to do their job?

It's Not Just Education, Qualifications And Licensing

As for educational requirements, the associations provide national conferences, training, seminars, courses, and local area meeting groups. In Ontario, as with other provinces and states, there are a number of colleges and independent training facilities that are endorsed by the associations as part of their education program. In Ontario, college programs consist of 10, 42-hour courses. The downside with the majority of these courses, however, is that most provide only classroom training. Over the years, a number of independent training facilities, private home inspectors and others have started their own home inspection courses or schools, many without any form of industry recognition. I'm continually hearing references from my students about 1- to 5-day courses that claim to qualify an individual as a home inspector. Anyone looking to take home inspection training should make a few phone calls and find out who you are dealing with. Remember, today anyone can claim whatever they want about themselves and their credibility on the internet. If it's a reputable course you should be able to get a reference from a ASHI or CAHPI chapter.

Although absent in the past, most inspection associations are starting to require mentoring programs (the first steps towards an apprentice program) for new inspectors. This is a very controversial issue as the latest ASHI figures show that over 76% of their members are one-man businesses, so mentoring someone often means that you're teaching that person to become your competitor and maybe even put you out of business! On the other hand, in areas that have become quite evolved for an inspector is looking to sell his business, it's an excellent way to attract a buyer. Yes, we've got our growing pains…

When I started performing home inspections, I was filled with a combination of confidence, nervousness and excitement. Even though it's now 15 years later, I can still remember inspections 1 and 2 as if I only did them yesterday. At 10 inspections, I started to get scared; at 50 inspections, the reality of my limitations began to set in; and at 100 inspections, I was wondering how much I had missed and why I hadn't been sued yet. At 500 inspections I started to feel that I knew what I was doing. It was around 1,000 home inspections (which represents over 5,000 hours on the job) that I really got comfortable, knew what I was doing and felt that I'd become a real home inspector! It's interesting to add here that while each varies slightly it takes about 8,000 hours of on-the-job apprenticing plus 700 hours of in the classroom study, to become an licensed electrician or plumber.

Today, with a few thousand inspections under my belt and continually adding to my education, teaching others and working with other inspectors, I'm constantly more aware of just how limited we are while performing pre-purchase inspections. Regardless of all the politics, there's nothing better than field experience and keeping up-to-date with fellow inspectors. Just this week, while writing this section, I consulted with three other inspectors regarding inspections that we were performing. From the bottom of my heart, I believe that we provide an extremely valuable service to our clients, but I also know that we could do better.

Over the years I, like other inspectors, have taken thousands of pictures during home inspections. Unfortunately the majority are taken for the purpose of documentation and not necessarily for re-production, so there have been some challenges in selecting those to share. Overall the editors and I have done our best to provide you a number of picture stories that show some of the things we come across as home inspectors. All pictures are from my personal files and are here to support the stories at hand and may not discuss every defect in the picture.

— CONDOMINIUM INSPECTIONS —

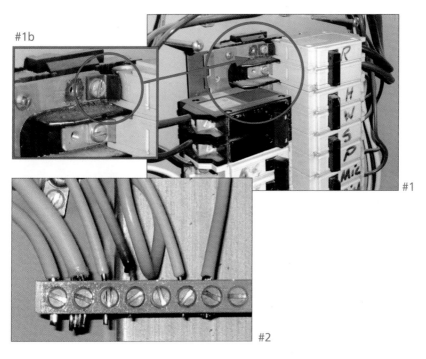

In pictures #1 & #2 we're looking inside the electrical panels of two different condominium units. In picture #1, and its close-up 1b, you can see where the electrical breaker is starting to melt which could lead to a fire. What you can't see is a second breaker in the opposite row that is doing the same thing.

Picture 2 is a close-up of the neutral termination bar in the second condominium unit. The neutral/white wire here is also overheating and again could lead to a fire. Immediately after this particular inspection, I was asked to check the electrical panel in a neighbor's unit and found exactly the same thing happening there.

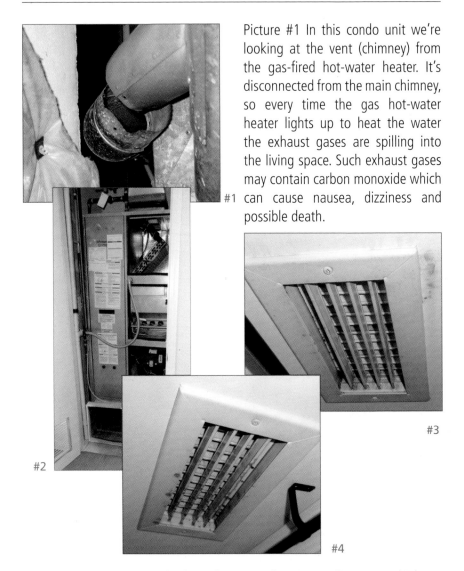

Picture #1 In this condo unit we're looking at the vent (chimney) from the gas-fired hot-water heater. It's disconnected from the main chimney, so every time the gas hot-water heater lights up to heat the water the exhaust gases are spilling into the living space. Such exhaust gases may contain carbon monoxide which #1 can cause nausea, dizziness and possible death.

#2

#3

#4

Picture #2 shows a standard condominium heating/cooling unit which are often oversized for the area to be heated or more critically, oversized for cooling. If you look closely at the air vents in picture #3 & #4 the discoloring is not dirt, it's mold. Because the air conditioner is dramatically oversized for this under 700sq. ft. condo unit (In this particular climate it could actually handle a 1,500 – 2,000 sq. ft. house) it is cooling the air much too fast. Because the air is being cooled too fast there isn't enough time for it to be dehumidified so condensation (water) is forming inside the duct work and growing mold to the point that it's coming out of the vents. This is a situation where mold can be a serious health issue.

Before taking these pictures I had to remove the items packed tightly around the furnace in this condo unit. Although this is a "zero-clearance" furnace, packing things up against it is never a good idea. There are a number of concerns here. First, starting at the top of picture #1, the brown color is rust caused by condensation (water) leaking from the air conditioning coil. Based on this, although we can't see it, it's logical to conclude that water may also be running down the inside and over the heat exchanger which can lead to premature failure of a furnace. Second, on the shelf in the middle of picture #2, what looks like crinkled-up aluminum is leftover water deposits from a defective induction fan (typically a $500 – $600 repair). Third, on the lower right-hand side of picture #1, the return air plenum (tin work) also shows a white trail caused again by water, this time leaking from the humidifier. (Note: because modern houses are very air-tight, extreme caution regarding humidifiers is advised as over-humidifying can contribute to mold growth amongst other problems.) With three different sources of water leaking from this furnace, it's no wonder that there was water running across the floor.

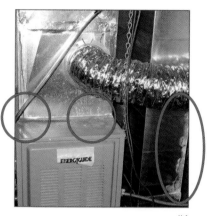

#1

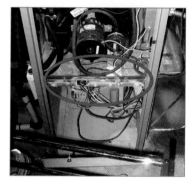

#2

#3

Picture #3 shows water damage in another condo. (In many cases this type of damage is actually caused by animal urine). Although this unit had been vacant for a number of weeks the area was saturated at the time of the inspection. Since there was no obvious plumbing in that wall it's logical to conclude that the water was coming from the unit above. However, there's no way of knowing what could be going on behind the wall (mold or rot) without cutting into it.

— NEW HOMES —

Picture #1 is not an optical illusion. This shows the bulge in the exterior second-story wall of this newer house. It's not uncommon for a single stud to warp inside a wall, but here, where there should be double or triple studs, the entire side of the window framing had warped or kicked out. As an inspector, when I see a single item like this it's one thing, but in this case the adjacent exterior wall, in the same room but without a window, was bulged out as well—that's another story.

Picture #2 shows that the warping at the window was equally bad on the inside. The hand you see is holding back the heavy curtain that was closed just enough to look natural, but far enough to hide the damage to the window casing. Although nothing appeared abnormal in the attic, this one definitely required further investigation.

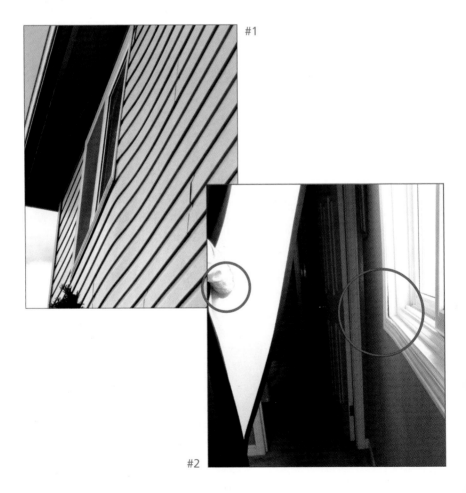

#1

#2

A birds' nest has plugged the roof vent, making it ineffective and causing water damage to this one-year-old house.

Not only is this an very crude job of installing an attic roof vent, but the roofer didn't cut out the shingles to allow for a large enough vent opening. Poor venting equals poor air flow and shortens the expected life span of shingles.

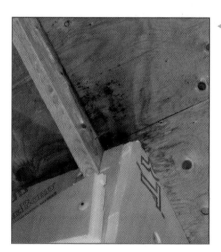

I tell all my clients that until about 1995 all skylights leaked; then we learned how to install them. Now only half of them leak! In this case the ceiling had been freshly painted along with the tunnel up to the skylight. (This should be a red flag for any inspector.) In the attic, this picture shows the real problem which could be an actual leak, condensation or both. Since this house was five years old everyone was impressed that the builder, once contacted, came back and fixed the problem at no charge. Then, to top it off, he went to the house next door that he'd also built, asked to inspect their skylight and again, without charge, repaired it. Yes, there still are good people out there.

#2

#1

In this case I was hired to perform a stepped inspection during construction in a rural area. The framing is complete and, although the municipal building inspector had not been there to sign off and approve the work, the builder was going ahead and starting to install insulation when I arrived.

The photos show the cathedral ceiling area over the kitchen. Cathedral ceilings require R-27 insulation (approximately 9 inches thick), plus a 2.5 – 3.5-inch air space between the top of the insulation and the plywood roof decking. Add that together and the roof members have to be a minimum of 11.5 inches deep, but the builder, using 2 x 6's & 2 x 8's providing only 5.5 and 7.5 inches respectively. Not only had he not allowed enough space for the insulation and venting, picture #2 shows that he used left over nocked members with the end cut down to fit into joist hangers for a 22 foot rafter span. Far beyond code in this specific geographical area. I don't know how this one turned out as I never heard from the client again.

◀ Earlier I've referred to "the house as a system". This picture shows an excellent example of things that can go wrong before all the components are put together to work as a system. Here the insulation would have been properly installed; however, without all the other parts of the roofing, venting and attic access port in place, larger than normal amounts of air was allowed to either blow or be drawn up through the soffit, displacing the insulation. Although this looks innocent enough, unchecked, it can lead to moisture and mold issues.

◀ Notice the two different sizes of plastic vent pipe. In our northern climate the smaller diameter pipe is required to be under (or wrapped in) insulation to avoid freezing of the warm moist air inside. Although venting is an issue here, the big problem is "someone forgot to insulate the attic".

During construction the waste pipes have to be capped and pressurized to ◀ make sure that there aren't any leaks. It's almost routine for inspectors to find test caps left on plumbing vent stacks. A plugged vent will affect the performance of all the drains and toilets in the house and can lead to sewer gas being drawn back into the house. Inspectors have to be careful calling this a defect as sometimes the glue holds too well and although the sides of the cap can be seen, the top has been carved out.

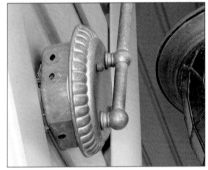

#1

Picture #1 shows a sample (I could have filled a full page with pictures) of the siding work on this six-month-old house in a higher-priced subdivision. I'm continually amazed at just how many of my clients tell me that they didn't even look at the exterior of the house.

#2

Picture #2, is the front porch light, as the builder left it. My question is, "Is this a poor siding job or an even worse electrical installation?" Unfortunately, this house had equally poor workmanship throughout.

Picture #3 and 4. The number one problem with heating and air conditioning systems today is not the furnace or the air conditioner, it's the distribution system (duct work). Every 90-degree angle in these pipes is equal to 10 feet of straight pipe and, during the cooling season, cold air is 3 – 5 times harder to move than hot air. Although I can't show it with pictures, the placement and/or lack of cold air returns is an equally common problem. Continually builders fail to take the design of the heating/cooling system into consideration when framing houses and home owners continue to wonder why their house doesn't heat or cool evenly.

#3

#4

Here we're looking at a sump pump pit. The sump pit collects water from the exterior weeping tile and the pump discharges the water away. This is a critical system designed to help keep our basements dry.

#1

Picture #1 shows the pit cover which should be found in the basement of most modern homes built in wet areas. In picture #2, we're looking inside the pit at the corrugated pipe, on the upper right-hand side, coming through the wall of the sump pit. This is connected to and is draining water from the exterior weepers into the pit. This one has been terminated correctly and you can actually see the water dripping out of it.

#2

Pictue #3 I find this problem often. The knock-out for the weeping tile has been cut out but the corrugated pipe is missing. In this situation you can see the pipe in the top left hand side of the wet gravel. Falling short of the pit and being partially clogged defeats the purpose of the weeper system. Are we surprised that the walls in the recently finished basement are extreamly damp.

#3

— LIFE SAFETY —

#1

In picture #1 we're looking at a clay tile roof on a six-year-old house. Notice the bow in the tile (that's not the camera lens!). Picture #2 shows the roof structure inside the attic that is holding up the clay tile. This roof structure was not adequately designed to hold the weight of clay tile hence the builder, after the fact, added the beam shown at the top of picture #2. This beam carries the point load (main weight) of the roofing system and rests on the lower beam, better shown in the picture #3 close-up. Notice the angle. One strong wind or heavy snow storm and the entire clay roof could quite easily end up in the basement on top of anyone or anything that had the misfortune to be in between. End result: possible injury or death to occupants and destruction of an otherwise beautiful house. After our inspection, engineers were brought in and recommended that the tile be taken off and the entire roofing structure (all the wood) be removed and replaced before the tile is put back on.

#2   #3

How many times have you heard about or read a news story regarding a house fire blamed on faulty electrical wiring? Here are some of the reasons. First, to help understand better, stop and imagine a little tiny garden hose; then figure a way to connect it to a fire hydrant and turn on the water. With electricity it's basically the same thing but instead of the garden hose swelling up and exploding immediately, the electrical wire typically heats up over a much longer period of time then bursts into flames.

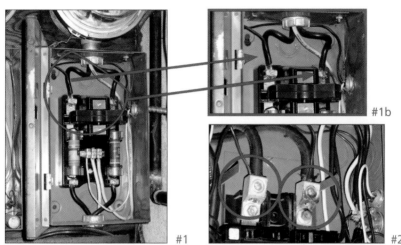

In pictures #1 & 2 we are looking at double taps (two wires should not be under one lug). Here it's not just the double taps, we're concentrating on the little wires that are tucked in with the big fat ones. The big fat ones are designed to carry more power, 60 or 100 amps, just as the fire hose carries more water while the little wires are designed to carry only 15 amps like the garden hose carries less water. In this case, because the two are connected, the little wires will actually try to carry the 60 or 100 amps which subjects them to an overload. As home inspectors we see this all too often and of course it's a serious fire hazard.

Now let's go back to picture #1, 1b closeup and look at the small black electrical wire in the top left corner that's clamped in with the larger black wire. Not only does this create a potential overload, but the wire is not protected by either a fuse or breaker. Because it's wired on the wrong (live) side of the main electrical disconnect, the circuit can not be turned off. It will always remain live even if the main panel switch is turned to the "off" position. Not only is this a fire hazard, it offers the potential for electrocution of anyone working on that circuit. Looking further at both pictures #1 & #2, you can see an arc/burn mark on the top right lug of each where someone caused a momentary short circuit / arch flash while working on the system without having turned the power off first—a serious life safety issue for the worker.

#1

#2

#3

Pictures #1 & #2 show a two-year-old furnace with a long list of problems, all related to a poor installation. Picture #1 shows an outdated vent (chimney) pipe being connected to the induction (vent) fan in picture #2 with the wrong size connection. The gap at the joint can allow leakage of exhaust gases, carbon monoxide and moisture back into the house. Although some of the rust was likely attributed to back drafting, the bulk appeared to be caused by a leaking air-conditioning coil that wasn't fastened solidly inside the plenum (duct work). The coil could be heard bouncing around when the furnace fan came on. This type of movement usually results in refrigerant lines leaking and failure of the air-conditioning system. When I tested the furnace it was overheating by 45 degrees F. (My heating contractor informs me that overheating is the number one reason for failure of modern furnaces). When I explained to my client that I had serious concerns about the furnace, the realtor created a big scene stating that the homeowner had installed the furnace himself and because he worked for a heating contractor there couldn't possibly be anything wrong.

Picture #3 Here we are in a basement where the furnace vent enters the base of the chimney. I'm using my pen as a reference to show the size of the holes that are allowing the exhaust gases and again, carbon monoxide, to leak into the house. Putting on my Indoor Air Quality Hat I questioned the home owner regarding her health. She explained that she had been having serious headaches and nausea for some time. Recently she'd been away from the house for three weeks during which she felt fine but the headaches came back once she returned home. There was no question in my mind that the furnace system could be the major cause of her health issues.

CHAPTER SIX: What's a Real Home Inspection All About

As I came to write this section initially I took for granted that it would a be quick and simple write, never thinking for a minute that it would be the hardest chapter for me to work with. Many people have their own idea as to what a home inspection is and what the home inspector should be doing. As we've said, although the inspection industry started to formalize in North American in the 1970s it has really only come into the forefront since the turn of the century. Since the industry remains unregulated in most provinces and many states, while others are still working out the bugs of their licensing programs, then add the vested interests of the real estate industry and the sensationalism fueled by the media, it's no wonder that there is confusion in the eyes of the public. Unfortunately, history shows that confusion often leads to mistrust.

For those inspectors who choose to follow them, the standards of practice spell out what the inspector is required to inspect, what they are not required to inspect and specifics that we are to report on. There is still no standard reporting system or inspection procedure. In most cases, if the inspector is using one of the better reporting systems that are commercially available, it will have a flow that, if followed by the inspector, should meet the standards of practice.

Because these reports come in a variety of shapes, sizes and formats, again we are left with an area of confusion.

As for inspection procedures, there is debate among inspectors as to whether we should be starting from the outside or inside. Once inside, should we be working from the basement up or the attic down? Although we're still debating, we all generally agree that there's no right or wrong way; however, once an inspector has standardized their personal approach, it's best to be consistent, do it the same way every time and don't deviate from it.

STORY #20: Older Gentleman, Get Me Out Of This

In this case, as I put my hand out to greet my client, he didn't even listen. He just blurted out, "Get me out of this! My kids and the realtor pushed me into it." We talked a bit and I got him calmed down before suggesting that we proceed with the inspection and see what we would find. Needless to say, he was quite relieved when we went into the house and found that, in one corner of the basement the water was deep enough, over that carpet, that we could actually splash in it. It was obvious that the recent basement renovation was a very short-term cover-up for a much bigger problem. (And people wonder why inspectors are always suspicious of fresh paint, repairs or renovations.)

Standards Of Practice

For over 30 years, the ASHI has shared CAHPI Standards of Practice, or a very close derivative of them. It's an ever-evolving document, and both associations are constantly in the process of formulating updates and changes.

It's recommended that inspectors make the standards of practice document available to their clients in advance of the inspection. A critical component of the standards is that they spell out not only what the inspector is required to inspect and required to report on, but also what the inspector is *not* required to inspect. It must also be noted that the standards are not meant to limit the inspector and we are allowed to exceed them, if technically competent in that particular area. Please note that it is against the code of ethics for an inspector to offer his or her services as a renovator or contractor to their pre-purchase or pre-sale home inspection clients. An inspector is allowed to provide other inspection or consulting related services, which they are qualified to perform. A home inspector is not allowed to practice real estate within his or her geographical area.

The following are two excerpts from a typical standard.

General:

2 PURPOSE AND SCOPE:

2.1 The purpose of these standards of practice is to establish a minimum and uniform standard for private, fee-paid home inspectors who are members of the _____ Association of Home Inspectors. Home inspections performed to these standards of practice are intended to provide the client with information regarding the condition of the systems and components of the home as inspected at the time of the home inspection.

(Section sample)

The Inspector Shall Inspect:

- Readily accessible systems and components of homes listed in these standards of practice

- Installed systems and components of homes listed in the standards of practice

The Inspector Shall Report:

- On those systems and components inspected which, in the professional opinion of the inspector, are significantly deficient or are near the end of their service lives

- A reason why, if not self-evident, the system or component is significantly deficient or near the end of its service life

- The inspector's recommendations to correct or monitor the reported deficiency

- On any systems and components designated for inspection in these standards of practice which were present at the time of the home inspection but were not inspected and a reason they were not inspected

Roof System:
The inspector shall:
A: inspect:
- the roof covering
- the roof drainage systems
- the flashings
- the skylights, chimneys and roof penetrations

B: describe the roof covering and report the methods used to inspect the roof

The inspector is not required to:
A: inspect:
- antennae
- interiors of flues or chimneys which are not readily accessible
- other installed accessories

Note: A typical standard will also include a glossary of terms in order to explain such terms as *Normal Operating Controls* or *Representative Number*

Standards Of Care, Duty Of Care And Code Of Conduct

Although The Standards of Care, Duty of Care/to Inform and Code of Conduct each have their own definitions, for many they all seem to blur together. Jointly, they represent the definitive statement that the inspector is/should be honest, working to an industry standard, without conflict of interest and in the best interests of their client.

Throughout the book we've talked in detail about the Standards of Practice. So what are the Standards of Care? While Standards of Practice are formalized and written Standards of Care are based on Tort Law and are not written anywhere. The Industry Standards/ Standards of Care are based on what other inspectors do in your area. If the majority of inspectors carry a 28-foot ladder, then that's the standard and a 28-foot ladder is what should be expected. If the majority of inspectors carry and use a moisture meter then it should be expected that an inspector carries and uses a moisture meter.

The Duty of Care/to Inform is a requirement that a person act toward others with watchfulness, attention, caution and prudence that a reasonable person in the circumstances would. Informing clients of limitations, restrictions and consequences would also fall under this topic.

A Code of Conduct is formally written and reference is given in the appendix and is quite straightforward. Basic highlights are that an inspector should not be paid from more than one source; the inspection report is confidential; and the inspector should not be offering to do contracting work as part of a real estate transaction-related inspection and an inspector should not be practicing real estate or be paying for referrals.

Limitations

It is standard for a home inspector's contract to spell out the basic limitations of the inspection, i.e. non-intrusive, visual only, the inspector is limited to standard operating controls. It's also important to understand that an inspection represents a snapshot of a specific moment in time. What an inspector sees today may not be the condition tomorrow. In addition to the standard limitations, all inspectors will have some kind of additional limitation on every inspection. In Northern climates, the air conditioning cannot be tested if the outside temperature is below 65° F, and on a hot summer day it's often not practical to fully run a heating system. However, inspectors shouldn't be using limitations as an excuse not to do something in order to perform a quick inspection.

Although I've had a number of clients surprised about what I can't or won't do, I can honestly say that I've had a lot more surprised by the extent of what I did. If I sense a client's expectations are unrealistic or the client is hesitant about my services, I'll either decline the inspection or offer to cancel it. To me it makes no sense to continue. At an annual meeting of the OAHI, I listened to the chairman of the discipline committee give his annual report regarding complaints they had received from unhappy clients regarding their home inspector. In summation, he explained that the bulk of complaints received were based on the fact that the inspector didn't communicate his limitations to the client.

I've had a number of clients over the years comment that "My lawyer, father, etc. asked that you make sure to look at the heat exchanger in the furnace." Because the heat exchanger is the only part of the furnace that's not worth replacing, failure requires a new furnace. This sounds like a very reasonable request but unfortunately home inspectors can't visually inspect heat exchangers. Occasionally we can see a very small area of them in older models, but nothing in modern units. Other common limitations or things that inspectors don't do (but clients may expect) as part of a basic home inspection are:

- Inspect wells and septic systems. (In most areas, a proper inspection of these systems actually costs more than a home inspection)

- Inspect wood-burning appliances or fireplaces (To be fully inspected, the interior of a chimney must be cleaned first)

- Inspect all aspects and function of appliances
- Walk on roofs (In some areas this is actually illegal)
- Inspect pools or pool equipment
- Inspect electrical panels (although this is one of the most common places to find serious issues, in some areas it's illegal for the inspector to remove the cover plate of electrical panel in order to expose the actual wiring)

Although some inspectors do provide these services for an additional fee, others will have references for specialized inspectors or will arrange such services on behalf of the client.

Risk Management

Understanding the concept of risk management may help to better grasp why there are things that your inspector won't do or why they have policies and procedures that they won't compromise or deviate from. To expand on this topic, I'm going to break risk management into two categories, again followed by a couple of stories.

1. **Risk Management/Health And Safety**
   Health and safety is naturally all about keeping oneself safe from injury. In many areas, government regulations stipulate, for example, workers, (in our case a home inspector) cannot go above 6, 8, or 10 feet on a ladder without fall protection and training, or cannot walk on a roof or remove the cover plate from an electrical panel. Inspectors have their own policies, such as not going into areas of a house that could cause health issues, wearing a respirator when going into an attic, wearing flash guard protection when opening an electrical panel or not getting off their ladder onto a

second-story roof. When booking an inspection, I explain to potential clients that when it comes to the roof inspection, I'll do my best, but I don't do acrobatics or put my life on the line for the sake of a $400 home inspection.

2. Risk Management/Legal

In today's world, lawsuits are more prevalent than ever. It's difficult to get three home inspectors in a room and not have the conversation turn to recent lawsuits. When the industry has seen lawsuits that range from involving a square yard of disturbed insulation because of the attic hatch design to a $13,000,000 suit over a loose handrail on a basement staircase, it's no wonder that inspectors want detailed contracts and report on things that some may consider trivial. While dealing with an issue unrelated to home inspection, I was recently shocked to discover that, in my jurisdiction, the small claims court limit is now up to $25,000 compared to $5,000 not many years ago.

Whether you're a home inspector, realtor or in any other business, in the past few years, risk management has become a much-used term. Risk management is a well thought-out plan and way of doing business that helps limit one's risk regarding legal action. We see examples such as a realtor recommending a home inspection as a means of passing liabilities on to the inspector or a lawyer selling title insurance to help limit both his and the clients' liabilities. Being the one that receives the least amount of money yet is expected to take on the greatest amount of risk in the real estate transaction, a home inspector's risk management strategy is paramount to staying in business. Hence professional home inspectors have very specific contracts and typically take great care to follow their standard procedure. I, like many other professional home inspectors, have been considered uncooperative and have lost many a potential inspection because I wouldn't deviate from my standard procedures or policies regarding the way I perform an inspection. It's also my policy to turn down a potential inspection if the person's expectation is unrealistic or things simply don't sound right.

STORY #21: On The Job Knee Infection

Often home inspectors don't think of workplace safety simply because we are in a residential setting doing non-intrusive work. In this case, I was inspecting a relatively new house which was extremely clean and well-kept. It was summer and on hot summer days, I wear short pants. During the furnace inspection, I'd knelt on the painted basement floor in front of the furnace. The next morning, I started to feel dizzy and lightheaded and could barely finish my morning inspection. Luckily I didn't have an afternoon client. By the end of the day, my leg had swollen and felt like it was on fire. The next day, my lower leg had swollen so far that I was sure that the skin was going to burst. I was in bed for 15 days, delirious for five of them and went through three different types of intravenous treatments before the swelling settled down. Five doctors were involved and the only conclusion they came to was that the infection, which they were unable to identify, was likely related to my kneeling on the basement floor.

STORY #22: Mold And Lawyer's Letter

Many individuals don't feel that a home inspection is worth the time and the effort required to take a morning or afternoon off work to attend. For me that's a warning, that the client is not serious about what I do, or has a different agenda. A short while back, I let my defenses down and let a realtor convince me to break my policy and do an inspection without the client present. Needless to say, it was only a matter of weeks before the lawyer's letter showed up threatening legal action. So for the sake of one $400 inspection, I spent three full business days preparing and reviewing documentation for and in meetings with my E & O (errors and omissions) insurance carrier to review the case. They informed me that the particular lawyer had a record of making similar threats, none of which had ever been successful and that in my case, I had done nothing wrong. My E & O carrier informed the lawyer the same way and stated that if he did proceed, they would be seeking costs against his client. That was some time ago and to date the only thing that came out of it – other than the loss of sleep and three days of my time – was a premium increase in my E & O at renewal.

STORY #23: Inspector Next Door At Same Time

Some time ago I had a realtor comment that I take longer inspecting the exterior of a house than most inspectors spend to do the entire house. More recently, I had just started an inspection when the realtor pulled in and commented that she didn't realize that I was the inspector and pointed out that I was at the wrong house. Quickly we realized that both (almost identical) houses were to be inspected at the same time, by two different inspectors. Shortly, both her client and inspector showed up and went about their business. My client arrived and we went about ours. Approximately 30 to 40 minutes later when I'd finished my exterior inspection and was getting ready to start inside, the inspector next door was already finished his inspection and getting in his car to leave.

STORY #24: Hurricane Destroys House

Recently a fellow inspector shared a story with me about one of his clients and the inspection. He'd done a morning inspection, business as usual, and thought nothing of it. Later that day, he got a strange phone call from his client stating that the inspection wasn't any good, nothing was like the inspector had said and on and on. The fact is the client was pulling the inspector's leg. A couple of hours after the inspection, a twister dropped down and flattened the house. An extreme story, but it sure drives home the point that an inspection only represents a particular moment in time!

Inspection Report

No matter how qualified and skilled an inspector is, if they can't communicate their findings in a clear, simplified manner while keeping them in perspective, there are going to be problems. The standards of practice state that a written report is required as part of the inspection process and makes direct statements such as "The inspector shall report on…" Although there are a vast number of formalized reporting systems available for the inspector to choose from, there is not a single standard reporting form. This leads to confusion in the marketplace results, as inspection reports range from a single handwritten page to 400-page books and computer-generated downloads. To simplify, I'll categorize the reporting systems into four groups:

1. Checklist Report:
    With these reports, the inspector simply checks off a number of boxes with pre-worded clauses and that's the basis of the report. The report may or may not have additional pages of general information.

2. Narrative Report:
    These are written reports, like essays, often with points and bullets that reflect the individual inspector's personal style. Typically they don't include much additional information.

3. Combination Report:
    These systems, while having a check list, leave lots of room for the inspector to write outside the box and provide more specific details. This report may or may not have additional pages of general information.

4. Computerized Reports:
    In recent years a plethora of computerized systems has popped up and the numbers seem be growing. These systems typically consist of a large database of pre-worded

statements that the inspector cuts, pastes and edits. These reports also may or may not have additional pages of general information.

Note: The taking of pictures and including them in the report will be discussed in the following paragraphs.

There is much debate between inspectors and the public as to which of these may be better than the others. I could easily write a page regarding the pros and cons of each, but that's not my purpose here. The real bottom line is that the report is only as good as the person writing it and the client's ability to understand it. As technology advances and the inspection market matures, things are constantly changing and the reporting systems are updated. It was only a few years ago, in many areas, that taking pictures in a seller's home and sharing them with the client was a serious no-no and considered an invasion of privacy. Today, with the advent of computerized reporting and digital cameras, this concern seems to have slipped under the radar unnoticed and isn't being talked about much.

Personally, I'm not embarrassed to say to my client, "Doing the inspection is the easy part; it's writing the report in such a way that you fully understand it that's the hardest part for me." I do a lot of writing outside the box and find that every report I write is skewed towards my client's knowledge base and ability to understand. (I often ask myself how inspectors who do inspections without their clients present handle this.)

Most seasoned inspectors whom I associate with agree that the inspection report is the most critical part of the inspection. They also agree that clear, concise and accurate report writing is a major weakness among inspectors. Often it's the realtors who find this vast diversity in report writing the most frustrating, as often, without the inspector's assistance, they have to interpret the report and explain it to the sellers in order to negotiate concessions. Other times, it's the lawyers and the courts that use a poorly written report against the inspector who wrote it.

Whereas some clients use the support material provided with the reporting system as a basic reference for home maintenance, it's the general consensus that the majority of clients never look at the report but just deal with the verbal report given by their inspector during the inspection. Many of the BEI (blind-eyed inspectors) use clients' habits like this to try to cover their tracks. During the inspection, they either play down or don't mention an issue, so that they don't upset the realtor ("blow the deal"), but then write it in the report, feeling that they've covered their tracks.

Overall, I again recommend that if you are purchasing a property, you want to be there with the inspector. If you notice something your inspector doesn't, question him. If you don't feel comfortable with your inspector, ask more questions.

Inspection Tools

With the advent of reasonably priced electronics such as moisture meters, digital cameras, combustible gas multi-meters and carbon monoxide detectors, many of these items have become standard tools for a home inspector. The biggest challenge is, does the inspector really know how and when to use the specific tool and is it the right tool or of high enough quality to really do the job? Pulling out many of these tools prior to detecting a problem or really needing them is often viewed as "grandstanding" in an attempt to create an illusion of the inspector's knowledge. Often such actions lead to a wild goose chase or backfire by creating unrealistic expectations for the client. In the section "Myths," we'll go into detail about infrared imagers, one of the latest tools to enter the inspection field.

One of my frustrations is with inspectors who think just because they have a specific tool, it qualifies them to use it.

STORY #25: First Day With Moisture Meter

In this example, the inspector had just purchased and used his new moisture meter for the first time. Excited, that evening he made a posting on the home inspectors' website chat page explaining what a great find he'd made that day. With his new moisture meter he had "saved his client's bacon" and kept them from purchasing the house. Then in detail he explained how he had used the meter and what his findings were. Unfortunately, what the inspector didn't know was that everything he did was wrong and now he was on-line explaining his mistakes in detail to his fellow inspectors. All of his findings were "false readings" which he misinterpreted to his client.

Not only should situations like this be embarrassing for the individual inspector, but both his attitude and lack of knowledge are an embarrassment to our industry. As a side note, his business didn't last two years.

STORY #26: Carbon Monoxide Meter

A quality carbon monoxide meter costs in the range of $400 to $600, reads down to 0/ppm (zero parts per million) and has a life span of approximately two years based on the usable life of the specific cartridge the manufacturer used. In this case, a fellow inspector told me that it wasn't necessary to purchase an expensive meter . He had gone to the hardware store and purchased a basic battery-operated carbon monoxide detector and fastened it to his tool kit, proud of the fact that it would be on at all times. What he didn't realize was that the standard hardware store model that he was using at the time only alarmed once the carbon monoxide level reached 70/ppm. Although any carbon monoxide level in a house should be considered an issue, Health Canada states up to 10/ppm over a 24-hour period or 25/ppm over a 1-hour period is acceptable. The USA's EPA (Environmental Protection Agency) specifies that 9/ppm over an 8-hour period or 35/ppm over 1 hour are the maximum acceptable limits. EPA's website also adds the caveat "one exposure per year."

The Inspection

Whereas the inspection procedure is subject to the individual inspector's style, a systematic process is critical in order to make sure that nothing is left out. Also, looking at things in a particular order can often save time when it comes to tracing household systems or suspected problems.

The home inspector's number-one skill is observation, and in many ways we are like a CSI Investigator you see on TV, trying to put together the pieces. The home inspector's focus is always on looking for signs of non-performance, things missing or not doing the job that they were designed for. Often even more difficult, we are always on the lookout for things that have been masked or hidden by an unscrupulous homeowner. Often clients don't realize that they, along with the inspector, are a guest in someone else's home and must treat it and its contents accordingly. In addition to being limited by time, the inspection is "non-intrusive" (can't take things apart or cut holes in walls) and is limited by "visual only" and the running of systems by "normal operating controls." For comparison I like to give the following example.

Think of yourself as the house, your doctor as the home inspector and this is your first visit ever to his office. He's never seen you before, doesn't know your history and can only deal with what he sees at the moment. He can't take X-rays or do further tests and it is all compounded by the fact that you can't talk to him!

I guess it could be said that a well-trained and seasoned home inspector "speaks house," or, if you're a fan of Monty Roberts (like myself), we could switch the phrase "horse whisperer" to "house whisperer." I'm not trying to say that some home inspectors have special powers here but I can honestly say that I've been in the situations where I felt the house was talking to me. One of my long-term peers "Brutal Bob" (As apposed to being called a "Deal Killer") assures me that I'm not actually hearing anything; it's what he calls experience!

Now I'm not going say that the following procedure is the only one; it's simply the format that many of my peers and I have followed successfully for a number of years. I've added a time frame so that you can get a feel for the flow.

Sample Inspection Procedure

Based on doing two inspections a day at 8:00 a.m. and 1:00 p.m., we will consider this a morning inspection and assume that the seller has been informed that the inspection will be at the house from 8:00 a.m. to approximately 10:30 or 11:00 a.m. The client has been requested to arrive at 8:30 and be available until 12 noon. This is by no means a definitive list of all the things I do, but I've tried to include enough detail that you'll get a feel for the flow.

7:45 a.m.
- Drive-by to confirm the address before a quick tour of the neighborhood to observe the adjacent houses.

7:50 a.m.
- Arrive at the house and park. Organize myself and walk across the street from the house I'm about to inspect, in order to get the macro view (the big picture).

- Check: is the house level, what's the condition of the grading, are there chimneys? What is the overall structure and what is it telling me about the interior systems?

- Formulate a plan to walk on the roof or inspect from the edge. Where is the best and safest location to put up the ladder for the best inspection results? Where are the typical weak spots in this design?

- Decide whether to walk around the house left to right or right to left.

- Take exterior frontal pictures.

8:00 a.m.

- Knock on door of house and introduce self to homeowner. Provide them with a brochure and explain briefly what I will be doing, how long I will be and areas that I'll be needing access to (I'm continually amazed at how many home owners look back in shock and state, "My realtor said that you'd only be 15 or 20 minutes...").

- Put up ladder and do roof inspection.

- Inspect roofing materials, flashings, and gutters. Inspect venting, vent pipes and chimneys components, anything installed on or through the roof system that is readily visible.

- On both the ascent and descent to and from the roof, view the exterior components of the house.

- Remove ladder (Never leave an unattended ladder set up).

8:15 a.m.

- Having started with the macro (big picture) view from across the street, I now proceed to circle the house performing the micro (close-up detailed) inspection of the exterior of the house, its components and grading, etc.

8:30 a.m.

- Client arrives

- Perform the "curb-side chat," a very critical part of the home inspection. Although expectations and limitations have been discussed at the time of booking, this is this chance to review, watch my client's body language and answer questions. I confirm that my client has read the inspection contract online as requested and have them sign the contract if they haven't already faxed it to me.

8:40 a.m.

- Start exterior inspection with client by reviewing the roof findings and grading before proceeding to go around the exterior with the client (this time in the opposite direction), explaining the details of the house while being careful to sort out serious concerns versus normal and/or maintenance issues.

9:00 a.m.
- The exterior inspection completed, it's time to enter the house. I start in the basement with the electrical, heating and plumbing.

9:45 a.m.
- Start the main and upper floor parts of the inspection.

10:20 a.m.
- Interior completed, it's time for the attic inspection.

10:25 a.m.
- Test furnace or air conditioning rate of rise and check the heating and cooling distribution system throughout the house.

10:30-10:45 a.m.
- Inspection portion at house wraps up with a quick recap and request for questions. This is where some inspectors part company, go home and write their report telling the client that it will be available the next day on the internet. Personally, I write the report then and there in my truck and make arrangements to meet with the client again in 45-50 minutes to review.

10:45 – 11:30 a.m.
- Write report in vehicle in front of house.

11:30 a.m.
- Regroup with client at coffee shop and present and review report in detail.

12:00 noon
- Ask for my check and part company.

Notes:
- A home inspector is not qualified to, and shouldn't, comment on the price of the house.

- Home inspectors do not "pass" or "fail" a house; they report on its condition and the buyer makes that choice.

- Although inspectors are advised not to provide cost estimates on possible repairs and renovations, a large percentage of us do.

So What Makes A Good Home Inspector?

So, what makes a good home inspector? This is an excellent question and definitely a passionate topic of debate for many. It's my opinion that home inspection is 75% communications skills and 25% technical knowledge. However, if you don't have the technical knowledge, it is not going to work!

One of my biggest shocks when entering the field of home inspection was discovering just how little the average homeowner knows about their house and how it works. Many of us spend considerable time educating our clients in order that they can understand what we are talking about. I shudder when I hear the many stories of uneducated clients who didn't attend their inspection, tried to understand a poorly written report and then found that the inspection was basically a waste of money. There's an obvious reason why a lot of these people aren't happy with their inspection.

I'm sure that by reading this far you've already started to develop your own idea of what you might be looking for in an inspector. Let's take a minute here and recap.

A Good Inspector:

1. Freely discusses your concerns and questions and clearly explains his or her services, qualifications and limitations before booking the inspection

2. Is punctual, organized, systematic and analytical

3. Is a good communicator and provides a formal written or computerized report

4. Has strong technical skills regarding building science, construction and the concept of the house as a system

5. Has formal inspection training

6. Is licensed, if required in your area

7. Belongs to ASHI or CAHPI and adheres to its standards of practice and code of ethics

8. When using tools, understands where, how and the reason for using them

9. Is professional and confident but is not embarrassed to admit when he or she doesn't know something

10. In our multi-cultural society I strongly encourage that the inspector speak the same language as their client

11. There is no gender issue in the inspection industry and although there are a number of successful female inspectors, there's definitely room for more

In the world of constant advertising, I've always been skeptical of someone's claims about how good their products and services are. Today, with technical advances, the internet has helped this evolve to a new level. In the past the success of many businesses could be partially judged by the level and cost of their advertising. For example, based on cost, a large ad indicated a large established business. Today, individuals with the appropriate computer skills can, for less than the cost of a single ad in a major newspaper, produce an elaborate website making them look like the biggest business in town, plus manipulate themselves into the top search engine rankings without doing even a single inspection. Whether it is home inspection or something else, many of these individuals or businesses end up being judged for their computer skills instead of the business or service they are promoting. The following story has always bothered me.

STORY #27: I'll Judge You By Your Web-Site

I'll never forget receiving a phone call from a techie who didn't want to communicate at all on the phone, which I can understand is becoming more common. When I tried to ask him about his needs and explain my services, he sarcastically snapped, "I'll judge you by the quality of your website". By the short conversation we had, I'm totally convinced he had no intention of looking at my actual qualifications; he was going to judge me on the technical savvy of my website. I guess that was his field of knowledge, but I've always thought that someone booked a home inspector based on their inspection qualifications and track record, not their computer skills.

CHAPTER SEVEN: Myths About Home Inspection

In reality a large portion of this book discusses many of the "Myths" related to home inspection, yet I feel that I'd be negligent if I didn't have a section appropriately titled.

The following bullets are a quick review to highlight a number topics and conditions discussed in other chapters. I feel that the topics covered in this chapter stand out and should be discussed as Myths. The biggest thing to remember is that a home inspector can't read minds, doesn't have X-ray vision and if he or she can't see it, they can't provide a "conclusive opinion" about it!

- The myth that licensing will solve the industry's woes and best protect the public is discussed in detail in the section "Who's Setting the Standards?"

- Looking up at the underside of a roof deck, through the attic access hatch, is not a conclusive way of checking for roof leaks. As the field of view and the angle from which one is observing the deck create serious limitations. The fact is the inspector is limited to reporting on the sample area that he can fully see.

- In a rural situation, walking over a septic bed is not a "septic inspection" and running water in a bathtub or from a garden hose into a five gallon pail is not a "well inspection". Both are explained in the section "Other Types of Inspections".

- Taking the service door off and looking inside a furnace does not allow an inspector to view the heat exchanger. In modern furnaces the inside of a heat exchanger cannot be seen at all. In older models where it can be seen, the view is extremely limited.

- A home inspection is not a guarantee, it's an visual-only inspection that's made at a specific moment in time.

- The point that a home inspector does not pass or fail a house is discussed in a number of sections of the book.

- Inspectors' qualifications. Is this a "myth" or "misunderstanding"? It seems that just about everyone you talk to has a different position on this one and it's one of the general themes throughout the book.

New Homes & Condominiums Don't Need A Home Inspection

To start, I believe the statement "new homes and condominiums don't need home inspections" presents one of the biggest myths in our industry today. For years I've been telling people that new homes are some of the biggest disappointments that I've seen as a home inspector. In our society today people are conditioned that everything revolves around price point and the lowest price. Add this to the fact that building codes stipulate the lowest possible acceptable standard, and it's only natural that builders are looking to do everything the cheapest way possible. Next, add the human element: individuals put all the pieces together, individuals who have good days and bad days, (we all remember the stories about cars built on Mondays), add blistering hot summer days and freezing cold winter days and, let's build a house....

When pulling together the material for this book I actually shocked myself with the number of pictures I'd taken over the years regarding condos that I've inspected and the problems that I've found.

Together, new homes and condominiums have a dedicated chapter that you may have already read.

The Inspector's Insurance Will Pay For That

Again as every industry comes of age there are many misconceptions and preconceived ideas. In the early days, in order to make themselves look more professional, a number of inspectors promoted that they were insured. That was virtuually painting a target on themselves; the public saw the word "insurance" and took it to mean that the inspectors were offering a guarantee. Needless to say, the lawsuits started to flow and, following the path of least resistance, the insurance companies began paying out instead of defending their inspector/client. It pretty much got to the point that lawyers didn't even bother with a lawsuit. Lawyers simply phoned up the inspector and asked for the name of their insurance company and that was that.

In the early 2000s Errors and Omissions Insurance premiums ranging from $5,000 to $10,000 and more had become unbearable for many inspectors. Then a major lawsuit against an individual inspector resulted in the vast majority of Canadian inspectors having their insurance canceled while the insurance companies re-evaluated their position with regard to insuring inspectors. Today premiums have become more realistic and insurance companies representing home inspectors diligently defend their inspector/clients against unrealistic claims.

Errors and Omissions Insurance is explained under the heading, "Hiring a Home Inspector".

STORY #28: Missing Heating Ducts

That last thing that I do in every house is run the furnace and confirm there is air supply in every room. In this case, I quickly found that there was no heat coming out of the registers in the upstairs of the house. When I went looking for my client and his realtor to explain, they'd gone outside for a break. When I explained to them what I'd discovered, the realtor looked away and my client's face turned red. Later my client confessed that it had been disclosed that the homeowner had removed the ductwork to the upstairs of the house when renovating the kitchen. He explained that his realtor had advised him that if he had a home inspection, the inspector would never find the problem and the inspector's insurance would have to pay to fix the heating system!

Infrared, The Latest Myth In Home Inspection

In 2010 a international television celebrity declared himself guru of the home inspection industry in North America and, because of his popularity, launched a television series promoting the same. There is an old business strategy, "Make yourself different from the others so you stand out." In this case, he proved the strategy correct when he chose to promote infrared cameras as a major home inspection tool. Along with sci-fi type support from movies and forensic science television programs that focus on entertainment with little concern for facts, he was well on his way to bringing something different to the viewing public. Overall, it was an extremely effective and successful business strategy, which, in this case, resulted in a successful TV series for him and a dramatic increase in sales for the manufacturers of infrared imagers. Yes, very successful for Mr. TV Celebrity, his sponsor and the infrared industry in general; however, not so good for the trusting public or the home inspection industry.

Yes, I.R. imagers are an excellent diagnostic tool having many applications. However, they cannot see through walls, they can't see through anything, they can't see water, and they can't see mold, all they measure is the infrared energy (a type of temperature) of a surface. Further, in order for them to provide any useful information they require a very controlled set of conditions and operating environment, which typically are not available at the time of a home inspection.

So let's back up here and share a little history. The knowledge of infrared has been around for over a hundred years. Although not a hundred years ago, I can remember the 1960s when Kodak tried to commercialize it by selling infrared film that could be used in my Brownie camera. At the time real I.R. imagers cost more than a half million dollars and required a small van to carry and transport the related equipment. At the end of the Cold War and with the advance of technology, these cameras eventually came down to a price level that some high-profile companies with specific applications could afford. Then, after the turn of the 21st century, a decent imager could be purchased for a mere $20,000. Like everything else revolving around technology and marketing it became a race of, how can these be made cheaper and how can the manufacturers increase sales volume? To date, they've succeeded to the point that imagers are available for under $1,000 with rumors that eventually we'll see them in cell phones. But don't get too excited. Like any low-end tool, what's missing and do they really work? Also a big issue here (as with any other tool), does the operator have the required knowledge and skill to use it?

So what is infrared photography? First, it's not photography and it's not a camera. It's called imaging and the tool is called an imager. Although not 100% accurate, this is a very simplified explanation that most people should be able to relate to. We all know what pixels are in our television or digital camera. Although this is not technically what it does, for simplicity, imagine the I.R. imager being able to read thousands of pixels (depending on the quality of the imager) being projected onto a surface and each of those pixels reads like a thermometer recording an individual reflective energy/temperature.

Got it? Now let's start to complicate things a bit and changing the term reflective energy/temperature to "the infrared energy being emitted from the surface or object." Using this data, the imager then converts it to colors in order that the human eye and brain can readily relate to it. Very simplified, that's what a thermal image is and the discipline of Thermography starts to get interesting.

Now, moving to the next level of complication, we'll introduce the fifty-cent word "emissivity." Emissivity explains that all surfaces, being made up of different materials, emit or reflect infrared energy differently. That means if you look at human skin, drywall or metal that are all at the same temperature, in infrared they'll register much differently. On a clear hot summer day, the imager may show a puddle of water on a flat roof as being -20° F, and it's not malfunctioning.

So now we come to the next step, interpreting, which is routinely the most complicated and the most susceptible to error. On occasion, especially if you know what you're looking for, images can be interpreted on the spot. However, in true thermography, the pictures will be downloaded to a computer via proprietary software for interpretation. Last in the process is confirming the findings by destructive investigation (taking things apart) which is, again, beyond the scope of a home inspection.

In the world of building science these imagers have been commercially used since the 1980s and have become an integral part of inspecting commercial electrical and flat roof systems. As their usage grew, organizations such as the ASNT (American Society for Nondestructive Testing) and ISO (International Standards Organization) established standards for imagers and operators. What the operator is looking for dictates which standard is to be used. Think of a standard as a recipe for baking a cake; if you don't follow the recipe closely, the cake probably won't turn out very well. Need I say much more than there is no standard for thermography as part of a home inspection. Also, although prices continue to drop, current imagers meeting the basic standards for commercial use start around $5,000, which is more than the cost of most home inspectors' entire tool box.

Now let's talk about operating the imager. Although they come with a manual and software, we're no longer in the world of point-and-shoot or plug-and-play. These are a scientific tool that, if misused, can get an operator into a lot of trouble. The following is a sample of the designations currently in use.

Thermography (A Basic Overview)

Level I: Training typically costs $1,600 to $2,000 and involves 30 hours of in-class training. This provides the operator with the skill required to take images along with a basic understanding of interpreting them. Notice that I am stressing *interpreting*.

Level II: Training typically costs $1,600 to $2,000 and involves 30 hours in-class with a prerequisite for over 1,000 hours of imager use, and focuses mainly on interpreting images.

Level III: Involves the same time and financial commitment and delves more into the science of thermography and trains one to teach thermography and lead a thermography team.

In the following I'll discuss a number of the limiting factors which help explain my position that I.R. imagers are not an effective tool for use during a pre-purchase home inspection.

- The operator of the imager must have a sound knowledge of building science and have been trained to take adequate images based on building science for interpretation.

- Since these imagers don't see water or mold, as many people have been led to believe, and are in reality a diagnostic tool, it's important to know what you're really looking for.

- In order to get a usable image, the accepted standards say there must be a 15° F differential across the surface one is looking at. For example, if taking the image of the wall of a house, there must be a 15° F difference between the side of the wall being viewed and the outside/backside.

- A wind of over 12/mph can change the temperature characteristics of a building, making imaging ineffective.

- The thermal effect of the sun shining on the house can play a major role, making imaging ineffective. Remember, a house has at least four sides in relation to the intensity of the sun's radiation, each having a different thermal load.

- Exterior imaging, including roofs, is best done around 11 p.m. or shortly before daybreak due to thermal loading of the building and building surfaces.

- In order to take an adequate picture of an electrical panel, the electrical system must be at 60% load. A properly designed panel should not exceed 80% load, so this means just about every possible device in the house that uses electricity needs to be turned on and operating. Without following this basic procedure, it's quite simple to take an image and get inaccurate information. Simply by plugging in something like a toaster, with the balance of the electrical panel at rest, it's very easy to take an image and make it look like the breaker feeding the toaster is over heating and ready to burn up.

- Reflected radiation, which can be one of the biggest challenges when taking an image is one of the major causes for misinterpretation of an image. Would you like to go on a ghost hunt? Without going into detail, I can show images of a ghost in just about any room of your house (*sounds like an opportunity for another TV program!*).

Note: When I'm saying "ineffective" or "must" in the above points, it has to be understood that these are not conditions that can be changed on the imager like adjustments on 35mm camera. These are environmental conditions that have to be right at the time the image is taken. If the control conditions are not right, they have

- Leave easy access to the electrical panel(s), furnace and attic. A competent inspector will be going everywhere.

- Move boxes and furniture away from basement walls.

- If you do things which limit the inspector's ability to inspect, you could be causing doubt, which in turn creates delays if the inspector has to report, "Inaccessible; further investigation is required."

- Make sure that your house is accurately advertised, e.g., size of electrical service, age of roofing materials and appliances.

- Avoid misrepresenting anything. One of the main reasons my clients walk away from a deal is because something was misrepresented, or they were outright lied to.

- Recent renovations are always of concern to an inspector. Invoices or saying that work was professionally done is little assurance. I recommend having both the permits and notices of compliance (confirmation that the final inspection of the work was done and passed) readily available. Don't try making things like this up on your own computer. That really gets people upset.

- Please, if you have dogs, either take them with you or have them in a cage. I've been bitten more than once by the "Don't-worry-he's-harmless."

STORY #33: Impressed Homeowner

I get a smile recalling this story. My phone rang and the conversation went like this. "Hi! You inspected my house last week and you cost me a new furnace. Guess I should be mad at you, but obviously you're the kind of inspector I want working for me. Can we book an inspection for the house I'm buying?"

Cover-Ups

Home inspectors are often criticized for overreacting, causing doubt in the minds of a buyer. The following are some of the reasons why we question things. I'm just one inspector and like the rest of my stories, the following are all true and have happened to me.

STORY #34: Plumbing Cover-Up

As home inspectors, other than opening our mailbox and finding one of those white #10 envelopes that seals on the end, the other thing that makes our hearts stop is picking up the phone and hearing the caller start off with, "You did a home inspection for me and..." I'll start this story by finishing the quote. "Well, every time that we use the washing machine, the hole in the basement floor overflows, and both realtors and both lawyers say that I'm supposed to sue you, but I don't think that's right."

Do you think that she had my attention? Now, as an inspector, I'm used to getting threatening calls from realtors, but this was my client and her voice had an edge to it. Once I got my heart restarted, I responded by politely asking for more information. After listening carefully to her story, I asked when I could come to the house and see the situation for myself. The minute we hung up the phone, I went to the files and pulled my copy of the inspection report and printed the pictures. Two hours later, we were standing in her basement comparing the pictures that I'd taken at the time of the inspection with the current condition. For clarification, the room had a dirt floor and the furnace was at the rear wall with the plumbing stack to its right and the laundry sink, washer and dryer on the left.

A: What I Saw At The Time Of The Inspection

At the time of the inspection, there had been a large blanket on a clothesline serving as a room divider hiding a wall of boxes, the furnace and plumbing stack. At that time, I did move the wall of boxes (beyond standards of practice) to gain access to both the furnace and the plumbing stack. I'd noticed something not right about the plumbing stack, but nothing wrong that I could comment on (note: this is where I joke about being a house whisperer or the house was talking to me!). Over by the laundry area I discovered that the laundry tub wasn't connected to a drain, but the washing machine was set up to drain into the laundry tub.

Based on the above findings, my report read, "Further investigation regarding basement plumbing is required. Laundry tub has no drain and a gray water pump will be needed." Fortunately for me, the first digital cameras had just come on the market and I had taken appropriate pictures.

B: What I Saw After My Client Moved In

Now that my client had moved into the house, all the storage boxes, etc. were gone from the basement. Other than moving in their personal effects, my client explained that they had made no changes in the room.

At the laundry tub, I found that a hose had been connected from the drain and run along the wall behind the furnace to the plumbing stack. At the bottom of the plumbing stack the clean-out access cap been removed. The end of the hose was placed loosely into the opening. In addition there was now a large "D"-shaped hole dug out from the foundation in the dirt floor. The hole went down to the bottom of the footing and under the footing there was a piece of plastic pipe sticking out. My client's explanation was that when they ran the washing machine, the clean-out hole in the plumbing stack overflowed into the hole in the dirt floor and the pipe under the footing wasn't taking the water away fast enough, hence was flooding the dirt floor.

C: Time To Compare

Now, standing there with 8" x 10" pictures, taken at the time of the inspection, we could see the plumbing stack with the clean-out cap in place (sealed) where it should be. There was no hole dug in the floor and no hose running from the laundry tub. The highlight of the picture was that we could see what appeared to be the outline of a "D" shaped hole, in the floor, that had been filled in at the time of the inspection. Further, there was even a pick and shovel in the picture, propped against the wall.

D: Outcome

- There was never an apology from the accusing realtors or lawyers.

- The realtors put the word out to the real estate community, blacklisting me, and I didn't do another inspection in that small town for years.

- When my client contacted a local plumber to fix the problem, the plumber confirmed that he'd advised the previous homeowners that they needed to add a gray water pump as I'd recommended at the initial inspection and in my report. Only problem was he dramatically over-charged my client to do the work.

STORY #35: No Septic / Realtor Says, "Don't Tell Anyone"

I'd arrived early and was greeted by a very obliging homeowner. He was very proud to take me through his house (which I don't typically do but something got my attention right off) and show me all the renovations he'd done to his century home. He was also quite pleased to answer all of my questions, in a number of cases explaining to me in great detail how he'd done much of the work incorrectly.

The backyard of the property was about half to three-quarters of an acre with a beautiful view of a river valley. During the first round of my exterior inspection (first round is before my client arrives and second round is with my client), I walked to the back of the lot to judge the degree of slope into the valley and if it might be an erosion issue. Looking down the slope, I noticed an abnormal pile of fresh pine boughs. Because "abnormal" is always an inspector's clue to look further, I worked my way down the slope. In the middle of the pile, I could just barely make out a black plastic pipe with signs of a heavy water flow below it. When the realtor arrived, I asked that they go inside and turn on some taps and flush the toilets a few times. Well, you guessed it! The pipe under the brush was the sewage drain from the house. It was simply draining raw sewage down the embankment instead of into a septic system. When I shared this information with the realtor their immediate reaction was, "You're not going to tell the client, are you?"

CHAPTER NINE: Hiring A
Home Inspector

In today's market, potential home-buyers and sellers usually look to their realtor for the bulk of their advice. Often, this results in the realtor selecting and booking the home inspector or recommending that particular inspectors should or should not be considered. In many cases realtors are advised to offer a choice of three inspectors and let the client make the final decision. Again in many cases, as an attempt to make it look like they did offer a choice, the realtor will lead the discussion with a comment along the line of, "Here are the names of three inspectors," followed by, "This is the one that I used for my house" or, "This is the one that most of my clients prefer." It's obvious that the relationship between inspectors and realtors is very important but you have to remember, who will the inspector be working for?

Now, when you try to contact and book an inspector, you'll find that the vast majority of businesses are single inspector firms so if you phone during the day you may not get to talk to the actual inspector. Some may be relying on voice mail, others may have an answering service or booking agency that takes your call, while others allow you to go online and book your inspection without any personal contact.

Questions You Should Be Asking

For most people, their house is the highest-priced purchase that they'll ever make. I find it shocking how many of my clients make comments like, "We only saw the house for a couple of minutes the other night, in the dark, before putting in our offer. We didn't even look outside..." or, "You know, I spent more time researching and picking out my new TV than I did buying this house..." However wrong these comments many seem, this is the accepted reality of how the buying and selling of homes works in North America. The one protection that buyers should have to insure a second sober look at the house is to make sure their offer to purchase has a bulletproof home inspection clause and that they hire a qualified and reputable home inspector who will be working for them to protect their best interest.

The following topics/questions should help create the appropriate conversation for things that you want to know and help with interviewing the potential inspector. Because they are all important issues, I have elaborated on most in other sections in the book.

- Independence: Is the inspector independent from other influences and truly working for you and your best interest?

- Attending The Inspection: Are you allowed to attend the inspection with the inspector and will the inspector be reviewing the report with you?

- Inspector's Qualifications: What is the inspector's experience and training? A lot of people automatically think that being an engineer or contractor qualifies someone to be an inspector. Although these are excellent attributes, nothing tops proper training. With so many questionable training facilities and qualifications, the best assurance of a professional home inspector is membership in ASHI or CAHPI.

- Association Affiliations: If an inspector claims to inspect to ASHI or CAHPI standards of practice and isn't a member, there's an important ingredient missing. If you have a problem with the inspector, they can't be held accountable by the association.

- About The Inspection: How long will the inspection take and when will it be? Although there are always variables, a standards-of-practice inspection for a 2,000 square foot house should seldom be less than 3.5 hours (including report writing) and often takes longer. An Inspection should not be done in the dark. If the inspector talks about doing more than 2 full inspections (including reports) per day you may want to question the quality of work.

- Report: What kind of report is the inspector going to provide? If there isn't a written or computerized report, the inspection does not meet the standards of practice.

- Limitations: What is your inspector not going to be doing that you might assume that he would be doing, e.g., checking appliances, wood-burning fireplaces, pool, hot tub, septic or well? If you have special concerns, make sure you ask up front in case additional arrangements need to be made.

- References: If you ask for references or read testimonials on a website, who are the people providing them? We all have friends who will say good things about us. You might want to ask if you could phone a recent client.

- Price: Of course, price is always a concern. As part of a consumer society, we've all been programmed to price-shop, but a home inspection is not comparable to getting prices on the same model TV or dishwasher at a variety of different stores. We're going to talk in detail about price in the final chapters of the book. Just remember, you are probably going to get only what you pay for. (Another tip from a long-term businessman) Never ask price up front. First make the inspector tell you about what you are getting for your money.

- Extra: Are there any other charges or services that the inspector will try to sell you at the actual inspection?

- Contract: Does the inspector have a contract, and can you read it before the inspection, along with the Standards of Practice?

- Insurance: I'm always nervous when a client asks me if I have insurance. My first reaction, along with many other inspectors, is, "Does this person want to sue me?" Maybe I don't want them as a client. Hence, I recommend that while asking this question is very important, do exercise diplomacy regarding how you ask it.

- Note: Be suspicious of any inspection business that advertises their "company" as being a certified ACI or registered RHI. Only individual inspectors receive these designations, not companies.

- Certified is a commonly used term in our society today and often misrepresented by inspectors who claim to be "Certified" by some self-proclaimed person or training body that has no official recognition.

Although this is not an exhaustive list, it provides the kind of questions that will create good dialogue to help you assess if the inspector you are talking to is the type of individual that you want to work with. Remember when calling around, many good inspectors are also interviewing you and deciding if your expectations are realistic and if they really want to work for you.

The Inspection Contract

Contracts have become a standard part of modern life. In relation to all the papers that an individual has to sign when buying or selling a house, the home inspection contract is a relatively short document. Because of the vast confusion surrounding home inspections, I do urge people to invest the five minutes that it takes to read the inspection contract before signing it. If you have questions, ask for clarification, and if you don't like it, don't sign it. A good contract should be straightforward and easy to understand. It should explain the inspector's limitations along with other key facts related to the transaction. I often joke with my clients after they read it, "I'm still going to inspect the house!"

Prior to the internet, clients often didn't see the contract until they showed up at the inspection. Today inspectors are urged to email the contract to their clients in advance or have them download it from the internet. Some will request that their client sign and return it prior to arriving at the inspection, while others will have it signed at the inspection. Most professional inspectors will have both their contract and a copy of the standards of practice posted on their website.

I've made this point elsewhere, but it's important to repeat it here. There are a number of inspectors out there who, although not members of the ASHI or the CAHPI, claim that their inspections are in accordance with their standards. This is misleading right from the start as, it may actually imply a relationship with ASHI or CAHPI that does not exist. Dealing with such individuals, you may want to ask yourself what else you're going to be misled about.

Franchises

As much as I have a "no holds barred" attitude toward making comments and criticisms about weaknesses in our industry, I do a lot of soul-searching when it comes to franchises because I know a number of quality inspectors who started out that way. But as I follow my mandate for this book, I'm simply trying to educate and provide information that you, the public, should know.

Ever since the trailblazing of Colonel Sanders and A&W restaurants, the world of franchising has become a way of life. These companies started as small businesses that worked. In order to grow, they formulated a simplified procedural system (today called a business model) that they could sell to others who paid them both an upfront fee and continuing royalties for the use of their model, name and products. However, today that formula has turned around and often the franchise comes before the successful businesses. An individual or a group identifies a market need or void, then builds a model and sells it to wannabe business owners. In the home inspection industry, franchises have developed from both perspectives. For potential home inspectors, having someone show them how to set up the business, with a formula for success, training them and providing professional national advertising can be very attractive. With all this support, the individual can set up shop and look like a well-established professional home inspector on their first day of business. This is an extremely attractive business plan, but how does this affect the consumer—in this case, the potential home inspection client?

Because the well-established franchises understand their market and the consumer, they provide competitive pricing and smooth professional advertising, giving the public valuable information the way they want to hear it. Also, these franchisors fully understand that realtors are their direct line to clients; hence they focus their main advertising and services towards the needs of the real estate community. Do I have to go any farther with that one?

Franchises cost in the range of $20-$40,000 and most include one to three weeks' training, after which the franchisee, with no other background or training, is considered a home inspector. (As scary as this seems, the training does surpass the qualifications for licensing in some states). Then the first day they officially start their new business, they can answer the phone and truthfully say, "We're ABC Home Inspections and we've been in business for years and done thousands of inspections," and not be lying. But what they are not telling you is that, for them, yours could be their first actual inspection. We all have to start somewhere, but let's be honest about it, OK? But for the next step, some franchisees go the next step and use their limited training to hire and train more inspectors to work for them. One more time, do your homework!

Errors And Omissions Insurance:

One of the hardest things for individuals to accept is the fact that a home inspection is not a guarantee. Considering what the average person pays, over the years, in premiums for house and car insurance to mammoth insurance companies, how can anyone realistically expect a single individual to invest half a day's time and underwrite a guarantee/insurance policy on a house for a onetime fee of $300-500?

So what's an inspector's insurance all about? Other than standard liability insurance (in case we damage something in your house during the inspection), just like your realtor, doctor or lawyer, a wise home inspector should have E&O (errors and omissions) insurance (Note: errors and omissions insurance is not yet mandatory for home inspectors in some areas). Traditionally, most people are more aware of the mega lawsuits against doctors than against home inspectors; however, in recent years the media have done a pretty good job featuring stories about home inspectors as well.

Again, errors and omissions insurance is not a guarantee of any kind for the house. Errors and omissions insurance comes into play if the inspector makes a major technical error and misses something. Unlike an insurance claim for a house fire or car accident, it has to be proven that the inspector was negligent. Occasionally the insurance company will concede and pay out if the inspector has made an obvious technical error but, if questionable, the claim will often go to court.

Although not nearly as expensive as doctor's or lawyer's insurance, my home inspection errors and omissions insurance is over ten times more expensive than my real estate errors and omissions insurance was. Even with a clean record. In many cases, insurance is a home inspector's largest expense.

Title Insurance

Although title insurance doesn't really involve the home inspection and enters into the transaction at the lawyer stage, I've again added it here because of confusion in the marketplace. Title insurance gained popularity in the USA in the 1980s and came to Canada in the 1990s. At a real estate convention in the late 1990s, an agent from one of the title insurance companies explained to me and a group of other inspectors how they were going to be putting us out of business by replacing the home inspection with an insurance policy. Although I've read about one case where title insurance covered a major structural issue, that's not the direction that the business went.

Here's the best explanation that I can offer. Other than title insurance, all insurance is designed to protect someone from a future event such as a car accident or a house burning down. Title insurance, on the other hand, is the only insurance designed to protect someone from a past event, e.g., something that has happened in the past, such as a mistake in a property survey or in the lawyer's past title search. It is not an insurance policy on the house. As part of their risk management, most lawyers both recommend and sell title insurance to their clients.

STORY #36: Old Furnace And Lawyer's Letters

This story revolves around a lawyer's letter. At the time of the inspection I had explained to my client while standing beside the furnace that it was over 30 years old, had outlived its life expectancy and would more than likely need replacing. I remember joking that the homeowner must have had a lot of time on his hands because he'd actually painted it. After the inspection, I reviewed my report page by page with my client as I always do. On the heating page, I filled in the section regarding the furnace and reported that it was old, required immediate investigation and wrote the estimated price for a new furnace. Once the client and I had gone over the report page by page, we finished with writing the summary page where I again wrote that the furnace was a probable expense and again included an estimated price to replace it.

A number of weeks had gone by when I received a letter from my client's lawyer stating that I owed her a new furnace because I hadn't put a tick mark in one of the boxes on the heating page under the line "Probability of failure/high". It took weeks and hours of letter-writing (I recall there were 7 in total) to get that lawyer off my back. Who was right? Who was wrong? Yes, I missed ticking off a box, but I'd also communicated to my client three times verbally and twice written (including a price) that a new furnace was required.

— LIFE SAFETY —

Picture # 1 This house didn't have a shower so a small electric water pump was hooked up with a hose and shower head to make one. In order to shower one first fills the tub, then standing in a tub of water reaches out with the electrical cord in hand and plugs it into a live electrical outlet, which didn't even have a GFI (ground fault interrupter). Please don't try this at your house unless you want to get electrocuted.

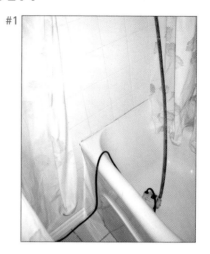

Picture #2 These are the main electrical lines coming into the house. The ground has settled leaving the live electrical lines exposed at the edge of the driveway right against the house. This is exactly in line to be hit with the blade of a snow shovel while cleaning the driveway. Again, possible electrocution or death to the snow shoveller.

Picture #3 A lot of work went into this project, yet it shows why people are required to have building permits. Someone rebuilt the old staircase. Although they didn't follow the standards for rise and run (step height and tread depth), here we are looking at the hand rail. For safety, this type of staircase is required to have hand rail approximately 34 inches above the steps. At the bottom it may be 34 inches (I didn't measure) but at the top it's about 15 inches high. Going down the stairs an adult must bend over and put their hand lower than knee level to hold onto the railing. Could there be a better way to throw someone off balance and have them fall down the stairs?

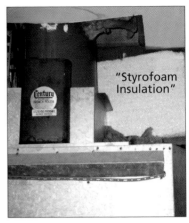

"Styrofoam Insulation"

#1   #2

Pictures # 1 & #2 show one of those instances where I asked myself, "What were they thinking?" At first glance photo #1 appears to show a very appealing marble-faced wood-burning fireplace. A closer look revealed that although it was wood burning, what appeared to be green marble was actually peel-and-stick vinyl floor tiles. Then, to add to the fire hazard, picture #2 shows that not only was the unit improperly installed (this is the back of the fireplace protruding into the garage) but there's an old rusted can of furniture polish sitting on top of the fire box and plastic foam insulation up against the chimney!

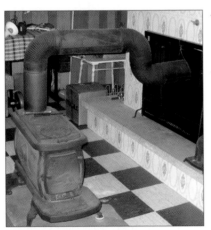

◀ Just when you think you've seen everything! Vent pipes are to have a minimum upward angle of ¼ inch per foot.

Picture #3 shows rust and corrosion caused by a leaking roof draining through the electrical panel. Electricity mixed with water is always a serious safety concern. ▶ #3

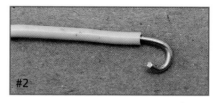

During this inspection I'd discussed the life safety issue and recommended that my client immediately bring in a qualified electrician to inspect and tail the aluminum wiring. Estimated cost of $1,200. – $1,500. After the inspection the realtor advised the client that this was not necessary and that an ESA inspection for $150. – $250. would qualify them for insurance. Naturally my client, wanting to save money, took the realtor's advice and not mine. Shortly after moving in the client phoned me explaining that they were having electrical problems. Picture #1 shows a sample of the charred and burnt wires the electrician found. Picture #2 shows what a wire should look like. As I often see, the realtor had no respect for the home inspector or safety of the client. It was all about down playing the issue in order to make the sale! However in this case, realizing his error in judgement, the realtor voluntarily paid the electricians bill.

Pictures #3 & #4 Again this is where I joke about "speaking house". The roof of this rental property was not one that I would normally climb on, nor was the chimney one that I would have looked down except some urge told me that I had to go there. Picture #3 shows what could be seen with the naked eye looking down the chimney while picture #4 shows what things look like with a strong flashlight. The inside of the chimney was almost 100% plugged and looked more like a compost pile. Once inside the house, we discovered that both a high-efficiency gas furnace and a conventional hot-water heater (not to be vented together) were vented into this chimney. I have no idea how either of the appliances was able to function, but I do know that the bulk of their exhaust gasses, including carbon monoxide, were building up in the house which didn't have a carbon monoxide detector.

#3

#4

— MOULD —

#1

#2

#3

Here I was called in to investigate an odor. After we moved some furniture and discovered the mold shown in picture #1, I was hired to supervise the cleanup. Although I don't have a photo to share with the baseboard still on, we successfully washed the area clean (as can be seen with the drywall in picture #2) before removing the baseboard. (In a home inspection scenario this mold could have been 100% washed away by a homeowner before the inspection). The middle photo shows what was hidden behind the baseboard in picture #1 after we started taking the wall apart. Picture #3 shows the mold growth on the back of the drywall in the same area. I always explain to my clients, if there is visible mold on the drywall or paneling of an exterior basement wall there is typically about ten times more on the backside. Drywall is like a buffet table for mold; add moisture (the food) and it grows like a healthy children.

These photos show another area of the same basement where there was no furniture in front of the wall. Although there was absolutely no visible sign of mold, my moisture meter picked up a reading just a little higher than I was comfortable with. Since things were being taken apart anyway, the homeowner agreed to let the contractor go further. (Note, the plastic that you see on the floor is part of the system used by the contractor to encapsulate this area of the room.) Picture #4 shows what was found when the baseboard was removed. For picture # 5 the contractor removed the lower drywall and laid it down so that you can see the back side. The blue strip was the bottom of the wall and the plastic to the right is the vapor barrier. Notice the mold on both areas.

The first part of this example discusses how simply a problem can be washed away while the second part shows what can be behind a perfectly innocent-looking basement wall. Overall my bottom line is, "If you want to live below grade (below the level of the ground outside) you have to be prepared for mold. After all, you've put together the ingredients for the "perfect recipe" to grow it.

#4

#5

— MISCELLANEOUS —

Problematic
Mold

Life Style
Mold

This was a student rental and the picture shows mold on the basement wall and around the water softener. The balance of the basement apartment had at least this much mold on all the exterior wall finishes. Unfortunately the other pictures were not high enough quality for print. When we rang the door bell a student answered, still in his house-coat. He immediately apologized that although he'd been asked to leave during the inspection he'd just been diagnosed with a collapsed lung and the doctor told him to stay in bed. Finding significant amounts of mold in the house, I was concerned. At the end of the inspection I sat down with the student and, based on my indoor air quality training, interviewed him. He explained that he had been in perfect health until he started university and moved into this particular house. We were working with a very professional realtor and as a result of our inspection and his involvement, the house was renovated and the mold problem remedied.

◀ Again this story revolves around my "speaking house". This was another student rental and something just didn't feel right to me regarding the basement washroom. Fortunately I was able to get my camera over the top of the wall to look down behind the shower and discover that the shower had been plumbed with garden hose.

◀ Although this was a relatively new house the furnace had recently been replaced. I expect that it was replaced because the humidifier (installed on the wrong side of the plenum) had leaked water onto the heat exchanger and prematurely destroyed the furnace. Obviously, by the water trails and water we found inside the furnace, the original problem hadn't been fixed and the new furnace was again incorrectly installed and destined for a very short life span.

This is an unbelievably dirty furnace filter. A filter this dirty dramatically ◀ lowers the air flow over the heat exchanger causing it to overheat during heating season. During the air-conditioning season the lack of air flow causes the evaporator coil to freeze into a block of ice. Usually when a filter gets this dirty, the air cannot pass and it is pulled into the furnace fan. All these are serious issues. After the inspection the listing realtor was asked to remind the homeowners to have the filter replaced with a new one. The realtor sarcastically answered that the homeowner had already changed it just before the home inspection.

◀ It's recommended that gas furnaces be serviced every two to three years and oil-fired units every year. Having this furnace serviced regularly would have added years to its life.

◀ Another very common problem that goes unnoticed until the chimney needs rebuilding: chimney caps. The top of a chimney has to shed water. It requires a solid mortar/cement surface sloping away from the center so rain can run off. In this installation, water will run down behind the brick and very quickly cause damage and dramatically shorten the lifespan of the chimney.

◀ I typically take my empties back to the store but in this case it was probably less expensive than buying the proper float for this make shift sump pump. By the way, the float worked perfectly!

Can you figure this one out without ▶ reading the rest of the sentence? We expect that additional space in the furnace room was more important to someone than an effective heating and air- conditioning system. The entire return air side of the duct system had been removed from the furnace!

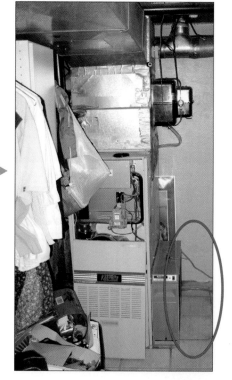

— LISTING INFORMATION —

Look carefully. Here we see a vinyl-covered wooden box with a Jenn-Air kitchen cook-top (stove burners) mounted into the top. Behind the fireplace doors there's what I call the "Boy Scout Church Basement Camp Fire", a couple pieces of wood nailed together with a light bulb placed under red paper. Also there was no support under the floor to hold the weight of the brick. My client was truly angry because the realtor had told them it was a "Wood-Burning Fireplace"!

◄ I think this is the most creative (or should I say disgusting) real estate listing that I've ever seen. This photo shows the top of a basement staircase and landing in a century home. There's barely enough room on the landing to safely get on or off the staircase. See the white electrical plug on the wall? My client stated that this was actually listed as a "Main Floor Laundry."

Picture #1 shows older shingles on the front of the house. The wavy pattern indicates that there is likely more than one layer of shingles which significantly shortens the life expectancy of the top layer. The left side of picture #2 shows the back side of Picture #1, while the right side shows the rear addition. You cannot see the wear on the left side of the picture as well as I'd like you to, but you can see where shingles are missing and others have broken loose because of old age and rot. Interestingly, it was the newer shingles on the addition that were leaking the most. At the time of the inspection the interior center wall was wet, top to bottom, from a recent rain fall.

About two hours after I arrived home from this inspection I received a very irate phone call from the listing realtor who claimed that he was at the house with another inspector who was saying that the shingles are good for another five years and that I'd better get right back there immediately and change my report. (He then got crazy and started ranting and accusing me, in detail, of all kinds of things that I'd supposedly done during previous inspections of his listings, none of which I was ever involved in nor towns that I'd gone to.)

◀ Unfortunately this one isn't even funny any more because I've seen it far too many times. In the realtor's listing and promotional materials these were described as "new shingles".

In this group of pictures we are starting on the exterior of a century home. In picture #1 you will see two round patches, in the brick work, which imply that at one time there had been an oil tank in the basement. Inside at a glance, picture #2 shows a typical century stone foundation that has been dug out and underpinned to provide head room in the basement. Looking much closer, at a better angle, picture #3 shows what looks like abandoned hot and cold water supply pipes sticking out of the wall. However, to a trained eye these could be the sign of a buried oil tank. With special permission, I came back for a second visit, took the caps off the pipes and pushed a fish-line, with a swab of cloth on the end, down the pipes. When I pulled the line back, the swab on the end was soaked with oil. The listing realtor basically accused me of putting the oil on the swab myself. Still interested in the house, my client invested $750 to have the ground X-rayed by an environmental specialist. The pink outline in picture #4 depicts the buried oil tank that was detected under the driveway. Again the realtor created a fuss and argued that there still wasn't any proof of a buried oil tank. It was later dug up and removed.

#2

#3

#1

#4

Picture #1 shows the effluent level and exit baffle of a properly functioning septic tank after the access lid has been removed. Picture #2 shows a close-up of the baffle (dam) that holds back any scum that forms on this side of the tank, allowing only clear liquids to flow under it and out the exit pipe into the weeping bed/tile. (In a conventional tank, like this one, all solids should remain in the input side)

Picture #3 is the exit baffle of the tank discussed in Story # 37, Septic Pumping. In this case the exit side of the tank is full of effluent solids mixed in with tree and plant roots, all of which are spilling over top of the baffle (which is almost totally plugged) allowing them to flow out into the weeping bed/tile. Solids should not be able to flow out of the holding tank as they will quickly fill and plug the weeping tiles causing the system to back-up and fail beyond repair. Picture #4 shows the input side of the tank after the pumper started to remove some of the effluent. Again, notice the roots growing out around the baffle. Although it doesn't show well, what looks like turbulence in the tank is actually plant roots which the pumper was trying to break up with a pole in order that they could be pumped out. Both compartments were packed full of tree and plant roots. Do you think that there was any chance that this system had been pumped the previous year as stated by the realtor?

#1

#2

WASTE IN...

#4

WASTE OUT!

#3

CHAPTER TEN: Other Types of Inspections

Most people, when the word "home inspection" comes up, associate it with what is referred to as a pre-purchase inspection, meaning an inspection that takes place on behalf of a buyer when purchasing a house. "Staging," the recent concept of cosmetically setting up the house to look warm and appealing for prospective buyers, should not be confused in any way with a home inspection. However inspectors must continually be on the lookout for cover-ups. When it comes to cosmetics of the house, many home inspectors, myself included, can't even tell you the color of the carpet once we've left the house. However, if you want to talk about a plumbing line somewhere in the basement ceiling, we can more than likely describe it in great detail, as we've trained ourselves to focus on the technical and performance systems of the house. At the end of an inspection I always do a quick review before leaving the house. After the umpteenth time of running back to the basement staircase to check if there was a handrail, and there always was, it finally sank in! I'd trained myself only to notice defects or issues of concern like a missing handrail. Although our focus is on negatives, it's important to keep everything in perspective.

In this chapter we're going to discuss other types of inspections that home inspectors may perform. Although this chapter may read more like a textbook, I feel it's important for people to understand the difference, as many assume they are part of a pre-purchase home inspection. The majority of these services are more investigative because the inspector is now working directly for the homeowner and is no longer handicapped by the limitation of being a guest in the house. Please note that this is not a conclusive list.

Pre-Purchase Inspection

Typically, when the home inspector is contracted for a pre-purchase inspection, the client/buyer is in the process of buying a house. The buyer's offer has already been accepted and they have 3 – 5 days to complete the inspection. Pre-purchase inspections make up the bulk of most home inspectors' business and as the main focus of this book, have been well covered elsewhere.

Pre-Offer Inspection

A pre-offer inspection is exactly what the name implies and the only difference from a pre-purchase inspection is that it takes place before an offer is made. Although having an inspection prior to placing an offer makes a lot of sense to many, it's seldom practiced. There are two main schools of thought on the topic.

1. One group feels that the pre-offer inspection is informative and makes them fully aware of what they are making an offer on.

2. The other group takes the position of "Let's make our offer and negotiate the best price possible. Then if after the offer is accepted and the inspection finds surprises, we can go back and use the inspection information as a re-negotiation tool."

New Home Or Pre-Delivery Inspection (PDI)

This topic covers delivery of new homes directly from the builder. This topic has already been covered in the section "New Homes and Condominiums." I've simply listed it here for consistency.

New Construction Inspection By Municipal Building Officials

In Ontario before a building permit is issued it's standard that blueprints and heat-loss analysis have to be presented and approved by the building authorities. At that point a building permit is issued and construction can start. The following list is a generalization of the stages when municipal inspectors visit the site to perform their progress inspections during construction:

- Prior to or after footings are poured

- Once foundation is built, but before the earth is back-filled around it

- When framing has been completed and before anything is hidden by insulation or other building materials

- Plumbing and electrical inspected before anything is covered up

- Insulation has to be inspected before covered up

- Final inspections confirm that all systems are completed and an "Occupancy Permit" is issued

The above may differ by jurisdiction, regardless, the builder must call for an inspection at each point and cannot proceed with work until each stage has been inspected and passed. It's important to understand that building officials are free to visit the site any time they wish and most will make surprise visits. Once everything has been completed, most jurisdictions issue what's called an *occupancy permit* which means the house is complete and all systems have passed their respective inspections. Although there are exceptions having an occupancy permit is standard in most jurisdictions before anyone can live in the house. I can recall showing up for an inspection one afternoon to find a very frustrated client sitting in front of the house with a fully-loaded moving van. It was closing day but there was no occupancy permit because a railing hadn't been installed on the front porch and the client wasn't allowed to move in.

As I've pointed out in a previous section, municipal inspectors are very busy and they are not policing the builder's individual contract with the purchaser; they are looking only at specific details required by code. As a result, some discriminating clients want an independent inspector to follow the construction sequence for them. Special attention should be taken to define a scope of work and the qualifications of the inspector being hired. In most cases the independent inspector is not shadowing the municipal inspector but focuses on following the builder's quality of work, good practices and obligation to specific terms and conditions of their contract with the client. These inspections can be very important, especially with homes in rural areas with limited development and in high-volume construction areas where municipal inspectors are taxed to the limit and labor turnover is high. Even a code-compliant house can have many serious issues that a consumer should be make aware of.

Rural, Well & Septic Inspection

In towns and cities most people simply take water and sewage for granted, only thinking about it when their monthly bill arrives in the mail. In the country or unserviced areas, wells and septic systems are very expensive to install and each requires respect and proper maintenance. Unfortunately I've heard stories of home inspectors that walk over the lawn and tell their client that there is no problem with the septic system while others run the bathtub or fill a water pail from the garden hose and imply that the well is adequate. Both septic and well inspections are very specialized and together will usually cost more than the home inspection itself. While there are home inspectors qualified for well and septic inspections, most will subcontract or recommend a qualified inspector for those services.

Septic Inspection:

Although most pumping companies do take a look at the holding tank, pumping out the septic tank is not a septic system inspection. A septic inspection starts with the inspector removing the lids (typically 2) of the holding tank, before it's pumped, to visually inspect the in and out baffles, effluent levels plus look for signs of non-performance in the tank structure itself. There may also be a reason to view the tank once it's pumped out. A more involved inspection will also include flushing dye into the system and digging up (intrusive) the corners of the weeping bed/field in order to confirm flow through the bed.

Well Inspection:

Mortgage lenders will typically require two things, a water sample and confirmation of the wells ability to produce water. A basic water sample is quite simple to take, can be performed by just about anyone and is recommended as an annual/semi annual (depending on one's area) maintenance practice. It must be understood that the basic "Bacteriological Analysis" is only testing for sewage and plant growth in the water. It is not testing for other contaminants or chemicals as those are more involved and costly tests.

Next to water quality the amount of water being produced by the well is of concern and is referred to by two terms, "recovery rate" and "flow rate".

Recovery Rate:

Recovery rate defines that amount of water that is coming into to well from the ground around it over a defined period of time. An example being 3 gallons of water per minute. This test starts by physically measuring the water level in the actual well at rest. (no water has been used and the well is at it's fullest/highest level). Then after pumping out a large volume of water the level is again measured and then timed to establish how long it takes to refill. Mortgage lenders will require recovery rates of 3 to 5 gallons of water per minute, for residential use. If you have other water needs like running a farm operation or using the well for a geo-thermal heating system a much higher recovery rate will be required. For specific applications, recovery rate testing may be performed over a longer period of time (possibly days) in order to confirm the consistency of the recovery rate.

Flow Rate:

Flow rate is often misunderstood by individuals and inspectors alike. Flow rate is the amount of water that the pump system can deliver to the house. The fact that I've seen a number of people fail to take into consideration is that the flow rate is totally dependent on the recovery rate explained above. By merely running and measuring 5 gallons of water (which I've heard of inspectors doing) it may appear that everything is good. However, if the well is not producing water fast enough (recovery rate) you'll be out of water as soon as the holding tank (15 to 60 gallons) and well reserve (varies greatly) are used up.

Well Report:

When a well is first dug or drilled the contractor provides a "well report" that states such basic information (there is more) as:

- at what level water *was* found

- how deep the well is

- the static level (when the well filled up with water how far below grade the water level *was*)

- what the recovery rate *was* at the time of commissioning the well

- if he provided the well pump, at what level the pump is hung (located)

Note, such a report *was* produced at a specific point in time and if conditions or water usage in the area have changed since, parts of the report may no longer be accurate. Seasonal conditions can have a very dramatic effect on a recovery rate and or static level.

STORY #37: Septic Pumping

This situation happened while I was practicing as a realtor. My client was a contractor purchasing a rural property because of the large detached shop. Although the listing realtor assured us that the septic tank had been pumped the year before, my client requested as part of the inspection clause, that it be pumped by a contractor of his choice. At sunrise one morning we arrived to locate the tank and meet the pumper truck. The home owners couldn't tell us for sure where the tank was and then they left. In most cases once the tank lids have been dug up there is a very identifiable pattern left in the lawn for a couple of years. We found non.

Doing some basic measurements, we located the tank dug down, and exposed the lids. It took the three of us together, pumper, client and myself to force the input lid up and lift it off. Once open we discovered that the effluent was flowing over top of the baffles and both compartments of the tank were totally packed with fine tree/plant roots. The pumper suggested that the tank may never have been pumped since it was installed and at this point would have failed in the very near future if it hadn't been pumped out. Although pumping the tank helped save the day, so to speak, the life of the tank is limited and left us all suspicious as to the condition of the weeping field.

Walk-Through Inspection

Just the term "walk-through inspection" puts a shiver up my spine! A walk-through inspection is *not* something that a competent home inspector will do. Often an inspector will get a call from a realtor stating, "We don't want a full inspection, we just want a quick walk through." In reality, what the realtor is asking is, "I don't want my client to know anything about the house, but I want someone else to be liable if there's ever a problem!"

Pre-Listing Inspection

Pre-listing inspections are done before the realtor lists the property for sale. The inspector could be working for either the homeowner or the realtor. Typically the pre-sale listing inspection is performed so that the seller can be pro-active in dealing with issues that may become problems when potential purchasers bring in their own inspector. Considering that many sellers are over-optimistic as to the value of their home and its actual condition, pre-listing inspections can bring excellent value to the selling process. Not only can the inspection help bring the seller up to speed with the realities of market competition, it can also play a critical role in selling the house faster for a higher price. Sellers must be cautioned that informed buyers will still want their own independent home inspection.

Some inspectors are resistant to these inspections or have special conditions as to how their report is going to be used. It should be clarified if this is simply to assist the seller or if it's to become part of the realtor's selling package. A prudent inspector is cautious to clearly specify what his obligations and liabilities are and to whom. As previously discussed, the home inspection is a report based on a specific moment in time and is intended for use by the original client only and is not transferable. A statement from a homeowner or comment from a realtor saying that everything noted in a report has been fixed means very little until said fixes have been confirmed by a qualified home inspection. Other inspectors will stipulate in their contract that they have no obligation to the future buyer and or will specify the terms and conditions for that buyer to hire them to re-inspect on their behalf.

I've seen inspection reports presented as part of the realtors' selling package where someone had gone through the report, ticked off everything that the inspector had commented on and written "fixed" beside when nothing had been fixed. Most disturbing was a home inspection report that had been cut apart, all the negative information removed, then pieced back together with the inspectors name on it, photocopied and presented as part of the listing package.

Maintenance Inspection

One of my biggest shocks when I first started in the home inspections business was discovering just how little the average person knows about their home, the required maintenance it needs, and how many had been the victims of bad advice. Over time dozens of clients have made comments along the line of, "This is my third house and you've taught me more in a couple of hours than I ever knew about houses!" Because of these observations and feedback, in 2010 I incorporated a property management company named CondoEase Your Home Canada Inc., with the concept of "Make your house as easy as a condo." In CondoEase we refer to the maintenance inspection as an audit. While a typical home inspection might take 3.5 – 4.5 hours, our audit is typically a full 8-hour day for a 2,000 square foot house in relatively good condition. As an inspector, I love doing these audits because I'm no longer limited to the visual only/guest scenario as I'm working for the homeowner in the problem- finding and solving mode.

The audit starts similarly to a home inspection but with the ability to poke and prod as we go along. At this point we will take things apart, cut holes in walls or call in specialists. Not only do we offer a report similar to that of a home inspector, we will also write a custom maintenance manual and provide hands-on training for maintenance specific to that individual house.

It breaks my heart to find renovations that have actually damaged a house. A person with limited or wrong information that has put insulation in the wrong place or caulked something incorrectly only to cause a bigger problem. However for many the policy still remains "Out of sight, out of mind" or "We'll clean up the mess and call a contractor when it gets too bad". I always find it interesting when telling a client that the shingles need to be replaced as soon as possible and then they turn to me and try to negotiate that they're good for another 3 – 5 years.

Limited/Partial Inspection

As opposed to a full home inspection, a limited/partial inspection may be restricted to inspecting only the roof, foundation, electrical or other single system. Again, most home inspectors will refuse to do partial inspections as part of a real estate transaction as we've been taught that judges have made rulings against inspectors on the basis, "Your are a home inspector, you were there, you should have seen it." Further I refer to the comments that I've made regarding walk-through inspections.

Where as a pre-purchase home inspection is visual only a partial inspection for a home owner routinely goes further. A partial inspection often surpass observation only and includes further investigation by taking things apart, problem solving or bringing in a specialist. Home owners are continually surprised that these inspections often take longer and cost more than a basic pre-purchase home inspection.

Callback Inspection

When inspectors get together, callbacks are often topics of discussion, as we all have them. By the time we get this call, the home inspection client has moved into the house and has found a problem. Reputable inspectors will return these calls promptly and deal with the matter.

Unfortunately, it's also at this stage that our associations often get a call from the client as well, complaining, "The inspector won't return my call!" This is a very legitimate claim, by the client, and you'll find that if the inspector is a member of CAHPI or ASHI, such calls will be taken seriously and dealt with. Inspectors who don't return calls are doing a disservice to both their client and our industry as a whole. Often these are the inspectors that end up giving their explanation in court.

Pre-Renovation Inspection

Often prudent home owners will contact a qualified home inspector in order to give them an unbiased opinion regarding renovation plans before hiring a contractor or proceeding on their own. Some inspectors are more qualified than others to do this and many also offer plan/quote review and/or project management services. The following story will help explain.

STORY #38: Renovation Quotes

In this case, my clients didn't really want to go through the stress and aggravation of moving, but needed a larger kitchen, work and eating area. They'd drawn their floor plan ideas and received three separate quotes from three separate contractors. Being unfamiliar with construction and because the quotes ranged from $25,000-$60,000, they were confused by what appeared to be three very different quotes, all to do the same thing. For an unbiased opinion, they contacted me, as I'd been their home inspector when they purchased the house.

Evaluating the plans, I explained that the two lower-priced quotations were to build the addition on pylons. Insulation would be mounted directly in the joist space on the underside of the floor sheeting and left exposed directly to outside air. Although an accepted construction technique and in compliance with local build code requirements, I explained to them that a basic principle of heating/comfort is that a cold space below equals a cold floors above. During the cold winter the floors (of what was to become their major living space) would be cold and clammy most of the time, and their heating bills higher. We then discussed that the higher price quote included a fully enclosed heated basement/crawlspace below, which would insure warm comfortable floors in the winter. They could have the additional living space for $25,000, but, if they wanted year-round comfort, it would cost $60,000.

Indoor Air Quality Inspection And Sick Homes

Since the 1970s, the rising cost of fossil fuels has focused a lot of attention on ways to control the cost of heating and cooling our homes and has lead to many changes in residential construction. During the 1970s and '80s, a concerted effort took place to increase public awareness towards efficiency. Almost overnight, the number-one accepted concept to save energy was the basic theory of "seal it up" and "make it air-tight" to keep the heat in (or out, depending on your climate).

Then, over the next decade a new term emerged, the "sick house." Without good air exchange between indoors and outdoors, the proper attention to the detailing of insulation, air barrier, vapour retarders and the building envelope, all kinds of things started to happen inside the walls of our homes and people started to develop health issues that appeared to be related to their household environment.

To best explain this point, I'll deal with the details in bullet form:

• Traditionally, our homes had resembled a loosely built box. These boxes were strong and, for the most part, kept the weather out, but they also had lots of air leaks and drafts. When minor water leaks or condensation got where it wasn't wanted, there wasn't typically a problem because the open air-flow evaporated the moisture. Using the "seal it up" theory, we changed the boxes into airtight "plastic bags."

- Next, picture a nice cold glass of ice tea on a hot summer day and all the condensation (sweat) that forms on the outside of the glass as the cold glass meets with the warm air around it. Can you picture that?

- Now, in a cold northern climate picture the exterior of your house (the plastic bag) as the glass, on a cold winter day. This time the hot air inside your house is like the hot summer day and the cold winter outside is the ice tea. Have you got that picture in your mind? If not, please back-up and work on it a bit harder......

- Now in that mental picture, what's missing? Where is the condensation (sweat)?

- Do you have an answer, or more questions?

- If your building envelope (the plastic bag) is all sealed and insulated correctly there shouldn't be a problem. But if it's not, that condensation is more than likely sweating somewhere in your walls. I'm sure that you have occasionally seen it on your windows.

- Now all this would be quite simple if everything was put together correctly right? The problem is that it's now 40 years later and the experts are still debating the proper way to seal our homes.

This is not a book on building science or the building envelope, but in the simplest of terms, I'm trying to explain that condensation in the wrong places is a major problem in our houses and can often cause mold growth, in addition to other issues. Now, add into the equation basement and plumbing leaks as other things going on in and behind walls and ceilings. The big problem here is that this can not usually be detected until it's too late and there is a problem.

Now, because we are living inside this plastic bag, we have to starting thinking seriously about all the other things inside with us. There's the possibly of carbon monoxide, but we've come to grips with that one and most homes now have (or should have) carbon monoxide detectors. But then there's the endless list of chemicals, gas, cleaning solutions, building products like asbestos, furniture and household items that off-gas, radon, smoking, pets, animal feces and so-called air fresheners, all of which can affect our health.

As a result of all the above, people are starting to put the pieces together and realize that indoor air quality is a serious issue and may be the major cause of many health problems. Hence the evolution of the "indoor air quality inspection". As with home inspections, there are a number of theories as to what an indoor air quality inspection is. My training comes from CMHC (Canada Mortgage and Housing Corporation) which focuses on health-related problems and as a surprise to many, seldom calls for air sampling. Their logic is, identify the problem and spend the money on remediation, not further testing.

Recently "mold inspections" have become big business however they are not "indoor air quality inspections" although indoor air quality inspections may find mold as a contributing factor. As for indoor air quality inspections, I'll break them into two major groups.

1. Health Issues Inspection:

Typically a health-related indoor air quality inspection starts by interviewing the people who live in the house to identify their symptoms so the inspector can establish what he might be looking for. Sometimes different symptoms in different rooms affect one member of the family but not others. For me, a typical indoor air quality inspection can take a full day. There is a good chance that I will be cutting holes in walls and I may need to make more than one visit to the house. Also there are things that the homeowner must to do up to two days in advance to prepare the house for the inspection, the simplest of these being removal of all the air deodorizers. Overall, I categorize houses with indoor air quality problems into three groups:

- Construction-related – poor design, systems or component failure, poor workmanship or something installed incorrectly

- Homeowner's lack of maintenance or understanding how their house works

- Life styles of the occupants

Although it's often a combination of all three, my experience is that second and third are the main contributors to poor indoor air quality.

2. Preventive Inspection:

This application may or may not include all the things listed in #1. Naturally, if this is being done as part of a pre-purchase inspection and limited to "visual only," the inspection will have serious limitations, hence air sampling may be the only solution.

If air sampling is required, the question becomes, how much money do you want to spend and what do you want to sample for? When samples are to be taken, it's very important that the person taking air and other samples is trained and qualified to do so. There are a number of questionable products on the market that are sold to both homeowners and inspectors that can be used for sampling. Personally, I always sub-contract sampling to a qualified lab.

All of this aside, to date in my practice, I've found sewer gas to be the number-one health issue in the houses that I've investigated.

Mold And Mold Inspections

As building science evolves, the experts continue to debate building envelope, air barriers vs. vapor barriers and detailing practices. There is no question that we've created excellent incubators for mold growth in our homes. I've attended seminars where speakers have stated that there are over 100 different types of mold, but only a handful are toxic. Further, with the advances of medical science and attention people are paying to personal health, mold has become one of the biggest scare words in relation to houses and workplaces. Although mold is a complex topic, for the sake of this book, I'm going to simplify mold into two categories: life style mold and problematic mold.

Life Style Mold

Based on the information that I've discussed earlier, it's reality that mold has become a product of our life style. For some time, I've been telling people that if their house is more than a year old, I can more than likely find mold in it. The real issue is, how much is too much? Mold around the bathtub tiles, bottom of the toilet, in your windows and on your water treatment equipment or a sweaty fridge in a warm climate has to be expected and remediation is called "good housekeeping practices" (OK, how many of you did I just insult?).

In a lot of the northern climates, mold in attics on the underside of the roof sheeting is very commonplace. A lot of companies are making good money convincing people it has to be removed while there are studies that claim the summer heat buildup will kill it naturally. Based on my experience in the field and being in thousands of attics, I don't agree with either. It's my stance that once mold is in the roof decking material the best solution is to change the roof decking the next time the home owner re-shingles. After all, if it's full of mold, it's more than likely rotten and needs to be replaced anyway. Seldom have I seen mold growing on the trusses or joists but when I have there were other serious things that needed to be dealt with as well.

Problematic Mold

How much mold is too much? When I took my indoor air quality training, CMHC defined too much as more than one square metre (a little over one square yard). Whereas this is a good, physically definable guideline, too much could more realistically be defined as the inhabitants' ability to withstand the environment. I've been in houses where black mold was coming two feet up from the floor or a foot down from the ceiling and the inhabitants claimed it didn't bother them. But my eyes were swollen and burning within minutes of entering the house. I find people often overreact to mold, but also do caution that it should not be downplayed. Often (but not always), mold on the interior of an exterior wall is a sign that something is going on inside that wall. I like to give my clients the iceberg example. When we were in school, they taught us that we only see about one-tenth of an iceberg and that nine-tenths of it is below the water. In the case of mold, if the moisture is coming from the back side of the wall it is usually much the same story. On our side of the wall we're seeing only the tip of the iceberg.

The Mold Inspection

Although "mold inspections" have become big business in recent years, just as with home inspections, there are a number of definitions as to what they should consist of and what the qualifications of the person doing the inspection are. Remember, if you have finished living space below ground level or continually maintain high moisture in your house, expect mold.

Again I'll cover this topic in bullet form.

- Do you want a mold inspection because of an existing health problem or are you simply being pro-active? *(Refer to the earlier section on indoor air quality and sick homes).*
- Remember, infrared imagers can't see mold; however when properly used, they can be useful to help detect suspect areas of mold growth. *(Refer to Infrared: the latest myth in home inspection.)*

STORY #39: Open House Mold

Back in 2009, I was attending a Sunday afternoon real estate open house when a guest came down the stairs, literally screaming out loud the house was full of mold, people shouldn't be in it and that it shouldn't be on the market for sale. Overall, she created quite a scene. When she took me up to the bathroom to show me her findings, she pointed out a sliver of mold approximately 4 inches long by 1/16 of an inch wide, in the caulking around the bathtub. Obviously she was the victim of too much media information and sensationalism.

STORY #40: Mold Inspection

In this instance I was working for the homeowner/landlord evaluating the extent of a mold problem. In the first area that I'll talk about there was heavy black mold on both the exterior and interior wall of a main floor bedroom. In this case we cut about an 18 inch square whole right through the side of the house. Although both the inside and outside surfaces where solid mold the interior of the wall was a clean and fresh as the day the house was built.

As for the rest of this twelve year old, three bedroom, single story house it wasn't so positive. In addition to the bedroom walls having high concentrations of visible mold (looked like black paint 2 feet up the walls), ceilings where covered with mold and kitchen ceiling was falling down do to high moisture content (there was not a roof leak above it). The bathroom walls where black with mold and the entire sink cabinet was damp and almost 100% covered with mold inside and out.

The end verdict was; it would be about the same price repair as it would be to tear down the house, sanitize the foundation and start over. There where three major contributing factors noted regarding the mold;

1/ As a factory build house it had been build under very exacting conditions which resulted in it being extremely air tight. Air tight is good however proper care was not being taken of either the house or it's mechanical systems.

2/ There were far to many people living in the house for it's size hence creating too much moisture through cooking, showers and body evaporation etc.

3/ The tenants had no respect for the containment of water or the control of wet articles resulting in excessive moisture in many places it should not be.

If there had simply been two or three people living in the house under normal conditions it is highly unlikely that there would ever have been a problem anywhere close to this extent. In my career this is one of two 12 year old homes where demolition was recommended.

Radon Inspection

Radon is an invisible odorless gas that's naturally present in the soil throughout North America. A large percentage of our houses have basements below grade, making us susceptible to radon penetration. It is estimated that radon is the cause of 10% (much higher when combined with smoking) of lung cancer in North America. Although radon testing has become a standard part of the real estate transaction in the USA, it seems to have slipped under the radar in Canada. There are a number of different testing methods for radon that range from a quick sample that can be taken during the home inspection to a more elaborate monitoring system that involves leaving an electronic logging system in the house for a number of days.

I've been aware for some time of the disparity between the USA and Canada regarding the dealing with radon; however, when compiling the information for this book, it's become obvious to me that radon should be taken far more seriously in Canada. The following headings highlight what is referred to as acceptable radon levels in Canada and the USA. Unfortunately it's hard for the layman to compare the standards as each country uses a different system of measurement which I'll try to explain.

Radon Levels Canada & USA:

Radon Measurements Defined:

Radon is measured in becquerel's per cubic metre. 1 Bq = 1 radioactive disintegration per second.

or

• Picocuries per litre (pCi/L) – measure of the potential alpha particles energy per litre of air.
   • 1 pCi/L is equivalent to 37 Bq/m3.

Canada

In 2007, Health Canada revised the acceptable guideline for radon levels indoors from 800Bq/m^3 (21.6 pCi/L) down to 200Bq/m^3 (5.4 pCi/L).

   • The Canadian Lung Association notes that any level of radon can be harmful and action should always be taken to lower the levels.

CAREX Canada National Map shows the estimated radon levels above 200Bq/m3 across the country.

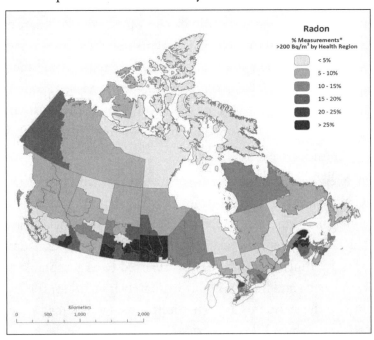

USA

In the USA, the EPA recommends that action should be taken if levels are over 4pCi/L (148 Bq per cubic metre) and that the average reading is about 1.3 pCi/L. (48 Bq per cubic metre.)

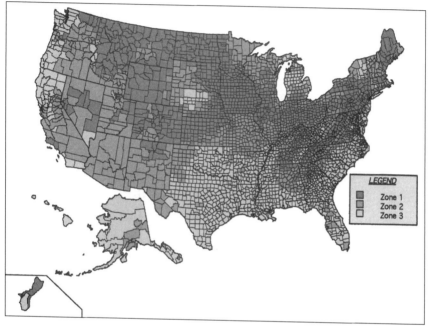

Zone 1 counties have a predicted average indoor radon screening level greater than 4 pCi/L (picocuries per liter) Highest Potential

Zone 2 counties have a predicted average indoor radon screening level between 2 and 4 pCi/L Moderate Potential

Zone 3 counties have a predicted average indoor radon screening level less than 2 pCi/L.

Note: These maps are re-printed with permission and are not intended to be used to determine if a home in a given zone should be tested for radon. These maps are simply to provided for general information only. However, it should be noted that EPA recommends that all home be tested

Higher quality versions for these maps can be found at www.carexcanada.ca/en/radon/ or www.epa.gov/radon/zonemap.html

Heat Loss Analysis/Energy Audit

The heat loss analysis is an elaborate computer-based program that takes in every factor that could affect the heating/cooling requirements of a building and calculates the size of heating/cooling system required. This information is typically gathered from the blueprint and takes into consideration the actual site location where the house is to be built. In many areas, this information is required as part of the building permit application.

Energy audits are performed on existing houses. Although not as elaborate as the heat loss analysis, they identify and input similar information into a computer program and combine it with a blower door test. For the blower door test, all doors and windows are closed and a large pair of fans/blowers is installed in place of an exterior door. Once turned on, the fan system depressurizes the house while interacting with a computer program to calculate the air loss of the house. The program then assigns a number which is defined as the energy rating for the building. Based on these findings, recommendations are typically given for upgrading the building's energy efficiency.

Insurance Inspections

In recent years insurance companies have become much more vigilant as to what they will and won't insure. Although governments do play their role, it's important to understand that it's the insurance companies that are driving the industry in requiring major upgrading of older homes. Few insurance companies will insure 60-amp electrical systems, galvanized water lines or knob-and-tube wiring. Depending on your area and insurance company the list can be much longer.

Although some insurance companies have their own inspectors, most rely on asking their client for such information. Although a home inspector should be able to help the client with most of these questions, a wise inspector will not comment on things they can not see, such as, "How much knob-and-tube wiring or how much galvanized water lines are there?" Although most insurance companies ask, like many realtors today, few home inspectors measure square footage because of liability issues.

Appraisal

Mortgage or bank appraisals (typically referred to as "the appraisal") are not part of the home inspection. Home inspectors are not qualified to, and should not comment on the price of a property. Appraisal is a very specialized trade. Whereas realtors may provide a "statement of opinion" regarding the value/price of a property, it's the appraiser who provides the acceptable, official report that's typically required by a mortgage lender.

In actuality, the appraiser spends very little time at the house once he has confirmed that it actually exists and its general condition. The bulk of the appraiser's time today is spent on the computer doing research. As with everything else, there are a number of different ways to go about appraising a house. The two most common types of appraisal calculations are the following:

1. **Cost Comparison**

   Involves comparing market conditions, and what prices other similar houses in the market have sold for. Often when calculating comparable values, the appraiser will use a charting system to add or delete the cost of double-car garage comparable to a single-car garage, house with pool or finished basement vs. one without and so on.

2. **Replacement Cost**

   Replacement cost sets a value for the basic lot and then estimates the cost to re-build the same house as new.

Infrared (Thermography) Inspection

I've already written an extensive piece on thermography and its general misrepresentation in the home inspection industry. However that is not meant in any way to discredit the true application of thermography. Thermography is a proven method for finding water and air penetration issues, electrical overheating, vulnerable spots in roofing systems, the lack of insulation and the list goes on. The 5 main differences between a home inspection and real residential infrared inspections (thermography) are the following:

1. An IR inspection must take place under the right environmental conditions. If such conditions are not present, there must be the time and opportunity to create them, which is not realistic at the time of a home inspection.

2. The IR inspector is not limited by the time restraint and visual-only restrictions of a home inspection.

3. A typical IR inspection takes place to help pinpoint and solve an already-identified problem. Further, results often require destructive investigation in order to be confirmed.

4. A full-house IR scan that is looking for a variety of possible issues takes considerable time at the house in addition to a number of hours at the computer to interpret the images.

5. A professional IR inspection by a qualified thermographer having adequate equipment will cost more than the average home inspection.

It must be noted that a professional thermographer will have the appropriate quality imager (camera) and training for the type of inspection that he or she is performing.

Wood-Burning Appliances WETT Inspection:

In Canada we refer to the inspection of wood burning appliances as WETT inspections (Wood Energy Technology Transfer). It must be pointed out that WETT Certified inspectors now offer three different levels of inspections:

- Level 1 "Readily Accessible"
- Level 2 "Accessible"
- Level 3 "Concealed Accessibility"

I must point out for someone purchasing a home with a wood-burning appliance that Level 3 (which includes all the requirements of Levels 1 & 2) is the only level that actually assures a full inspection of the unit and its concealed areas such as the chimney flue and smoke chamber. If there is any question regarding the integrity of fireplace, wood stove or any part of their system I always recommend a full inspection (by a qualified inspector or chimney sweep) which should start with cleaning of the chimney.

Pest Control Inspections

Termite and other insect-related inspections are again a very specialized inspection service and often even more specialized based on the region or area of the country. Whereas termite inspections and exterminating procedures are a fact of everyday life in warmer, moist southern climates, it is only in that past few decades that they have became an issue further north. Although signs of termites, carpenter ants, and/or mice may be visible at times, such inspections often become intrusive as opposed the "visual only" limitation of a home inspection.

Other Inspection Services Provided By Home Inspectors

It is ASHI and CAHPI policy that a professional home inspector cannot provide contracting services for pre-listing or pre-purchase inspection clients or practice real estate. However, inspectors are allowed, if qualified, to offer other consulting or inspection-related services. Many inspectors offer additional services or add-ons for their clients, but again, it is up to the client to confirm that they are satisfied with the inspector's qualifications for such services.

CHAPTER ELEVEN: When Things Don't Work Out

It's important for clients to understand that there is no such thing as the perfect house and that there will always be some surprises after moving in. The real question remains, what's a little surprise versus a big surprise? When teaching new inspectors, we always explain that having their client attend the inspection helps both parties understand each other's expectations and limitations and if, after the inspection there is a problem, respond immediately.

As a client if you have a problem, I always recommend that you call your inspector first, stay calm and explain your concern. You should find a reputable inspector very cooperative at this stage. Often in such cases, I find that by jogging the client's memory they quickly remember our talking about the concern during the inspection and we end pleasantly discussing possible solutions. A word of caution: if in your complaint phone call, email or letter you mention any type of legal action, don't expect immediate assistance from your inspector other than possibly a confirmation that they've received your information. This shouldn't be interpreted as lack of cooperation by your inspector as most error and omissions insurance policies stipulate that the inspector is not to deal with the such matters until they, the insurance company, have had the opportunity to review the complaint. This can take weeks; however, if there is no cooperation, legal action is always an option.

In areas of licensing, often governments' only involvement is making sure that the inspector is licensed; and do not have a process for assisting unhappy clients. If the inspector is a member of ASHI or CAHPI, the client will get assistance by contacting the association where formal complaints are passed on to the discipline committee for review and possible action. As a former board member of OAHI/CAHPI Ont., I can assure you that complaints against inspectors are taken very seriously. It's also important to remember that a similar complaint process is available in the real estate industry, and a legitimate complaint against a realtor can involve some very substantial fines.

STORY #41: My Plumbing Doesn't Work!

I was about to start the morning inspection when I received a phone call from a previous client with a problem. They'd recently moved into the house that I'd inspected for them and now none of the plumbing worked. I tried to get more information but all she could say was "none of the plumbing worked." I explained that my day was fully booked but that I could be there that evening to take a look. Would they be OK until then? It was difficult to put the call out of my mind and stay focused on the day's inspections. I kept questioning myself should I call a plumber and send him over as soon as possible?

That evening when I arrived at the house where none of the plumbing worked my client led me to the bathroom to show me the problems. The screw type drain plug, in the bathtub, wasn't closing all the way and needed to be turned a couple of times in order to make a perfect seal and keep the water in. Also the shower diverter (the lever that lifts up to make the water come out of the shower head) was letting a little water drip out of the bathtub spout (a very normal condition) when they used the shower.

Although I'd sweated over this all day I was quite happy that those two small items were the entire problem. As I talked with the clients it was my observation that they had a case of "buyers' remorse" (wished they hadn't bought the house) and now were angry at it and anyone involved in their buying it. Very nice people, but a very troubling situation.

Unhappy Seller And Unhappy Realtors

Often homeowners are very upset if the potential purchaser backs out of the deal after the home inspection. Although this can be very legitimate concern, many homeowners have a lot of trouble accepting the fact that a well-qualified home inspector will typically have a better technical understanding of their home than they do themselves. It must also be realized that the home inspection is confidential information between the client and the inspector, and the inspector must have his or her client's permission before entering into discussion about the report with anyone.

Often complaints by the homeowner occur because no one took the time to explain the inspection logic and process to them. They are left with the impression that the inspector "failed" their house. One of the most frustrating things for me is hearing comments like, "The inspector passed or failed the house" is one of the many reasons I wrote this book.

Home inspectors provide an objective overview of the condition of the house and its systems. The potential buyer then takes that information and makes the decision to "buy or run." I've seen clients go ahead and buy some really scary houses while I've seen others walk away over a $300 repair. It's difficult for everyone and often reflects negatively on the home inspector when the buyer simply decides not to buy the house and uses the home inspection as their escape. Other times, I've had my report misrepresented to the sellers, by the buyer, as a bargaining tool, then losing all objectivity both parties get wrapped up in the negotiating process and forget that the objective of the exercise was to buy and sell a house.

Most inspectors whom I've talked to over the years agree that their number-one source of complaints (some very violent and threatening) come from unhappy realtors because we "blew their deal" and, in extreme cases, lost them the client. One of the things I was surprised to learn as a realtor was just how many clients rely on the realtor to say, "This is it. This is the one you should buy." So when the home inspector discovers major issues with the house, he's no longer just dealing with the inspection, he's also jeopardizing the realtor's credibility for having recommended that house to his or her client.

STORY #42: Re-Build Roof, Mold, Aluminum Wiring?

In this case, a few days after the inspection, I received a phone call from a contractor asking about the house. The conversation went in such a way that I assumed I was listening to my client's (the buyer's) contractor. I didn't offer any information until I had to say, "I didn't say that," to which he responded, "I didn't think you would have, but that's what I was told." It was only then I realized that I was talking to the homeowner's (seller) contractor. Now in this case, I didn't worry about going back to my client for permission to disclose information based on the fact that my client had grossly misrepresented me and my report.

There had been a couple of sheets of siding falling off the house so my client told the seller that I reported all the siding had to be replaced. I had reported that the shingles needed replacing and she told the seller that I said the entire roof structure had to be replaced. I had reported that the aluminum wiring required tailing* and explained the process, but again she told the seller that I'd said that all the electrical wiring had to be taken out of the walls and replaced. The tiny, almost insignificant patch of mold at the bottom of the basement stairs behind the boot tray had been blown up to be a major mold infestation.

*Tailing is the term used for a common process by which
an electrician changes the aluminum/copper terminations
at a switch, receptacle and light fixture.

STORY #43: Sump Pump Not Connected To Weepers

When I arrived at this house, the curb was piled with a line of house-purging-type garbage that was longer than my truck and as wide as the boulevard. When I got out and walked around my truck, I was gagging on the smell of mold and mildew which appeared to be coming from the garbage. The house that I was about to inspect was a newer bungalow with a wooden foundation and crawl space as opposed to a full basement. The street was on a hill. There were at least two houses on higher ground channeling water directly at this one. Inside the house, the musty smell was obvious.

What I found in the crawl space (while wearing a respirator) under the house was:

- The crawl space was a return air plenum, which means all the house air circulated openly through the crawl space on its way back to the furnace before being heated/cooled and blown back through the house

- There was mold on the wood foundation and the crawl space was very musty-smelling

- The sump pump motor worked but there was no water in the sump pit which surprised me based on the exterior grading

- Upon closer examination, I discovered that the weeper system which collects water from around the exterior of the foundation and drains it to the sump pump/pit for disposal had never been connected

With the weeper and sump system not working properly excessive moisture was building up around the foundation making the crawl space very damp. We were able to confirm that all the moldy garbage at the curb had come out of the crawl space. In this case the builder actually came back and repaired the weeper system. A few weeks later I was having a conversation with a realtor in another town who informed me that the realtor involved in the house with the moldy crawl space had taken on a phone campaign to call other realtors telling them to stay away from me, again, because I "didn't know what I was doing" and "had blown the deal."

STORY #44: I'll Buy You A Can Of Tar

I was doing a home inspection for one of my students and the realtor didn't arrive until part way through the inspection. By that time, I'd discovered a problematic chimney flashing and major drywall damage to the exterior bedroom wall below it, which indicated the possibility of insulation and mold issues inside the wall. My client and I were in the basement below the subject area, discussing the size of the large water stain that followed from above, down the foundation wall and across the floor when the front door opened and the realtor bellowed, "*Where are you?*" When she came downstairs, I politely started to explain the issue when she again bellowed at our mutual client, "I'll buy you a can of tar!" Later while reviewing the report with my client at a coffee shop, my cell phone rang. When I answered it was the realtor yelling at me. I set the cell phone on the table, without the speaker phone option turned on. The people at the tables on both sides of us turned to look as they listed to her scream at me and threaten with all the people she was going to complain to about me. Complain about how I'd been so unethical by tying up her client and taking too long to do the inspection and review the report with them.

One of the things that made the situation even more interesting was the fact that my client was also a student in the college home inspection program. Now he could go back to class with his own first hand war story about realtors and report to the other students that the instructors were not just making this stuff up.

STORY #45: Wait And Watch The Shingles

Evaluating the shingles during my morning inspection had been limited due to rain. This was further complicated by my client's unrealistic expectations that I should be able to tell her almost exactly the day the shingles would fail. Since the house was close to where I lived I did offer to come back the next day, if the conditions were right, and take a second look. It continued to rain that night and most of the next day so there was nothing that I could do. That evening I got a very aggressive phone call from her realtor whose basic argument was that I should have stayed at the house until the shingles dried out, and besides, her husband was a contractor and I didn't know what I was doing. I set the phone on the table and my dinner guests 12 feet away listened to her yell at me for about 10 minutes.

STORY #46: Carbon Monoxide Detector

I must also say that I've had realtors call me very respectfully and question my findings and, although not agreeing with me, remain civil and professional. Recently I got a serious carbon monoxide reading when doing my furnace inspection. Following my standard procedure when something like that happens, I repeat my testing sequence which begins with re-calibrating the meter outside the house in fresh air. On the second attempt I got the same results. In this case, the homeowner called in a heating contractor who didn't find anything wrong. The listing realtor called me, again very respectfully, but was obviously upset. He basically accused me of not knowing what I was doing, that my carbon monoxide meter was either defective or that I didn't know how to use it. I explained to him that I had a high-end meter, that it was less than a year old with an anticipated life span of two years, that this didn't happen often and that I was quite competent using the meter. Further, I would be negligent if I didn't report my findings to my client. We all know the story about taking our car to the garage for the mechanic to hear the noise and ....

Overall the realtor was upset that my client didn't buy the house and although there was a long list of other more serious issues (one being that the main staircase was about to fail), this is the one that the realtor used to blamed me for blowing the deal.

STORY #47: I Don't Want This House / The Peach

In this case, I inspected a beautiful, well-maintained 100-year-old peach of a house. My client appeared troubled beyond the typical stress level I often see. He didn't appear to be paying much attention to what I was saying and was very agitated. By the time we made it to basement, I stopped, put my hands up like an umpire calling for a time out and asked, "What's going on here? Have I offended you? Do we have a problem?" My client just about broke down and started to explain, "My wife and the realtor have pushed this house down my throat...I don't want this house, I don't want an old house...I want a new house in a new sub-division...Please, get me out of this!" In this case, the realtor had made sure that there was a bulletproof escape clause in the offer to purchase contract and was able to get them out of the deal and made sure that I wasn't accused of being the deal killer.

Electricity Supply Issues, Another Surprise

To help make the point that home inspectors are not immune to extreme unforeseen problems, we're going to go a little off topic here and talk about my latest house purchase. When, as a teenager I first heard my father talking around the dinner table about underground water lines heating a house I was curious. After researching the theory in the early 80s I've fantasized about having a house with a geo-thermal heat pump for heating/cooling. In the early fall of 2011 our home inspectors group heard a very dynamic individual, the president of a geothermal manufacturing company, speak at one of our meetings. At lunch he and I paired off, got into a heavy conversation about geo-thermal and the die was cast. Again, to show you that I'm occasionally driven by emotions just like other home buyers, the next day I proceeded to purchase a country property that I'd been eyeing and set the closing date to allow time for the installation of a geo-thermal system before the ground froze.

On Friday, December 16th I took possession of the house and, with the full co-operation of mother nature, on the following Monday and Tuesday helped dig an 800-foot trench 6 feet wide and 5 feet deep in the yard and buried 2,400 feet of pipe. With the scurry of trades, excavation, electrical, plumbing and HVAC (heating ventilation and air conditioning) by Friday, December 23rd the system was up and running. Now this wasn't just a basic geo-thermal system, it had most of the bells and whistles. Because it was initially being used for forced air heating/cooling we had to double the size of the existing duct work in a finished basement which proved to be a big challenge. In our climate, contractors typically include a small electric emergency/back-up heating coil just in case there's a problem in extreme cold spells that the geo-thermal heat-pump can't keep up. In this case I'd decided, just to be safe, to include a full size electric back up system that met the full heating requirements for the house. Further the system was designed to heat the household hot water, provide in-floor hot-water heat along with the ability to heat a future hot tub or swimming pool. It also had optional electrical safety devices, a high tech ECM (Electric Commutated Motor) fan motor and the latest advancement in electronic air filtering. And yes, just like anyone else the project was under estimated and came in over budget. But after all, I'd been dreaming about it for years.

The first thing that we discovered during excavation and installation of the underground piping was the fact that the house was sitting on a natural spring (water) which, in most situations, is a very bad thing. During the process we also discovered the modification that had been made to the lower sump pump, by a previous homeowner, which hid the excessive water condition. However, understanding the issue, the spring water was diverted into a drainage/weeper tile placed over top of the underground piping to enhance the thermal conductivity of the earth to the system. (in the world of geo-thermal there is a saying "the wetter the better"). How often does a major problem turn out to be a positive benefit?

Since there was a part tank of oil left from the old heating system allowance was made to use up the oil before removing the old system so initially we bounced back and forth between the oil heat and geo-thermal. As for the geo-thermal everything checked out and the system was initially running text-book perfectly. Then, once fully moved in and settled we started to sense that something was wrong after which the manufacturer ended up replacing the compressor. Later both the geo-thermal manufacturer and the compressor manufacture reported that the failure had been due to high electrical voltage. At that point I got directly involved with the technical staff of both manufacturers in order to, as a layman, get the best possible understanding of the issue.

I then immediately contacted my electricity supplier, Hydro One and they sent out a technician who took some readings. Eventually they installed a logger system to the meter base at the side of the house in order to record voltage readings over a few days. From this they assured me that nothing was wrong on their side. Shortly there after, one afternoon, my house filled up with smoke and the smell of burning electronics. Ignoring the advice that I'd give others to call the fire department, I went to work finding the source of the problem and found that the circuit board of the ECM motor on the circulating fan had burned up. It actually melted. The geo-thermal manufacturer lent me a standard motor, without sophisticated electronics, so the system could run. I contacted Hydro One again. Again Hydro One claimed that there was nothing wrong with the electrical power that they were delivering to my residence. Shortly thereafter the second compressor burned out, again due to high voltage. This time the compressor burned so badly that it contaminated the refrigerant lines and the 450-pound, $14,000 air handler (furnace) had to be disconnected, dragged up from my basement and completely replaced.

Fortunately I'd built a strong relationship with the geo-thermal manufacturer and he has loaned me an entire new air handler unit as we continue to deal with the issue of "who's to blame". At that point expenses were over \$20,000 in addition to weeks of lost time. Although a new system was installed and operational I was afraid to turn it on for fear of burning it up as well.

I spent the balance of the 2012 winter with no heat, followed by the summer without air conditioning and the first two months of the fall heating season without heat. I must note at this point Hydro One had begrudgingly replaced the transformer at the end of my driveway, while still denying any responsibility. Unfortunately the electrical readings by my electrician and the local ESA (Electrical Safety Authority) inspector showed that the new transformer made no difference.

Realizing that talking to Hydro One, even going as high as the board of directors, was like trying to communicate with a brick wall, I began to research my battle. Then discovering the standards for the delivery of electrical power to our homes in the USA and Canada things became interesting. Because it's easier to follow I'll continue in bullet form:

- In the USA and Canada we operate on 110/220-volt electrical supply which translates to, 120/240 volts at our homes.

- Products manufactured for use in the USA and Canada are required to meet CSA/ULA standards. Part of those standards require that electronic products be manufactured and tested to operate at 110/220 plus or minus 15%. This means that products like compressors, cloths dryers and kitchen stove controls designed to run at 220 volts must be able to withstand an overload up to 253 volts.

- The USA / Canada standard for the delivery of electricity to our home is broken into 3 categories as stated by CSA Standard CAN3-235-83 Table 3 (Single Phase 120/240)

    - Extreme Low 106/212 volts

    - Normal operating conditions nominally 110/220 – actually 125/250 volts

    - Extreme High 127/254 volts

Do you see anything wrong with the basic math here? The maximum that anything in our houses is designed to run at is 253 volts but our suppliers are allowed to deliver 254 volts? Ever wonder why that new electric appliance you bought lasted only a couple of months? (Note, low voltage and brown-outs are just as dangerous to our electronic goods.)

Based on these findings I started to track the voltage at my house with a clamp meter and eventually purchased my own electronic logging system that records 64 voltage readings per second, 24 hours a day, 7 days a week. What we discovered is that although CSA, the governing body, defines 250–254 Volts as Extreme Operating Conditions, Hydro One considers delivering 250– 54 volts (almost daily) their definition of Normal Operating Conditions. It's also not uncommon for them to exceed 254 volts or provide extreme brown-outs as low as 9 volts.

In the quest for answers I have letters from ESA (Electrical Safety Authority), CSA (Canada Standards Association), the Premier of Ontario's office and the Ontario Minister of Energy all either giving me the brush-off or defending Hydro One, saying that they are operating within acceptable parameters. Did none of these people pass rudimentary math? I may be old and understand that a lot of things have changed over the years but my understanding is, that numbers like 254 and above are still higher than 253. Has that changed when I wasn't paying attention? It's no wonder that so many people have such little faith in large corporations and government.

So maybe at this point you're wondering what I am doing about heat? After months of research, talking to electricians, engineers, electrical inspectors, CSA, ESA, Government, Hydro One or anyone that would listen, but no one had a solution. Then my local newspaper, *The Elmira Independent*, published a feature article about my problem.

That night I received an e-mail from a local factory owner who told me about a temporary solution. The next day I purchased the specified part (less than $200) and within a two-hour service call by an electrician the system was up and running. The device he installed drops the voltage supply to my geo-thermal unit by 13 volts. When Hydro one supplies 254 volts my unit only sees 241 volts. Still higher than the compressor manufacturer wants to see on a regular basis, but it's relatively safe. Unfortunately this solution does not deal with brown-outs; on days when the power swings from the 250s down into the 220s I'm now afraid of low-voltage problems.

At time of writing, my latest correspondence from senior management at Hydro One continues to deny that they have done anything wrong. But, they say, for a little over $2,000 they will install the proper transformer at my house to insure that the problem doesn't happen again. (I'm not a lawyer here, but is that not extortion?) Also, co-incidentally, Hydro One is re-constructing the transformer relay station closest to my house. To date my readings show that the new transformer is delivering higher voltage levels more regularly than over the past months with the older station.

The battle continues.

Now back to the book and home inspections. I've added this story so you understand that home inspectors are not immune to the trials and tribulations of home ownership and when I say to a client, "there could be issues", I've been there and am not making a frivolous statement.

STORY #48: Surprise Electrical Bills

When purchasing a property it is extremely important to see recent utility bills. Although the issue discussed in the previous paragraphs was nothing that could reasonably have been foreseen, I'm currently investigating two situations that are quite different. Both are dealing with the same electrical supplier as myself. We all have similar houses with similar electrical usage. Where my electrical bills average around $250 – $300. pr month the first person is claiming to have monthly hydro bills in excess of $2,000. pr month and the second's are over $1,000. pr month. I've been contacted because neither are getting any cooperation from our supplier.

CHAPTER TWELVE: The Future

Throughout the book I've attempted to talk about both the positive and negative sides of the home inspection industry and the overall aches, pains and bruised knees involved with the "coming-of-age" process. As our children grow, we try to guide them and teach them our values, but then one day we have to take the training wheels off the bicycle and let them ride on their own. Some will fail, some continue doing everything exactly as they were taught while others will become the visionaries, take chances, make changes and risk success or failure at a new level.

Today I see myself in the middle of this process. I wasn't around early enough to be a founder, but I did show up soon enough to pick up and believe some of the old ways and misconceptions that fuel resistance to change. As my effort to assist the industry, I've chosen to step outside the box and disclose what's really going on in an effort to educate both the general public and legislators in hope that they can make more informed decisions. Although I will not call myself a visionary, this chapter will sum up my personal observations and opinions as to the current state and future needs of the home inspection industry. Although my daily business is focused in Canada, my international contacts and research reflect that, in the big picture, neither country is unique and we both share similar challenges and frustrations as discussed here in this book.

In many sections of the book, I've talked about the inspector's individual limitations. Now I'm going to talk about the industry's limitations. Although overall quite basic to identify, they are extremely complex and sensitive issues to be dealt with. In this section, I will discuss those before sharing my "dream list" and making final comments.

Who's In Charge?

If you ask any group of home inspectors in North America about who controls their industry, the answer will be an overwhelming, "The realtors." Until the home inspection industry is taken out of the control and direct influence of the real estate community and becomes a truly independent transaction between the home inspector and his or her client, the industry will remain flawed. Inspectors will continue to fight for respect, simply because realtors dramatically outnumber us and are the first line of contact and have the most influence over our potential clients.

The Public's Perceived Value And Willingness To Pay

Until the realtors' direct influence over home inspection is brought under control, there is little chance of the public ever truly trusting the home inspection process and its value. On a daily basis, the general public confirms their lack of understanding and/or value of home inspections simply through their lack of willingness to pay for the service. Because of a lack of standards, formal procedures and through misguided trust placed in licensing, home inspectors, as a group, are all too often painted with the same brush and are selected by price alone. With little chance for making a reasonable income, low-end and part-time inspectors will continue to come and go as the higher-qualified and good businesspeople take their skills elsewhere, or fight to re-invent themselves.

Unfortunately, in our society, just about everything revolves around money. For home inspectors, their fee dictates how much time they can invest in performing an individual inspection, invest in follow-up, training, association memberships, tools and insurance. I think I can safely say, along with a vast majority of other professional inspectors, that for every hour that I spend at an actual inspection, I spend a minimum three more running my business, being involved in association activities and continuing my education in an effort to keep up and do quality work.

The length of time that's required to inspect a property does have variables. One of my first surprises was that a 1,000-square-foot house can take longer to inspect than a 2,000-square-foot house! Once you think about it, the logic is quite simple. Both have the same basic components: exterior, roof, plumbing, heating etc. The big difference is that the person in the small house usually has just as much "stuff" but it's packed into a smaller space making it much more difficult for the inspector to get around. Further, a smaller house often represents a lower income level and more do-it-yourself issues to contend with, especially when there have been multiple owners.

In the courses that I facilitate we teach that, although every house and client is different, a true standards-of-practice inspection averages 3.5 to 4.5 hours (including report writing and review) for a typical single-family house under 2,000 square feet. Often the client or home owner doesn't realize the inspector's true time commitment, especially when the inspector prepares his report off-site. However, if your inspector is doing more than two full inspections a day, you may have reason to question the quality of his or her work. Whereas there are inspectors who argue we wouldn't do any better job if we were there longer, in many cases I would argue otherwise. Unfortunately and again, based on our clients' unwillingness to pay, we can't afford to give them any more time than we already do. Although I exceed the standards of practice on just about every inspection that I do, my training and experience tells me that in many cases inspectors could do more for their clients if we had more time and greater freedom in the houses we inspected. If inspectors were prepared to step up and realtors would back off and let us do our job, our industry could provide a much better service to the public. By going to the next level, which involves better training, more time on-site when required, and surpassing the limitations of visual-only and standard operating controls, inspectors could go further and more likely answer questions on the spot that we otherwise have to report as, "Further investigation required."

I find it amusing that realtors fight against the discount brokerages that charge lower commissions, but perpetuate the idea that the lowest price is the best criteria for selecting a home inspector.

Price / Pie Chart

In the grand scheme of things I feel that the following pie chart speaks volumes as to the public's perceived value of a home inspection.

Breakdown of the $31,300. in costs required to purchase a $400,000 home in Ontario

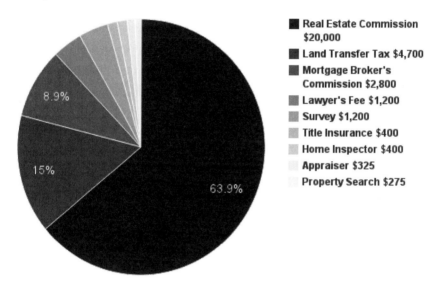

- Real Estate Commission $20,000
- Land Transfer Tax $4,700
- Mortgage Broker's Commission $2,800
- Lawyer's Fee $1,200
- Survey $1,200
- Title Insurance $400
- Home Inspector $400
- Appraiser $325
- Property Search $275

Note: Expect variations province to province and state to state. If this transaction were in the Greater Toronto Area, the tax portion would be approximately double.

My first question as I study this chart based on dollars is, why do people see so little value in a home inspection? Is this because they have so little faith in home inspectors or is it simply because they don't understand? While I truly believe that it's a combination of both, it's my position that people just don't get it. When an individual is prepared to pay $20,000 to a broker for helping find a house (typically today the serious consumer is doing the bulk of that themselves searching on the internet) and negotiating a price, how can they realistically expect to pay between $300 – $500, for independent advice regarding the largest purchase of their life which could possibly turn around to be the largest liability of their life? What's the hourly rate charged by a good lawyer?

In our consumer society, price is so often the only thing that people look at. Unfortunately, some inspection companies actually fuel this by offering quick inspections, coupons and other promotions instead of quality service. Overall, while most people say they want quality, the vast majority simply aren't prepared to pay for it. It's my observation that in the world of home inspection, the typical consumer relies on price mostly because they don't understand the service that they should be getting. It's often hard for those receiving a regular paycheck to relate to people who are self-employed in the service industry. Many see that their home inspector as making $100 an hour. They push the basic math along the idea, "He does 2 or 3 inspections a day, 5 or 6 days a week," and a light goes on: "This guy's making a fortune!"

As usual, the grass always looks greener on the other side. Just as I've told you that 10% of the realtors are doing 90% of the business, the latest estimate that I've heard quoted in Canada is that 75% of home inspectors are considered part-time workers. It's not part-time because they want to be, it's simply because there are too many of us competing for the business. In another comparison to real estate, every month a large number of wannabes enter both the real estate and home inspection fields because it looks easy and profitable while there is a relatively similar sized group dropping out because they couldn't pay the bills.

Bottom line, if an individual can't make a decent living, they can't provide a decent service. It's interesting that, in the home inspection courses that I teach, we find that the majority of students drop out or don't make it through the first year in business, once they find out what is really involved. Of the approximately 40 students in the group that I took my basic courses with, only three of us became inspectors, two full-time and one part-time. Fifteen years later, I'm the only one left.

A few years ago I mentored a new home inspector. I don't do this for just anyone, but this individual really seemed to have the right stuff. In the beginning I explained to him, if you're charging $425, which was my price at the time, you actually take home about $175 after expenses and then get to share that with the tax man. A year or two later we were talking at a conference when he turned to me and said, "Of all the things you taught me, you were wrong on one. Charging $425, there is no way I can take home $175 after expenses. There are just too many other expenses involved if you're going to do it right."

My Dream List

Although sellers agree to have their home inspected, they often don't understand what the home inspection process is. Many simply don't want us there. As I've stated previously, I'm continually greeted at the door by homeowners who state, "Well, the realtor said that you'd only be 15 or 20 minutes" or make some rude remark about how stupid it is to have their home inspected.

Speaking as both a home inspector and recently licensed realtor, I feel strongly that in the process of standardization and licensing throughout the USA and Canada, there should be a specific form in the realtors' offer of purchase and sale package that deals with the home inspection as a separate item. Such a form would provide an official consent by the homeowner for the inspection, spell out the seller's obligation to co-operate, make note of areas that need to be accessible to the inspector, explain what a real home inspection is plus include the standards of practice to which the home inspector is to work under in that province or state.

Actually, my dream list is not long. It's simply five points listed below. Unfortunately, without points 1 and 2 being addressed first, the rest of the exercise remains relatively futile and home inspections will, in my eyes, remain a questionable part of the real estate transaction.

The Dream List

1. That the home inspection clause be removed from the standard real estate offer of purchase and sale form and become a separate document. (This has been done in Quebec)

2. That home inspectors and inspections become truly independent and fully out of the control and or influence of the realtor or real estate community.

3. That a minimum 45 – 90 hour course involving the house, its systems, construction techniques, maintenance and home inspection be added to the basic real estate curriculum as part of the mandatory qualifications for a real estate license.

4. That legitimate two-year college courses for home inspection are implemented and that such courses be designed in cooperation with and taught by qualified home inspectors and tradespeople and include dedicated shop time and field work.

5. That governments respect the fact that our two countries, via ASHI and CAHPI, have worked together at the professional association level for 30 years to set standards and raise the bar. Even competitive groups that try to start up independently eventually realize that the wheel has already been invented

and resort to copying the ASHI and CAHPI models. With an ever-mobile populace, why can't we all work together, sensitive of our geographical differences, to standardize licensing requirements as well as standards of practice, codes of conduct and ethics, inspection procedures and set a base standard for reporting?

It's my opinion as a front-line home inspector, recently licensed realtor, professional educator, long-standing association supporter and lifelong businessman, that the combination of the above can dramatically improve home inspections, better serve the public, and bring the home inspection industry to a level where 75% of the inspectors are full-time instead of the 75% part-time (in Canada) and make a legitimate living as professional home inspectors.

Although I've witnessed the real estate industry begrudgingly, accept home inspectors as part of the real estate transaction, I challenge them to step up to the plate and move up to the next level. The home inspection industry, although trying to make changes, does not have the numbers, respect or finances to take any more action than they have. In many areas, our colleges are not prepared to invest in legitimate full-time courses until the Government sets standards and recognizes the home inspection industry as they have other trades and professions.

Untapped Opportunity / North America's Used Housing Inventory

A number of years ago I was surprised to receive an e-mail from a manufacturer of electrical GFIs (ground fault interrupters) that are used in bathrooms and for out-door receptacles. Because these devices were (still are) sold by general retail outlets and often installed by do-it-yourselfers, it was being discovered that many of the devices were installed incorrectly. The manufacturer, realizing that home inspectors are out there testing GFIs, was requesting our assistance to help estimate just how many devices were not working. At that time I was finding that the majority of the GFIs I tested were faulty. In the circles that I travel it was generally agreed that the installation instructions where too technical. Not long after doing their research the manufacture revised their instructions to a more novice level. Today I can confidently report that I find far fewer units misinstalled. *(However, today the biggest problem that I find with GFI's is that they are seized. Likely do to the lack of exercising/testing.)*

What I'm trying to point out is that we home inspectors are the only people "randomly" auditing the used housing inventory in North America. "Randomly" we inspect the intimate workings of all sizes and shapes of houses. One day it's a house that needs recycling (a "tear down"), the next, a breath- taking, text-book perfect model of construction. "Randomly" we see first hand many products that work and many that don't. Sometimes it's the product, sometimes it's the installation while other times it is a matter of life safety. When news, television programs and contractors sensationalize possible issues such as mold or vermiculite insulation in attics, just stop and think, "How many attics in North America are inspected in any one day by home inspectors?". So I ask, who else has a better understanding regarding the condition of our housing inventory through-out North America other than our home inspectors? Are there more positive ways this information can be used beneficially?

Overall, home inspectors as a group have the best access to, and first hand knowledge of, the used housing inventory in North America. We not only witness the aging process of the house and its systems, we see inherent problems with specific products, their usage or misunderstood installation procedures and possible improvements that could be made. Regularly we see that damage done by overzealous homeowners who, with good intentions but too little or wrong information. Although the details of our individual inspections are confidential, generalities could be valuable to various housing authorities, insurance companies or manufacturers for future planning and product development.

In the past few years Ontario has had a number of government grant programs designed to improve the energy efficiency of our homes. Much of this work was such that municipal permits were neither required nor taken out. Understanding the objective of the programs and technology involved, many of us have to report that the work was not done effectively. From this it's easy to conclude that a program, being politically correct, and with very good intentions was compromised by a lack of follow-up to insure the work was done correctly. Yes, in this specific case, our information could be very valuable for future programs.

Final Comments

In the first pages of the book, I challenged you to put aside your preconceived ideas regarding home inspection so that you could read with an open mind. I hope I've provided some insights that have caused you to think and quite possibly have a better understanding of our home inspection industry. Through reading this book, I'm sure that you've formulated a number of your own opinions and even discussed them with friends. In conclusion, I leave you with these questions:

1. **Who** is in charge of and driving the home inspection industry today?

2: **Who should be** in charge of driving the home inspection industry today?

3: **How** can we better protect the best interests of the house-buying public today?

Appendix

- Sample Inspection Contract (Courtesy of Carson Dunlop) ... 172
- *ASHI Standards of Practice 175
- ASHI Code of Ethics 182
- *CAHPI Standards of Practice.. 183

*Note: At the time of printing, both the ASHI & CAHPI Standards of Practice are currently under review. The updated versions will be available on their respective web-sites, listed below, once available. Both web sites will lead you to State and Provincial Chapters and offer a wealth of other information regarding Home Inspections. They will also assist you to find a qualified Home Inspector in your area

www.AHSI.org

www.CAHPI.ca

Published by:

The Inspectors International Press Inc.
www.TheInsepctorsInternationPress.com

Sample Inspection Contract

HOME INSPECTION REPORT – AUTHORIZATION FORM PART 1   THE HOME REFERENCE BOOK®

AUTHORIZATION FOR HOME INSPECTION

Property	Address:
	Inspection Date: _____ Inspection Time: _____

Client	Name:
	Address:
	Home Phone: _____ Business Phone: _____
	Mobile Phone: _____ Fax: _____
	E-mail:

Fee	Base Fee: $ _____
	Tax: $ _____
	Total Fee: $ _____ payable before or at the time of the inspection.

**THIS CLAUSE LIMITS THE LIABILITY OF THE HOME INSPECTOR:
PLEASE READ CAREFULLY BEFORE SIGNING.**

The Inspection of this property is subject to the **Limitations and Conditions** set out in this Agreement.
The report is based on a visual examination of the readily accessible features of the building.

The Inspection is performed in accordance with the **Standards of Practice** of the _____
_____ . A copy of these Standards is available at
no charge from the inspector.

The attached Report is an opinion of the present condition of the property. It is not a guarantee, warranty or an insurance
policy with regard to the fitness of the property.

**The liability/liquidated damages of the Home Inspector and the Home Inspection Company arising out of this
Inspection and Report, for any cause of action whatsoever, whether in contract or in negligence, is limited
to a refund of the fees that you have been charged for this inspection.**

I have read, understood and accepted the terms of this Agreement including the Limitations and Conditions
on the following pages.

Client Signature: _____   Date: _____

On Behalf of: (Company) _____

Payment Received in Full: (Signature) _____

Home Inspector: (Print Name) _____

Note: The inspection report is for the exclusive use of the client named above. No use of the information by any other party is intended.

Sample Inspection Contract Con't

HOME INSPECTION REPORT – AUTHORIZATION FORM PART 2   THE HOME REFERENCE BOOK®

THIS CONTRACT LIMITS THE LIABILITY OF THE HOME INSPECTION COMPANY. PLEASE READ CAREFULLY BEFORE SIGNING.

The Inspection is performed in accordance with the **STANDARDS OF PRACTICE** of the American Society of Home Inspectors and the Canadian Association of Home and Property Inspectors. These **STANDARDS** explain what an inspector must do and what an inspector is **NOT** required to do. To review the **STANDARDS**, go to www.ashi.org (USA) or www.cahpi.ca (Canada). Home inspections are **NOT** code compliance inspections.

In addition to the limitations in the **STANDARDS**, the Inspection of this property is subject to the Limitations and Conditions set out in this Agreement.

LIMITATIONS AND CONDITIONS OF THE HOME INSPECTION. There are limitations to the scope of this Inspection. It provides a general overview of the more obvious repairs that may be needed. It is not intended to be an exhaustive list. The ultimate decision of what to repair or replace is yours. One homeowner may decide that certain conditions require repair or replacement, while another will not.

1) THE INSPECTION IS NOT TECHNICALLY EXHAUSTIVE. The Home Inspection provides a basic overview of the property condition. Because your Home Inspector has only a limited amount of time in the property, the Inspection is not technically exhaustive. Because it is a sampling exercise, some visible issues will not be identified.

Some conditions noted, such as foundation cracks or other signs of settling in a house, may either be cosmetic or may indicate a potential problem that is beyond the scope of the Home Inspection.

If you are concerned about any conditions noted in the Home Inspection Report, we strongly recommend that you consult a qualified Licensed Contractor or Consulting Engineer. These professionals can provide a more detailed analysis of any conditions noted in the Report at an additional cost.

2) THE INSPECTION IS AN OPINION OF THE PRESENT CONDITION OF THE VISIBLE COMPONENTS. The Home Inspection Report is an opinion of the present condition of the property. It is based on a visual examination of the readily accessible features of the building.

A Home Inspection does not include identifying defects that are hidden behind walls, floors or ceilings. This includes wiring, heating, cooling, structure, plumbing and insulation that are hidden or inaccessible.

Some intermittent problems may not be obvious on a Home Inspection because they only happen under certain circumstances. As an example, your Home Inspector may not discover leaks that occur only during certain weather conditions or when a specific tap or appliance is being used in everyday life.

Home Inspectors will not find conditions that may only be visible when storage or furniture is moved. They do not remove wall coverings (including wallpaper) or lift flooring (including carpet) or move storage to look underneath or behind.

3) THE INSPECTION DOES NOT INCLUDE HAZARDOUS MATERIALS. This includes building materials that are now suspected of posing a risk to health such as phenol-formaldehyde and urea-formaldehyde based insulation, fiberglass insulation and vermiculite insulation. The Inspector does not identify asbestos roofing, siding, wall, ceiling or floor finishes, insulation or fireproofing. We do not look for lead or other toxic metals in such things as pipes, paint or window coverings.

The Inspection does not deal with environmental hazards such as the past use of insecticides, fungicides, herbicides or pesticides. The Home Inspector does not look for, or comment on, the past use of chemical termite treatments in or around the property.

4) WE DO NOT COMMENT ON THE QUALITY OF AIR IN A BUILDING. The Inspector does not try to determine if there are irritants, pollutants, contaminants, or toxic materials in or around the building. The Inspection does not include spores, fungus, mold or mildew that may be present. You should note that whenever there is water damage noted in the report, there is a possibility that mold or mildew may be present, unseen behind a wall, floor or ceiling.

If anyone in your home suffers from allergies or heightened sensitivity to quality of air, we strongly recommend that you consult a qualified Environmental Consultant who can test for toxic materials, mold and allergens at additional cost.

5) WE DON'T LOOK FOR BURIED TANKS. Your Home Inspector does not look for and is not responsible for fuel oil, septic or gasoline tanks that may be buried on the property. If the building had its heating system converted from oil, there will always be the possibility that a tank may remain buried on the property.

If fuel oil or other storage tanks remain on the property, you may be responsible for their removal and the safe disposal of any contaminated soil. If you suspect there is a buried tank, we strongly recommend that you retain a qualified Environmental Consultant to determine whether this is a potential problem.

6) TIME TO INVESTIGATE. We will have no liability for any claim or complaint if conditions have been disturbed, altered, repaired, replaced or otherwise changed before we have had a reasonable period of time to investigate.

7) REPORT IS FOR OUR CLIENT ONLY. The inspection report is for the exclusive use of the client named herein. No use of the information by any other party is intended.

8) NOT A GUARANTEE, WARRANTY OR INSURANCE POLICY. The inspection is not a guarantee, warranty or an insurance policy with regard to the fitness of the property.

9) LIMIT OF LIABILITY/LIQUIDATED DAMAGES. The liability of the Home Inspector and the Home Inspection Company arising out of this Inspection and Report, for any cause of action whatsoever, whether in contract or in negligence, is limited to a refund of the fees that you have been charged for this inspection.

I have read, understood and accepted the above Limitations and Conditions of this Home Inspection.

Client Signature: _____   Date: _____

The inspection report is not complete unless accompanied by the Home Reference Book.

The Standards of Practice and Code of Ethics of
THE AMERICAN SOCIETY OF HOME INSPECTORS®

www.ashi.org

The Standards of Practice and Code of Ethics of the American Society of Home Inspectors

TABLE OF CONTENTS

Page

ASHI Standards of Practice 3

Section Description

1. Introduction 3

2. Purpose and Scope 3

3. Structural System 3

4. Exterior 3

5. Roofing 4

6. Plumbing 4

7. Electrical 4

8. Heating 5

9. Air Conditioning 5

10. Interiors 5

11. Insulation and Ventilation 5

12. Fireplaces and Solid 5
    Fuel Burning Appliances

13. General Limitations 6
    and Exclusions

Glossary 7

Code of Ethics 8

Distribution of this material is not an indication of ASHI® Membership. For a free listing of the Membership go to"Find an Inspector" at www.ashi.org. To obtain additional copies or request permission to reprint The ASHI® Standards of Practice and Code of Ethics, contact:

The American Society of Home Inspectors, Inc.®
932 Lee Street, Suite 101
Des Plaines, IL 60016

800-743-ASHI/2744

HOME INSPECTION

Home inspections were being performed in the mid 1950s, and by the early 1970s were considered by many consumers to be essential to the real estate transaction. The escalating demand was due to a growing desire by homebuyers to learn about the condition of a house prior to purchase. Meeting the expectations of consumers required a unique discipline, distinct from construction, engineering, architecture, or municipal building inspection. As such, home inspection requires its own set of professional guidelines and qualifications. The American Society of Home Inspectors (ASHI) formed in 1976 and established the ASHI Standards of Practice and Code of Ethics to help buyers and sellers make real estate transaction decisions based on accurate, objective information.

American Society of Home Inspectors

As the oldest, largest and highest profile organization of home inspectors in North America, ASHI takes pride in its position of leadership. Its Membership works to build public awareness of home inspection and to enhance the technical and ethical performance of home inspectors.

Standards of Practice

The ASHI Standards of Practice guide home inspectors in the performance of their inspections. Subject to regular review, the Standards of Practice reflect information gained through surveys of conditions in the field and of the consumers' interests and concerns. Vigilance has elevated ASHI's Standards of Practice so that today they are the most widely-accepted home inspection guidelines in use and are recognized by many government and professional groups as the definitive standard for professional performance.

Code of Ethics

ASHI's Code of Ethics stresses the home inspector's responsibility to report the results of the inspection in a strictly fair, impartial, and professional manner, avoiding conflicts of interest.

ASHI Membership

Selecting the right home inspector can be as important as finding the right home. ASHI Members have performed no fewer than 250 fee-paid inspections in accordance with the ASHI Standards of Practice. They have passed written examinations testing their knowledge of residential construction, defect recognition, inspection techniques, and report-writing, as well as ASHI's Standards of Practice and Code of Ethics. Membership in the American Society of Home Inspectors is well-earned and maintained only through meeting requirements for continuing education.

Find local ASHI Members by calling 1-800-743-2744 or visiting the ASHI Web site at www.ashi.org.

The Standards of Practice and Code of Ethics of the American Society of Home Inspectors

ASHI STANDARDS OF PRACTICE

1. INTRODUCTION

The American Society of Home Inspectors®, Inc. (ASHI®) is a not-for-profit professional society established in 1976. Membership in ASHI is voluntary and its members are private home *inspectors*. ASHI's objectives include promotion of excellence within the profession and continual improvement of its members' inspection services to the public.

2. PURPOSE AND SCOPE

2.1 The purpose of the Standards of Practice is to establish a minimum and uniform standard for home *inspectors* who subscribe to these Standards of Practice. *Home inspections* performed to these Standards of Practice are intended to provide the client with objective information regarding the condition of the *systems* and *components* of the home as *inspected* at the time of the *home inspection*. Redundancy in the description of the requirements, limitations, and exclusions regarding the scope of the *home inspection* is provided for emphasis only.

2.2 **Inspectors shall:**

A. adhere to the Code of Ethics of the American Society of Home Inspectors.

B. *inspect readily accessible*, visually observable, *installed systems* and *components* listed in these Standards of Practice.

C. *report*:

1. those *systems* and *components inspected* that, in the professional judgment of the *inspector*, are not functioning properly, significantly deficient, *unsafe*, or are near the end of their service lives.

2. recommendations to correct, or monitor for future correction, the deficiencies *reported* in 2.2.C.1, or items needing *further evaluation*. (Per Exclusion 13.2.A.5 *inspectors* are NOT required to determine methods, materials, or costs of corrections.)

3. reasoning or explanation as to the nature of the deficiencies *reported* in 2.2.C.1, that are not self-evident.

4. *systems* and *components* designated for inspection in these Standards of Practice that were present at the time of the *home inspection* but were not *inspected* and the reason(s) they were not *inspected*.

2.3 **These Standards of Practice are not intended to limit inspectors from:**

A. including other inspection services or *systems* and *components* in addition to those required in Section 2.2.B.

B. designing or specifying repairs, provided the *inspector* is appropriately qualified and willing to do so.

C. excluding *systems* and *components* from the inspection if requested by the client.

3. STRUCTURAL COMPONENTS

3.1 The *inspector* shall:

A. *inspect*:

1. *structural components* including the foundation and framing.

2. by probing a *representative number* of *structural components* where deterioration is suspected or where clear indications of possible deterioration exist. Probing is NOT required when probing would damage any finished surface or where no deterioration is visible or presumed to exist.

B. *describe*:

1. the methods used to *inspect under-floor crawl spaces* and attics.

2. the foundation.

3. the floor structure.

4. the wall structure.

5. the ceiling structure.

6. the roof structure.

3.2 The *inspector* is NOT required to:

A. provide any *engineering* or architectural services or analysis.

B. offer an opinion as to the adequacy of any *structural system* or *component*.

4. EXTERIOR

4.1 The *inspector* shall:

A. *inspect*:

1. *siding*, flashing and trim.

2. all exterior doors.

3. attached or adjacent decks, balconies, stoops, steps, porches, and their associated railings.

4. eaves, soffits, and fascias where accessible from the ground level.

5. vegetation, grading, surface drainage, and retaining walls that are likely to adversely affect the building.

6. adjacent or entryway walkways, patios, and driveways.

B. *describe*:

1. *siding*.

EXTERIOR 4.2, Continued

4.2   **The *inspector* is NOT required to *inspect*:**

A. screening, shutters, awnings, and similar seasonal accessories.

B. fences.

C. geological and/or soil conditions.

D. *recreational facilities.*

E. outbuildings other than garages and carports.

F. seawalls, break-walls, and docks.

G. erosion control and earth stabilization measures.

5. ROOFING

5.1   **The *inspector* shall:**

A. *inspect*:

1. roofing materials.

2. *roof drainage systems.*

3. flashing.

4. skylights, chimneys, and roof penetrations.

B. *describe*:

1. roofing materials.

2. methods used to *inspect* the roofing.

5.2   **The *inspector* is NOT required to *inspect*:**

A. antennae.

B. interiors of flues or chimneys that are not *readily accessible.*

C. other *installed* accessories.

6.   **PLUMBING**

6.1   **The *inspector* shall:**

A. *inspect*:

1. interior water supply and distribution *systems* including all fixtures and faucets.

2. drain, waste, and vent *systems* including all fixtures.

3. water heating equipment and hot water supply *system.*

4. vent *systems*, flues, and chimneys.

5. fuel storage and fuel distribution *systems.*

6. drainage sumps, sump pumps, and related piping.

B. *describe*:

1. water supply, drain, waste, and vent piping materials.

2. water heating equipment including energy source(s).

3. location of main water and fuel shut-off valves.

6.2   **The *inspector* is NOT required to:**

A. *inspect*:

1. clothes washing machine connections.

2. interiors of flues or chimneys that are not *readily accessible.*

3. wells, well pumps, or water storage related equipment.

4. water conditioning *systems.*

5. solar water heating *systems.*

6. fire and lawn sprinkler *systems.*

7. private waste disposal *systems.*

B. determine:

1. whether water supply and waste disposal *systems* are public or private.

2. water supply quantity or quality.

C. operate *automatic safety controls* or manual stop valves.

7.   **ELECTRICAL**

7.1   **The *inspector* shall:**

A. *inspect*:

1. service drop.

2. service entrance conductors, cables, and raceways.

3. service equipment and main disconnects.

4. service grounding.

5. interior *components* of service panels and sub panels.

6. conductors.

7. overcurrent protection devices.

8. a *representative number* of *installed* lighting fixtures, switches, and receptacles.

9. ground fault circuit interrupters.

B. *describe*:

1. amperage and voltage rating of the service.

2. location of main disconnect(s) and sub panels.

3. presence of solid conductor aluminum branch circuit wiring.

4. presence or absence of smoke detectors.

5. *wiring methods.*

7.2   **The *inspector* is NOT required to:**

A. *inspect*:

1. remote control devices.

2. *alarm systems* and *components.*

3. low voltage wiring *systems* and *components.*

4. ancillary wiring *systems* and *components.* not a part of the primary electrical power distribution *system.*

B. measure amperage, voltage, or impedance.

The Standards of Practice and Code of Ethics of the American Society of Home Inspectors

Continued

8. HEATING

8.1 The *inspector* shall:

A. open *readily openable access panels*.

B. *inspect*:

    1. *installed* heating equipment.

    2. vent *systems*, flues, and chimneys.

C. *describe*:

    1. energy source(s).

    2. heating *systems*.

8.2 The *inspector* is NOT required to:

A. *inspect*:

    1. interiors of flues or chimneys that are not *readily accessible*.

    2. heat exchangers.

    3. humidifiers or dehumidifiers.

    4. electronic air filters.

    5. solar space heating *systems*.

B. determine heat supply adequacy or distribution balance.

9. AIR CONDITIONING

9.1 The *inspector* shall:

A. open *readily openable access panels*.

B. *inspect*:

    1. central and through-wall equipment.

    2. distribution *systems*.

C. *describe*:

    1. energy source(s).

    2. cooling *systems*.

9.2 The *inspector* is NOT required to:

A. *inspect* electronic air filters.

B. determine cooling supply adequacy or distribution balance.

C. *inspect* window air conditioning units.

10. INTERIORS

10.1 The *inspector* shall *inspect*:

A. walls, ceilings, and floors.

B. steps, stairways, and railings.

C. countertops and a *representative number* of *installed* cabinets.

D. a *representative number* of doors and windows.

E. garage doors and garage door operators.

10.2 The *inspector* is NOT required to *inspect*:

A. paint, wallpaper, and other finish treatments.

B. carpeting.

C. window treatments.

D. central vacuum *systems*.

E. *household appliances*.

F. *recreational facilities*.

11. INSULATION & VENTILATION

11.1 The *inspector* shall:

A. *inspect*:

    1. insulation and vapor retarders in unfinished spaces.

    2. ventilation of attics and foundation areas.

    3. mechanical ventilation *systems*.

B. *describe*:

    1. insulation and vapor retarders in unfinished spaces.

    2. absence of insulation in unfinished spaces at conditioned surfaces.

11.2 The *inspector* is NOT required to disturb insulation. See 13.2.A.11 and 13.2.A.12.

12. FIREPLACES AND SOLID FUEL BURNING APPLIANCES

12.1 The *inspector* shall:

A. *inspect*:

    1. *system components*.

    2. chimney and vents.

B. *describe*:

    1. fireplaces and *solid fuel burning appliances*.

    2. chimneys.

12.2 The *inspector* is NOT required to:

A. *inspect*:

    1. interiors of flues or chimneys.

    2. firescreens and doors.

    3. seals and gaskets.

    4. automatic fuel feed devices.

    5. mantles and fireplace surrounds.

    6. combustion make-up air devices.

    7. heat distribution assists (gravity fed and fan assisted).

B. ignite or extinguish fires.

C. determine draft characteristics.

D. move fireplace inserts and stoves or firebox contents.

The Standards of Practice and Code of Ethics of the American Society of Home Inspectors

Continued

13.   GENERAL LIMITATIONS AND EXCLUSIONS

13.1   General limitations:

A. The *inspector* is NOT required to perform any action or make any determination not specifically stated in these Standards of Practice.

B. Inspections performed in accordance with these Standards of Practice:

1. are not *technically exhaustive*.

2. are not required to identify concealed. conditions, latent defects, or consequential damage(s).

C. These Standards of Practice are applicable to buildings with four or fewer dwelling units and their garages or carports.

13.2   General exclusions:

A. *Inspectors* are NOT required to determine:

1. conditions of *systems* or *components* that are not *readily accessible*.

2. remaining life expectancy of any *system* or *component*.

3. strength, adequacy, effectiveness, or efficiency of any *system* or *component*.

4. the causes of any condition or deficiency.

5. methods, materials, or costs of corrections.

6. future conditions including but not limited to failure of *systems* and *components*.

7. the suitability of the property for any specialized use.

8. compliance with regulatory requirements (codes, regulations, laws, ordinances, etc.).

9. market value of the property or its marketability.

10. the advisability of purchase of the property.

11. the presence of potentially hazardous plants or animals including, but not limited to, wood destroying organisms or diseases harmful to humans including molds or mold-like substances.

12. the presence of any environmental hazards including, but not limited to, toxins, carcinogens, noise, and contaminants in soil, water, and air.

13. the effectiveness of any *system installed* or method utilized to control or remove suspected hazardous substances.

14. operating costs of *systems* or *components*.

15. acoustical properties of any *system* or *component*.

16. soil conditions relating to geotechnical or hydrologic specialties.

B. *Inspectors* are NOT required to offer:

1. or perform any act or service contrary to law.

2. or perform *engineering* services.

3. or perform any trade or any professional. service other than *home inspection*.

4. warranties or guarantees of any kind.

C. *Inspectors* are NOT required to operate:

1. any *system* or *component* that is *shut down* or otherwise inoperable.

2. any *system* or *component* that does not respond to *normal operating controls*.

3. shut-off valves or manual stop valves.

D. *Inspectors* are NOT required to enter:

1. any area that will, in the opinion of the *inspector*, likely be dangerous to the *inspector* or other persons or damage the property or its *systems* or *components*.

2. *under-floor crawl spaces* or attics that are not *readily accessible*.

E. *Inspectors* are NOT required to inspect:

1. underground items including but not limited to underground storage tanks or other underground indications of their presence, whether abandoned or active.

2. items that are not *installed*.

3. *installed decorative* items.

4. items in areas that are not entered in accordance with 13.2.D.

5. detached structures other than garages and carports.

6. common elements or common areas in multi-unit housing, such as condominium properties or cooperative housing.

F. *Inspectors* are NOT required to:

1. perform any procedure or operation that will, in the opinion of the *inspector*, likely be dangerous to the *inspector* or other persons or damage the property or its *systems* or *components*.

2. describe or report on any *system* or *component* that is not included in these Standards and was not *inspected*.

3. move personal property, furniture, equipment, plants, soil, snow, ice, or debris.

4. *dismantle* any *system* or *component*, except as explicitly required by these Standards of Practice.

The Standards of Practice and Code of Ethics of the American Society of Home Inspectors

ASHI STANDARDS OF PRACTICE GLOSSARY OF ITALICIZED TERMS

Alarm Systems
Warning devices *installed* or free-standing including but not limited to smoke detectors, carbon monoxide detectors, flue gas, and other spillage detectors, and security equipment

Automatic Safety Controls
Devices designed and *installed* to protect *systems* and *components* from unsafe conditions

Component
A part of a *system*

Decorative
Ornamental; not required for the proper operation of the essential *systems* and *components* of a home

Describe
To identify (in writing) a *system* or *component* by its type or other distinguishing characteristics

Dismantle
To take apart or remove any *component*, device, or piece of equipment that would not be taken apart or removed by a homeowner in the course of normal maintenance

Engineering
The application of scientific knowledge for the design, control, or use of building structures, equipment, or apparatus

Further Evaluation
Examination and analysis by a qualified professional, tradesman, or service technician beyond that provided by the *home inspection*

Home Inspection
The process by which an *inspector* visually examines the *readily accessible systems* and *components* of a home and which *describes* those *systems* and *components* in accordance with these Standards of Practice

Household Appliances
Kitchen, laundry, and similar appliances, whether *installed* or free-standing

Inspect
To examine any *system* or *component* of a building in accordance with these Standards of Practice, using *normal operating controls* and opening *readily openable access panels*

Inspector
A person hired to examine any *system* or *component* of a building in accordance with these Standards of Practice

Installed
Attached such that removal requires tools

Normal Operating Controls
Devices such as thermostats, switches, or valves intended to be operated by the homeowner

Readily Accessible
Available for visual inspection without requiring moving of personal property, *dismantling*, destructive measures, or any action that will likely involve risk to persons or property

Readily Openable Access Panel
A panel provided for homeowner inspection and maintenance that is *readily accessible*, within normal reach, can be removed by one person, and is not sealed in place

Recreational Facilities
Spas, saunas, steam baths, swimming pools, exercise, entertainment, athletic, playground or other similar equipment, and associated accessories

Report
Communicate in writing

Representative Number
One *component* per room for multiple similar interior *components* such as windows, and electric receptacles; one *component* on each side of the building for multiple similar exterior *components*

Roof Drainage Systems
Components used to carry water off a roof and away from a building

Shut Down
A state in which a *system* or *component* cannot be operated by *normal operating controls*

Siding
Exterior wall covering and cladding; such as: aluminum, asphalt, brick, cement/asbestos, EIFS, stone, stucco, veneer, vinyl, wood, etc.

Solid Fuel Burning Appliances
A hearth and fire chamber or similar prepared place in which a fire may be built and that is built in conjunction with a chimney; or a listed assembly of a fire chamber, its chimney, and related factory-made parts designed for unit assembly without requiring field construction

Structural Component
A *component* that supports non-variable forces or weights (dead loads) and variable forces or weights (live loads)

System
A combination of interacting or interdependent *components*, assembled to carry out one or more functions

Technically Exhaustive
An investigation that involves *dismantling*, the extensive use of advanced techniques, measurements, instruments, testing, calculations, or other means

Under-floor Crawl Space
The area within the confines of the foundation and between the ground and the underside of the floor

Unsafe
A condition in a *readily accessible*, *installed system* or *component* that is judged to be a significant risk of bodily injury during normal, day-to-day use; the risk may be due to damage, deterioration, improper installation, or a change in accepted residential construction standards

Wiring Methods
Identification of electrical conductors or wires by their general type, such as non-metallic sheathed cable, armored cable, or knob and tube, etc.

The Standards of Practice and Code of Ethics of the American Society of Home Inspectors

ASHI® CODE OF ETHICS
For the Home Inspection Profession

Integrity, honesty, and objectivity are fundamental principles embodied by this Code, which sets forth obligations of ethical conduct for the home inspection profession. The Membership of ASHI has adopted this Code to provide high ethical standards to safeguard the public and the profession.

Inspectors shall comply with this Code, shall avoid association with any enterprise whose practices violate this Code, and shall strive to uphold, maintain, and improve the integrity, reputation, and practice of the home inspection profession.

1. Inspectors shall avoid conflicts of interest or activities that compromise, or appear to compromise, professional independence, objectivity, or inspection integrity.

    A. Inspectors shall not inspect properties for compensation in which they have, or expect to have, a financial interest.

    B. Inspectors shall not inspect properties under contingent arrangements whereby any compensation or future referrals are dependent on reported findings or on the sale of a property.

    C. Inspectors shall not directly or indirectly compensate realty agents, or other parties having a financial interest in closing or settlement of real estate transactions, for the referral of inspections or for inclusion on a list of recommended inspectors, preferred providers, or similar arrangements.

    D. Inspectors shall not receive compensation for an inspection from more than one party unless agreed to by the client(s).

    E. Inspectors shall not accept compensation, directly or indirectly, for recommending contractors, services, or products to inspection clients or other parties having an interest in inspected properties.

    F. Inspectors shall not repair, replace, or upgrade, for compensation, systems or components covered by ASHI Standards of Practice, for one year after the inspection.

2. Inspectors shall act in good faith toward each client and other interested parties.

    A. Inspectors shall perform services and express opinions based on genuine conviction and only within their areas of education, training, or experience.

    B. Inspectors shall be objective in their reporting and not knowingly understate or overstate the significance of reported conditions.

    C. Inspectors shall not disclose inspection results or client information without client approval. Inspectors, at their discretion, may disclose observed immediate safety hazards to occupants exposed to such hazards, when feasible.

3. Inspectors shall avoid activities that may harm the public, discredit themselves, or reduce public confidence in the profession.

    A. Advertising, marketing, and promotion of inspectors' services or qualifications shall not be fraudulent, false, deceptive, or misleading.

    B. Inspectors shall report substantive and willful violations of this Code to the Society.

Canadian Association Of Home & Property Inspectors

2012 NATIONAL STANDARDS OF PRACTICE

The National Standards of Practice are a set of guidelines for home and property inspectors to follow in the performance of their inspections. They are the most widely accepted Canadian home inspection guidelines in use, and address all the home's major systems and components. The National Standards of Practice and Code of Ethics are recognized by many related professionals as the definitive Standards for professional performance in the industry.

These National Standards of Practice are being published to inform the public on the nature and scope of visual building inspections performed by home and property inspectors who are members of the Canadian Association of Home and Property Inspectors (CAHPI).

The purpose of the National Standards of Practice is to provide guidelines for home and property inspectors regarding both the inspection itself and the drafting of the inspection report, and to define certain terms relating to the performance of home inspections to ensure consistent interpretation.

To ensure better public protection, home and property inspectors who are members of CAHPI should strive to meet these Standards and abide by the appropriate provincial/regional CAHPI Code of Ethics.

These Standards take into account that a visual inspection of a building does not constitute an evaluation or a verification of compliance with building codes, Standards or regulations governing the construction industry or the health and safety industry, or Standards and regulations governing insurability.

Any terms not defined in these Standards shall have the meaning commonly assigned to it by the various trades and professions, according to context.

INDEX
1. Introduction
2. Purpose and Scope
3. General Limitations and Exclusions
4. Structural Systems
5. Exterior Systems
6. Roof Systems
7. Plumbing Systems
8. Electrical Systems
9. Heating Systems
10. Fireplaces & Solid Fuel Burning Appliances
11. Air Conditioning Systems
12. Interior Systems
13. Insulation and Vapour Barriers
14. Mechanical and Natural Ventilation Systems

Glossary   Note: Italicized words are defined in the Glossary.

1. INTRODUCTION

1.1 The Canadian Association of Home and Property Inspectors (CAHPI) is a not-for-profit association whose members include the following seven provincial/regional organizations: CAHPI-British Columbia., CAHPI-Alberta, CAHPI-Saskatchewan, CAHPI-Manitoba, OAHI (Ontario), AIBQ (Quebec), and CAHPI-Atlantic. CAHPI strives to promote excellence within the profession and continual improvement of inspection services to the public.

2. PURPOSE AND SCOPE

2.1 The purpose of these National Standards of Practice is to establish professional and uniform Standards for private, fee-paid home inspectors who are members of one of the provincial/regional organizations of CAHPI. Home Inspections performed to these National Standards of Practice are intended to provide information regarding the condition of the systems and components of the building as inspected at the time of the Home Inspection. This does NOT include building code inspections.

These National Standards of Practice enable the building being inspected to be compared with a building that was constructed in accordance with the generally accepted practices at the time of construction, and which has been adequately maintained such that there is no significant loss of *functionality.*

It follows that the building may not be in compliance with current building codes, standards and regulations that are applicable at the time of inspection.

These National Standards of Practice apply to inspections of part or all of a building for the following building types:

- single-family dwelling, detached, semi-detached or row house
- multi unit residential building
- residential building held in divided or undivided co ownership
- residential building occupied in part for a residential occupancy and in part for a commercial occupancy, as long as the latter use does not exceed 40% of the building's total area, excluding the basement.

2.2 THE INSPECTOR SHALL:

A. inspect:
   1. *readily accessible,* visually observable *installed systems,* and *components* of buildings listed in these National Standards of Practice.

B. report:
   1. on those *systems* and *components* installed on the building inspected which, in the professional opinion or judgement of the *inspector, have a significant deficiency* or is unsafe or are near the end of their *service lives.*
   2. a reason why, if not self-evident, the *system* or *component has a significant deficiency* or is unsafe or is near the end of its *service life.*
   3. the inspector's recommendations to correct or monitor the reported deficiency.
   4. on any *systems* and *components* designated for inspection in these National Standards of Practice which were present at the time of the *Home Inspection* but were not inspected and a reason they were not inspected.

2.3 *These National Standards of Practice are not intended to limit inspectors from:*
   A. including other inspection services in addition to those required by these National Standards of Practice provided the *inspector* is appropriately qualified and willing to do so.
   B. excluding *systems* and *components* from the inspection if requested by the client or as dictated by circumstances at the time of the inspection.

3. GENERAL LIMITATIONS AND EXCLUSIONS

3.1 GENERAL LIMITATIONS:

   A. Inspections performed in accordance with these National Standards of Practice
   1. are not *technically exhaustive.*
   2. will not identify concealed conditions or latent defects.

A. The *inspector* is not required to perform any action or make any determination unless specifically stated in these National Standards of Practice, except as may be required by lawful authority.

B. *Inspectors* are NOT required to determine:
1. condition of *systems* or *components* which are not *readily accessible.*
2. remaining life of any *system* or *component.*
3. strength, adequacy, effectiveness, or efficiency of any *system* or *component.*
4. causes of any condition or deficiency.
5. methods, materials, or costs of corrections.
6. future conditions including, but not limited to, failure of *systems* and *components.*
7. suitability of the property for any use.
8. compliance with regulatory requirements (codes, regulations, laws, ordinances, etc.).
9. market value of the property or its marketability.
10. advisability of the purchase of the property.
11. presence of potentially hazardous plants, animals or insects including, but not limited to wood destroying organisms, diseases or organisms harmful to humans.
12. presence of any environmental hazards including, but not limited to toxins, carcinogens, noise, and contaminants in soil, water, and air.
13. effectiveness of any *system* installed or methods utilized to control or remove suspected hazardous substances.
14. operating costs of *systems* or *components.*
15. acoustical properties of any *system* or *component*
16. design adequacy with regards to location of the home, or the elements to which it is exposed.

C. *Inspectors* are NOT required to offer or perform:
1. any act or service contrary to law, statute or regulation.
2. *engineering, architectural* and technical services.
3. work in any trade or any professional service other than *home inspection.*
4. warranties or guarantees of any kind.

D. *Inspectors* are NOT required to operate:
1. any *system* or *component* which is *shut down* or otherwise inoperable.
2. any *system* or *component* which does not respond to *normal operating controls.*
3. shut-off valves.

E. *Inspectors* are NOT required to enter:
1. any area which will, in the opinion of the *inspector*, likely be hazardous to the *inspector* or other persons or damage the property or its *systems* or *components.*

F. *Inspectors* are NOT required to *inspect*:
1. underground items including, but not limited to storage tanks or other indications of their presence, whether abandoned or active.
2. *systems* or *components* which are not *installed.*
3. *decorative* items.
4. *systems* or *components* located in areas that are not readily accessible in accordance with these National Standards of Practice.
5. detached structures.
6. common elements or common areas in multi-unit housing, such as condominium properties or cooperative housing when inspecting an individual unit(s), including the roof and building envelope.
7. test and/or operate any installed fire alarm system, burglar alarm system, automatic sprinkler system or other fire protection equipment, electronic or automated installations, telephone, intercom, cable/internet systems and any lifting equipment, elevator, freight elevator, wheelchair lift, climbing chair, escalator or others;
8. pools, spas and their associated safety devices, including fences.

G. *Inspectors* are NOT required to:
1. perform any procedure or operation which will, in the opinion of the *inspector*, likely be hazardous to the *inspector* or other persons or damage the property or it's *systems* or *components.*
2. move suspended ceiling tiles, personal property, furniture, equipment, plants, soil, snow, ice, or debris.
3. *dismantle* any *system* or *component*, except as explicitly required by these National Standards of Practice.

4. STRUCTURAL SYSTEMS

4.1 THE INSPECTOR SHALL:
A. inspect:
1. *structural components* including visible foundation and framing.
2. by *probing* a sample of structural components where deterioration is suspected or where clear indications of possible deterioration exist. *Probing* is NOT required when *probing* would damage any finished surface or where no deterioration is visible.

B. describe:
1. foundation(s).
2. floor structure(s).
3. wall structure(s).
4. ceiling structure(s).
5. roof structure(s).

C. report:
1. on conditions limiting access to structural components.
2. methods used to *inspect* the *under-floor crawl space*
3. methods used to *inspect* the attic(s).

4.2 THE INSPECTOR IS NOT REQUIRED TO:
A. provide any *engineering service* or *architectural service*.
B. offer an opinion as to the adequacy of any *structural system* or *component*.

5. EXTERIOR SYSTEMS

5.1 THE INSPECTOR SHALL:
A. inspect:
1. exterior wall covering(s), flashing and trim.
2. all exterior doors.
3. attached or *adjacent* decks, balconies, steps, porches, and their associated railings.
4. eaves, soffits, and fascias where accessible from the ground level.
5. vegetation, grading, and surface drainage on the property when any of these are likely to adversely affect the building.
6. walkways, patios, and driveways leading to dwelling entrances.
7. landscaping structure attached or adjacent to the building when likely to adversely affect the building.
8. attached garage or carport.
9. garage doors and garage door operators for attached garages.

B. describe
1. exterior wall covering(s).

C. report:
1. the method(s) used to inspect the exterior wall elevations.

5.2 THE INSPECTOR IS NOT REQUIRED TO:
A. inspect:
1. screening, shutters, awnings, and similar seasonal accessories.
2. fences.
3. geological, geotechnical or hydrological conditions.
4. *recreational facilities*.
5. detached garages and outbuildings.
6. seawalls, break-walls, dykes and docks.
7. erosion control and earth stabilization measures.

6. ROOF SYSTEMS

6.1 THE INSPECTOR SHALL:
A. inspect:
1. *readily accessible* roof coverings.
2. *readily accessible roof drainage systems*.
3. *readily accessible* flashings.
4. *readily accessible* skylights, chimneys, and roof penetrations.

B. describe
1. roof coverings.

C. report:
1. method(s) used to inspect the roof(s).

6.2 THE INSPECTOR IS NOT REQUIRED TO:
A. inspect:
1. antennae and satellite dishes.
2. interiors of flues or chimneys.
3. other *installed* items attached to but not related to the roof system(s).

7. PLUMBING SYSTEMS

7.1 THE INSPECTOR SHALL:
A. inspect:
1. interior water supply and distribution *systems* including all fixtures and faucets.
2. drain, waste and vent *systems* including all fixtures.
3. water heating equipment and associated venting systems.
4. water heating equipment fuel storage and fuel distribution systems.
5. fuel storage and fuel distribution *systems*.
6. drainage sumps, sump pumps, and related piping.

B. describe:
1. water supply, distribution, drain, waste, and vent piping materials.
2. water heating equipment including the energy source.
3. location of main water and main fuel shut-off valves.

7.2 THE INSPECTOR IS NOT REQUIRED TO:
A. inspect:
1. clothes washing machine connections.
2. wells, well pumps, or water storage related equipment.
3. water conditioning *systems*.
4. solar water heating *systems*.
5. fire and lawn sprinkler *systems*.
6. private waste disposal *systems*.
B. determine:
1. whether water supply and waste disposal *systems* are public or private.
2. the quantity or quality of the water supply.
C. operate:
1. safety valves or shut-off valves.

8. ELECTRICAL SYSTEMS

8.1 THE INSPECTOR SHALL:
A. inspect:
1. service drop.
2. service entrance conductors, cables, and raceways.
3. service equipment and main disconnects.
4. service grounding.
5. interior components of service panels and sub panels.
6. distribution conductors.
7. overcurrent protection devices.
8. a *representative number* of *installed* lighting fixtures, switches, and receptacles.
9. ground fault circuit interrupters (GFCI) (if appropriate).
10. arc fault circuit interrupters (AFCI) (if appropriate).
B. describe:
1. amperage and voltage rating of the service.
2. location of main disconnect(s) and subpanel(s).
3. *wiring methods*.
C. report:
1. presence of solid conductor aluminum branch circuit wiring.
2. absence of carbon monoxide detectors (if applicable).
3. absence of smoke detectors.
4. presence of ground fault circuit interrupters (GFCI).
5. presence of arc fault circuit interrupters (AFCI).

8.2 THE INSPECTOR IS NOT REQUIRED TO:
A. inspect:
1. remote control devices unless the device is the only control device.
2. alarm *systems* and *components*.
3. low voltage wiring, *systems* and *components*.
4. ancillary wiring, *systems* and *components* not a part of the primary electrical power distribution *system*.

5. telecommunication equipment.
B. measure:
1. amperage, voltage, or impedance.

9. HEATING SYSTEMS

9.1 THE INSPECTOR SHALL:
A. inspect:
1. *readily accessible* components of *installed* heating equipment.
2. vent systems, flues, and chimneys.
3. fuel storage and fuel distribution *systems*.
B. describe:
1. energy source(s).
2. heating method(s) by distinguishing characteristics.
3. chimney(s) and/or venting material(s).
4. combustion air sources.
5. exhaust venting methods (naturally aspiring, induced draft, direct vent, direct vent sealed combustion).

9.2 THE INSPECTOR IS NOT REQUIRED TO:
A. inspect:
1. interiors of flues or chimneys.
2. heat exchangers.
3. auxiliary equipment.
4. electronic air filters.
5. solar heating *systems*.

B. determine:
1. system adequacy or distribution balance.

10. FIREPLACES AND SOLID FUEL BURNING APPLIANCES
(Unless prohibited by the authority having jurisdiction)

10.1 THE INSPECTOR SHALL:
A. inspect:
1. system components
2. vent systems and chimneys
B. describe:
1. fireplaces and solid fuel burning appliances
2. chimneys

10.2 THE INSPECTOR IS NOT REQUIRED TO:
A. inspect:
1. interior of flues or chimneys
2. screens, doors and dampers
3. seals and gaskets
4. automatic fuel feed devices
5. heat distribution assists whether fan assisted or gravity
B. ignite or extinguish fires
C. determine draught characteristics
D. move fireplace inserts, stoves, or firebox contents

11. AIR CONDITIONING SYSTEMS

11.1 THE INSPECTOR SHALL:
A. inspect
1. permanently *installed* central air conditioning equipment.

B. describe:
1. energy source.
2. cooling method by its distinguishing characteristics.

11.2 THE INSPECTOR IS NOT REQUIRED TO:
A. inspect
1. electronic air filters.
2. portable air conditioner(s).

B. determine:
1. system adequacy or distribution balance.

12. INTERIOR SYSTEMS

12.1 THE INSPECTOR SHALL:
A. inspect:
1. walls, ceilings, and floors.
2. steps, stairways, and railings.
3. a *representative number* of countertops and *installed* cabinets.
4. a *representative number* of doors and windows.
5. walls, doors and ceilings separating the habitable spaces and the garage.

B. describe:
1. materials used for walls, ceilings and floors.
2. doors.
3. windows.

C. report
1. absence or ineffectiveness of guards and handrails or other potential physical injury hazards.

12.2 THE INSPECTOR IS NOT REQUIRED TO:
A. inspect:
1. *decorative* finishes.
2. window treatments.
3. central vacuum *systems*.
4. *household appliances*.
5. *recreational facilities*.

13. INSULATION AND VAPOUR BARRIERS

13.1 THE INSPECTOR SHALL:
A. inspect:
1. insulation and *vapour barriers* in unfinished spaces.

B. describe:
1. type of insulation material(s) and *vapour barriers* in unfinished spaces.

C. report
1. absence of insulation in unfinished spaces within the building envelope.
2. presence of vermiculite insulation

13.2 THE INSPECTOR IS NOT REQUIRED TO:
A. disturb
1. insulation.
2. *vapour barriers*.

B. obtain sample(s) for analysis
1. insulation material(s).

14. MECHANICAL AND NATURAL VENTILATION SYSTEMS

14.1 THE INSPECTOR SHALL:
A. inspect:
1. ventilation of attics and foundation areas.
2. mechanical ventilation *systems*.
3. ventilation systems in areas where moisture is generated such as kitchen, bathrooms, laundry rooms.

B. describe:
1. ventilation of attics and foundation areas.
2. mechanical ventilation *systems*.
3. ventilation systems in areas where moisture is generated such as: kitchens, bathrooms and laundry rooms.

C. report:
1. absence of ventilation in areas where moisture is generated such as: kitchens, bathrooms and laundry rooms.

14.2 THE INSPECTOR IS NOT REQUIRED TO:
1. determine indoor air quality.
2. determine system adequacy or distribution balance.

GLOSSARY

Adjacent
Nearest in space or position; immediately adjoining without intervening space.

Alarm Systems
Warning devices, installed or free-standing, including but not limited to; carbon monoxide detectors, flue gas and other spillage detectors, security equipment, ejector pumps and smoke alarms.

Architectural Service
Any practice involving the art and science of building design for construction of any structure or grouping of structures and the use of space within and surrounding the structures or the design for construction, including but not specifically limited to, schematic design, design development, preparation of construction contract documents, and administration of the construction contract, adequacy of design for the location and exposure to the elements.

Automatic Safety Controls
Devices designed and installed to protect *systems* and *components* from unsafe conditions.

Component
A part of a *system*.

Confined Spaces
An enclosed or partially enclosed area that:
1. Is occupied by people only for the purpose of completing work.
2. Has restricted entry/exit points.
3. Could be hazardous to people entering due to:
a. its design, construction, location or atmosphere.
b. the materials or substances in it, or
c. any other conditions which prevent normal inspection procedure.

Decorative
Ornamental; not required for the operation of the essential *systems* and *components* of a building.

Describe
To *report* a *system* or *component* by its type or other observed, significant characteristics to distinguish it from other *systems* or *components*.

Determine
To find out, or come to a conclusion by investigation.

Dismantle
To take apart or remove any component, device, or piece of equipment that would not be taken apart or removed by a homeowner in the course of normal and routine home owner maintenance.

Engineering Service
Any professional service or creative work requiring engineering education, training, and experience and the application of special knowledge of the mathematical, physical and engineering sciences to such professional service or creative work as consultation, investigation, evaluation, planning, design and supervision of construction for the purpose of assuring compliance with the specifications and design, in conjunction with structures, buildings, machines, equipment, works or processes.

Functionality
The purpose that something is designed or expected to fulfill.

Further Evaluation
Examination and analysis by a qualified professional, tradesman or service technician beyond that provided by the *home inspection.*

Home Inspection
The process by which an *inspector* visually examines the *readily accessible systems* and *components* of a building and which *describes* those *systems* and *components* in accordance with these National Standards of Practice.

Household Appliances
Kitchen, laundry, and similar appliances, whether *installed* or freestanding.

Inspect
To examine *readily accessible systems* and *components* of a building in accordance with these National Standards of Practice, *where applicable* using *normal operating controls* and opening *readily openable access panels.*

Inspector
A person hired to examine any *system* or *component* of a building in accordance with these National Standards of Practice.

Installed
Set up or fixed in position for current use or service.

Monitor
Examine at regular intervals to detect evidence of change.

Normal Operating Controls
Devices such as thermostats, switches or valves intended to be operated by the homeowner.

Operate
To cause to function, turn on, to control the function of a machine, process, or system.

Probing
Examine by touch.

Readily Accessible
Available for visual inspection without requiring moving of personal property, *dismantling*, destructive measures, or any action which will likely involve risk to persons or property.

Readily Openable Access Panel
A panel provided for homeowner inspection and maintenance that is within normal reach, can be removed by one person, and is not sealed in place.

Recreational Facilities
Spas, saunas, steam baths, swimming pools, exercise, entertainment, athletic, playground or other similar equipment and associated accessories.

Report
To communicate in writing.

Representative Number
One *component* per room for multiple similar interior *components* such as windows and electric outlets; one *component* on each side of the building for multiple similar exterior *components*.

Roof Drainage Systems
Components used to carry water off a roof and away from a building.

Sample
A representative portion selected for inspection.

Service Life/Lives
The period during which something continues to function fully as intended.

Significant Deficiency
A clearly definable hazard or a clearly definable potential for failure or is unsafe or not functioning.

Shut Down
A state in which a *system* or *component* cannot be operated by *normal operating controls*.

Solid Fuel Burning Appliances
A hearth and fire chamber or similar prepared place in which a fire may be built and which is built in conjunction with a chimney; or a listed assembly of a fire chamber, its chimney and related factory-made parts designed for unit assembly without requiring field construction.

Structural Component
A component that supports non-variable forces or weights (dead loads) and variable forces or weights (live loads).

System
A combination of interacting or interdependent components, assembled to carry out one or more functions.

Technically Exhaustive
An inspection is technically exhaustive when it is done by a specialist who may make extensive use of measurements, instruments, testing, calculations, and other means to develop scientific or engineering findings, conclusions, and recommendations.

Under-floor Crawl Space
The area within the confines of the foundation and between the ground and the underside of the floor.

Unsafe
A condition in a *readily accessible, installed system* or *component* which is judged to be a significant risk of personal injury during normal, day-to-day use. The risk may be due to damage, deterioration, missing or improper installation or a change in accepted residential construction Standards.

Vapour Barrier
Material used in the building envelope to retard the passage of water vapour or moisture.

Visually Accessible
Able to be viewed by reaching or entering.

Wiring Methods
Identification of electrical conductors or wires by their general type, such as "non-metallic sheathed cable" ("Romex"), "armored cable" ("bx") or "knob and tube", etc.

Note - In these National Standards of Practice, redundancy in the description of the requirements, limitations and exclusions regarding the scope of the Home Inspection is provided for clarity not emphasis.

(CAHPI acknowledges The American Society of Home Inspectors®, Inc. (ASHI®) for the use of their Standards of Practice (version January 1, 2000)

(AUGUST 22/12 VER. F)

Brian Mulroney

Brian Mulroney
The Boy from Baie-Comeau

Rae Murphy/Robert Chodos/Nick Auf der Maur

James Lorimer & Company, Publishers
Toronto 1984

ISBN 0-88862-693-2 cloth
Design: Don Fernley

Photographs are reproduced courtesy of: Mrs. Benedict Mulroney
(1-3); Mrs. Olive Elliott (4-7, 12, 13); Mulroney family (9, 14);
Progressive Conservative Party of Canada (8, 10, 26); Peter White
(11); Canapress Photo Service (cover, 15-19, 21, 24, 25, 28, 32,
35-37); Arthur Campeau (20); Richard Holden (22, 23); United
Press Canada (27, 29-31, 33, 34).

Canadian Cataloguing in Publication Data

Murphy, Rae, 1935-
   Brian Mulroney, the boy from Baie-Comeau

Includes index.

1. Mulroney, Brian, 1939- 2. Politicians —
Canada — Biography. 3. Progressive Conservative
Party of Canada — Biography. I. Chodos, Robert, 1947-
II. Auf der Maur, Nick, 1942- III. Title.

FC631.M85M87 1984   971.064'6'0924   C84-098200-3
F1034.3.M85M87 1984

James Lorimer & Company, Publishers
Egerton Ryerson Memorial Building
35 Britain Street
Toronto, Ontario M5A 1R7

Printed and bound in Canada
6 5 4 3 2 1   84 85 86 87 88 89

CONTENTS

Acknowledgements   *vii*
Introduction   *1*

1 The View from Baie-Comeau   *4*
2 School and Politics   *24*
3 Laval: The Team Takes Shape   *45*
4 Lawyer on the Rise   *58*
5 The Search for a Winner   *84*
6 The View from Head Office   *110*
7 Waiting in the Wings   *134*
8 This Time No Mistakes   *162*
9 The Great Negotiator   *190*

Bibliography   *215*
Index   *218*

ACKNOWLEDGEMENTS

The authors wish to express their appreciation to Richard B. Holden, who provided great assistance and support through all phases of the preparation of this book.

The final result has been enriched by many formal and informal interviews. In particular we would like to thank Brian and Mila Mulroney, members of their immediate families, and a number of personal and political friends, including Michel Cogger, Peter White, Jean Bazin and Michael Meighen. Our thanks go as well to many other individuals active in the Progressive Conservative party, too numerous to name here.

Others were also generous with their time and assistance; to mention only a few, we are grateful to Alex Pathy, Stanley Hartt and officials at the Hanna Mining Company, the Iron Ore Company of Canada, the Tribune Company and its subsidiaries, the United Steelworkers of America, the Maritime Employers Association, the Steel Company of Canada, and the law firm of Ogilvy, Renault.

We owe a final thank-you to Constance Chodos for her invaluable assistance in the research phase of the book.

Some of our debts to published sources are listed in a bibliography at the back of the book.

INTRODUCTION

When Brian Mulroney emerged victorious from the Progressive Conservative leadership convention in June, 1983, there was more than the usual high level of euphoria in party ranks. The atmosphere owed something to the purging of a certain reluctance to name Mulroney leader. But what heightened the excitement of having a new leader more was the expectation, some would say knowledge, that before long this new leader would become the prime minister of Canada.

To many Canadians, however, Mulroney is just an image: handsome, charming and superficial. To many Conservatives he is all things — for Mulroney has made it his policy not to say what his policy is. What lies behind the image, behind the ambivalent political stance, of this prime minister-in-waiting?

In this book we have tried to place Brian Mulroney in the context of his background, a background that is markedly different from that of most of his predecessors and competitors.

Perhaps most obviously, Mulroney is the first Conservative leader since Confederation who has any real ties to French-speaking Canada. From his boyhood fascination with the Duplessis regime, to the role he played in the Cliche Commission and events more recent, Mulroney has been immersed in a distinct political culture that is alien to most English Canadians.

And Mulroney's roots are neither middle class nor metropolitan. His boyhood in the remote company town of Baie-Comeau instilled a sense of self-advancement and community solidarity that influences his worldview to this day.

Finally, while most leaders serve their apprenticeship in cabinet posts, or at least as MPs, Mulroney came to the leadership direct from a career in labour negotiations topped by a five-year stint as the president of a major corporation.

Mulroney places a very high value on each of these aspects of his personal history: his credibility in Quebec will make the Conservative party a home to French Canadians; his Baie-Comeau background gives him a sense of social compassion; and his experience as a labour lawyer and company president will bridge the chasms between the federal and provincial governments, and awaken Canada from its economic dormancy. In sum, a perfect package to present as an alternative to the Liberal dynasty in Ottawa.

We first became interested in Brian Mulroney while researching and writing our book on the 1976 Tory leadership convention, *Winners, Losers*. Joe Clark's resignation as leader early in 1983 led to the scheduling of a rematch between Clark and Mulroney. But the outcome of the contest, after seven years of what was widely perceived to be a failed leadership, was all too obvious to write about again. The natural topic was the man whom fortune would likely favour — Brian Mulroney.

We followed Mulroney on the campaign trail, at the convention, and throughout his early months as leader. We interviewed scores of his party confreres, friends, aides, family members and business associates. And we drew on many books on politics and business in Quebec to better understand the influences that have operated on Mulroney.

This is neither an "unauthorized" nor an "authorized" biography. Mulroney, and those close to him, all readily consented to interviews, and many points of fact were verified by an aide.

But there were none of the tradeoffs of access and approval to which many political biographies owe their genesis.

We hasten to add that this is a political biography, not an intimate one. This emphasis reflects our feeling that in the long run, Brian Mulroney's background — as a working-class teenager in a company town, as an anglophone raised in a francophone milieu, as a labour lawyer, as a party wheelhorse and corporate executive — will have far more importance for Canada than his looks, tastes, habits and pastimes. We hope the portrait presented in the pages that follow will suggest what Canadians can expect from ''the boy from Baie-Comeau.''

CHAPTER ONE

The View from Baie-Comeau

The Mulroneys are among the millions of families that owe their origins in North America to the Great Migration that followed the end of the Napoleonic Wars in 1815. More than 800,000 emigrants, mainly from the United Kingdom, arrived in the British North American colonies, while many times that number settled in the great republic to the south. Any old tub that could float carried timber to Europe and returned with a human cargo jammed below deck.

This migration transformed all parts of the North American continent, and its impact on the vast, virtually empty collection of British colonies, whose estimated population before the turn of the nineteenth century had been less than 400,000, was enormous. For the immigrant, whatever the dangers and hardships of the voyage to America, the opportunity to escape the poverty and, in many cases, the religious oppression of the old country seemed to make any risk worthwhile.

Irish immigration to North America began in the early nineteenth century as a trickle and grew to a flood in the middle decades of the century as the potato famine gripped Ireland. It was in this period, in the 1840s, that the Mulroneys came to the British colony of Canada East, joining other Irish families in the area of Sainte-Catherine-de-Portneuf, just west of Quebec City near where the Valcartier military base is today. It was a typical farming area, neither exceedingly prosperous nor poor, where the new arrivals had to carve their fields out of the woods. The work was hard, but a living could be made.

Sainte-Catherine-de-Portneuf was one of those Quebec farming regions where the French formed the majority but the Irish existed in significant numbers and retained their character. The rural Celts had more in common with the *Canayen* farmers than with the Protestant English of Quebec City and Montreal. It was in these areas that mixed marriages often produced French Canadian families with names such as Johnson, Ryan, MacAndrew and Sullivan. This cultural miscegenation and coexistence also produced the distinctive French Canadian fiddle and accordion music, derived from the Irish and Scottish traditions.

Benedict Mulroney was born in the family home in this Irish/French community in 1903. Here he went to school, receiving his basic primary education in French and then studying a few years in English. As a teenager, he taught himself Morse code and telegraphy, and eventually he decided that the life of a farmer was not for him. He enrolled in a Chicago-based correspondence course in electricity and went to work as a construction electrician on projects throughout Quebec.

Back home in Sainte-Catherine-de-Portneuf, he chanced to notice Irene O'Shea at mass one Sunday morning. In a move remarkably similar to his son Brian's courtship of Mila Pivnicki many years later, Ben Mulroney showed up with his family in a horse and carriage at the O'Shea home that same afternoon. Although the O'Sheas had been farming in the area since the 1830s — almost a decade longer than the Mulroneys — this particular Sunday marked the first time one of the families had visited the other. Ben was thirty-one, Irene was seventeen. They were married in 1934.

Ben Mulroney was working on a hydro project near Ottawa when their first child, Olive, was born in 1936. A second daughter, Peggy, was born in Quebec City while Ben was working on another project 420 kilometres down the St. Lawrence River, at the site of the future town of Baie-Comeau. Ben spent the Depression winter of 1937 living in a tent on the construction site in what until then had been part of the vast wilderness of northern Quebec. When the Baie-Comeau paper mill was completed the following year, he was offered a permanent job as an electrician and he accepted it. The Mulroneys travelled to Rimouski on the South Shore, and then by boat across the wide St. Lawrence to the company town Ben had helped build. And on March 20, 1939, their third child, Brian, was born in a hospital in Baie-Comeau.

The move from Sainte-Catherine-de-Portneuf to Baie-Comeau was a move from the Quebec heartland to a pioneer area where communication with the outside world could be accomplished only with difficulty. But it was also, paradoxically, a move from the relative economic backwater that constituted Quebec's farming communities into the industrial mainstream of North America. For while Quebec political leaders, who were interested in opening up the northern part of their province, and an energetic local priest played a role in the creation of Baie-Comeau, the most significant force in its development was a burgeoning business empire based in Chicago, at the other end of the St. Lawrence/Great Lakes system.

This empire was built by another family of nineteenth-century Irish immigrants to North America, Protestant this time — the Medills. The Medills came to New Brunswick from Northern Ireland in 1819, and Joseph Medill was born near Saint John four years later. In 1832 the family moved on to Ohio, where young Joseph got started in the newspaper business; he soon bought his own newspaper in Cleveland, which was just beginning its climb from frontier outpost to great city. Then he moved on again, to another western town with even greater promise, and became part-owner and editor of the Chicago *Tribune*.

At the site of Chicago, the Mississippi River system and the St. Lawrence/Great Lakes system are separated by only a few kilometres, and by the time Joseph Medill arrived, the two systems were joined by a canal. Chicago built on this advantage to become the marketing and manufacturing centre for the expanding Midwest; even the great fire of 1871 only temporarily stalled its growth. In the wake of the fire, Joseph Medill served a brief term as mayor, and soon afterward bought the *Tribune* outright.

One of Medill's two socially ambitious daughters married into the McCormick family, which had helped spur Chicago's growth by establishing the farm machinery manufacturing firm that later became International Harvester. The other daughter married the son of Rev. Robert W. Patterson, Chicago's most influential Presbyterian minister. From these two unions issued Joseph Medill's four extraordinary grandchildren, one of whom became a United States senator while the other three became publishers of major American newspapers.

As a young man in Cleveland, Medill was active in a new anti-slavery political organization and is generally credited with giving it its name: the Republican party. He also made the acquaintance of Cleveland industrialist Mark Hanna, later one of the party's most powerful figures. At the 1860 Republican convention in Chicago, Medill helped secure the presidential nomination for Abraham Lincoln of Illinois. The family's connection to high Republican circles continued even after Joseph Medill's death in 1899. President Theodore Roosevelt was a guest at the Cleveland wedding of Medill's grandson J. Medill McCormick (the future senator) to Mark Hanna's daughter in 1903.

In 1912 Medill's grandsons Robert McCormick and Joe Patterson took over the *Tribune*. McCormick's chief talents lay in the business side of running a newspaper. One of his first decisions was to secure a source of newsprint by opening the *Tribune*'s own paper mill. The removal of the tariff on Canadian newsprint and the advantages of the Great Lakes shipping route favoured a location north of the border; so the mill was built at Thorold, Ontario. One McCormick biographer, Joseph Gies, stated flatly that "the *Tribune* owes its life to McCormick's far-sighted Canadian newsprint enterprise."

McCormick's management of the *Tribune* was interrupted by

the First World War, from which he returned with the rank of colonel, a title he used for the rest of his life. In the heady postwar years, he and Patterson undertook another significant expansion, starting a newspaper in New York. While Colonel McCormick remained in Chicago, Patterson took charge of this new enterprise and gave his genius for popular journalism free rein, making the New York *Daily News* the largest-circulation newspaper in the United States. Meanwhile, Colonel McCormick's search for pulpwood to feed the Thorold mill took him to northern Quebec, where he established the logging community of Shelter Bay on the North Shore near the mouth of the St. Lawrence River. As his newspapers grew, Colonel McCormick kept looking for new areas to cut pulpwood, and he was especially attracted by the region drained by the Manicouagan and Outardes rivers, about 150 kilometres upriver from Shelter Bay. This region offered not only vast stands of spruce but also the prospect of cheap hydro power from the two rivers. The colonel conceived a scheme in which logs would be driven down the Manicouagan and a pulp mill would be built using power from the Outardes. Work on damming the Outardes was begun in 1925, and a wharf (partially paid for by the federal government) was built on a bay a few kilometres downriver from the mouth of the Manicouagan that had been chosen as the site of the pulp mill. This bay would later be named after Napoléon Alexandre Comeau, a legendary local hunter, trapper and naturalist.

According to the terms on which the company leased the timber limits on the Manicouagan, the pulp mill was supposed to be in operation by 1930, but market conditions in the newsprint industry caused second thoughts. Headlong expansion in the 1920s — especially in Quebec — brought about a drop in the price of newsprint from $130 a ton in 1921 to $70 a ton in 1927 (it hit a low of $40 a ton in 1934) and led to numerous bankruptcies and mergers in the late 1920s and early 1930s. The company asked the Quebec government of Premier Louis-Alexandre Taschereau for a postponement, and it was granted. When market conditions failed to improve, additional postponements were requested and agreed to, until the Tribune Company finally decided to go ahead with the project in 1935. By this time its plans had changed and now included building a complete paper mill on the shores of Baie-Comeau and shipping the output of the mill to New York through the Gulf of St. Lawrence and down the Atlantic coast. The slopes of Mont Sec, a 120-metre knoll of granite on the rim of the bay, were chosen as the site of the new town that would rise around the mill. A new Tribune subsidiary, the Quebec North Shore Paper Company, was incorporated, and the Baie-Comeau mill opened in 1938.

Like many newspaper publishers, Colonel McCormick was fiercely conservative, and became more so as he grew older. He was highly critical of trade unions, and especially the militant Congress of Industrial Organizations (CIO), although he treated his employees well in a paternalistic sort of way; during the Depression, he not only kept employment and salaries at the Tribune Company stable but even maintained Christmas bonuses every year except 1931, when he thought it well to remind the employees that such things are not automatic. From Hoover through to Eisenhower, administration after administration in Washington failed to measure up to the colonel's standards. Where he differed from most publishers was in his isolationism — his belief that the United States should avoid "foreign entanglements" and his ingrained distrust of the rest of the world. McCormick's distrust of foreigners was especially pronounced in the case of the British and anyone connected with them, but he made an exception in the case of Canada, and especially Quebec. Surveying the sad state of the world before a meeting of the *Tribune*'s advertising salesmen in 1932, he noted that the only part of the British Empire still solvent was not even British, but French; the reference was to the province where he was planning his new paper mill.

In 1945 the *Tribune* took the unusual step of assigning a full-time correspondent to Canada, which it referred to in an editorial as "one of the most interesting countries in the world." In another editorial, the *Tribune* praised a forthcoming measure by the government of Prime Minister Mackenzie King that would make

Canadians "Canadian citizens" instead of "British subjects," and expressed the hope that this might be the first step towards a new Canadian constitution with an amending formula and a charter of rights, anticipating the constitutional position of Pierre Elliott Trudeau — and Brian Mulroney — by some thirty-five years.

Perhaps nowhere was the colonel's influence felt as strongly as in Baie-Comeau. A party of his engineers arrived there on April 12, 1936, finding only the wharf and five small, weatherbeaten buildings that had been put up when the project was first under consideration in the 1920s. Rations had to be borrowed from the motor ship *Jean Brillant*, which brought them over from the South Shore. When Ben Mulroney arrived, his son likes to say, "there wasn't a goddamn thing there. . . . There was no road, everything went by boat and they lived in a tent." Workers had to blast through granite to build foundations for homes and lay sewers and water mains. At a reception marking the twenty-fifth anniversary of the paper mill at Baie-Comeau in 1963, Arthur Schmon, McCormick's wartime adjutant whom the colonel later appointed to head his paper operations, described the construction of the mill and town:

> Twenty months after that landing [by the engineers], the first roll of newsprint ever produced on the North Shore came off number 1 machine and there was a beautiful planned town. Building the mill and the town was a construction achievement that warmed the hearts of all who took part in this great pioneering adventure. There was no precedent to follow; nobody had every built anything like this on the North Shore. . . . Everything had to be brought in by water; there were no rail lines, nor roads connecting Baie-Comeau with Quebec City and the interior of Canada. . . .
> Shipping stopped at the end of November and no water traffic moved again until spring. But construction had to

go on. . . . Finally granite and forest gave way to industry
and civilization, and an efficient paper mill and a neat
orderly community rose around the slopes of Mount Sec.

In its early years, Baie-Comeau had to overcome a number of
difficulties. The town was threatened by a severe forest fire in
1941. The danger of German U-boat attacks and wartime restrictions on using ships for carrying non-essential commodities made
it impossible to follow the original plan to ship newsprint to New
York. However, the company received permission to ship newsprint by an inland route using the New York State Barge Canal
in return for a commitment to carry bauxite to the Aluminum
Company of Canada smelter on the Saguenay. This complicated
scheme allowed the company to keep the Baie-Comeau mill
operating at full blast throughout the war, and in the flush postwar
period the mill was expanded substantially.

Baie-Comeau is a pleasant town in a picturesque location on
the St. Lawrence, just before it broadens into the gulf. There are
many small rivers and lakes nearby, hilled forests with the fresh,
sweet smell of jackpine and pulp in the air. There are large scenic
beaches — although the cold waters of the St. Lawrence don't
encourage swimming for more than a few summer weeks.

And then there was the Baie-Comeau winter. "I remember
the winters," Brian Mulroney says, "my God Almighty, they
were never-ending. . . . They started in October, and by the time
June came along it seemed like the ice was just starting to break
up. . . . I have a Stanley Cosgrove painting at home, the first
piece of art I ever bought, a painting of the Rivière Saint-Maurice.
I bought it because it looked exactly like Baie-Comeau at four
in the afternoon in the middle of February. Bleak, dreary, cold —
the wind coming off the bay, the snowbanks as high as the
houses."

Nevertheless, the Mulroneys recall those years in Baie-
Comeau as a very happy time. Three more children followed
Brian — Doreen, Gary and Barbara. Ben Mulroney always came
home for lunch, so there were big family meals twice a day. And
friends were always joining them.

There was one part of Baie-Comeau where the English-speaking families lived; the Mulroneys lived on that side of town, but they certainly weren't part of the English establishment. Nor were they completely at one with the French. A former mayor of Baie-Comeau, Henry Leonard, recalled Ben Mulroney as "a good Irishman": "You stick together when you have names like Mulroney and Leonard in places like Baie-Comeau because you're a minority." As a kid, Brian Mulroney claims to have been oblivious of both class and national distinctions. He recalls playing with the mill manager's son who was distinguished from the other kids only insofar as he had better clothes. He also says:

> I grew up bilingual. I never had any sense of there being a difference between French and English. To this day, it isn't Christmas without *la tourtière* and Irish music after Christmas Eve midnight mass. I went to the Catholic school, l'Académie Saint-Emélie, which was run by nuns. There were one or two English classrooms among thirty or forty French classrooms, but you walked to and from school with your French friends and you even took some of your courses in French, if only because the teacher didn't speak any English.

Ben Mulroney supported his wife, six children and company home on a weekly take-home pay of seventy dollars. "Sometimes we read in the papers nowadays that we were poor," says Olive, the eldest of the children. "Well, we weren't poor. We weren't rich but we didn't really seem to lack much. Thursday was payday and Thursday night was steak night. As for the rest, well, mother was a good cook."

Ben was a remarkable man who exerted a great influence on his family. A frequent visitor to his house who later became his son-in-law describes him as "a rather shy man, but friendly and obviously totally devoted to his family." He was a natural with his hands, able to fix just about anything. He could craft furniture out of rough-hewn wood and quickly fathomed the workings of all the new gadgets that became widespread in North America during his lifetime — radios, automobiles, refrigerators. Ben's ability to tinker with machines made it possible for the Mulroneys to have a car and a refrigerator when nobody else in town did except for the wealthier families. Even with a car, however, travel was something of an adventure. Until the late 1950s, Baie-Comeau's link with southern Quebec was a dirt road interrupted by two ferry crossings. In a speech reminiscing about Baie-Comeau, Brian Mulroney recalled the family's 1938 Pontiac and the annual trip to see relatives in Quebec City:

> My father at that time was inclined to think of himself as a Gilles Villeneuve. He would begin our fourteen-hour odyssey at four in the morning — my parents, the six children, the dog, fourteen sandwiches, and a six pack — to begin a mad race over unpaved roads to catch the ferry at Bersimis, followed by an heroic gallop to catch the ferry at Baie Sainte-Catherine, followed by a leisurely ride at seventy miles an hour to Quebec; the children crying, the dog barking and my father grinding his teeth, and my mother saying her beads for the third time that day. . . . [There was] an imposing billboard situated at the entrance to the village of Sacre-Coeur . . . with a picture of the Lord with the caption: "Why do you use the name of the Lord in vain?" During my entire childhood, I always thought that the message was directed exclusively at my father.

If in the summer it was possible to travel in and out of Baie-Comeau by boat, and in a manner of speaking by car, during the winter months the town was almost completely isolated. There was no television or regular newspapers, and only one radio station — CJBR from Rimouski. For the most part, the entertainment was home-made.

After meals, the Mulroneys would sit around the piano and sing Irish folk songs. Olive played, while Brian, she recalls, "always loved to sing. He just loved it. He sang for anybody, any time, anywhere. All you had to do was ask him." His favourite song in those days was Bing Crosby's version of "Dear

Hearts and Gentle People (who live in my home town)." When Mary Schmon, Arthur Schmon's daughter-in-law, organized a choir, Brian was one of its members. The July, 1950, issue of the *Observation Post*, the employee magazine of the Tribune Company's Canadian operations, contained a description of "a delightfully refreshing program of musical entertainment, sponsored by the British Empire Service League, and entitled A Spring Fantasy." Among the performers were "several promising young local artists," including "Brian Mulrooney [sic], who sang Dear Hearts and Gentle People and Sipping Cyder on the Zuyder Zee." And he sang for Colonel McCormick.

The colonel was an avid hunter and fisherman whose attachment to the North Shore went well beyond his appreciation of its value as a source of pulpwood and newsprint. He was a regular visitor to Baie-Comeau. He liked to spend his birthday there (it fell in July), and for a number of years conducted an annual meeting of the Tribune Company's board of directors in the remote mill town. Whenever he was in town, young Brian Mulroney would be summoned to sing "Dearie," "Danny Boy" or "When Irish Eyes Are Smiling." The colonel paid him fifty dollars — almost as much as his father made in a week. Everyone insists that he turned the money over to his mother. Mulroney recalls one occasion when he was eight or nine, " . . . standing in front of the piano with Jack Dempsey sitting right in front of me. The colonel had brought him up for some fishing. I just about had a heart attack. . . . "

Young Brian was a boy about town, always poking into the stores, the plant, other people's homes, making himself the kid everybody in town knew. When he was ten, he got a job delivering Hudson's Bay Company Wednesday store circulars, enlisting his sisters' help (the money earned was usually given over to their mother, who apportioned it in allowances and savings). On the whole, he was not greatly different from his contemporaries — perhaps a little more outgoing and with a little more hustle than most. And he had an early and intense interest in politics.

While the Mulroneys voted Liberal, the family was essentially apolitical, and Brian's main contact with the world of politics was through the radio, to which he was an attentive listener. From the time he was five until he was twenty, Quebec provincial politics was dominated by a powerful leader with deep roots in the rural areas of the province: Premier Maurice Duplessis. In the 1930s, Duplessis, who was leader of the provincial Conservative party, made an alliance with dissident Liberals to form the Union Nationale. In 1936 this alliance defeated a Liberal administration that had governed Quebec for almost forty years. Duplessis was defeated in 1939, but came back five years later and ruled the province until his death in 1959.

Politically, the Duplessis regime was a paradox. While professing to stand for the traditional values of rural Quebec, it was an active partner in promoting economic changes that were undermining those same values. The industrialization of Quebec, which had begun in the nineteenth century and accelerated under the Liberal governments of the early twentieth, continued apace under Duplessis and was extended to parts of the province where it had hitherto been unknown. "Under him," wrote Duplessis's biographer, Conrad Black, "Quebec ceased to be a backward place in every respect except, perhaps, political methodology." These changes were felt especially strongly on the North Shore. The first Duplessis government sponsored a measure authorizing the construction of a company-controlled town at Baie-Comeau. And after his return to power, Duplessis reached an agreement with another business empire based in the Midwest (this one founded by Mark Hanna, Joseph Medill's Cleveland friend and Medill McCormick's father-in-law) to carry out an even more audacious scheme: mining the vast iron ore deposits of the Labrador Trough to supply steel mills in the American industrial heartland.

The premier was on excellent terms with the industrialists who were bringing these changes to the province — including Colonel McCormick and Arthur Schmon. The colonel's relations with Duplessis were in marked contrast to the bellicose posture he

adopted towards successive presidents of the United States, and
the premier frequently accompanied him on his July visits to
Baie-Comeau. In his biography of the colonel, Frank Waldrop
wrote that in Baie-Comeau his subject "played the pacific role
of monopoly capitalist with concern only for things that count;
getting the buildings up, the work force assembled and the operation going, among some of the most fractious elements of
religious, ethnic, social and political disaffection to be found in
North America. It would be hard to match Quebec stresses anywhere, then or now." Waldrop's point was that the colonel could
be the perfect diplomat when he wanted to, but much of the credit
for the easy political ride he and others like him enjoyed in
Quebec in the Forties and Fifties has to go to Duplessis, whose
efforts were directed towards making the rich and potentially
troublesome province safe for outside investors. "Colonel
McCormick, you have played here the role of the pioneer,"
Duplessis said at the formal inauguration of work on a new
Tribune Company power project on the Manicouagan in 1951.
"You have great newspapers in the United States which I am in
no position to appreciate. All I can say is that no matter how
important the role your newspapers play in the United States,
such a role is no more important than that of the great pioneering
you have done in this region of the Saguenay. The Province of
Quebec is grateful to you."

Robert M. (for McCormick) Schmon, Arthur's son and later
his successor as head of the Tribune Company's paper operations,
remembers dinners with his father and Duplessis at the Garrison
Club in Quebec City. At one such occasion, Duplessis pointed
to Robert, who towered over both Arthur Schmon and the premier, and said, "You may be taller than your father but you're
not greater." For his part, Arthur Schmon annually sent Duplessis
"four brace" of pheasants, and once wrote to him after the Union
Nationale had seen to the passage of a bill desired by the company: "I marvel at the amount of energy and time that you
sacrificially devote to your beloved province. You carry many,
many burdens, and as you have wished for me so many times,

I can only wish for you a much greater reward — that you so richly deserve — in Heaven.''

The Duplessis government's labour policies were a major element in its strategy of maintaining good relations with both domestic and foreign industrialists. As a result of these same policies, Quebec's increasingly militant trade union movement became the chief focus of opposition to Duplessis. And in the eyes of a significant minority of Quebecers — whose most prominent members were labour organizers such as Jean Marchand, journalists such as Gérard Pelletier and Réne Lévesque, progressive clerics such as Father Georges-Henri Lévesque, dean of Laval University's new Faculty of Social Sciences (who has been called ''the father of the modern left in Quebec''), and Archbishop Joseph Charbonneau of Montreal, lawyers such as Jean Drapeau, and intellectuals such as Pierre Elliott Trudeau — the Union Nationale regime came to be seen as dictatorial and an obstacle to progress in Quebec. Duplessis's use of the highly politicized provincial police to ''keep order'' during major strikes reinforced this impression. Three such strikes — at Asbestos in 1949, Louiseville in 1952 and Murdochville in 1957 — became *causes célèbres*, pitting the Duplessis government and its corporate allies against the rather motley opposition coalition.

The authoritarian aspect of the Duplessis regime could be seen in its treatment of its political opponents and others who displeased the powerful premier. Its harshest measures were reserved for two tiny minorities: Communists and Jehovah's Witnesses. Communists were subject to the notorious Padlock Law, according to which a home or office could be padlocked if it was being used to promote communism, or rather if it was so deemed by the provincial attorney general — a portfolio Duplessis retained for himself. Taken to the courts, the Padlock Law was declared unconstitutional by the Supreme Court of Canada in 1957, twenty years after its adoption. Duplessis's harassment of the Jehovah's Witnesses also produced a celebrated civil liberties case; here too Duplessis's target was vindicated by the Supreme Court in 1959. In addition, Duplessis abetted his allies in the Catholic church in their intrigues against the two leading clerical opponents of the regime, Archbishop Charbonneau and Father Lévesque. These intrigues, which were carried to Rome, resulted in the removal of Charbonneau as archbishop in 1950, while Lévesque was placed on trial for "heresy, excessive laicization, positivism, experimentalism, and socialism"; he was eventually exonerated.

Perhaps the most pervasive component of the Duplessis system was the Union Nationale's vast patronage machine, which extended to virtually every community in Quebec. The Union Nationale's war chest, the Caisse Electorale, functioned almost as a parallel public treasury. There was $18 million in the Caisse at Duplessis's death in 1959, and an almost equal sum, in total, had been spent on the re-election campaigns of 1948, 1952 and 1956 (not to mention the amounts spent between elections). While Duplessis himself was personally frugal and indifferent to financial gain, the system over which he presided was clearly open to abuse, and abuses there undoubtedly were.

Despite Duplessis's welcoming and accommodating attitude towards American and English Canadian capital, he was a forceful defender of Quebec's autonomy in its relations with the federal government. Although he willingly deferred to private capital in the economic sphere and to the church in the educational field, he would not yield an inch to Ottawa on anything. This was perhaps the aspect of Duplessis's policy that was most widely approved in French Canada, and even such a confirmed *anti-duplessiste* as Pierre Trudeau backed the premier in his refusal to participate in the federal university grants program in the mid-1950s.

In the late 1940s and 1950s, Duplessis seemed to incarnate Quebec, and especially rural Quebec. In Conrad Black's words, "He became a great helmsman, defending the nation from threats from without, exorcising rotten elements within, helping the little, collaborating with the big, for the greater good of all." But the mystique did not survive the man. After Duplessis's death, the period of his rule became known in Quebec as *la grande noirceur* — the Great Darkness. A statue of the late premier commissioned by the government mysteriously disappeared before it could be put on public display. The labour organizers, journalists and intellectuals who had fought Duplessis became the new leaders of Quebec, and eventually of Canada as a whole. With the growth of a new form of Quebec nationalism, however, Duplessis's autonomist battles against Ottawa came to be regarded with increasing respect, and the statue was finally brought out of the closet by the Parti Québécois government of René Lévesque in the 1970s.

Both Baie-Comeau and the North Shore constituency of Saguenay as a whole remained loyal to the Union Nationale throughout the Duplessis years, although after Duplessis's death they went Liberal in the 1960 election that ushered in Quebec's "Quiet Revolution." Federally things were less clear-cut. The great majority of Quebec seats went Liberal, at least until the Diefenbaker sweep of 1958. But Charlevoix-Saguenay (as it then was) elected a Tory-backed independent, Frédéric Dorion, in a 1942 by-election and re-elected him in 1945. In 1949 Dorion lost the new riding of Saguenay to a Liberal, Henri Brisson, but in Baie-Comeau Brisson ran a poor third behind an independent Liberal, Mme Victor Gladu, and Dorion. In the 1958 federal election, Premier Duplessis saw his chance to score a decisive victory over the federal Liberals, his adversaries for more than twenty years. With the Liberals at a low ebb, Duplessis put his Union Nationale machine at the disposal of John Diefenbaker's resurgent Conservatives, and set his sights on fifty Quebec seats; the Conservatives took all fifty. Among these seats was Saguenay, and Baie-Comeau went Conservative by a solid majority of five hundred votes.

The Rimouski radio station that reached Baie-Comeau aired a large number of political broadcasts, particularly by the Union Nationale government. By the time he was thirteen, Brian Mulroney was a political junkie. One childhood friend, Pierre Rocque, describes him as an ordinary kid, good at sports and speaking up for himself, who began to think of politics as a career at the age of thirteen: "We'd be playing outside somewhere and he'd rush home all of a sudden to catch a Union Nationale speech on the radio. It was something he had to do." He also announced to his surprised friends that he intended to become prime minister.

Almost everybody who knew Brian in Baie-Comeau remembers him as a nice boy, a good student, "just a great kid to grow up with," in the words of his sister Olive. His first teacher, Sister Rosa Rita, says he was "a splendid student, very cooperative and most eager to learn. . . . We had three grades in one room. Brian not only succeeded in his regular grade but followed the work of the other grades. But on reaching grade three, he became bored, nothing to which to aspire except to read every available book in the class library." Virtually the only person who paints a different picture is Brian Mulroney himself, who prefers to be recalled as a tough little urchin, always getting into scrapes:

> No doubt about it. I was one tough little kid. Big mouth too. I think it had a lot to do with my size. I was always smaller than the other kids, right up until I was seventeen. . . .
>
> I used to hang around with Jacques "Pom-Pom" Provencher, mainly because we were about the same size. In the winter we used to wear what we called *les pitchous*, the Indian trapper's winter boots, and to save a nickel fare we'd wait for the bus to stop, then grab the back bumper and slide the mile-and-a-half to school. . . . One time the two of us were barrelling along and hit a patch of pavement. We both went ass-over-tea-kettle, and I broke my jaw.

A neighbour, a Mr. Bernier, was known as a bit of an eccentric, and Brian enjoyed going by his house, sticking his hand through the open bathroom window and flushing the toilet. Brian and his friends would hide and laugh when they saw Bernier come into the bathroom looking puzzled. Another stunt Mulroney remembers, "and to this day I don't know why we did it, was the time

Jimmy Green and I tried to burn down Mr. Bodker's house. We had plenty of wood and we got the fire started all right, but we were pretty stupid: we built the fire against a cement wall. Greenie and I were busy fanning the thing, and who came around the corner but Mr. Bodker. He nailed both of us, and I got the lickin' of my life.''

Mulroney's recollections of himself as a tough kid can be at least partially shrugged off. There is, however, no reason to doubt his driving ambition, as well as the overpowering ambition of his father for Brian and for all his children. One "lickin'," Irene Mulroney recalls, occurred when Brian broke Ben Mulroney's strict standards of behaviour by going to the town poolroom. "So Ben spanked him and gave him another lecture about wasting his time in a poolroom . . . but after it was over, Brian said, 'It was worth it.' "

"Did he ever go back to the poolroom?" Irene Mulroney was asked.

"Of course he did."

On the other hand, his success in school made his father very happy. Brian also developed his talent for public speaking early on. Sister Rosa Rita remembers that "he was exceedingly ambitious and gloried in attempts at public speaking and the other types of competition." From the age of ten, he won most of the Lions' Club speaking contests in Baie-Comeau. His first winning speech was on comic books. His sister Olive won the girls' prize that same year with a speech entitled "Welcome Newfoundland." It was 1949, the year Joey Smallwood became Canada's "only living Father of Confederation." During one of the contests, when Brian was delivering his speech, a man sitting behind Ben Mulroney tapped the proud father on the shoulder and said: "Ce gosse-là, il va faire un Chris' de bon évêque [That kid is going to make a hell of a good bishop]."

As they were about to start high school, Brian and a group of his friends were attracted by a company apprenticeship plan for children of employees. "Over my dead body," said Ben Mulroney, and he and Irene would have none of it. To make his point, the elder Mulroney moonlighted for years as an electrical contractor to provide the extra money for the children's education. And while he worked the "extra hour," both parents instilled in the kids the notion that the way out of the mill was through university and that the ambition to go to college had to be accompanied by the willingness to work towards that goal. A secure maintenance job in a new mill during the height of the Depression may have seemed a great opportunity for the elder Mulroneys, but they made it quite clear to their children that it was not to be for them.

There may be some political hokum and exploitation in Mulroney's constant references to life with family and friends in Baie-Comeau, and there is sometimes a quality of Walt Disney fantasy in his recollections. But his attachment to his family and his roots, his pride of place and sense of community with Baie-Comeau are genuine. What is more, the view from Baie-Comeau has profoundly influenced Brian Mulroney's outlook and politics. When he speaks of the ideal of finding success by having the opportunity and being willing to work the extra hour, to make the extra effort, he can remember the example of his father and his own ambition and achievement. More important, perhaps, Brian Mulroney's sense of power, order and civility can be traced to his background in that company town on the North Shore, during the reign of Maurice Duplessis.

When Brian Mulroney was growing up, the modern paper mill was serving an insatiable market. There were jobs, and the jobs were secure and steady. Baie-Comeau grew and prospered, reaching a population of ten thousand by the late Fifties. By that time, the economy of the town was no longer dependent on paper alone. The paper company had outgrown the original power station on the Outardes, and in 1951–52 it built the McCormick Dam to harness the mighty Manicouagan, the first power development on a river that would later, under the direction of the provincially owned utility Hydro-Quebec, supply a large portion of the province's electricity needs. Taking advantage of the cheap power, British Aluminum established an aluminum smelter in

Baie-Comeau in partnership with the Chicago Tribune interests. And with the opening of the St. Lawrence Seaway, Cargill Incorporated of Minneapolis, a giant in the world's grain trade, opened a huge, multimillion-dollar grain elevator at Baie-Comeau that allowed it to shave fifteen cents a bushel from the cost of delivering midwestern grain to European buyers. Through it all, the paternalistic Quebec North Shore Paper Company appeared to share the wealth — it built the homes, the hospitals, the schools. In 1963, at the reception marking the twenty-fifth anniversary of the mill, Arthur Schmon noted that the whole period was marked by the absence of any strike or serious labour dispute.

In spite of the good life in Baie-Comeau, which the family now fondly recalls, Ben and Irene Mulroney were determined that none of the children would stay in town to work in the mill. And none of them did.

School and Politics

When he reached grade ten, Brian was enrolled at St. Thomas High School, a Catholic boarding school in Chatham, New Brunswick. That same year, his two sisters, Olive and Peggy, were shipped off to Iona Academy, a school run by the Sisters of the Holy Cross near Alexandria, Ontario.

Family and friends came down to the dock to see the three Mulroneys and Andy Morrow, a friend of Brian's, board the *Jean Brillant* for the voyage to Rimouski. "There were a group of nuns on the boat with us," Olive recalled. "They were singing 'Partons, la mer est bonne' as we waved to the wharf. . . . Brian looked so young. He was so short. And when we got to Rimouski, we took the train west and he took the train east." In Brian's recollection, he felt like Marco Polo as he was shipped off to school clutching a cardboard suitcase. But his mother can produce a photograph with Brian holding a plaid suitcase. "We like to get sentimental about it," Doreen adds. "Life was a struggle, but we weren't poor. Dad got him a proper suitcase."

A few days after arriving at the boarding school, Brian saw his friend Andy Morrow talking on the telephone to his family: "It only hit me then that I wasn't going to see my family for another four months or so. . . . I also called home. . . . There we were, bawling our eyes out, but my father said, 'You just have to stay there.' " And he did. He soon adjusted and is remembered at the school as an active and popular student.

Located on the Miramichi River in New Brunswick's salmon-fishing country, Chatham is an English-speaking pocket in the primarily Acadian northeastern part of the province. At the turn of the century, it had launched one of Canada's more notable political careers by electing a young lawyer named R. B. Bennett to its town council; Bennett's campaign manager in that race, Max Aitken, also went on to greater things.

St. Thomas High School, affiliated with St. Thomas University, attracted students from all over the Maritimes, Quebec and eastern Maine. Réal Deschênes, now a successful civil engineer in Montreal, was a student at St. Thomas at the same time as Mulroney. Deschênes arrived at St. Thomas from the tiny town of Hébertville in the far-off Lake St. John region of Quebec when he was fifteen. He was sent to Chatham to learn English, with which he was totally unfamiliar. In addition, he had a physical handicap that left his legs and hip crooked. Brian Mulroney was the only person at St. Thomas who spoke French, and immediately became Deschênes's special friend. Brian took his fellow Quebecer under his wing, helped him in the off-hours with his English, introduced him to the other students and generally made him feel comfortable. "That was very important to me," Deschênes says. "He was the first person I met, outside of my family, who seemed genuinely blind to my handicap."

It was a great financial burden on the Mulroneys to provide private education for their children, and Brian returned every vacation to Baie-Comeau to work at one job or another around the paper mill. (It was understood that the company would provide summer employment for employees' children.) Over the Christmas holidays, he would work at the post office. After finishing his studies at St. Thomas, Brian went on to St. Francis Xavier University in Antigonish, Nova Scotia, which was the destination for many St. Thomas graduates. He continued to spend his summers working at various jobs around Baie-Comeau (in-

cluding a stint as a waiter at the Hotel l'Auberge du Roc) throughout his college years until, as a law student at Laval University,
he accepted a summer job on Parliament Hill in Ottawa instead.

The Mulroneys' close family life resumed during those school
vacations. Dick Elliott, a young civil engineer from Saskatchewan who arrived in Baie-Comeau to work on the construction of
the aluminum smelter and was befriended by the Mulroney family, says that "the door was always open and the dinners were
usually crowded. There was an atmosphere in the house that
suggested the most important thing in the world was that families
hang together. They seemed to enjoy each other." The Mulroneys
extended their characteristic warm welcome to Elliott, and hardly
a day passed that he wasn't in their house. In May, 1958, two
years after his arrival in Baie-Comeau, he and Olive Mulroney
were married.

After dinner, Dick, Olive, Peggy and Brian would do the dishes.
Then they would sing a couple of songs or else sit around the
living room reading books, most of them from the library. "The
house was full of books," Elliott says. "Everybody, especially
Brian, loved words." Brian's relationship with Irene Mulroney
was particularly close. Olive remembers that when Brian came
home from a party, "he would always see if his mother was still
awake and he'd sit down on the bed and tell her all about it, who
was there, what music was played, and who said what to
whom. . . . He was just naturally happy and enthusiastic. . . .
Those were the days of home-made fudge, sitting around the
piano and beach parties."

Presumably Brian didn't tell his mother everything, for he cut
a wide swath around Baie-Comeau those summers. His pranks
became a little more sophisticated than reaching into an open
bathroom window to flush a toilet. Olive tells the story of the
time Marlene Blanchard left town to get married:

> She had been friends with Wilber Touche, but she was mar-
> rying somebody else. We all drove down to the wharf to
> see her off. Even poor Wilber came down driving his fath-

er's car. Brian kept singing, "Marlene is breaking up that old gang of mine."

When we got to the wharf and were all saying our good-byes, Brian slipped away to tell the wharf manager that the car was also going on the boat with Marlene. And as the boat was pulling out, poor Wilber saw his father's car on the deck with his old girl friend. . . . Fortunately they were able to call the boat back.

Brian was a confident young man who knew everybody in town — a charmer who had a way with both his peers and his elders. He was a good athlete and played second base on the town's baseball team. It was also in Baie-Comeau that he first developed his love of tennis, winning the town's junior championship one year. Friends in those days recall Brian as "street-wise," but he was more of a lover than a fighter. Girls were attracted to him, and he had several girl friends, although no one in particular. His small stature made him look young, but he seemed older than he was because of his deep voice and the way he handled himself. When he was nineteen, he started growing again and didn't stop until he was twenty-one.

Meanwhile, new influences were operating on Mulroney, and he was developing the attitudes towards power and politics that would shape his subsequent career.

He realized that for all his easy mingling with the mill managers' children, Baie-Comeau was not an egalitarian society. The Mulroneys had a good life, but they didn't call the shots. He told Dick Elliott at a stag one night, "My Dad is a great guy, but he is not a guy who moves things, who makes things happen." He saw how the company managers pulled all the strings, and how everybody deferred to management (for Elliott, coming from the more democratic traditions of Saskatchewan, this was something of an eye-opener). But he saw how in the wider world even the mill managers were relatively powerless compared to people in political office. Brian wanted to call the shots. And politicians were the people with clout. So despite his family's lack of political involvement or interest, he would make politics his life.

In the spring of 1957, Dick Elliott picked Brian and Peggy up in Quebec City on their way home from school, and they went to Valcartier to spend the night with relatives. The two young men shared the attic bedroom and sat up all night talking politics. Brian told Elliott of his intention to pursue a political career and to become Tory leader and prime minister. Mulroney "has an instinct for power, coupled with an understanding of it, of how and why it works," says his brother-in-law, who is perhaps as well placed as anyone to assess both the development of his politics and his vaulting ambition. "Later when Trudeau was in, he'd say, 'Trudeau has imposed his will on the country, you can argue about what Trudeau has done but you can't do anything about it unless you have power. You can have the best ideas, but without power, it's meaningless.' "

If the instinct for power is at the core of Mulroney's political drive, it is coupled with something else he learned in Baie-Comeau. This was that there were great differences between French and English Canadians living in Quebec. As an Irish Catholic who moved easily between the two cultures, his attitude towards this phenomenon was rather complex. He knew that he was not part of the WASP establishment, but he wasn't a French Canadian either. And he was aware that the WASP establishment was "there by virtue of birth and history, rather than by knowledge and competence," as Dick Elliott put it. He didn't share the antagonism that many members of each language group felt towards the other, and he believed that he could fill the gap between the two. But he did sympathize with the resentment that French Canadians felt. He foresaw a long period in which the rest of Canada would have to come to terms with French Quebec. "There was going to be a coming of age and a breaking of privilege," Elliott says.

In the summer of 1959, when the Cargill grain elevator opened, Brian was twenty years old and working as a truck driver. One day he came home from work steaming with anger. Two guys, one English and one French, had turned up late for work at the elevator. The French guy was fired and the English guy was given a short lecture. Both were acquaintances of Brian's, but he knew the one who was kept on better. If one was fired, he felt, both should have been. "There must be even-handed justice," he said.

Mulroney was also eager to help people from outside Quebec understand his native province. On one occasion, after meeting Dick Elliott's father and discovering that he had little grasp of Quebec, Brian sent the westerner a copy of Mason Wade's *The French Canadians*, then fairly recently published and by far the most comprehensive history of Quebec available in English, as a casual gift. "It wasn't his birthday or anything," says Dick Elliott. "He just wanted him to try and understand. It was an expensive book, and Brian, being a student then, didn't have any extra money. He didn't have two cents to rub together."

While Baie-Comeau was the source of Mulroney's appreciation of power and his belief in the need for a change in the relationship between Canada's two founding peoples, another set of influences was operating on him in Antigonish. As the home of St. Francis Xavier and headquarters of the diocese of Antigonish, the picturesque cathedral town was the centre of Catholicism and Catholic education in eastern Nova Scotia. And from the 1920s onward, the destitute farmers and fishermen of the surrounding rural areas, many of them descended from Catholic highlanders driven out of Scotland in the eighteenth century, came to look to Antigonish as the symbol of the struggle against poverty, ignorance and exploitation and of hope for a better life.

For while St. Francis Xavier was a small college (it had about seven hundred students at the time Mulroney was there) in a part of Canada generally considered a backwater, it was a remarkable, innovative institution that had acquired an international reputation as a result of its pioneering efforts in the field of adult education. The "Antigonish movement," as it became known, arose out of the tradition of Catholic social activism inspired by the encyclicals *Rerum Novarum* and *Quadragesimo Anno*, through which the church tried to participate in the modern world instead of blindly resisting it. In 1921 Rev. Dr. J. J. (Father Jimmy) Tompkins established the first People's School in Antigonish. His work was carried on by his cousin Rev. Dr. Moses Coady, who headed the Department of Extension at St. FX from its formation in 1928 until 1952.

Under Tompkins and Coady, adult education in Nova Scotia acquired what St. FX professor Alexander Laidlaw called "its down-to-earth, racy flavour," and had a vast impact in the farming and fishing communities. The leaders of the Antigonish movement believed in spreading knowledge not only for its own sake but also as a means of helping people gain control of their own economic lives. "With the help of his co-workers" in the Extension Department, wrote Gregory Baum in *Catholics and Canadian Socialism*, Coady "organized study clubs among the farmers and fishermen to teach them how to set up stores for buying and selling goods, cooperatively owned factories and mills, and eventually, when greater numbers were involved, credit unions or cooperative banks." A 1953 *Maclean's* article entitled (perhaps prematurely) "How FX Saved the Maritimes" called the Antigonish movement "the strongest social force in the Maritimes" and noted that the work of the Extension Department "has earned for St. FX the title, 'the People's University.' "

The Antigonish movement propagated its teachings not only throughout the Maritimes but abroad as well. Dr. Coady became one of the most influential Canadians of his time, and his book *Masters of Their Own Destiny* was translated into seven languages. At the time Mulroney was there, the university's student population included an unusually large number from developing countries, and the Coady International Institute, established after Coady's death in 1959, promoted a philosophy of aid to emerging nations. "The Coady International Institute," says Mulroney, "has probably had more influence on and been of more benefit to the developing countries than all our CIDAS and CUSOS."

The radical imprint of Dr. Coady, and the emphasis on public service and social activism that he stood for, was still strongly felt at St. FX when Mulroney was a student. "At the university everybody was involved in politics, what we considered left-wing politics," he says. "I was president of the student co-op one year." Considering the size of the university, there are a great number of prominent political figures who were first imbued with the notion of political and social activism at St. FX — from Liberal-MP-turned-Newfoundland-trade-union-leader Richard Cashin through Allan MacEachen through to Brian Mulroney.

Mulroney clearly feels comfortable with at least some aspects of the St. FX tradition, for through the years he has kept his ties with the university he likes to call his second home. And Robert McKenzie of the *Toronto Star* quoted an alumnus as saying that the university "practically ordained him [Mulroney] a saint" for his chairmanship of a special 1979–82 fund-raising effort that brought in $11.1 million, $4 million more than the original target. However, there is at least one element of the St. FX tradition that is somewhat at odds with Brian Mulroney's subsequent career.

St. FX was the "People's University" especially for the Celtic Catholic population of the Maritimes. And it reflected a Maritime political tradition that the political home for Catholics was the Liberal party. Dr. Coady himself, while looking for inspiration to the CCF experiment in Saskatchewan, the Labour governments of Australia and New Zealand, and the Social Democrats of Scandinavia (he would have regarded the "Swedenizing" of Canada as almost a realization of his life's work), continued to consider himself a Liberal — an independent and critical one, but a Liberal nonetheless. Thus, he concluded a 1942 letter to Nova Scotia Conservative Leader Leonard Fraser in the following terms: "I know some of the delegates that attended your past conventions, and for braying asininity and intolerance of any new ideas they surpassed everything that I ever knew, with the possible exception of the top men in the Antigonish County Liberal machine for the last fifty years — and this is from a man who was nearly always a Liberal."

However, things did not appear in quite the same light to a young Celtic Catholic from Quebec. By the time Brian Mulroney reached university, he not only had political ambitions, he also had his political party. He was ready and eager to get involved in student politics, and he joined the campus Conservative club.

Mulroney's conservative beliefs are straightforward and unvarnished. They spring from his background in the well-ordered company town and his acceptance of that order. They are also a natural outgrowth of his deeply held religious convictions, although he is categorical in stating that his private religious principles do not carry over into politics. With all that, there is nothing in his political makeup that is incompatible with membership in the Liberal party. Moreover, Mulroney's political drive does not issue from his ideology, but from his sense of power, who has it and how to get it. Or, as he expressed to his brother-in-law, he wanted to have clout, to be able to make things happen.

At the time, it was by no means obvious that the Conservative party offered the best road to power for a young man with political ambitions. The Liberals had been in office for more than twenty years both federally and in Nova Scotia and were by far the dominant federal political party in Mulroney's home province of Quebec. This is not to say that the political culture in which Brian Mulroney had grown up was monolithically Liberal. As we've seen, Quebec was dominated provincially by Duplessis's Union Nationale, and the Liberals represented primarily the urban and anglophone population. And Baie-Comeau had not been consistently Liberal even on the federal level. Nevertheless, on the whole the Conservative party was out of the picture federally in Quebec; conservatism maintained its grip at the provincial level only by establishing a separate identity as the Union Nationale and keeping its distance from the Conservatives in the rest of the country.

The historic weakness of the Conservative party in Quebec, the reversal of which would be one of Mulroney's major goals as an adult politician, dated back to the last years of the nineteenth century. Immediately after Confederation, the Conservatives were the majority party in Quebec, as they were in the country as a whole. Among French Canadian voters, their cause was helped by large sections of the Catholic clergy, which regarded Liberalism as incompatible with church doctrine and openly attacked its exponents; it took a papal encyclical in 1897 to put an end to the clergy's anti-Liberal crusade. By this time, Conservative support in Quebec had in any case begun to wane, largely as a result of the hanging of the French-speaking, Catholic, Métis rebel leader Louis Riel by Sir John A. Macdonald's government in 1885 — the first of a series of actions by Conservative administrations that were widely seen as offensive in French Canada. French Canadian anger at Riel's death was translated into support for two outstanding Liberal leaders — Honoré Mercier at the provincial level and Wilfrid Laurier at the federal. Mercier became premier in January, 1887, at the head of a coalition of Liberals and dissident Conservatives (his government, an activist administration that in some ways presaged the Parti Québécois, was to dissolve in scandal in 1891). And in the February, 1887, federal election the Tories barely held on to their lead in Quebec — thirty-three seats to the Liberals' thirty-two. The Conservatives would not win more seats than the Liberals in Quebec again until Maurice Duplessis lent a hand in 1958.

In 1896 Laurier was elected prime minister, and the next year the provincial Liberals swept to office. A majority of Quebecers approved of the provincial Liberals' policies of support for industrialization (much of it through American investment), fiscal conservatism, and very hesitant social reforms, notably in education. The Liberal hold on the provincial government became so taken for granted that in two elections (1904 and 1919) the Conservatives fielded candidates in only a minority of the seats, ensuring the Liberals of victory before the voting even took place. The Tories were not able to offer a coherent alternative to the government, and brief revivals of the party (which always stopped well short of electoral victory) were separated by long periods of disarray.

Federally, however, many Quebecers became disillusioned with Laurier as a result of his accommodations with British imperialism on such issues as participation in the Boer War and the formation of a Canadian navy pledged to imperial service. In the 1911 election, Quebec nationalists, led by Henri Bourassa, backed the Conservatives. The Tories captured twenty-seven Quebec seats, and — partly as a result — a majority in the House of Commons.

But the Conservative-nationalist alliance was short-lived. In Ontario, a Conservative provincial government limited the educational rights of Franco-Ontarians by passing its controversial Regulation 17. In Ottawa, Prime Minister Robert Borden's Conservative federal government supported the British Empire even more firmly than had Laurier's Liberals. The government's imposition of conscription for service in the war in Europe in 1917 was heavy-handed and accompanied by anti-French overtones, and the 1917 election divided the country along ethnic lines, with English Canadian Liberals supporting Borden's "Union" slate while French Canadians returned overwhelmingly to Laurier. Quebecers, historians Paul-André Linteau, René Durocher and Jean-Claude Robert have written, "were now overwhelmingly opposed to everything *bleu* (Conservative). Not only were they not concerned about being isolated, they were proud of it. Whenever any French-speaking politician who had agreed to collaborate with the Borden or Meighen government dared to face the French-Canadian electorate of Quebec, he could be certain of a resounding defeat. Never had French-Canadian voters been so unanimous as they were during this crisis."

Laurier's successor, Mackenzie King, was a unilingual, Protestant English Canadian who did not claim to understand French Canada. But he had opposed conscription, and he had the good sense to leave Quebec affairs largely in the hands of his able lieutenant, Ernest Lapointe. After Lapointe's death in 1941, another distinguished French Canadian, Louis Saint-Laurent, was brought into the government, eventually to succeed King as prime minister. French Canadians of the stature of Laurier, Lapointe and Saint-Laurent were conspicuously lacking in the federal Conservative party.

Only once during the King era, in the Depression year of 1930, did Quebec fail to give the Liberals an overwhelming majority of its seats. In that year's election, twenty-four Quebec seats helped produce a national Conservative majority. But the Depression became even worse under the government of R. B. Bennett, and most of those seats went Liberal again in 1935. Between 1935 and 1953, Conservative strength in Quebec ranged from zero to five seats. Not even the imposition of conscription by the King government in 1944 made much of a dent in the Liberals' Quebec support. Unlike the Tory government in 1917, King defused the conscription issue by resorting to the techniques of obfuscation and delay, at which he was a master. The Tories, meanwhile, were as rabidly pro-conscription as ever, and their position was symbolized by the brief return of the architect of the First World War conscription policy, Arthur Meighen, as Tory leader in 1942.

The relationship between the Conservatives' difficulties in Quebec and the infrequency with which they formed the government in Ottawa was direct. In a number of elections, Quebec provided the Liberals with their margin of victory. On the two occasions when the Tories made a respectable showing in Quebec (1911 and 1930), they won a majority; this would happen again in 1958. These were the only Conservative majority governments in the twentieth century (not counting the pro-conscription "Unionist" majority of 1917).

It would not have been surprising if this history had weighed heavily on Brian Mulroney when he first became involved in politics as a student at St. Francis Xavier. And yet he decided to join the campus Conservative club. Some people who knew him at St. FX insist that Mulroney's adherence to Conservatism was simply a matter of practical politics. The Liberal club was large and crowded. They were also an exclusive and arrogant bunch. "You should have seen those campus Liberals," Mulroney says. "They were arrogant enough to make anyone a Tory." It was too big a pond for the skinny kid from Baie-Comeau with no pedigree to make much of a splash. Outside of the Liberals, there appears to have been a great deal of interchange among the student political groups. Mulroney remembers his friend and occasional debating partner Richard Cashin as being a member of four political parties. "Rick founded one or two himself," he says. "I forget their names — one was the Democratic Republicans or something." In Mulroney's case, another friend insists that the budding politician was interested in politics, not party. It could have been the CCF or the Liberals, but the Tories asked him to join first.

During his first year at St. Francis Xavier, Brian Mulroney met the provincial leader of the Nova Scotia PCs, Robert Stanfield. Stanfield had taken over leadership of the almost moribund party in the late 1940s and had already lost one election to the powerful Liberal premier Angus L. Macdonald. However, Macdonald had since died and his successor, Henry Hicks, had won the Liberal leadership only after a bruising battle with Harold Connolly that split the party on religious grounds. In the fall of 1956, before the wounds had healed, Hicks called a provincial election, and a newly reorganized and revitalized Tory party beat him.

Brian Mulroney, student politician, became involved in the successful campaign. He canvassed door to door, and advised on the translation of election material into French. As a young teenager, he did not play a particularly prominent role in the campaign, but he worked hard, and more important, he made friends.

The end of Liberal rule in Nova Scotia could seem to some to presage a wider Tory renaissance. In the mid-1950s, the arrogance and unresponsiveness of the aging Liberal government in Ottawa were becoming increasingly apparent. The government's economic czar, C. D. Howe (who contributed the phrases "Who's to stop me?" and "What's a million?" to the Canadian political vocabulary), was treating Parliament with what his biographers Robert Bothwell and William Kilbourn have described as "a contempt he made no effort to hide." In 1955 an attempt by Howe to extend emergency powers accorded to him during the Korean War as minister of defence production caused a parliamentary uproar, which proved to be only a prelude to an even more tumultuous controversy the next year: the epochal Pipeline Debate. Howe used the parliamentary "guillotine" of closure to suit the convenience of the American company building the trans-Canada gas pipeline, which had a construction schedule that didn't allow for extended deliberation in the House of Commons. This heavy-handed manoeuvre provided a focus for the growing discontent with the Liberal regime. Later, in 1956, George Drew resigned as federal Conservative leader, making way for a leadership convention that was to elect John Diefenbaker and serve as Brian Mulroney's initiation into politics.

Even in Quebec it was possible to see the prospect of change. As long as the popular Louis Saint-Laurent was in office, Quebec would be Liberal territory federally; but "Uncle Louis" was seventy-four years old, and once he retired, continued Liberal mastery of Quebec could not be taken for granted. Thus, there were currents in the country encouraging Brian Mulroney in his decision to become a Tory in 1956. What is not so easy to explain is his decision, as a lawyer and businessman in Montreal through the Sixties and Seventies, when the Conservative party in Quebec was sinking into increasing obscurity, to remain one.

He never made any secret of his ambition nor of his determination to achieve his goals, which even in the charade of student politics can be defined as political clout or power. Yet he seems not to have fit the mould of the typical student politician — especially the Tory variety who give the impression of having entered the world wearing three-piece pin-stripes and once provoked Dalton Camp to remark that there is "no shirt too young to stuff."

Five weeks after the Nova Scotia election, Mulroney attended the federal Progressive Conservative leadership convention as a delegate. He was chairman of Nova Scotia Youth for Diefenbaker and vice-chairman of the National Youth for Diefenbaker Committee, positions whose main function was to tape Diefenbaker posters around the convention site under the direction of George Hees. Young Mulroney developed a friendship with the new leader, which was to last until Mulroney broke with the Chief and supported Davie Fulton in the 1967 leadership race that resulted in the election of Robert Stanfield. As a student, Mulroney made much of his relationship with Diefenbaker. He would often boast about his friendship with the leader, soon to be prime minister, and the telephone calls that would be exchanged between the prime minister's office and the student's rooms. In casual conversations with his friends, he would let it out that "the Chief just phoned" or "as I told Diefenbaker."

The relationship between the young Brian Mulroney and John Diefenbaker, which continued after Mulroney's graduation from St. FX and through his years as a law student at Laval University in Quebec City, was a curious and complex one. As we have seen, Mulroney was early very sensitive to the problems of French Quebec. In his honours year at St. FX, he wrote his major paper on relations between Quebec and the Canadian federal state, and in a debate that year in Charlottetown, Mulroney caused a sensation by speaking in French. All of which makes his friendship with John Diefenbaker, whose term in office appeared to constitute a series of insults to Quebec and to French Canadians, somewhat incongruous.

Diefenbaker had never been known as a friend of French Canada; he had risen repeatedly during the conscription debates of the Second World War to attack French Canada's military record or the lenient penalties being handed out to draft dodgers in Quebec. In the 1956 leadership campaign, a majority of the Quebec Tories, led by former national party president Léon Balcer, opposed Diefenbaker, but by the time of the convention, most were reconciled to the inevitability of his victory. As was traditional, a French Canadian, Pierre Sévigny, was prepared to second his nomination. At the last minute, however, Diefenbaker decided to have Premier Hugh John Flemming of New Brunswick do the honours. At this point in the convention, Balcer and most of the Quebec delegation staged a brief walkout in protest. And the young Baie-Comeau native attending the convention as a student delegate from Nova Scotia sympathized with them.

Diefenbaker's insensitivity towards Quebec became more marked after he received his huge majority in 1958, and the deterioration of his relationship with French Canada was not seriously mitigated by token gestures such as simultaneous translation in the House of Commons and bilingual cheques in the civil service. Because Diefenbaker's domination of English Canada was so secure, the Quebec caucus had little leverage and less power in Ottawa. The Chief distrusted most of the Quebec MPs, regarding them as nationalists who were closer to Duplessis than to him. One Quebec Tory who was active in the party during Diefenbaker's leadership recalls that he didn't understand and was contemptuous of Quebec politics: "He thought we were all a bunch of crooks." Diefenbaker relegated the French Canadians in his cabinet to minor portfolios, except for his reluctant appointment of Balcer as minister of transport in 1960. (Balcer later quit the party after an unhappy term as Quebec lieutenant under Diefenbaker in 1964–65. He ran unsuccessfully for a provincial seat as a Liberal in 1966, and his political journey culminated in his active support of the "*oui*" option in Quebec's sovereignty-association referendum in 1980.)

Nevertheless, Mulroney developed an almost filial relationship with the Tory leader. In his 1963 account of Diefenbaker's term as prime minister, *Renegade in Power*, Peter C. Newman portrayed Mulroney as an adviser to the Chief: "He was politically mature beyond his years and had a perfect appreciation of Quebec's political aspirations. Unlike most of the other men who had access to the Prime Minister, he was unafraid to be openly critical. It was largely because Mulroney's advice went unheeded that the Tories lost the confidence of Quebec." In his own recollection of his relationship with Diefenbaker, however, Mulroney maintains that it is "oversimplifying things" to describe him as an adviser:

> We would talk often, and I remember him and Olive in Quebec City on their way to a Commonwealth conference inviting me to their suite for dinner. But it was a personal, almost a family gesture.

Oh, I remember trying to give him advice on occasion. Once while visiting his office in Ottawa I complained to him that his gestures toward Quebec were being construed as "Uncle Tomism." He looked at me for a moment and called old Gilbert Champagne into the office and sent him down to the library for a Saskatchewan law report of 1922 or '23. [Gilbert Champagne had functioned in Conservative headquarters since the days of Robert Borden, although what his function actually was never seemed clear.]

Sure enough Gilbert returned with the book, and Diefenbaker quickly found the report of an attempt to dissolve a French school board by the government, and the lawyer defending the school board was John Diefenbaker. "Take that," he said — I think I still have it — "I was fighting for French rights before you were even thought of."

In the early years most Tories, and especially the younger members of the party, were under the spell of Diefenbaker's forceful and dominating personality. "We would go up to Ottawa to speak to him about our grievances and complaints, ready to demand some changes," one Tory recalls. "Dief would start to speak and a few minutes later we were in the palm of his hand. We would all leave believing that everything was solved and that the Chief understood and supported us." As Brian Mulroney's politics matured and Diefenbaker's stubbornness hardened in defeat, the political differences between them grew, but it is not surprising that when Mulroney was a young student activist down in the Maritimes, the dominant element in his view of the Tory prime minister was faith in his obvious good will.

It is difficult to discuss "high politics" and issues such as relationships between Quebec and Confederation, language rights and constitutional guarantees, in the context of the fun and games of student politics. And for the most part, Mulroney concentrated on the stuff of winning elections at the student level and on being an active foot soldier in the campaigns of the party on the provincial and federal levels. In the name of the campus PCs, he won all the debates. In his senior year he pulled off a big political upset by winning the student elections and becoming the PC prime minister in the Combined Atlantic Universities Parliament.

At St. FX, Mulroney demonstrated his ability to take charge without offending the people over whom he is taking charge — no mean feat in student politics where egos soar even higher than ambitions and expectations. He also showed signs of what is perhaps his outstanding characteristic as a mature politician: the ability to win and maintain personal friendships with political opponents.

From Baie-Comeau through St. FX and everywhere he went, Brian Mulroney demonstrated the politician's talent for making and keeping friends. This is something he works at all the time. Mulroney made a number of good friends at St. FX, and for the most part he can still count on them; they have formed a network based upon personal loyalties that go far beyond Tory politics, and indeed beyond politics altogether. Probably his closest personal friend, Toronto lawyer Sam Wakim, the former MP for Don Mills, is a fellow St. FX graduate. Wakim suggests that a politician's ability to make and keep friends lies in his capacity for giving rewards. Until 1983, however, Mulroney was never in a position to reward his friends. Thus, the Mulroney network, centred around a politican without office or access to patronage, appears all the more remarkable.

Mulroney did not get involved in politics alone at St. FX, but in everything the university had to offer. "I can still see him arriving with his cardboard suitcase" (will Brian Mulroney ever get rid of that cardboard suitcase?), says a friend who was a year ahead of him. "He didn't know anybody and he wanted so hard to be liked. The older kids would shove him around a bit and he'd look at them with eyes like saucers and keep trying to get accepted."

Another friend, Gerald Doucet (later to be PC education minister in Nova Scotia), remembers Mulroney "taking the campus by storm. Within six months he was in everything: varsity debating, drama, politics — you name it, he was part of it. It's a hard act to achieve coming in from the outside like that and taking over without arousing antagonism, but he did it. He really towered over most people in the way he handled himself and he was tremendously popular — with guys and girls.''

Robert Higgins, former leader of the Liberal party in New Brunswick and now associate justice of the New Brunswick Supreme Court, remembers that when Mulroney first came to St. FX, he ''was rather shy and quiet.'' But he developed rapidly into ''an outstanding public speaker with a great presence. He was a good mixer and, at the student union, was willing to take on practically any job anyone would ask him to do.'' And Sam Wakim recalls Mulroney's capacity for a good time: ''He was always good company.''

Mulroney clearly loved to party as much as he loved his Party. Stories abound about after-hours dorm parties, beer smuggling and the like. In those days there were so many more university rules to break than there are today, and it seems apparent that Mulroney and his buddies broke most of them. And he got caught on enough occasions to raise the question of his expulsion at least once.

Through all the high jinks of university and all the extracurricular activity, Mulroney was a hard-working and diligent student, and he graduated with an honours B.A. in political science in 1960. He moved to Halifax to begin studying law at Dalhousie University, but after a year he decided to move on again. ''I had been in the Maritimes six or seven years,'' he says, ''and was sort of thinking: 'This is a great place; I might settle down here.' Then I suddenly thought: 'Hell, all my roots are in Quebec. I'd better hightail it back home.' ''

It sounds like an easy decision, but why would the young man with the goal of being Tory prime minister of Canada decide to return to Quebec? And once deciding that, why would he not choose an English university such as McGill instead of heading to Quebec City and French-speaking Laval University?

Part of the reason may have been personal. The Mulroney family had lived in the Quebec City area for almost a century

before Ben and Irene moved to Baie-Comeau; and Quebec City
— much more than the far-off metropolis of Montreal — served
as the "big city" for the rural areas of eastern Quebec.

However, another answer suggests itself. As the decade turned,
so did life in Quebec. In September, 1959, Premier Duplessis
flew to the iron ore port of Sept-Îles, 150 kilometres downriver
from Baie-Comeau, and then north to the iron-mining company
town of Schefferville on the Labrador border. There he suffered
a cerebral hemorrhage, and died four days later in the Iron Ore
Company of Canada guest house. He was succeeded by Paul
Sauvé, who had been the most respected and independent-minded
member of the Duplessis cabinet. In his inaugural speech, Sauvé
pronounced the portentous word *désormais* (henceforth). Henceforth things would change, and indeed they would, but not under
Sauvé, who suffered a fatal heart attack after only three months
in office. Another Duplessis cabinet minister, Antonio Barrette,
assumed the premiership, but a few months later he had to lead
his dispirited party, deprived of its revered "Chef" and his only
credible successor, into an election against the resurgent Liberals
led by Jean Lesage.

The result was a narrow victory for the Liberals, and the
changes that this election ushered in were so extensive that they
soon became known collectively as the Quiet Revolution (Laval
sociologist Gérard Bergeron thought it would be more accurate
to call the process a "noisy evolution" — he was probably right,
but the term never caught on). There were few areas of Quebec
life that were not affected. The role of government was redefined
and expanded, the educational system was restructured, the influence of the church declined precipitately, and cultural life
showed a new vitality. The provincial government, under the
direction of a few key cabinet ministers, such as René Lévesque
(who would nationalize the province's private electrical companies) and Paul Gérin-Lajoie (who would revolutionize its
educational system), and a group of capable and innovative
technocrats attracted to the civil service, showed unprecedented

vigour and replaced the Catholic church as the central institution in Quebec society.

At the time Brian Mulroney decided to switch to Laval in 1961, the Quiet Revolution was well under way. Quebec City was where the action was, and it was where Mulroney wanted to be.

CHAPTER THREE

Laval: The Team Takes Shape

W hen Mulroney arrived at Laval, although the venerable university had recently completed its move from its former quarters in the old walled city to a new and rather characterless campus in suburban Sainte-Foy, the Faculty of Law remained, virtually alone, in the old Latin Quarter. Laval's Faculty of Social Sciences, under the leadership of Father Georges-Henri Lévesque, had been a centre of opposition to Duplessis and a training ground for the new and more modern generation of Quebec leaders who would supersede him (Laval graduates were, in Mason Wade's words, "the true makers of the 'Quiet Revolution,'" and included future federal Liberal cabinet ministers such as Maurice Lamontagne and Jean Marchand and future provincial Parti Québécois ministers such as Claude Morin and Louis O'Neill). At the same time, other parts of the university — including the law school — had retained their historic role as the apex of Quebec's traditional educational system. But in 1962, while Mulroney was a student there, the replacement of Guy Hudon as dean of law by Yves Pratte (later president of Air Canada and a Supreme Court justice) heralded an expansion of the curriculum and a new openness to the forces of change that were penetrating the campus.

The presence of an anglophone student such as Mulroney at

the prestigious French-language law school was very much a novelty. The first English Canadian to study law at Laval had arrived in 1928. He was Theodore Roosevelt Meighen, son of former Conservative Prime Minister Arthur Meighen. The elder Meighen, who as the architect of conscription during the First World War was regarded in French Canada as the embodiment of English Canadian insensitivity towards Quebec, was fully conscious of the extent to which the unceasing opposition of Quebec had damaged his political career, and sent his son to Laval in a personal effort to bridge the gap. In the early 1960s, Michael Meighen, the prime minister's grandson, was studying law at Laval as part of what was by then a family tradition. Another student in a similar position was Peter White, a member of a prominent Tory family from London, Ontario, whose uncle John Stairs had studied law at Laval. Both Meighen and White became firm and lasting personal friends and political associates of Brian Mulroney. So did two bilingual francophone students, Michel Cogger and Jean Bazin.

Mulroney had been at Laval only a few months before he was able to talk the local English television station into letting him host a public-affairs program, and he had hosted the show for only a few weeks before he was able to talk Premier Lesage into an appearance. Meanwhile, he was up to his ears in Conservative politics. He was active in the Progressive Conservative Student Federation, of which he became vice-president in 1962. But while active in student politics, his interests extended to the wider arena. The phone calls to and from John Diefenbaker in Ottawa and other Tory movers and shakers around the country that had begun while he was at St. FX, continued.

Evening time that Mulroney did not devote to studying or political phone calls was often spent with his fellow students at Aux Délices, a Greek restaurant and bar near the Quebec Basilica. "Huddled in the high-backed wooden booths," writes Robert McKenzie, "the students would launch endless political discussions, often about the corruption of the previous Union Nationale regime of the late Maurice Duplessis." But it was not only Duplessis and the past that animated the group. They had some plans of their own: the 1961 Laval Congress on Canadian Affairs.

The new directions in Quebec society that accompanied the change of government in 1960 were felt with particular force in the areas of federal-provincial relations and, more generally, in the relationship between French and English Canada. Conflicts between the government of Quebec and the government of Canada were not new; they had been a recurring feature of the Duplessis era. But the autonomism of Duplessis and his predecessors was reactive and defensive. Lesage and his ministers, by contrast, were eager to involve the provincial government in new fields of endeavour, and adopted a newly aggressive posture towards Ottawa.

At the same time, a movement was taking shape in the province that favoured an end to the federal pact and the creation of an independent Quebec. This too was not a new idea, but in the past it had been associated with a religious and mystical — almost messianic — view of French Canada that had consigned it to the political margin. In its new manifestation, the independence idea was couched in the modern phraseology of political nationalism and thus potentially had a much wider appeal than had been the case in the past. English Canadians were not so much reassured by the admittedly small size of the pro-independence groups as they were disturbed by the fact that they existed at all. The most credible of the new groups was the Rassemblement pour l'Indépendance Nationale (Coalition for National Independence), headed by a federal civil servant with the Defence Research Board, Dr. Marcel Chaput.

Part of the response to these new currents was a sudden desire on the part of English Canada to understand what was happening in Quebec. The time for English Canadians to try to come to terms with French Canada, foreseen by Brian Mulroney a few years earlier, had arrived. This was the era when the phrase "What does Quebec want?" first became widespread. It was believed that the problems of Confederation could be solved through dialogue and understanding. There was an explosion of conferences

and symposiums, and the most spectacular of these was the 1961
Congress on Canadian Affairs at Laval University.

Brian Mulroney and his Conservative friends — Meighen, White,
Cogger and Bazin — were the driving force behind the symposium. But it was not a sectarian affair. Among the other law students who worked with them to organize the symposium were
Clément Richard and Jean Garon, who became ministers in the
provincial cabinet of the Parti Québécois.

The initial idea for the event came from Peter White, who had
been impressed by a similar conference on world affairs at McGill.
When White left for a summer World University Service seminar
in Europe, Michel Cogger was left in charge. The students had
no funds for their conference and began to approach private sources
for donations — starting with the president of Quebec North
Shore Paper of Baie-Comeau, Robert Schmon. "The money started
to trickle in," remembers Cogger. "Well, we had to put on a
conference. So we'd phone Mason Wade and say we had André
Laurendeau [publisher of *Le Devoir* and later co-chairman of the
Royal Commission on Bilingualism and Biculturalism], and while
he was thinking about it, we'd phone Laurendeau and say we had
Wade."

The title of the conference was "Le Canada, expérience ratée
ou réussie? [The Canadian Experiment, Success or Failure?]."
The students got all the provincial lieutenant governors to lend
their names as sponsors, but Governor General Georges Vanier
wrote back saying: What if the conference concludes Canada is
a failure? They had to respond assuring him it was just a discussion and there would be no definite conclusions. Dean Hudon of
the law school was upset because he felt the students were putting
too much time into the event. Nevertheless, the organizers succeeded in staging the conference and assembled an impressive
cast: Lesage, Wade, Laurendeau, Chaput, provincial Natural Resources Minister René Lévesque, federal Justice Minister Davie
Fulton, New Democratic MP Douglas Fisher, future federal Liberal cabinet ministers Maurice Lamontagne and Gérard Pelletier,

and future Union Nationale Premier Jean-Jacques Bertrand, among others.

For five days in November, 1961, the event made front-page headlines. Fulton took the occasion to announce that the government would shortly be proposing an amending formula making it possible for Canada to repatriate its constitution; this proposal, which was based on the principle of the unanimous consent of the provinces for major constitutional changes and, as modified by a subsequent Liberal justice minister, became known as the Fulton-Favreau formula, was the chief focus of the constitutional discussions of the Sixties. Lévesque came to the conference fresh from a visit to Manicouagan, the huge power station north of Baie-Comeau that was then under construction and would become the symbol of technological progress in Quebec. After expressing regret that he was not still in Manicouagan, the outspoken cabinet minister observed that English Canada needed French Canada more than the reverse. Taking offence at this, Fisher, representing "the average English Canadian view," described French Canada's contribution to the country in the following terms:

> I suppose for us the greatest impact of French Canadian culture has been made by Maurice Richard and Lili St-Cyr. We did have Gisele, of course, but she became Gisele McKenzie and went off to the United States. I wonder whether we are to be fascinated by your marvellous police tradition. . . . I wonder if we are to be impressed with your tradition of literary censorship or whether your educational system has a great deal to offer us in a society where technocracy is becoming so much more important.

But by far the most dramatic event at the conference was the appearance of Dr. Chaput. Unlike Lévesque or Fisher, Chaput spoke calmly, soberly and unemotionally, delivering his speech, in the words of *Montreal Star* commentator John Maffre, as if it were "the reading of a yearly bank statement." And yet, Maffre wrote, "the effect was amazing. To an English Canadian sitting in the crowded audience, the emotional response that he evoked was almost a tangible thing, a physical thing. Somehow he expressed the deep and abiding sense of insult — the word is not too strong — that his young listeners felt about the French Canadian minority position in a largely Anglo-Saxon country," The content of his speech, however, was overshadowed by the circumstances that surrounded his presence at Laval. This is how Brian Mulroney told the story twenty years later:

> I was chairman of a panel discussion that made national headlines. On the panel was Marcel Chaput, the Quebec civil servant who worked for the Ministry of National Defence and made no attempt to hide his separatist leanings. Chaput had been forbidden by his employer, the Minister of National Defence, from appearing at the symposium and espousing the separatist cause. When Chaput put in his appearance, the federal minister, Douglas Harkness, sent Chaput a telegram that arrived during the panel discussion. Its contents were read aloud. He was fired on the spot. Chaput did not flinch.

Actually, Chaput was not fired on the spot. The Defence Research Board (DRB) denied him leave without pay to attend the conference. Harkness said that if he went anyway he would be suspended. Chaput did go anyway. He spoke on a Friday. When he showed up for work Monday morning, he was given a two-week suspension for "wilful disobedience." He subsequently resigned to save the DRB the trouble of firing him. In any event, Chaput did speak at the conference, and his career at the Defence Research Board did come to an end as a consequence.

The conference "was what they call an epochal event," says Michel Cogger. "It was a huge success, there were massive amounts of publicity, we were all heroes and they threw us a party at the Bois de Coulonges [the Quebec lieutenant governor's mansion]."

Brian Mulroney's part in the organization of the symposium reflected the distance between his own views and the anti-French insensitivity of the Conservative party of the day. In hindsight, Mulroney described the aims of the conference: "We were hoping

— inexperienced students that we were — that our elders and our political leaders would use certain of the ideas and a major part of the enthusiasm generated by the Congress in evolving new approaches to old problems. But this did not seem to happen.''

The careers of the organizers of the conference were to diverge on the question of how to resolve the problems surrounding Quebec's relationship with the rest of Canada, if indeed there was to be a place for Quebec in Canada at all. Some chose the independence option, some remained federalists. In Quebec, the issue is seen mainly as being between the federalists, represented by the Liberals, and the pro-independence forces, represented by the PQ. What middle ground there may be is not occupied by the PCS. The Tory tide of 1958 ebbed quickly in the 1960s, and the party soon resumed the marginal position it had occupied through most of the century. The younger generation of Quebecers has seen the Tories either as being hostile to the aspirations of French Canada or, more commonly, as being irrelevant to them. For a young, ambitious politician such as Brian Mulroney, one who has been pictured as the consummate political opportunist, the decision to remain both a staunch federalist and a staunch Conservative was also a decision to remain on the political margin in Quebec throughout the 1960s and 1970s.

On a narrower but perhaps equally important level, the 1961 Laval Congress on Canadian Affairs was the event that drew Brian Mulroney, Michael Meighen, Peter White, Jean Bazin and Michel Cogger together. The team that was to capture the leadership of the federal Progressive Conservative party in 1983 was in place.

Brian Mulroney is a gregarious sort who likes to be with people. He likes to talk to people — he even sometimes considers reporters to be people and on occasion has been burned by his openness. Mulroney seeks advice and he gives it. But with all that said and done, he has a core group of personal friends and political advisers (with this group, there is no distinction between the two roles) who from the early Sixties at Laval to the Tory leadership race of 1983 were as close to being a team as it is possible to define one in politics.

Michel Cogger comes from a roughly similar background to Mulroney and became his closest confidant. He was born in Quebec City, the son of an accountant for the Canadian National Railways. After preparing to become a teacher by receiving a traditional classical education — philosophy, literature, history and Latin — at the Séminaire de Québec, he decided to study law at Laval, "just to keep my options open." At Laval, Cogger became editor of the student paper. Through the paper he met Joe Clark, then editor of the *Gateway*, the student paper at the University of Alberta. He also became involved in student politics. Recalling the beginnings of his friendship with Brian Mulroney, he says:

> We were always broke then, but one of the things I had in Quebec City that the others didn't was a home. I had three brothers, one of whom died at nineteen in 1958 and another who went to Africa as a missionary. My mother always liked it when she could cook spaghetti dinner. Brian would always come around, because it was a lot better at our table than sitting around on a Sunday night in a rooming house on St. Louis Street.

Jean Bazin, Peter White and Michael Meighen were also Sunday night regulars for dinner at the Cogger home. Bazin later became a prominent corporation lawyer in Montreal, with a list of clients that included the Iron Ore Company of Canada.

The two other anglophones in the group, Meighen and White, both came to Laval after doing undergraduate studies at McGill. They had become friends there (White's father had been a college roommate of Meighen's father in the 1920s) and both had served on the McGill student council in the late 1950s.

Like Meighen, White has an unassailable Tory pedigree. His mother was a Stairs from Halifax whose grandfather, John F. Stairs, was Nova Scotia's leading financier at the turn of the century and gave his fellow Maritimer Max Aitken (later Lord Beaverbrook) his start in both high finance and Conservative politics.

Peter White was born in Brazil, where his father was South American sales manager for Sperry Gyroscope. With his father overseas during the Second World War, White grew up in the Montreal home of his grandfather, Gilbert Stairs, a prominent lawyer in a firm that included Liberal cabinet minister Brooke Claxton. After the war, White and his family moved to the Eastern Townships, and later White enrolled at McGill. White decided to study law at Laval because he had "had enough of McGill" and wanted to get away from home and get the feel of a French university. In spite of his Tory background, White claims (as does Cogger) that he didn't have much connection with politics until he became friendly with Brian Mulroney.

One result of White's new interest in politics was his first meeting with his future business partner, Conrad Black. Early in 1962, Mulroney dragged White up to Ottawa for the Tory annual meeting. Black, who was studying at Carleton and was then a staunch Liberal, arranged to meet White and Jeremy Riley (Black's double first cousin) at noon for lunch. "Of course," White says, "Conrad rolled in around two," and they spent the afternoon arguing about Lester Pearson. Of such things are enduring partnerships built. Black and White (a good name for a publishing firm) together took over a small Quebec weekly and built their publishing interests into the Sterling chain. After Black's successful bid for Argus Corporation in 1978 (in which he outgunned Col. Maxwell Meighen, Michael's uncle), White became a director of Argus and its associated corporations, Hollinger Mines and Labrador Mining and Exploration (this is discussed further in chapter six). White also claims to have convinced Black to study at Laval, where he pursued his deepening interest in Quebec politics and especially in the Union Nationale, which eventually led to his richly detailed biography of Maurice Duplessis.

"Long before the introduction of Quebec's law to reinforce

the position of the French language," Robert McKenzie has written, "the Mulroney-Meighen-White group looked like a new breed of Quebec anglos — a growing bilingual elite." As it turned out, it was a new breed that never really materialized. But one distinguishing characteristic of Mulroney and his friends that became more and more striking as the years went on was their adherence to the Conservative party.

"I think we started out as a team," says Michel Cogger, "and then we went on to develop our thinking. I don't want to sound cynical, but at age twenty or twenty-three, I don't see a lot of substantial philosophical differences between all of us. Maybe it was a question of the Ins and Outs. But you have to remember, we went to school with people [Liberals] who have never really been out of power."

Cogger denies that this is a matter of substituting a Tory trough for a Liberal one, and stresses that the Liberals do not have a monopoly of talent in the country. His reasons for joining the Tories amount to a fairly classic statement of the rationale for a two-party system — the idea that there is, or should be, an alternative government (even when they actually formed the government, at least on the federal level, the Tories still felt like the Outs). And he gives Jules Lesage, the premier's son, at least partial credit for his decision to become a Conservative. Apparently the younger Lesage and the other student Liberals were strutting about the Laval campus figuring they were the only ones with both the questions and the answers. "When you're exposed to the Grits," says Cogger, "your Conservatism — no not Conservatism — your Toryism gets reinforced. You know, when it comes to arrogance, on a scale of ten, most of them [Liberals] score at least nine and a half."

Meanwhile, the five friends, by now all active Tories, began to make plans for life after Laval.

In the summer of 1962, Brian Mulroney didn't return to Baie-Comeau. He went to Ottawa instead to work as a special assistant to Agriculture Minister Alvin Hamilton for four months. Hamilton's assistant Roy Faibish was seconded to the Diefenbaker staff for the 1962 election, and he recommended that the Laval law student travel with Hamilton. Mulroney used the time to make some contacts in western Canada (whenever he was in the West during the 1983 leadership contest, he used every occasion to remind Tories of this rather tenuous connection of his with agriculture and cattle ranching). He also spent a lot of time listening to Alvin Hamilton, who was arguably the brightest and certainly the most loquacious member of the Diefenbaker cabinet. Hamilton suggests that it was he who advised the young Mulroney that if he wanted a career in politics he should first establish himself in a business or profession, although Mulroney says Hamilton actually confirmed a decision he had already made.

When he returned to Laval, Mulroney announced his plans to his buddies. He was going to return to Baie-Comeau, set up a legal practice, make some money and wait for his chance. Before he ran for political office, he needed a secure financial base. "There is nothing sadder than some guy in politics who is at the mercy of financial backers," he said. "If you're not a free man, what's the point?"

As it was to happen, Michel Cogger discovered a better option for a young Tory than the unlikely prospect of trying to get both rich and elected on the Quebec North Shore. Cogger heard from a friend who was about to accept a position as a *stagiaire* (apprentice lawyer) with the Montreal firm of Howard, Cate, Ogilvy, Bishop, Cope, Porteous & Hansard that another opening was available with the same firm. The firm was the largest in Quebec and one of the best connected, and the small number of *stagiaire* positions that it offered each year were eagerly sought by graduating law students. Cogger had his friend recommend Mulroney, who was tempted but first had to check it out with his father. "You can come home any time," said Ben Mulroney, "this is an opportunity for you." Brian was offered the position and took it.

Meanwhile, Bazin was elected president of the Canadian Union of Students (CUS), and it was during his term that the strains in the dialogue that Mulroney and his friends were trying to promote became evident, at least at the student level. Students at Quebec's

French-language universities had been considering establishing their own union, separate from CUS. Laval and the universities of Montreal and Sherbrooke withdrew from CUS just as Bazin was taking office, and organized the Union Générale des Étudiants du Québec a few months later. (Coincidentally, one of Bazin's predecessors as president of the Canadian student federation was Walter McLean, now the Tory MP for Waterloo, Ontario. McLean and his wife Barbara spent their honeymoon in 1961 at the Laval Congress on Canadian Affairs, and were strong Mulroney supporters during the 1983 leadership race.)

After his term of office at CUS, Bazin came to work in Montreal, as did Michael Meighen. Cogger remained in Quebec City where he married and divorced. In 1966, after the break-up of his marriage, Cogger was at loose ends when he received a phone call from Mulroney. "It seemed to me," he says, "my options were to be a ski instructor in Europe or to study at Stanford in California. But Brian phoned me up to tell me Fulton was looking for an executive assistant and was gearing up for a leadership run. Mulroney said, 'You'll enjoy this stuff. It'll be like meeting old friends. You'll meet everybody in the country.' Well, I signed on."

In 1964 Peter White went to work for Liberal cabinet minister Maurice Sauvé. The two had met when White was trying to get Sauvé to attend the Laval symposium. White told Sauvé before agreeing to work for him that he was a Tory. "That's okay," Sauvé said, "I've got a Créditiste in my office now — I may as well have a Tory." Sauvé was minister of forestry and rural development and was responsible for the administration of the Agricultural Rehabilitation and Development Act (ARDA), one of Alvin Hamilton's more successful brainstorms and most important legacies to the country. The idea was to redevelop depressed rural areas, improve use of rural land, and retrain rural people and involve them in the development of their own communities. White ended up working on ARDA and subsequently spent two years running the Brome County Rural Development Association in the Eastern Townships.

So after Laval the members of the group went their separate ways, but they all kept in touch, and many years later, when Brian Mulroney made his successful run at the Conservative party leadership, they would all be on board. Including Alvin Hamilton.

CHAPTER FOUR

Lawyer on the Rise

T he firm that Brian Mulroney joined as a *stagiaire* in 1964 had been at the centre of Quebec's economic and political life for eighty-five years. Formed in 1879 as Carter, Church & Chapleau (the name changed every few years as old partners died or retired and new ones were brought in until, under new Quebec legislation, the firm adopted the permanent name of Ogilvy, Renault in 1979), its original partners were all prominent Tory politicians. Joseph-Adolphe Chapleau (later Sir Joseph) was leader of the provincial Conservative party and about to become premier of Quebec. He subsequently served in the federal cabinet of Sir John A. Macdonald, and he ended his career as lieutenant governor of Quebec.

Although Tory in its origins, over the years the firm was home to a substantial number of leading politicians of both parties, as well as non-partisan figures such as Georges Vanier, who practised law with the firm in the 1920s on his way to becoming governor general of Canada. Bud Drury, Guy Favreau and Francis Fox (whose brief stay at the firm as a student coincided with Mulroney's entry there) all went on from service with the firm to positions as federal Liberal cabinet members. Firm members Levi Ruggles Church (one of the original partners), John Hall and Albert Atwater had each held the portfolio of provincial treasurer — at the time generally reserved for English Quebecers — in nineteenth-century Conservative provincial governments, while Stuart McDougall briefly occupied the same position in a Liberal government in 1936.

From the early years of the twentieth century until the 1930s, the firm was dominated by three men, Albert Brown, George Montgomery and Robert McMichael, and it was under their leadership that it became one of the leading law firms in Montreal's rapidly expanding corporate world. The three possessed complementary talents — Brown was a knowledgeable corporation lawyer, Montgomery a skilled courtroom pleader, and McMichael a legal scholar who studied the Quebec Civil Code the way a medieval rabbi studied the Talmud — and their partnership was an extraordinarily successful one. In 1907 the firm consisted of the three partners plus one associate, but by the 1930s Brown, Montgomery & McMichael was the largest law firm in the British Empire. It continued to grow, to the point where in the years after the Second World War it became familiarly known in Montreal legal circles as "the factory."

In 1907, the year the firm took the name of Brown, Montgomery & McMichael, two notable financial institutions moved their head offices to Montreal from Halifax. One was Max Aitken's Royal Securities, which the future Lord Beaverbrook had established with the help of Peter White's great-grandfather, John F. Stairs. The building Aitken bought to house Royal Securities included Brown, Montgomery & McMichael among its tenants, and during his brief but spectacular career in Montreal before he headed for England, the financier employed Brown as his chief legal adviser. Brown was involved in the deals through which Aitken forged the Canada Cement Company (uniting virtually all of the country's significant cement producers outside of British Columbia) and the Steel Company of Canada (bringing together such major companies as Montreal Rolling Mills and the Hamilton Steel and Iron Company). He became a director of Stelco in 1916.

In the long run, however, of even greater importance to the

law firm was the relationship it established with the other transplanted financial institution from Halifax, the Royal Bank of Canada. Brown and McMichael were both well versed in banking law and became legal advisers to the bank; Brown was the first of a series of the firm's partners to serve as a Royal Bank director. The Royal Bank's president, Sir Herbert Holt, was Montreal's most powerful businessman, and he controlled numerous other corporations as well; several of these became Brown, Montgomery & McMichael clients, including Montreal Light, Heat and Power (of which Montgomery had been head of the legal department before going into partnership with Brown and McMichael) and the Montreal Trust Company. When the bank moved into an imposing new head office building on St. James Street in 1928, Brown, Montgomery & McMichael was one of its tenants, and when it moved uptown to the just-completed Royal Bank of Canada Building in Place Ville Marie in 1962, it was again closely followed by the law firm (in 1981 Ogilvy, Renault moved to a new building two blocks north of Place Ville Marie).

While the firm as a whole continued to handle a broad range of legal matters, as it grew, its individual lawyers increasingly became specialists in one area of the law or another. In the new Place Ville Marie office, a lawyer's area of specialization determined which quadrant of the cruciform building he was placed in, and this arrangement soon became institutionalized with the creation of formal groups. At the time Mulroney joined the firm, the head of the business and finance group was Jack Porteous, whose son Timothy later became an adviser to Prime Minister Pierre Trudeau and head of the Canada Council. Porteous's clients included a rising entrepreneur from Sudbury named Paul Desmarais (many of whose corporate takeovers would be financed by the Royal Bank). In addition to the Royal Bank and various Desmarais enterprises, corporations on whose boards of directors firm members were represented in the mid-1960s included Sogemines Limited (later Genstar), Dominion Steel and Coal, Imperial Life Assurance, Canadian Petrofina, Domtar, Canadian International Paper, Dominion Bridge, and Northern Electric.

Mulroney arrived at the firm after graduating from Laval in 1964, and immediately began to make a big impression. True to the spirit of the crusty, formal Albert Brown, the firm maintained a policy of not allowing employees to take their jackets off in the office. During Mulroney's first weeks there, a partner noticed him working at his desk with no jacket and his sleeves rolled up. "We always keep our jackets on at the office," the partner said. "So I've noticed," Mulroney answered, smiling broadly. "I don't."

"Everyone took a liking to him right away," recalls a fellow lawyer. "Old Angus Ogilvy [soon to become senior partner] used to ring for him and call him in — this young kid — just to talk things over." Another partner was so impressed by the young lawyer that he later named him an executor of his estate. Mulroney also quickly learned to find his way around the firm's most important clients. William Bennett, the president of the Iron Ore Company of Canada, a former executive assistant to C. D. Howe and head of a number of Howe's crown corporations, became a patron of the young lawyer. Bennett introduced him around town and surprised him one Christmas with a huge television set. He eventually groomed Mulroney to be his successor at Iron Ore.

The rare personality trait of being able to be popular with one's peers and one's elders at the same time, which Brian Mulroney developed as a kid in Baie-Comeau, served him well in the big city. The "street smarts" he learned on the North Shore also came in handy. But it wasn't merely charm and personality that earned him entrée. Mulroney quickly gained a reputation as a glutton for work. He was always a meticulously prepared lawyer with a superb courtroom presence. "Brian wasn't known as an intellectual," one colleague recalls, "but he always knew his brief. He could judge people and his timing was perfect. He was a great courtroom tactician."

Another prominent Quebec lawyer, Stanley Hartt, who worked with Mulroney on a series of cases involving the Montreal waterfront, gave the following insight into the young Brian Mulroney: "His early strength was his combination of rough and tough paper mill town background and an air of perfect urban sophistication.

All of us growing up have a little roughness in our demeanor, but I knew Mulroney in his early twenties and he was already a sharpie, a smoothie. I never knew him as a country bumpkin."

Brash and flashy, he cut a big figure in downtown Montreal. Even when he couldn't afford it, he enjoyed what he would call the good life: good food and drink and fine stylish clothes, which became more expensive as he became more established. "Brian always had to be going somewhere," says someone who knew him at the time, "and he was always making the big impression. We all knew he was broke, but Brian was going what he thought was first-class all the time. He was always flashing a bankroll, and it was always drinks in the Ritz-Carlton or some other expensive bistro."

Above all, Mulroney enjoyed good company, both male and female. His girl friends were mostly casual dates, and Michael Meighen has been quoted as saying that "very few women who were young and pretty escaped him." Mulroney kept in touch with his early buddies, but his network of friends grew. And he gained a reputation as the kind of person who genuinely liked helping others. He could dig up hockey tickets, put in a good word for somebody who needed a job, help somebody out with a legal problem or just make a thoughtful phone call. One such incident concerned Robert Morrow, a senior counsel with Howard, Cate, Ogilvy (and nephew of former senior partner Robert McMichael), who took the young Mulroney under his wing. Much later, when he had retired from the firm and Mulroney was president of the Iron Ore Company of Canada, Morrow was struck with a serious illness. Morrow's daughter Louise Wickson remembers that even though Mulroney had lost contact with the Morrow family, "he heard Father was sick and needed heart surgery in Cleveland, and out of the blue, Brian was on the phone. He had Father flown on the company plane to the hospital, and it was also made available for my mother to visit with him."

Had Mulroney been a carpenter or a computer technician, it would have been simple to regard all this as straightforward generosity and the author of these good deeds as a considerate and thoughtful soul. But he became a politician, and in politics more than in any other profession, favours are currency. As a result, Mulroney's friends are defensive, always making the point that his generosity just comes naturally, that it is personal and non-political or at least non-partisan: "Look, he is just good company, a good guy to have as a friend, and don't quote me."

In 1965, just as he was beginning his career with the law firm, Brian had a serious family responsibility thrust on him. Ben Mulroney died of cancer, leaving a widow and two school-age children: Gary, sixteen, and Barbara, twelve. The elder Mulroney was only sixty-one and his death was a shattering blow to the close-knit family. As his father would have wanted and expected, Brian assumed responsibility for supporting the remaining family members. He moved them down from Baie-Comeau, set up an apartment for them in Montreal, and took over the burden of educating his younger brother and sister.

Mulroney's attachment to family is another element of his personality and value system that has become interwoven with his political persona. He often uses the example of his father in speeches about work, devotion to family, dedication and self-sacrifice, and says that "carrying a lunch bucket was always considered a badge of honour in my family." The image of his father is still with him. Interviewed by David Frost, he spoke of how his father had died before he could even begin to express his love and respect for him in the smallest material sense — tickets to an NHL game he'd never have the chance to see, a vacation south he'd never have the opportunity to take. As he conveyed his sense of loss in these simple, direct terms, for a moment his eyes misted and his voice broke. On another occasion, he recalled his mother taking him to hear Maurice Duplessis speak at a construction-site ceremony: "It must have been a Sunday, because my father didn't come. The old man worked every Sunday." And when he was taunted during the 1976 leadership campaign about being the big-money candidate, he replied bitterly that "if my father were alive he would have had a laugh about that. We Mulroneys never had anything given to us. We worked for everything we had.''

Dedication to family, like kindness to friends, has its political uses. And Mulroney's unashamed ambition to be rich and power-ful and his Diamond Jim style (''If ya got 'em, ya wear 'em'') have encouraged suspicion as to the sincerity of his attachments. Yet behind the façade, he is seen by those who know him best as the good son, the devoted husband and father, and the loyal friend.

The year his father died, Mulroney flunked one of his bar exams. Under pressure to support his family, he almost decided to get out of law to take a job that would pay more than his stipend as a *stagiaire*. The firm, however, thought enough of him to begin paying him a full lawyer's salary while giving him a chance to take another run at his bar admission exams. He passed on his second try.

As a *stagiaire*, Mulroney was given a taste of the firm's various departments, and the one that interested him the most was the relatively new field of labour law. When he joined the firm on a permanent basis, he immediately went to work in the labour law group under Paul-F. Renault, a member of a prominent Liberal family and a nephew of Louis Saint-Laurent. Although many of the other lawyers in the office looked down on labour law, it actually represented a good opportunity for a young man with ambition. The Lesage government's new Labour Code had made negotiations more difficult, especially for employers, and there was an increasing demand for specialists to serve the management side. In addition, there was a growing tendency among unions to insist on negotiating in French, which meant that companies owned outside Quebec needed local experts who were fluent in the language. Before Mulroney joined the group, Renault had only one other lawyer working for him, and the amount of busi-ness was expanding rapidly as industrial relations in Quebec entered an explosive period. As a result, it was not long before Mulroney became involved in some fairly important cases.

In the spring of 1967, workers went on strike at the Canadian

British Aluminium plant in Baie-Comeau and froze the pot in which the aluminum was smelted. The company approached Renault to handle the case for its side, but he was busy representing an asbestos company in Thetford Mines at the time. He recommended the young Baie-Comeau native in his department, and Mulroney was quickly dispatched to the North Shore. Sitting across the table from one of the ablest negotiators for the Confederation of National Trade Unions (CNTU) — the labour central that had grown out of Quebec's old Catholic unions to become the most militant section of the province's labour movement — Mulroney obtained a settlement that was highly favourable to his client. The company retained the right to take disciplinary action against the workers involved, and to sue the union for damages (which it subsequently did, winning an award of more than $1 million), while no significant concessions were made to the union side. For a novice labour lawyer, it was an impressive performance.

By this time, Mulroney had already become involved in the dispute that would occupy the major portion of his time during his decade with the law firm. Under the pressure of technological change, labour relations on the Montreal waterfront (as well as in the smaller ports of Quebec City and Trois-Rivières) had erupted into crisis. Containerization and other new developments were reducing the numbers of longshoremen needed to load and unload ships. Organizationally, the shipping industry was in chaos. It consisted of a large number of shipping companies, each one wanting to get its ship loaded or unloaded as quickly as possible and none of them concerned with the long-term interests of the port. In addition, the bargaining unit on the management side consisted of the shippers (loosely organized as the Shippers' Federation of Canada), but the longshoremen's direct employers were the stevedoring contractors. In this anarchic situation, one strong force had emerged — the International Longshoremen's Association (ILA), which effectively controlled the labour supply. Longshoremen were organized into gangs, and when half a gang worked (as was commonly the case), the whole gang got paid.

"The strongest stayed home," says Arnie Masters, an executive assistant to Labour Minister Bryce Mackasey in the late 1960s, "while the oldest and weakest worked." Pilferage was another notable feature of the freight-handling system.

Despite this system's obvious deficiences, the industry was able to live with it until the early 1960s. As new freight-handling methods were introduced, however, the industry wanted to take advantage of them to lower labour costs and increase productivity. On the other hand, the longshoremen, for whom featherbedding was compensation of a sort for the total absence of job security, saw technological change as a threat to their livelihood. Between 1960 and 1965, there was a series of work stoppages and wildcat strikes. These difficulties culminated in a thirty-nine–day strike in 1966, which was settled in the office of Prime Minister Lester Pearson with a promise to appoint two commissions of inquiry to study waterfront labour relations. The more significant of these commissions, headed by Laurent Picard (later president of the Canadian Broadcasting Corporation [CBC]), was mandated to delve into the issues of productivity and job security. To represent its interests before this commission, the Shippers' Federation of Canada engaged Paul-F. Renault, and Renault soon turned the case over to Mulroney.

The Picard Commission was the beginning of a restructuring of the whole relationship between longshoremen and their employers that eventually resulted in labour peace on the waterfront, and Brian Mulroney was one of the people primarily responsible for bringing this about. Because the shippers were so loosely organized, they had no central spokesman, and Mulroney soon came to fill this role. He not only gained the confidence of the shippers, but was also able — not being a shipper himself — to establish considerable credibility with the stevedoring contractors. His skill as a debater made him a valuable asset in the Picard Commission's hearings and the court cases that followed. And his fluent bilingualism allowed him to move easily between the commission hearings, which were conducted almost entirely in French, and meetings with the shippers, most of whom spoke only English.

Stanley Hartt, who represented the stevedoring contractors, remembers one case in which he was barred from the courtroom because his clients were technically not the longshoremen's employers and hence were not a party to the case. Mulroney quickly wrote out a mandate in longhand making Hartt the lawyer for one of the shipping firms, got it signed and said to Hartt, "Here, take this." With the mandate, Hartt was allowed to stay.

Another case before the Labour Relations Board in Ottawa involved an attempt by the ILA to organize checkers, clerical workers whose job it is to verify deliveries. The case revolved around the question of exactly who could be included in the bargaining unit, and just before it was to be heard, Mulroney and Hartt got wind of a just-issued Supreme Court decision establishing that a union's internal constitution could have a bearing on this question. Quickly thumbing through the ILA's constitution, they discovered a clause saying that checkers had to pass a test as a condition of employment. Mulroney, armed with that knowledge, asked puzzled union witnesses whether they had passed a test. The chairman of the board, equally puzzled, asked what kind of test he was referring to. "Well," said Mulroney, "you could ask questions like, 'If three checkers working on a Thursday can steal six boxes, how many boxes can twelve checkers working double-time on a Sunday steal?'" Hartt recalls that "the place went into absolute bedlam. The union representative [on the board] ran out of the room and refused to come back and they couldn't have a quorum without him. It was a total shambles and we ended up winning on a technicality."

The Picard Commission recommended concessions by both labour and management. Federal legislation had made its recommendations binding on both sides; but this had occurred only over the union's protest, and another wildcat strike ensued. The solution to the waterfront's problems was still a long way off. The idea of a strong employers' association with power to bargain with the union first came from the shippers, and especially from a shipping company executive named Alex Pathy (now vice-president for business affairs of the University of Toronto), but its realization was largely due to Mulroney's skills as a conciliator. In working for the establishment of the employers' association, Mulroney had to deal not only with the shippers, the stevedoring contractors and the longshoremen but also with the federal government, which through Labour Minister Mackasey provided important moral support for the creation of a strong employers' group.

The Maritime Employers' Association (MEA) came into being in 1970, and hired Mackasey's aide Arnie Masters as its president the next year. In 1972 the MEA negotiated its first collective agreement with the union, which Masters calls ''the most modern collective agreement in the history of the industry.'' It provided for the elimination of work gangs and featherbedding and the institution of a computerized dispatch system that allowed work to be assigned on a basis that was generally recognized as fair. Six weeks after the agreement was concluded, the longshoremen were again out on strike, and they eventually had to be legislated back to work by Parliament. ''They thought we wouldn't use the rights we had acquired in the area of flexibility,'' Masters says. ''We used them.'' Mulroney was vacationing in Europe when this strike broke out, and was called back to Montreal to help deal with it.

As a consequence of these events, the shippers had agreed to reduce the work force by buying out 1,000 longshoremen at $12,000 each. Put into effect, this agreement caused financial problems for many shippers, and loans had to be negotiated with the banks and the federal government. Again Mulroney played an instrumental role. At the same time, labour-management conflict continued. ''There were wild grievances, wild court cases, and shouting in court,'' Masters remembers. The waterfront had a permanent mediator, Judge Allan Gold (now chief justice of Quebec's Superior Court). In 1975 the union's rejection of one of Judge Gold's conciliation reports led to another strike; although he was then a member of a commission of inquiry into labour relations in Quebec's equally troubled construction industry, Mulroney was called in to help plan management strategy. Parliament eventually enforced Judge Gold's report through legislation.

The 1975 strike was the last act of a dying era. The effects of the MEA, the computerized dispatch system and a vastly reduced work force (from 3,300 in 1965 — the last year any new longshoremen were hired in Montreal — to 1,000 in 1983, despite a 25 per cent increase in tonnage handled in the same period) had begun to be felt. Nowadays, stevedoring companies phone the MEA with their labour requirements for the next day, and longshoremen are assigned to jobs through the computer according to a rotation system that ensures equitable distribution of work. Tape-recorded phone conversations facilitate settlement of disputes, and under a job-security arrangement, longshoremen get paid a fixed amount regardless of the number of days they have actually worked.

People who were involved in this modernization and rationalization of waterfront labour relations are agreed that Mulroney's role in it was a highly valuable one. In some ways, the service Mulroney performed for the shippers was similar to the one rendered by William Lyon Mackenzie King to John D. Rockefeller, Jr., in much harsher circumstances half a century earlier. In the aftermath of a bitter miners' strike in Colorado that had culminated in the odious Ludlow Massacre, in which women and children as well as miners were killed, King had persuaded Rockefeller to soften his uncompromising stand against the organization of workers, shepherded him on a highly publicized tour of the mines and undercut the militant United Mine Workers by inventing the company union. As a result, labour peace was brought to the mines of Colorado and their owner was restored to public repute. Mulroney, similarly, had to persuade his clients to abandon outworn methods that were no longer in their best interests. He got them to understand their long-term stake in labour peace, a reduced work force and more efficient methods of job allocation, and to appreciate that if they wanted to achieve those goals they would have to give something in return.

"Brian was constantly trying to achieve a consensus," says
Arnie Masters. "He was never part of the problem but always
part of the solution, and that's the best thing you can say about
someone in this business." Alex Pathy pays tribute to Mulroney's
skill as a debater: "He was very good on his feet. He understood
collective bargaining, and had a good understanding of power.
Along with Masters and myself, he was one of the people who
brought this together." Stanley Hartt says that Mulroney "does
himself something of a disservice when he projects this kind of
smoothie Bill-Davis-deflecting-the-substance-of-a-question kind
of image. He's really much more substantial than his image
conveys. I'm not worried about them taking the country and
sticking it in his hands tomorrow — and I'm a Liberal." Even
Mulroney's adversaries in the waterfront dispute speak highly of
him. Phil Cutler, a top Quebec labour lawyer who represented
the ILA, says that "no matter how difficult a situation may be,
he comes through as a stabilizing influence. He's a stabilizer and
we need fewer destabilizers and more stabilizers like Brian Mulroney." Former union president Leo Taylor echoes Cutler's words:
"We were on opposite sides of the fence but Mr. Mulroney was
a straight shooter. His word was his bond."

As Mulroney's reputation as a lawyer grew, he drew in more
money and an ever-widening circle of influential friends. He was
now better able to support his fast-lane life. The bachelor lawyer
took to frequenting the posh Beaver Club in the Queen Elizabeth
Hotel — onetime private preserve of the city's fur traders — and
the bar at the Ritz-Carlton, a venerable English hotel with a
board that includes Brian Mulroney.

At the same time, he was one of the most important people
behind the scenes in the Conservative party in Quebec, holding
a succession of executive positions and working tirelessly to
breathe new life into an organization whose fortunes had deter-
iorated still further now that the Liberals were led by Pierre Elliott
Trudeau (these activities are the subject of the next chapter). He

also joined the Mount Royal Tennis Club — more of which later. However, one labour negotiator who sat across the table from Mulroney says he never lost the common touch: "He didn't behave like someone who thinks he's great. But he wasn't down on his knees either. A lot of management lawyers behave like they've got a guilt complex or something — very defensive. Never Brian Mulroney. He'd mix it like a union strike leader. He respects you, but he's very tough."

In 1971 a series of lockouts at the largest French-language newspaper in Canada grew into Quebec's most explosive labour conflict in years. As with the waterfront dispute, technological change triggered what became known as the *"La Presse* affair." In this case, however, a host of other issues soon became involved — especially control of information and the effects of corporate power on society. The initial dispute involved *La Presse*'s plan to introduce a new computerized printing process, threatening the jobs of many of its production workers. The newspaper adopted a tough bargaining strategy, locking out its pressmen, stereotypers, photo-engravers and typographers. Eventually, the conflict spread to *La Presse*'s journalists, who attacked the paper's news policies and demanded greater control over its content.

Before the *La Presse* affair, Quebec's major trade union centrals — the Quebec Federation of Labour (QFL), representing the Quebec affiliates of Canadian and international unions, the home-grown Confederation of National Trade Unions, and the province's largest teachers' union, the CEQ — had devoted much of their energy to squabbling with one another. They had also, with the exception of sections of the CNTU, remained faithful to the North American conception of a trade union and kept their distance from politics, and especially the radical, extraparliamentary politics that became a major feature of Quebec life in the late 1960s. Now, however, in response to what they regarded as provocative tactics on the part of the *La Presse* management and its political allies, the rival unions displayed a new spirit of solidarity. In addition, union leaders who had previously been known as moderates and had been regarded as sellouts by Quebec's radical movement now called for the overthrow of capitalism and re-emerged as radical heroes. The feisty QFL president, Louis Laberge, symbolized the transformation. For a time it appeared that a united opposition movement capable of issuing a serious challenge to Quebec's existing political and economic order might develop.

One of the reasons *La Presse* was such a powerful symbol for Quebec's radicals and labour leaders was that it had since 1967 been one of the numerous holdings of Paul Desmarais, the corporate empire-builder whose domain had been expanding at what some considered a disturbing rate. Desmarais had acquired a cash-rich holding company, Power Corporation of Canada, in 1968, and the companies under his umbrella included the Voyageur bus line, Canada Steamship Lines, the Consolidated-Bathurst paper company, and the Great-West Life and Imperial Life insurance companies.

What had attracted the most public attention, however, was the commanding position Desmarais had attained in the field of information. He had gained control of four of Quebec's eight French-language daily newspapers (*La Presse*, *La Tribune* of Sherbrooke, *Le Nouvelliste* of Trois-Rivières and *La Voix de l'Est* of Granby), seventeen weeklies (including the three largest weeklies in the Montreal area), and ten radio and television stations (including Montreal's CKAC, the largest French-language radio station in Canada). These acquisitions raised the spectre of a virtual information monopoly during a very tense period in Quebec. Desmarais's critics regarded his approach to newspaper publishing as being excessively oriented towards the bottom line. And his close relations with politicians, and especially with the Liberals then in office in both Ottawa and Quebec City, were a further source of resentment. Thus, even though Desmarais was one of the few French Canadians to make it in the corporate big leagues, he became a major target of a wide-ranging opposition movement in French Canada, one based on lines more of class and politics than of language. An attempt by *La Presse* to blame the conflict on "American unions" backfired.

In late October and early November, the *La Presse* affair escalated dramatically. The unions called a mass demonstration to show their solidarity with the locked-out workers. The newspaper, which had been publishing despite the lockouts, abruptly closed down, and tight security was instituted at its downtown building. The company issued hints of impending violence. Montreal Mayor Jean Drapeau invoked his anti-demonstration by-law, the validity of which was then before the courts. The demonstration took place anyway, and culminated in a bloody confrontation between marchers and police, resulting in the death of a young woman and hundreds of injuries. Four days later, the unions staged a huge rally in the Montreal Forum. Desmarais went on television to declare that he would not be pushed around by "Communists" even if the paper were to close permanently and he were to lose his entire $22 million investment.

Looking for a way out of the impasse, Desmarais turned to the law firm of his long-time legal adviser, Jack Porteous, and engaged the services of the rising young labour lawyer, Brian Mulroney.

"He defused a very tense situation," Claude Beauchamp, then president of the journalists' union at *La Presse*, told Robert McKenzie. "He came in, talked to everybody, sized up the situation and then, I suppose, reported to Desmarais. You've got to assume that Mulroney brought him around to a more realistic appraisal of the facts. Within three or four days, negotiations had resumed and we were on our way to a settlement."

La Presse finally resumed publication in early February of 1972. Management retained the right to introduce technological changes, but some financial concessions were made to the unions. And while the journalists did not gain the veto power over appointment of the managing editor that they had sought, the company did agree to consult their union in appointing the managing editor and editor-in-chief. The unions held another march, with placards reading VICTORY and WE'RE RETURNING WITH OUR HEADS HELD HIGH. The new union alliance generated by the *La Presse* affair turned its attention to the provincial government and staged a common front strike in the public sector in April and May. Provincial anti-strike legislation and the jailing of Laberge and other trade union leaders at first provoked widespread resistance, but finally succeeded in breaking the strike. The spirit of revolt that had been in the air for six months ebbed. The union centrals resumed their squabbling, and the CNTU faced an internal split.

And Paul Desmarais was sufficiently pleased with the work of the labour lawyer who had helped him settle the *La Presse* conflict that he became a key backer of Brian Mulroney's political ambitions. He is often named as having contributed generously to Mulroney's 1976 leadership campaign and as having been one of his principal supporters in 1983.

In the early 1970s, Mulroney also helped settle a long and bitter strike at the 7-Up bottling plant in the suburban Town of Mount Royal. But his clients weren't all management. Tom McPhail, now director of communications studies at the University of Calgary and a media adviser to Mulroney, met him in Montreal during his years as a labour lawyer:

> I was teaching at Loyola [College], and they were getting set to get university status and decided to use the occasion to rid themselves of some teachers. I think they fired about thirty. A defence committee was established and somebody mentioned a hot-shot lawyer from Ogilvy. A few of us were skeptical, but anyway, Brian came down and said he could handle these Jesuits, and you know he got most of the teachers reinstated. That was the first time I met Brian Mulroney, but we've been friends ever since, and we've kept in touch.

In the spring of 1972, Mulroney was vacationing in Spain with Michel Cogger, who by then was also practising law in Montreal; the two friends were planning to go over to Morocco when Mulroney was called back to Montreal to deal with the latest waterfront strike. He was, at that time, also involved in the delicate negotiations that led to Judge Claude Wagner's decision to run as a Conservative candidate in the next federal election

— a move Mulroney would later have cause to regret. And that summer, he spent a great deal of time at the Mount Royal Tennis Club.

Although Mulroney was and is an avid tennis player, the main attraction at the club was Mila Pivnicki, then an eighteen-year-old engineering student at Sir George Williams (known as Concordia University after 1974). The Pivnicki family came to Montreal from Yugoslavia when Mila was five years old. At first, the family lived in a modest apartment above Pines Pizza, a student hangout on Pine Avenue near McGill University. But like Ben and Irene Mulroney, the Pivnickis (Mila's father is head of psychiatry at the McGill-affiliated Royal Victoria Hospital) attached great importance to their children's education, and sent Mila to a fashionable private girls' school in Westmount, Miss Edgar's and Miss Cramp's.

The story is told that Brian saw Mila on the tennis courts, introduced himself to her and asked for a date. Mila denies this and says that "we were introduced properly through a mutual friend." In any case, the thirty-three-year-old lawyer and the teenaged student began to date. She says she didn't know of him before they met, and then thought he was interesting but too old for her. Brian was also concerned about the age difference: "I didn't tell many people because Mila was rather young and I had a reputation, well, as a ladies' man." The age difference — there was a similar age difference both between Ben and Irene Mulroney and between the older Pivnickis — did not long stand in their way as they found other things in common. Mila was also something of a political junkie, and a Conservative one at that. During the 1972 election campaign, she worked as a volunteer in Michael Meighen's unsuccessful effort to unseat Treasury Board President Bud Drury in Westmount. Mila was also very poised, sophisticated, and mature not only beyond her years but also, in a sense, beyond Brian's. Mulroney says of Mila simply: "She civilized me."

Meanwhile, Michel Cogger returned to Canada just in time to travel with Robert Stanfield in the 1972 federal election campaign, and met his future wife on the Stanfield plane. "After the campaign," he says, "I invited Bones [Brian] over to my place for a drink. 'I have a surprise for you.' 'Well, I have one for you also.' He brought Mila over, and I introduced them both to my future wife, Ericka." Brian and Mila were married in 1973.

In 1974 the labour and political situation in Quebec and Brian Mulroney's career simultaneously took another major turn. This new development originated with an incident at the far-off LG-2 construction site, part of the massive James Bay hydro-electric project. As conceived by Quebec Premier Robert Bourassa, James Bay was intended to do more than just meet Quebec's electricity needs. In the words of a subsequent Science Council of Canada report, Bourassa and his government regarded it as "a project that could in some way galvanize the enthusiasm of the Quebec collectivity" at a time when the province was economically stagnant and politically volatile, just as the Manicouagan project on the North Shore had in the 1960s. Bourassa described it as the "project of the century," and the 1971 Liberal party rally in Quebec City at which it was officially announced was highlighted by a film in which the gathering was told that "the world begins today."

In its early stages, however, James Bay seemed to have an effect that was precisely opposite to the one Bourassa intended. The project was the object of a major power struggle within the government between the premier and his supporters on the one hand and the powerful publicly owned utility, Hydro-Quebec, on the other. The mounting cost of the project (nobody knew just how many billions the final figure would be) and the decision to award the main management contract to a San Francisco–based multinational engineering firm, Bechtel, generated public criticism. Cree and Inuit who lived in the James Bay area and saw their way of life threatened by the project tried to stop it and succeeded in convincing an independent-minded Superior Court judge named Albert Malouf of the merits of their case.

Malouf (who now sits on the Quebec Court of Appeal) issued an injunction in the fall of 1973 ordering a halt to the project; the injunction was reversed on appeal, but it necessitated a costly settlement with the native peoples.

Most serious of all, however, was the labour violence that broke out at LG-2 in early 1974. Tension at the site had been running high both between labour and management (exacerbated by a widely publicized statement by a Bechtel administrator that "you Canadians know fuck all") and between the rival construction unions of the QFL and the CNTU. In part, the tension was a product of the living and working conditions that are universal at isolated northern construction sites. In part, it was fed by the workers' grievances, related to the condescending attitude of Bechtel's American administrators. But the explosion at James Bay was also part of a complicated power play in which the QFL and CNTU construction unions, the construction contractors, elements of the underworld, and the provincial government were all involved in one way or another.

After the period of demoralization that followed the provincial government's breaking of the Common Front strike in 1972, the Quebec labour movement had recovered much of its militancy but not the unity of the 1971–72 period. Hostility between the CNTU and the QFL was especially intense in the construction industry, an industry that had a number of common features with the longshore trades that had occupied so much of Brian Mulroney's attention as a lawyer: employment was sporadic, job security unknown, and the employers fragmented and often financially precarious. In construction as on the waterfront, union muscle had arisen as a rudimentary instrument of order in an otherwise chaotic situation.

The 1973 QFL convention was held on the theme of "*le combat inevitable* [the inevitable struggle]" to be waged against multinational corporations and their servants in the political, economic and judicial systems of Quebec. The same convention passed a resolution allowing unions to break away from their international parents and affiliate directly with the QFL. Construction unions were among the first to take advantage of the new provision. While this softened the "American" face of the QFL unions and thus was regarded as a victory for nationalists and progressives and a concession to the rival CNTU, it also helped concentrate more authority in the hands of growth-minded QFL officials.

The chief agents of the QFL's monopoly drive were shop stewards at the major construction sites around Quebec. These officials were appointed by central union authorities rather than elected by workers at the sites, and some of the appointments were highly dubious and suggestive of the shop stewards' real function. One shop steward on a contract held by Bot Construction at James Bay had recently served five years in jail for his part in one of Montreal's most celebrated foiled bank robberies. He was dispatched with a message that "Christmas time is right around the corner" if the Bot firm cooperated with the QFL. Most construction firms, wanting to complete their contracts as quickly as possible, having only a short-term relationship with their employees and placing a high value on avoiding labour troubles, found it in their interests to go along.

As the largest construction site in Quebec, James Bay naturally became the major focus of the activities of certain QFL organizers, and it was at James Bay that the incident that would bring these activities to public attention occurred. On March 21, 1974, Yvon Duhamel, business agent for a QFL union local, got into a bulldozer and ploughed into the construction camp's three electrical generators. A small group of men ruptured two huge fuel storage tanks and set fire to a large part of the camp. The riot forced the evacuation of the site and a delay of several months in the project.

The CNTU blamed corruption in the QFL, which in its quest for a monopoly had already obtained a large majority of the jobs at James Bay, and intimidation tactics used by its officials for the violence. Premier Bourassa responded by establishing an inquiry commission with sweeping powers to investigate the "exercise of union freedom in the construction industry," and he appointed Judge Robert Cliche, onetime Laval University law professor and former leader of the Quebec wing of the New Democratic Party, to head it.

Despite his NDP background, Cliche (who died in 1978) was a respected non-partisan figure. The other two members of the commission were to represent labour and management respectively. Guy Chevrette, then vice-president of the CEQ (teachers' union) and a Parti Québécois activist (he is now minister of recreation, fish and game in the Lévesque government), was named as labour representative. For management, Cliche chose a former student of his at Laval who had become one of Quebec's top labour negotiators on the corporate side, Brian Mulroney. As had been the case on the waterfront, Mulroney's effectiveness on the Cliche Commission would depend on his ability to serve more than his clients. Although a noted management lawyer and the management representative on the commission, he also had to be part of the solution to a problem that was created in part by the actions of management. He was a member of a team that had to be seen as impartial.

The Cliche Commission was formed on May 3, 1974, and presented its report exactly one year later. Its inquiry turned out to be a more wide-ranging one than anybody anticipated — especially Premier Bourassa. As the commission investigated the labour situation in the construction trades, the web of corruption it unravelled extended beyond inter-union rivalry, beyond the labour movement, even beyond the construction industry, and led into the offices of provincial Liberal cabinet ministers. Through months of public hearings in late 1974 and early 1975 and the testimony of almost three hundred witnesses, a spectacular story of violence, intimidation, loan-sharking, government corruption, payoffs by companies to avoid strikes, and almost every form of criminal activity emerged before fascinated television watchers and newspaper readers. The *Financial Post* called the commission's sessions "the best show in town" and compared them to the U.S. Senate Watergate hearings. The Cliche Commission's witnesses included some of Quebec's top labour leaders, government officials and several cabinet ministers, and the commission stopped just short of calling Premier Bourassa himself.

A former Bourassa advisor (who had left the premier's employ by the time the Cliche Commission began its work) was found to have discussed a QFL union monopoly at James Bay with a QFL official the same day the union man offered to help the Liberal cause in a by-election. An executive assistant to Bourassa's first labour minister, Pierre Laporte (kidnapped and killed by the Front de Libération du Québec during the 1970 October Crisis), was found to have taken a $2,000 payment to ensure an appointment to the Quebec Minimum Wage Commission. Revelations about lesser figures at the commission's hearings were so damaging that a number of union officials and members of the government-sponsored Construction Industry Commission resigned before the Cliche Commission even issued its report.

Mulroney played a large role in the hearings, and overnight emerged from obscurity to become a public figure in Quebec. As the management representative on the commission, Mulroney came under attack by many trade union leaders. He was accused of manoeuvring the commission into concentrating on labour wrongdoing while merely lobbing softballs at management. And a federal Liberal MP against whom suspicions were raised at the hearings accused Mulroney of acting out of Tory partisanship. But Judge Cliche was quick to defend his colleague's integrity, and the MP had to retract his allegation. In the end, the work and findings of the commission were accepted among the public. While the respect gained by the crusading Judge Cliche was largely responsible for this, it was also significant that there was little evidence to support a charge of bias against either of the other two commissioners.

Mulroney's work on the commission also provided an occasion for a glimpse at some of his personality traits and certain aspects of his pragmatic outlook. In one incident, Michel Chartrand, Quebec's aging *enfant terrible* and president of the CNTU's Montreal Council, accused Mulroney of "going easy" on Robert Boyd, president of the James Bay Energy Corporation. Mulroney, who for all his agility has never quite figured out how to turn the other cheek, shot back that "the members of the CNTU who pay Mr. Chartrand's fat salary and expense account should take care of him." Chartrand was making less than $14,000 at the time.

In the course of its investigations, the commission began to rely heavily on telephone taps and other forms of covert evidence gathering. Mulroney later claimed that the commission was reluctant to resort to these covert methods but they were being lied to and such methods were the only ways to "confront the perjurers with the clear evidence of their crimes."

A similar pragmatism in the area of civil rights was manifested in the commission's controversial recommendation 53, which Mulroney is believed to have written. This clause — which like many of the commission's other recommendations was enacted into law — called for a presumption of guilt in the case of any employer accused of discriminating against workers on the basis of which union they belonged to and any union member or official accused of organizing illegal strikes or work slowdowns. Mulroney defended this measure as necessary to establish the rule of law in an industry that was in "anarchy."

The commission's other recommendations included placing four union locals in trusteeship, the reorganization of the Construction Industry Commission and the establishment of a strong central authority on the management side, somewhat along the lines of the Maritime Employers' Association.

If sections of the trade union movement were critical of Brian Mulroney's work on the commission, he was clearly the darling of the media. He was definitely the most available commissioner, and some people suggest that during the days of the Cliche Commission, Brian Mulroney learned to play the press like a virtuoso. Who played whom is now moot. Mulroney's love affair with the Quebec press had moments of intense passion, degenerated into stormy recriminations and then settled down, as these things usually do, to a weary coexistence, a state that is also being reached with the national media.

By the time the Cliche Commission submitted its report, the atmosphere surrounding the James Bay project had changed. In the era of oil price escalation and growing doubts about nuclear power, a big hydroelectric development, even at a relatively high cost, increasingly seemed like a good idea. A clear consensus in favour of the project finally developed in Quebec, even if it never generated the enthusiasm Bourassa had hoped for. The budget eventually plateaued in the neighbourhood of $15 billion, and despite the delay caused by the 1974 riot, LG-2 ultimately opened ahead of schedule. All this, however, happened too late for Robert Bourassa. The evidence of corruption uncovered by the Cliche Commission, along with other revelations that emerged around the same time, surrounded his government with an aura of scandal that led to his stunning election defeat at the hands of the Parti Québécois in 1976.

The conclusion of the Cliche Commission's work left Brian Mulroney at a crossroads. He had been away from the law firm a full year. The challenge had largely gone out of the waterfront labour situation, which after one last strike was about to settle into something approaching routine. One opportunity arose in the form of an offer from his old patron William Bennett, president of the Iron Ore Company of Canada, to become executive vice-president of the corporation. Bennett was nearing retirement age and Mulroney would be next in line.

However, in late summer 1975, another possibility appeared. Mulroney began to think seriously about his prospects as a candidate to succeed Robert Stanfield as leader of the Progressive Conservative Party of Canada. Mulroney had been active behind the scenes as a Tory throughout his decade as a labour lawyer: he had raised money, been a strategist in three election campaigns and helped bring Claude Wagner into the party. The Cliche Commission had gained him a certain public reputation. And becoming Tory leader had, of course, been his ambition since he was a teenager.

But it was not at all obvious that this was the best time for Mulroney to pursue this ambition, for it is somewhat out of the ordinary for a thirty-six-year-old man who has never been elected to anything and is virtually unknown in the country at large to be considered for the leadership of a major political party. To understand why a cool-headed tactician such as Mulroney would have thought he had a shot at it — and although he ultimately was not elected leader in 1976, it was not an unreasonable estimate of the situation — it is necessary to examine the evolution of the Progressive Conservative party under Robert Stanfield, and especially its singular relationship with the province of Quebec.

CHAPTER FIVE

The Search for a Winner

Organizing the removal of John Diefenbaker from the leadership of the Progressive Conservative party was a long, messy war of attrition that began in 1963 and didn't really end in 1967 with his actual replacement by Robert Stanfield. Indeed, it could be argued that the end of the Diefenbaker era of the party was not signalled until the election of Brian Mulroney in 1983, some twenty years after the first caucus "termites," as Diefenbaker called them, began to undermine the Chief.

The issue went far beyond the person of John Diefenbaker, although the first ten years of the struggle could be so personalized. The problem for the party was to remake itself in the context of the politics of a new Canada. This new Canada was highly urbanized, it teemed with millions of postwar immigrants, particularly from eastern and southern Europe, and above all, its politics was increasingly characterized by a set of issues that were conveniently gathered under the rubric of Quebec's Quiet Revolution and the response of the rest of Canada to this revolution. These issues were expressed in such code words as "special status" and "two nations" on the one hand and "unhyphenated Canadians" and "royal symbols" on the other, and illuminated by emotional debates over a "distinctive national flag" and the patriotic merits of various anthems.

Moreover, the remaking of the party had to be accomplished in public, in the full glare of television, so that political questions, no matter how neatly disguised, were not the only ones involved. The process also entailed the creation of a new image for the party. It required a break with the tarnished past of the unfortunate Diefenbaker cabinets, and a new leader who could be shown to be both experienced in government and a successful administrator. This new leader had to appear open to new ideas (this was the decade of studies and thinkers' conferences), yet steady and reliable. Above all, he had to be someone who was never associated with the Diefenbaker government.

The task was complicated by the image and personality of John Diefenbaker, who, particularly in western Canada, was seen as a man of the people. In this view, Diefenbaker was a populist leader who had ripped the party out of the hands of the Bay Street oligarchs, the imagined successors of R. B. Bennett and his friends who had brought us the Great Depression. He had gone on to achieve a massive voter mandate, only to have it destroyed by the unreconstructed establishment, aided by uncomprehending Quebecers and, many thought (not without evidence), by what would today be described as an organized destabilizing effort directed from the United States.

Inside the Conservative party, the anti-Diefenbaker element saw themselves as "progressives," and their goal, at least in the beginning, was not so much ousting Diefenbaker as changing the face of the party. First and foremost, this meant creating a responsiveness within the party to the demands of the new Quebec. As a Tory student leader at Laval, Brian Mulroney was one of the "progressives" (as was his contemporary in Alberta, Joe Clark, and the whole generation of party activists who were to mature and become prominent and eventually position themselves to take over the party during the Stanfield years). By the time the movement to endow the party with a new leader had crystallized, Mulroney was a young labour lawyer in Montreal handling his first important cases. At the same time, his influence in Tory circles was beginning to grow, and he was appointed to the party's policy committee and the finance committee of the Quebec party.

Since the core political issue was Quebec and the developing constitutional crisis, Mulroney was particularly attuned to the need for a political change inside the party. His sensitivity to this issue was a product of the political and social milieu in which he grew up and was expressed in such activities as his involvement with the Laval Congress on Canadian Affairs. He could also read the voting pattern in Quebec, where the party progressed from a disaster in 1953 to a larger vote than the Liberals in 1958, but by 1963 was back to its level of ten years earlier. In addition, he felt that in the wake of the inconclusive elections and the intraparty bickering, something had to be done about the party leadership, if only to clear the air. His personal relationship with Diefenbaker turned sour as the struggle for a leadership review grew intense, and he had other friends and other loyalties in the party, especially to Davie Fulton, whom Diefenbaker could not abide.

In his book on the politics of this era, *The Distemper of Our Times*, Peter C. Newman wrote about an annual meeting of the Quebec Progressive Conservative Association in Quebec City. James Johnston, Diefenbaker's national director of the party, was in attendance and organized a group of pro-Diefenbaker delegates to leave the meeting to swell the crowd at the airport for the arriving Chief:

> Johnston took aside some of the party's Young Turks who seemed to be running the session and told them patronizingly that they should keep the meeting discussing non-controversial matters until he returned with the Chief. Unfortunately for Johnston, the three young Tories he chose, Michael Meighen . . . Brian Mulroney . . . and Peter White . . . , were young in years but not in political experience. White had previously arranged for Diefenbaker to be driven from the airport to the provincial legislature for a courtesy call on the Quebec premier. This — plus the fact that most of Diefenbaker's supporters were at the airport —

gave the young Tories and their friends enough time to rush back into the meeting and ram through a series of resolutions calling for the federal leadership to be reviewed every four years, starting in 1967.

The problem was to find a credible new leader. Party President Dalton Camp, who was doing most of the thinking for the Tories in those days, hit upon two provincial premiers, Duff Roblin in Manitoba and Robert Stanfield down in Nova Scotia. Roblin dithered too long, and Stanfield was conscripted. Stanfield was both a successful premier of Nova Scotia and a Diefenbaker loyalist through the early Sixties. Whatever his personal doubts about Diefenbaker, Stanfield kept them to himself. In the federal election campaign of 1965, Stanfield's intervention in Nova Scotia was crucial. He stumped the province with Diefenbaker, and the three Nova Scotia seats the Tories gained from the Liberals were just enough to prevent Lester Pearson from forming a majority government. Moreover, when Diefenbaker's leadership was challenged at a party executive meeting in 1965 by Léon Balcer and the Quebec wing of the party, the Nova Scotia group, at Stanfield's urging, supported the leader.

On matters of political substance, however, Robert Stanfield had already made his break with Diefenbaker. In a speech to the Canadian Club of Montreal in 1964, he said:

> I realize some Canadians, perhaps many Canadians, feel we should have only one culture in Canada, a Canadian culture. I suppose they really have in mind a common culture with English as the common language. Any such concept is abhorrent to a French-speaking Canadian. There is surely no reason why we cannot have two languages and two cultures existing side by side and yet have an effective nationhood.

Stanfield went on to agree with the Liberals that Canada should have a distinctive national flag and anthem. He even endorsed Lester Pearson's ideal of a bilingual civil service: ''English Canadians ought surely to be prepared to accept measures that the federal government considers necessary to assure equality of opportunity for French Canadians in the federal service.'' In 1965 Stanfield denied any federal ambitions. He said he had considered federal politics ''in much the same way as I have considered ski-jumping.'' However, by the time the Camp wing of the party was able to force a leadership convention, Stanfield had been convinced to put on his ski boots.

In the process leading up to the leadership convention, a Tory thinkers' conference was held in Montmorency Falls, just outside of Quebec City. The conference was both a serious examination of policy options and an exercise in public relations to demonstrate the openness of the party to new ideas and showcase some of the new talent that was being attracted to the party. One of the conference's proposals was the statement that ''Canada is composed of the original inhabitants of this land and the two founding peoples (*deux nations*) with historic rights, who have been, and continue to be joined by people from many lands.''

''*Deux nations*'' reminded John Diefenbaker of Berlin Walls and Checkpoint Charlies, and he used this issue to contest the leadership. However, he was defeated by the third ballot, and the issue was squelched by William Davis, who saw to it that the whole thing was tabled. The statement was never even debated at the convention, and whenever it arose, it was simply dismissed as a problem of translation. The *deux nations* formulation had been dealt with for the moment, but it turned out to be a delayed-action land mine.

Meanwhile, Brian Mulroney was active in the leadership campaign of Davie Fulton, who was one of the first prominent Tories to express his distaste for the Diefenbaker leadership and also one of the first to signal his interest in being the Chief's successor. Mulroney was close to Fulton at the time, and even before the former justice minister actually declared his candidacy, Mulroney urged his friend Michel Cogger to move from Quebec City to Ottawa to become Fulton's executive assistant, in preparation for the eventual campaign. Mulroney had already committed himself to Fulton by the time Stanfield decided to contest the leadership. And he remained with his candidate until it became apparent that Fulton had lost. Mulroney then helped convince Fulton to join with Stanfield and, having done that, jumped back into the fray festooned with Stanfield buttons and badges.

Canada was well into the era of television, and Canadian television audiences had already enjoyed a few ding-a-ling American political conventions. Thus, television was a key element in the plans of those Tories who believed that their problems could be solved by electing Robert Stanfield leader. The hoopla and pizazz just needed money and choreography. Stanfield could be packaged and provided with a national image overnight. That worked distressingly well, as the first image of Stanfield most Canadians saw was that of a gaunt, phlegmatic individual eating a banana — and that was the image that remained.

Nevertheless, despite these untidy elements, in the space of a few weeks Robert Stanfield became a national figure and the likely next prime minister of Canada. To this day, nobody can recall what he said or did during the leadership campaign. As far as most Canadians were aware, Stanfield just stood there and let the organization do its work — for the new breed of political technician, it looked easy. The 1967 leadership convention was what is called ''a terrific learning experience'' for Brian Mulroney and his young political associates. They were in at the beginning of the modern political convention in Canada. And they developed an early appreciation of the technology and tactics of organization and packaging in the new era.

Reflecting back on that whole period in the party's history, Mulroney blames John Diefenbaker for turning it into such a bitter and personal struggle. One had to be either for him or against him. It was, he says, ''a sad and tragic period for the party. And one of the most tragic aftermaths of the affair was that a most decent man and brilliant politician, Dalton Camp, became a pariah in his own party.''

When Stanfield was elected leader of the party, the Pearson government was so tattered and torn that its position in the public

opinion surveys was approximately the same as that of the Trudeau government fifteen years later when Mulroney became leader.
The public seemed to like Stanfield, and he had momentum when
he entered Parliament in a by-election that the Liberals didn't
contest. The first sign of trouble brewing appeared when John
Diefenbaker failed to do the new leader and member the courtesy
of introducing him to the Speaker. As the session wore on, Diefenbaker's seat in the Tory front benches was usually empty, and
it stood as a storm warning while Stanfield plodded through his
initial days as leader being civil, decent and generally ineffective
in the House.

After Lester Pearson had announced his retirement and while
his would-be successors were out and about scrambling for delegate votes, the Conservatives caught the Liberals in a surprise
vote of no-confidence and the government was defeated in the
House. Stanfield could have forced an election then and there,
and with the Tories still riding high and the Liberals with a lame-
duck leader, he could probably have won. But Stanfield was talked
out of it, mainly through the intervention of Louis Rasminsky,
then governor of the Bank of Canada, who convinced the Tory
leader that an immediate election campaign would greatly harm
the stability of the Canadian dollar, then under severe pressure.
Stanfield bit, and allowed the Liberals to wriggle out of the vote,
to the open anguish of John Diefenbaker and the displeasure of
the Tory caucus, many of whose members remained loyal to the
Chief and resented the new leader in any case.

But Stanfield's troubles were just beginning.

The Tories had a new "high-profile, credible Quebec public
leader" who was going to be the answer to their problems in
French Canada. His name was Marcel Faribault, a prominent
Quebec businessman and financier who for the past number of
years had been expressing a desire to get into politics if certain
conditions, both political and financial, could be met. He had
approached John Diefenbaker once with an offer to join the Tories
if he was named deputy prime minister and provided with a substantial sum of money. This turned out to be an offer that the

Chief could quite easily refuse. Now, with new federal Tory leadership, Faribault was cast as Stanfield's Quebec lieutenant, in the tradition of Sir George Étienne Cartier, who had held Quebec for the Tories at the time of Confederation.

Meanwhile, Pierre Trudeau emerged as leader of the Liberal party, and his political baggage included more than just a personality in which many Canadians, riding high in the immediate aftermath of the Centennial and Expo 67, saw a mirror image of themselves. Trudeau was also a staunch federalist who had absolutely no time for any Quebec nationalist talk about *deux nations*. In the 1968 election campaign, Trudeau and John Diefenbaker both made sure Canadians did not forget about the "two founding peoples — *deux nations*" proposal thought up at the Montmorency thinkers' conference the year before. The ill-starred formulation would not go away, and neither, for the unfortunate Tories, would Marcel Faribault. Diefenbaker shot at Stanfield from one side, Trudeau shot from another, and Faribault, who began talking about the right of Quebec to determine its own future by itself, shot him in the feet. Stanfield, never adroit when under attack to begin with, was on the defensive. There were other problems too. While Trudeau spoke of an exciting future, Stanfield evoked a lost past. The Tory leader's rallies opened with bagpipes and renditions of "Pack Up Your Troubles in Your Old Kit Bag." Trudeau rallies had rock music and flowers strewn at the leader's feet by what were then known as teeny-boppers.

The 1968 general election was a disaster for the Tories, and nowhere more so than in Quebec, where Brian Mulroney was assistant to the chairman of the campaign committee. On election night, before the results came in, Stanfield spoke by phone with Mulroney about how the campaign had gone in Quebec. Michel Cogger, who was working at party headquarters in Ottawa, remembers that "he had to kind of give Stanfield an optimistic forecast. 'I can't see us getting less than twelve seats in Quebec,' he said." When the results were in, they had four. Election deposits, the heady prospects of 1967, and Marcel Faribault all disappeared together.

The day after the election, Mulroney and Cogger went to their favourite vacation spot at the time, the Massachusetts resort island of Nantucket. "I was really just a minor player," Cogger says. "It wasn't psychologically shattering for me. I really didn't know Stanfield, but for some of the others . . . " After their vacation, Mulroney went back to work at his law practice and at behind-the-scenes Tory politics, while Cogger remained for a time at party headquarters in Ottawa as the link with Quebec. Cogger also learned the ins and outs of the party machinery — payroll, budgets and who was who. While he was in Ottawa, Cogger got to know two other young Tories who were working in Stanfield's office at the time — Lowell Murray, a friend of Mulroney's from St. FX days, and Joe Clark from Alberta. The three for a time shared a classy apartment in the Rideau Terrace. "Brian was my close, close friend," Cogger says. "Living with the other two, well we had a good relationship, but it was sort of strange. I felt more empathy with Brian. Politics is one thing — I respected Joe Clark's political sense — but let me put it this way: when it comes to renting a winter cottage for weekends, Brian is a lot more interesting."

After the election defeat in 1968, Robert Stanfield went doggedly about the task of trying to rebuild the party federally. Reflecting later on the outcome of the election, Stanfield ruefully observed that the party "even lost the bigot vote." Worse, a number of the Tory brighter lights, including Dalton Camp, went down to defeat while many of the old Diefenbaker stalwarts survived. Surrounded by a hostile caucus, Stanfield told his friend Senator Grattan O'Leary that it was his misfortune in 1968 that all the "bonks" got elected while all the good members were defeated. The party seemed to have problems everywhere, but nowhere were these problems more manifest than in Quebec, where it had been swept from sight. In two federal by-elections held in the wake of the 1970 FLQ kidnappings, the murder of Pierre Laporte and the invocation of the War Measures Act, the Tories lost their deposits.

Brian Mulroney worked tirelessly for the party in Quebec. But although he was gaining a reputation inside federal Tory circles and power among the small band of Tory faithful in Quebec, as far as the public was concerned, he was nowhere. His mission to bring the Tories out of the wilderness in Quebec was a difficult one, and part of the problem was that the federal Liberal party cast a wide net in the province. It seemed to have room for virtually every political tendency except the independence option represented by the Parti Québécois — and even some Péquistes supported the Liberals on the federal level, reasoning that despite the Liberals' intransigence towards anything smacking of Quebec nationalism — epitomized by their harsh response to the FLQ kidnappings of October 1970 — they were at least a party with deep roots in Quebec.

There were areas of rural Quebec that were resistant to the Liberals' appeal, but they were loyal to the Créditistes, not the Tories (the Liberals were to chip away at these areas through the 1970s, finally overrunning the last Créditiste bastions in the 1980 election). The traditional Tory constituency in Quebec had consisted of conservative French Canadian nationalists who still wanted to keep Quebec in Confederation — the people who provincially were the backbone of the Union Nationale. By 1970, however, the Union Nationale was visibly dying, and Mulroney and his colleagues were faced with the task of finding a credible successor to this constituency.

Thus, Mulroney organized a lot of meetings, chartered empty buses to go to empty meeting halls, called press events that went unreported, found suitable candidates for the election abattoirs, stroked bruised egos, raised money and then raised more. Through the years of frustration and decline, Mulroney had an opportunity to gain a good deal of experience in the practical affairs of running a political party organization. His formal campaign and committee positions expressed only part of his role, and he was in the thick of everything that happened Tory-wise in Quebec — he was in the trenches and he was at the command posts. His hand was in everything, but — as someone once described a former editor of the *New York Times* — "he rarely left his fingerprints."

A friend of Mulroney's suggests that he stayed with the Progressive Conservatives because of his friends and his loyalty. This is no doubt part of the explanation, and a general ideological affinity to conservative politics is another part. But perhaps a more significant reason for Mulroney's ever-deepening commitment to the party lies in his personal bent for activism and his joy at being at the centre of things. In addition, his first political efforts, back in his student days, had been crowned with success. He could, he thought, be successful once more. And there were enough near misses in the generally unfortunate leadership of Robert Stanfield to keep a pusher such as Brian Mulroney trying and trying again.

Much of Mulroney's attention was devoted to planning for the federal election expected sometime in 1972. Mulroney would be one of the key Quebec organizers for the election and vice-chairman of the campaign committee in the province. As early as the summer of 1971, he met with Graham Scott, then Stanfield's executive assistant, and Michel Cogger to discuss prospects in Quebec and to find a "star" candidate for the election. They considered a number of people, one of whom was Claude Wagner.

Joseph-Napoléon Claude Wagner was, at the time, a very popular figure in Quebec. He had earned an early reputation as a hard-nosed fighting prosecutor, and in 1963, at the age of thirty-eight, he was named the youngest sessions court judge in the province's history. And he was a tough one. In one of his first cases he sentenced a man to ten years for a holdup that netted $1.90. In 1964 Liberal Premier Jean Lesage offered him a position in the cabinet as solicitor general. He was soon promoted to attorney general and then named the province's first justice minister. Through this series of rapid promotions, the crew-cut Wagner, with his flamboyant public style, attracted considerable media attention. It was his wont to make charges about the power of organized crime, claiming he and he alone would break this power while working "to instill in our province a new conception of justice."

The Quebec Liberal government was replaced by the Union Nationale in 1966, and Wagner was banished to the relative obscurity of the opposition benches. By 1969 Wagner had had enough of obscurity and began a campaign for the leadership of the provincial Liberal party. This seemed a little pushy to the party's establishment, since the Liberals already had a leader who had expressed no intention of stepping down. But Wagner forced the issue and Lesage was pressured out.

Wagner appeared to have the ensuing Liberal leadership race all sewn up. He had a clear majority of the elected delegates, but he also had a number of powerful enemies. Pierre Trudeau and his chief Quebec allies in the cabinet, Jean Marchand and Gérard Pelletier, liked Claude Wagner not at all. Indeed, while Pelletier was still a journalist, he had described Wagner as a prejudiced, hidebound conservative who demonstrated, with disconcerting enthusiasm, the limits of his own horizons. In spite of Wagner's large lead among the elected delegates, the party establishment found room for 1,000 ex officio delegates at the convention. And these delegates voted for, and elected, the hitherto obscure Liberal finance critic, Robert Bourassa.

Wagner was angry at his loss and had to be literally dragged onstage by his friend Bryce Mackasey to accept his defeat. He was soon reappointed to the bench by Union Nationale Premier Jean-Jacques Bertrand, who was about to lose an election to Bourassa. But by 1971 Claude Wagner was looking around for a way to return to politics. He was being wooed as a prospective leader of both the Union Nationale and the Créditistes. He was also about to be given the Mulroney treatment.

Wagner, who by now had let his hair grow and appeared increasingly concerned with softening his public image, had a few meetings with Robert Stanfield, and the two men seemed to be getting along well. "I'm not a separatist," Wagner once said, "but I found his [Stanfield's] federalism flexible. . . . He sought to avoid the confrontation of the Trudeau style." And Brian

Mulroney was at his persuasive best. "I hate to think how much money I spend buying lunch for that guy," he laughed. It wasn't only politics that caused the wooing of Wagner to become a protracted affair. Wagner needed money and some form of security should things go wrong, as they are wont to do with the Tories and their Quebec stars.

In early 1972 Mulroney commissioned the American pollster Robert Teeter to do a survey on Wagner's popularity. It was a small but expensive poll, and the results seemed worthwhile, for they showed that Wagner was more popular in Quebec than the Man Himself — Pierre Elliot Trudeau. After the results of the poll were circulated among leading Conservatives, money was no object: Wagner had to be brought on board. At a meeting in a Montreal hotel in July, Wagner, Mulroney, national campaign committee chairman Finlay MacDonald and party fund-raiser Eddie Goodman worked out the details of a trust fund to be established for the judge — a not unusual practice in Canadian politics (the Liberals had provided both Louis Saint-Laurent and Lester Pearson with financial help). But even after this meeting, Wagner still hesitated. Finally Mulroney told him, "This bus only passes once. If you want to get on, this is the time." Wagner got on the bus, forty-eight hours before the 1972 election was called.

The Tory high command also insisted that this campaign be run differently from the Faribault disaster. Plenty of money would be devoted to Quebec, and everything would be done to stroke Wagner's prickly nature; but while Wagner was to be the first among all Quebec candidates, Stanfield was to be the leader and Wagner had to be a member of the team. And this time, there would be no communications screw-up. In 1968 Stanfield had appeared to say one thing at one end of the country while Faribault said the opposite at the other end, and this would not be allowed to happen again. With this in mind, the day Michel Cogger returned from his summer vacation in Europe, Mulroney invited him to dinner and explained his new job. Cogger would travel with Stanfield as a French presence, dealing with the French media, while Peter White would travel with Wagner as an English presence. "If we slip up," Mulroney told Cogger, "you guys get together and take care of it."

The Conservatives came close in 1972. The Liberals were forced into a minority government, only two seats ahead of the Tories, and everybody knew another election would come at any time. But in Quebec the party's situation had, if anything, gotten worse. Wagner got himself elected in the riding of Saint-Hyacinthe, and Heward Grafftey, who distanced himself from Wagner, got himself elected in Brome-Missisquoi. But that was the sum total of Tory seats in Quebec, and the Tory popular vote was even lower than in 1968. Wagner was not, at least in Mulroney's eyes, the solution. In fact, as things were developing in the party, Wagner was part of the problem.

After the 1972 election, Mulroney became the principal Tory wheelhorse in Quebec, along with Claude Nolan and Claude Dupras. He also became a married man in 1973, and a father a year later when his first child, Caroline, was born. And he was at the height of his reputation as a labour lawyer, having negotiated an end to the *La Presse* strike for Paul Desmarais and having helped work out what now appeared to be a viable solution to the chaos on the Montreal waterfront. At the same time, Michel Cogger was developing his own law practice, establishing himself as an expert in securities and making lots of money.

A swing to the left by the Liberals allowed the minority government to stay in office with NDP support through 1973, but a budget introduced in defiance of the NDP's conditions in the spring of 1974 ruptured the uneasy alliance and precipitated the expected electoral rematch. Now the Tories had their chance to finish the job they had started in 1972. Mulroney had just been appointed to the Cliche Commission and could not take on any formal campaign position, but he was active behind the scenes and persuaded Cogger to travel with Stanfield again. This time, however, the constitutional issue was in the background. Wagner was a candidate in Saint-Hyacinthe again, but not even the most optimistic Tory thought that his presence would bring about a breakthrough in Quebec. Instead, the party believed that it had an issue on which it could capture the country as a whole. Canada was facing double-digit inflation, and the Tories had a policy to deal with it: a wage and price freeze to be followed by controls.

This proved as inspired a campaign vehicle as *deux nations* had been in 1968. Trudeau succeeded in ridiculing the Conservatives' proposal: would Stanfield tell Arab oil producers, "Zap, you're frozen?" The hapless Tory leader was left to try to explain, or explain away, his party's policy. Stanfield also talked a lot about discipline and frugality, and that didn't help either. The election that was supposed to produce a Tory victory ended up returning the Liberals to a majority position (from which they implemented their own wage and price controls program a year later and proceeded to demonstrate that everything Trudeau had said about the idea during the campaign was true). In Quebec, Conservative strength rose from two seats to three, but only because Roch LaSalle, a Conservative who had contested the 1972 election as an independent, had by now returned to the Tory fold. The Liberals' Quebec campaign slogan, "C'est solide," said it all.

Having now lost three in a row, Stanfield offered his resignation to the first post-election meeting of the caucus. Even given the demoralization of a party losing an election it had expected to win, it could have been expected that Stanfield's resignation would be either not accepted or at least put aside to allow him to remain leader of the opposition throughout most of the new Parliament and then be replaced in an orderly leadership transition as the next election loomed. However, his resignation was accepted in relative silence. And the weakened opposition was made even weaker as various leadership hopefuls started jockeying for position and the bitterness that had surrounded the Diefenbaker debacle and the party's subsequent losses became the dominant spirit of the as yet undeclared campaign.

Brian Mulroney supported Robert Stanfield throughout his leadership, and when he heard of Stanfield's intention to resign, he got on the phone to try to convince him to stay on. However, it was soon clear that Stanfield's position was untenable. In the summer of 1975, after it became obvious that, ready or not, the leadership race was on, Brian Mulroney visited Michel Cogger at the latter's farm in the Eastern Townships. Cogger recalls:

> He brought his wife and kid, and we were sitting around as you do in the country. And he talked about the IOC [Iron Ore Company of Canada] job and the possibilities — he had an impressive offer. Then we went for a walk down a dirt road, into the woods. He said he was thirty-six and we talked about the leadership. He said he was interested. We had walked quite a way from the house, but Mila knew what we were talking about. Well, instead of commenting directly, I took the tack: what are the pros and cons, the considerations? We don't want to be insulted by ending up with a horrible showing — by looking stupid.

In 1967 the major candidates had all been either former cabinet ministers or provincial premiers — whatever their deficiencies, they had at least been able to claim a certain credibility based on political experience. This time around, however, the situation was different. The only potential candidate with national stature was Premier Peter Lougheed of Alberta, but his reputation as the blue-eyed Arab of Edmonton would be a serious liability in the East and his entry into the race was, in any case, by no means certain (in the event, Lougheed stayed out). Most of the other proto-candidates were MPs who had first been elected in the Tory near-miss of 1972. The most prominent of these were Flora MacDonald, the member for Kingston and the Islands who would attract a lot of support in the Ontario party, and Mulroney's Quebec recruit, Claude Wagner. There was also a host of minor contenders: Jim Gillies, John Fraser, Joe Clark, Sinclair Stevens and others.

"Look at the other players," Mulroney told Cogger. "Look at the names. Is there anybody inspiring? No, there are no great players, nobody who transcends. None.'' Cogger pointed out that ''co-chairmanships, vice-presidencies, positions like that open up all the time. But the leadership?'' They sat on Cogger's lawn weighing the arguments, but came to no definite conclusion.

A week later, the president of Labatt's Breweries, Don MacDougall (an active Tory who later prepared a report on privatizing Petro-Canada for Prime Minister Joe Clark), dropped in on Mulroney in Montreal on his way to Prince Edward Island and suggested that he take a look at the leadership. Shortly afterwards, Mulroney and Cogger met for lunch at La Veille Poule in Old Montreal and agreed to let the idea float around to see what the reaction would be. Cogger went down to the Maritimes. He spent some time with Lowell Murray, met MacDougall and then went off on a different kind of fishing trip with Graham Scott, Stanfield's former assistant. And everybody worked the phones, keeping in touch. By midsummer Michael Meighen — by then national president of the party and perforce a neutral — thought the idea interesting and was open. Murray was very cool. He felt Mulroney hadn't addressed the country and policy very much. Graham Scott asked: ''Are you serious?''

''The bottom line,'' according to Cogger, ''was that by early fall we had satisfied ourselves that Brian's candidacy would not be seen as a joke, that the result would not make us a laughing–stock. We'd have at least a respectable showing. And then we drifted into the campaign.'' Cogger made a quick ten-day tour of the West, and Brian Mulroney announced his candidacy in Montreal on November 13, 1975.

Mulroney has told people that he was initially quite reluctant to get into the race. However, Judge Cliche recalled that as the two worked on the commission, they became very close and that Brian confided in him many of his political ideas as well as aspirations. Cliche was not surprised at all by Mulroney's decision to run.

A few weeks before he officially declared, Mulroney outlined his campaign strategy in an interview. He felt the delegates, in the end, would vote for someone who looked like a winner; the

Tories were tired of being in opposition, so he had to look like someone who could command wide public support. He had to find a way to appeal to both factions of the party, and this meant he should not get caught out on any ideological or even contentious policy issues. He had credibility in Quebec, which he was going to make the most of, and finally, he would turn his most glaring liability, his lack of electoral experience, into an asset. Given what was known about some of the more prominent candidates, being an unknown might not be so bad.

The key to this strategy was for Mulroney to keep a low profile, let the front-runners kill each other off, make as few enemies as possible and come into the convention as the candidate who was least unacceptable to a broad spectrum of the party. But Mulroney's situation also suggested another strategy, the one that had captured the 1967 convention for Robert Stanfield. In the intervening years, the modern political wonder of television wedded to solid backroom organization and sharp media relations had been greatly reinforced by the phenomenon of Trudeaumania. With an attractive candidate, an experienced and sharp machine, and some razzle-dazzle media hype, the party could be taken again. Diefenbaker was now out of it. Mulroney had a good relationship with Stanfield, friends around the country, and access to money. And above all, he would never be caught eating a banana on prime-time.

Mulroney's statement announcing his candidacy in 1975 makes interesting reading today. It is remarkably similar to the pitch he would use in 1983. Yet it also expressed — if only by omission — the glaring defects in his position. He began with his assertion that the party needed a winner and he was the man: ''I undertake this challenge with confidence. I am in this race to stay. I am in this race to win. My purpose is to lead the party to victory.''

In 1975 Brian Mulroney was already a very successful lawyer who had carved himself a specialized niche in the labour relations field. He had handled some major cases, and his clients included such prominent corporations as the Iron Ore Company of Canada (whose president had already approached him about joining the company as vice-president with the clear perspective of assuming the presidency) and Power Corporation. He had worked extremely hard for the Conservatives in Quebec during Stanfield's star-crossed attempts to gain credibility in the province. He was the money raiser and the chief organizer. Through the Cliche Commission, he was a public figure in the province. He was a handsome man with a handsome family. In many respects, he was a publicist's dream. However, being the key man in federal Tory backroom politics in Quebec didn't cut much ice in the party at large. And the fact that he had never run for any kind of public office made his claim that he was a sure winner seem rather odd.

Despite the similarities between this campaign and the appeal to the party Mulroney would successfully make in 1983, there were also two significant differences, and these illustrate the inherent difficulties of the task he had set for himself in 1975–76. In his first campaign, Mulroney went out of his way on several occasions to speak highly of the incumbent leader of the party, in this case Robert Stanfield. He also did not make Quebec a major theme of the campaign and spoke about it only in passing.

''I start,'' he said, ''from the premise of an indivisible Canada. There can be no compromise on this point. I shall attempt to bring to the ongoing debate regarding Canadian federalism and its attendant problems the sense of civility and responsibility that has characterized Mr. Stanfield's intervention.'' What he said about Stanfield may have been quite true, and no doubt Mulroney believed it. But that was just the problem. The party, or a goodly section of it, wanted nothing to do with Stanfield's softness towards Quebec. It had, they felt, cost them elections, and indeed his ''moderation'' in things relating to French — these were the days when many good Tories started their morning with indigestion from reading French on their corn flakes boxes — was just part of the watering down of ''conservative principles'' that began with the ouster of ''the Chief'' and continued through Stanfield's tenure. Thus, Mulroney's statement that ''I make no apologies for the record of the Conservative leadership on this vital question'' would win him no friends among the many Conservatives who felt that the party had a great deal to apologize for in this area.

Another problem was that Mulroney was not the only Quebec candidate in the field. He could not really draw too much attention to Quebec and the debate on federalism because of the presence in the race of Claude Wagner, whose credentials as a spokesman for Quebec appeared much stronger than Mulroney's. In addition, Wagner was a real two-fisted conservative's Conservative. Mulroney by now had cooled on Wagner, who he felt had had his chance.

While pre-empting much of Mulroney's appeal to English Canadian Tories as a native Quebecer, Wagner also undermined Mulroney within Quebec. The early stages of the campaign were characterized by a bruising delegate fight in Quebec which Mulroney lost, although the support he gathered was enough to deny Wagner the clean sweep of Quebec delegates that would have made him unstoppable at the convention. While the distinctions were a bit fuzzy around the edges (like most political divisions within the Conservative party), the delegate fight could be seen as a struggle between two identifiable segments of the party in Quebec — in a sense between two generations. For despite Wagner's inability to win any degree of public support, he had been able to shift the influence in the party in Quebec away from Mulroney and his friends to the old-guard remnants of the Union Nationale; Jean-Yves Lortie, who typified the Duplessis school of political organization in the Quebec Conservative party, was working for Wagner (while Claude Dupras, whom Lortie had helped elect provincial party president, was in the Mulroney camp).

The struggle was waged with methods straight out of the Duplessis era (it would not be the last such campaign). One nominating meeting was held at 2 p.m. on Grey Cup day, another at 7 p.m. on Christmas Eve. One riding's delegates had been apportioned between Mulroney supporters and forces loyal to Joe Clark, until the local motorcycle gang, all card-carrying Tories, entered the nominating meeting and delivered the riding to Wagner. Mulroney himself was denied status as a delegate-at-large by Wagner, who had his wife and son appointed — an insult to Mulroney that would cost Wagner dearly. Mulroney's setbacks were not made any less bitter by the fact that he had recruited Wagner, worked as best he could to support him (at least in 1972), and in fact helped organize the wherewithal that had enabled Wagner to have his chance on the national political scene.

Then the story of the trust fund that had been set up for Wagner surfaced. The story got quite messy, and Wagner did not handle it well. While Wagner did not deny the existence of the fund, he maintained that it had not been set up until after the 1972 election. However, using information supplied by Peter White, the *Globe and Mail* and the *Toronto Star* reported that a suitcase filled with $20,000 in cash, an advance payment on the fund, was delivered to Wagner's front door four days before the election. White, who had been Wagner's assistant in 1972, urged Wagner in 1975 to either stop receiving payments or forgo a run at the leadership, because of the political liability of the fund; White turned up at the convention as a Mulroney supporter. (Conrad Black, on the other hand, helped raise Wagner's campaign funds.) The leakage was traced to the Mulroney camp, and in the end, the story damaged the Mulroney campaign more than Wagner's.

Mulroney could do nothing about Wagner except fight him. But he also had another set of enemies within the party, those Tories for whom his identification with Stanfield placed him among the big-money Dalton Camp boys who had stabbed John Diefenbaker in the back before stabbing him in the chest. He attempted to neutralize this faction by trying to show that way down deep he was really a Diefenbaker loyalist. He arrived uninvited at Diefenbaker's eightieth birthday party in Ottawa and took to telling everyone who asked and many who didn't how really close he was to the Old Chief. He repeatedly produced a photograph showing himself with Diefenbaker when he was a member of the Youth for Diefenbaker Committee. It was all to no avail. The Diefenbaker people had some accounts to settle, and this time that brash young Mulroney guy was going to get stamped "Paid in full."

It mattered little that Flora MacDonald was an unrepentant charter member and major tactician for Dalton Camp's faction. Diefenbaker had had Flora fired from the Tory national office and, in one of his most famous lines, more than once referred to her as "one of the finest women who has ever walked the streets of Kingston." It mattered even less that Joe Clark had been part of the Get Diefenbaker cabal from the beginning. In the eyes of the Diefenbaker faction, Brian Mulroney became identified as the man to beat. As Mulroney's profile rose, the determination to get him grew. And there wasn't much he could do about it. Indeed, the only thing he could do actually made matters worse.

Mulroney did not stick to his early low-key strategy. "We really didn't expect to win in the beginning," said a Mulroney campaigner, "but things really started to roll and by December, we thought we had a real shot at it." Tom McPhail remembers Superbowl Sunday, 1976. "That was the weekend when we realized that we had a good chance of winning it all. The English media was taking the candidacy seriously — the *Globe and Mail* had just run a great piece on Brian, and we felt we were on the way." In part forced into a change of strategy by his weakness in Quebec and the opposition to him in the party as a whole, and in part swept up by the attention he was getting in English Canada, Mulroney launched a high-profile public campaign that appeared designed to take the convention by storm.

Mulroney did become the focus of media attention. A writer in *La Presse* described Mulroney as "dynamic, bilingual and seductive." Out in Calgary, the *Herald* wrote that he has "that carved in granite, made in heaven look that political publicists love to sell in public." The Edmonton *Journal* gushed, "The eyes are Paul Newman blue, his hair has the swoop of the Robert Redford style and the voice the resonance of a Lorne Greene school of broadcasting. The jaw is by Gilbraltar." Richard Gwyn of the *Toronto Star* wrote a piece announcing that the media were going to choose the next leader of the PCs and that Brian Mulroney was the man they would choose. Reading the press, it would be quite natural for the Mulroney people to believe that they could do an end run around the party, much as Stanfield had in 1967. Mulroney had the look of a winner and the style of a leader for the Seventies, and that, after all, was what the party really wanted. That was all true enough as far as it went. But first of all, the party (or at least a healthy minority within it) had some scores to settle. And second, the party did not like the media and was suspicious.

Then Brian Mulroney started spending money. It was not really much more money than the other major candidates spent, and it could be argued that he even spent less than one or two of them, but there was a glitter to the Mulroney gold that did not sit well. It was ostentatious, glitzy and offensive to many of the delegates. A corporate jet leased by Mulroney at one point came to symbolize the campaign. The financing of the Mulroney campaign caused him further trouble, and Mulroney finally refused to disclose either the amount spent or the sources of it. Most of the unfavourable publicity surrounded the extent to which the campaign was being financed by Paul Desmarais's Power Corporation (falsely rumoured as being the source of the corporate jet), which was unpopular both because of its previous support of Trudeau and the Liberals and because of its nervy though unsuccessful attempt to take over Toronto's Argus Corporation in 1975. Desmarais did contribute some money, and helped raise a lot more. Jack Porteous, the well-connected Tory fund raiser and head of the business and finance group at Ogilvy, Cope, Porteous (as the law firm was now called), and Jacques Courtois, then president of the Montreal Canadiens hockey team, assisted in bringing money into the Mulroney campaign as well. And a good deal of money came from some prominent Liberals who were a little fed up with Trudeau and were looking for a PC leader who could conceivably be a credible alternative in Quebec.

Meanwhile, the original low-key Mulroney strategy was being

followed almost to the letter by another thirty-six-year-old back-room veteran with virtually no national reputation — Joe Clark.

The writing was on the wall for the Mulroney campaign even before the convention. What was surprising at the convention was the extent of the bitterness directed against Mulroney. Even the presence at the convention of the extremely shy and extremely pregnant (with Benedict) Mila Mulroney was held against Brian. "I'll never vote for a man," said one young delegate, at a time when a distressingly large number of reasons were being invoked for not voting for Brian Mulroney, "who makes his pregnant wife stand for hours at some stupid reception." But even if Mulroney's fate was sealed, it took two events in the convention hall to make sure that all concerned knew exactly what that fate was.

The first of these was John Diefenbaker's speech the night the convention opened. Among the many leadership candidates with whom Diefenbaker had scores to settle, he singled out Brian Mulroney by decreeing that the new leader must have years of parliamentary experience. Diefenbaker's motive in raising this question was not immediately apparent. One theory was that it was a disguised pitch for the Tory MP with far and away the most parliamentary experience — himself. Another was that he was referring to Stanfield's early stumbling in the House. But most people concluded that he was reacting against the apparent dismissal of Parliament displayed by that outsider, Brian Mulroney.

The party for Diefenbaker was always the caucus, the House. Throughout his political career he felt victimized by the backroom party boys. Indeed, he was finally brought down by a man, Dalton Camp, who could never win a seat. Brian Mulroney looked upon the party somewhat differently. There was no love lost between him and the caucus, many of whose members had sent out letters to delegates urging them, in effect, not to vote for Mulroney. He resented what he called "the club," and felt he had paid his dues to the party, more so than some of the members of caucus who joined the party to run for Parliament and whose commitment to it went no further and lasted no longer than their term in office.

In any case, the effect of Diefenbaker's speech in many delegates' eyes was to disqualify Brian Mulroney from the leadership. Without pausing to ask themselves how much parliamentary experience was necessary or why any was needed at all, they could now vote for whomever they pleased and still remain in the Chief's good graces so long as they voted for somebody other than Brian Mulroney. Mulroney himself believed then, and continues to believe now, that the speech was aimed directly at him. When the Chief had finished, he leaned over to Mila and said, "We're dead in the water." Nevertheless, Mulroney does not think that Diefenbaker was being personal and says, "I know for a fact that he later regretted that speech. I think he just could not conceive of anybody becoming leader of the party without coming up the way he did." (Mulroney and Diefenbaker re-established their personal friendship, and before he died the old Chief named Mulroney to be an honorary pallbearer at his funeral.)

Then there was Mulroney's own speech two days later. The convention as a whole was marked by overwrought, underthought and just plain silly speeches. Mulroney's was not noticeably worse than some of the other candidates' speeches, although it was certainly not any better. What was extraordinary, however, was the reaction to the speech — a thin ripple of applause and a complete absence of enthusiasm. The Mulroney bandwagon had been brought to a screeching halt.

Before the first ballot in 1976, it looked as if Claude Wagner might have it wrapped up. The CBC virtually declared Wagner the winner on the basis of a leaked count before the result was given. In the event, he received 531 votes — close, but no cigar. Mulroney was second with 357, a surprisingly good showing. Then Brian had to sit and watch as candidate after candidate — first Heward Grafftey, then Jim Gillies and finally Sinclair Stevens — walked by his section to toss in with Joe Clark, who was third with 277 votes. Even though Clark had fewer votes than Mulroney, he had become the focus of the stop-Wagner movement developing in the convention hall. For any leadership candidate, and especially as proud a man as Mulroney, that was bound to hurt.

On the second ballot, Clark passed Mulroney, and Wagner was slowed. By the third ballot, Mulroney was finished. The majority of his delegates seemed to be moving to Clark. Mulroney was begged from one side to move to Clark along with them, and from the other to go with his fellow Quebecer to unite the party, at least in Quebec. Roch LaSalle approached Mulroney to vote for Wagner. Mulroney reminded LaSalle that he had no vote to deliver. The Wagner campaign had made sure of that. Mulroney had nothing to do but sit.

The final vote was Clark 1,187, Wagner 1,122. There was a cold murderous silence in the Wagner half of the arena, and outraged delegates began streaming towards the doors. In the minds of many, Brian Mulroney had first split the Quebec vote and then, when all was lost for him, had refused to back his fellow Quebecer.

Thus, the 1976 convention created a new set of scores to settle. There would be more than a few Quebec delegates at the 1983 convention who would work hard to defeat Mulroney, remembering that Sunday in 1976.

CHAPTER SIX

The View from Head Office

Mulroney returned to Montreal smarting from his loss, and went through a period in which he took a hard look at himself and his future. The ambition he had nursed since adolescence of becoming leader of the Progressive Conservative party and prime minister had been thwarted, and for all he knew the opportunity would never arise again. He also knew that if he could not become the leader, he was not going to accept any subordinate role in caucus or, if the party should win the government, in cabinet. He rejected offers from Joe Clark to run for Parliament in the expected election, and he also turned down Pierre Trudeau, who, according to Mulroney, offered him a cabinet position on two occasions. "I didn't run for the Conservative leadership to become Justice Minister for Pierre Trudeau," he said, "and I didn't even run so I could get a cabinet job from Joe Clark. I ran because I thought I would be a leader of the Progressive Conservative party who could win an election." Like another man of thwarted ambitions, Nelson Rockefeller, Mulroney didn't want to be vice-president of anything.

"It seemed like a turning point in his life," says Mila Mulroney. "He had to decide whether he wanted to get into active politics again, or get on with something else. He had gotten tremendous support from his friends and family, but a defeat is a defeat. And it was really the first time he was defeated. He usually accomplishes what he sets out to accomplish. He works extremely hard at what he does. He is very committed, and he usually succeeds.'' Mila was to give birth to the Mulroneys' second child and first son, Benedict, a few weeks after the convention. Having tried to combine the roles of student, mother and political wife (their daughter Caroline went to day nursery while Mila went back to university), spending a good part of her pregnancy as an active participant in Brian's leadership campaign, she now gave up her engineering studies at McGill, a few credits short of graduation.

There was some residual bitterness about the convention in the Mulroney camp. The resentment did not focus so much on the loss itself (curiously, it is impossible to find anyone in the Mulroney entourage who confesses to believing that he had a chance to win in 1976; yet somehow Mulroney, the Great Listener, thought he was going to take it, apparently right up to the convention). It was the manner of the loss that rankled — the procession of anti-Wagner candidates to Clark when Mulroney felt that they should rightfully have gone to him. Memories of what Michel Cogger called ''the negative things that were said against us'' did not fade, and a feeling persisted that Mulroney had been done in. However, there was not much thought of ''wait until next time,'' since nobody really thought there would ever be a next time. And a decision was made against trying to keep the Mulroney campaign team together in an organized way. ''None of that 195 Club,'' said Cogger, referring to the group John Turner had maintained after his defeat by Pierre Trudeau at the 1968 Liberal convention (Turner received 195 votes on the final ballot). Mulroney and his friends kept in touch, but they devoted most of their energies to the business of raising families and making a living.

When Mulroney returned to his desk in Place Ville Marie, he had been away from his law practice for almost two years. The cases he had been involved in had been either resolved or taken over by other lawyers. He had grown accustomed to being in the limelight. At the age of thirty-seven, he was receptive to the idea of a career change.

One of the first calls he took was from Robert Anderson, executive vice-president of Cleveland-based Hanna Mining, and chairman of the board of its associated company, the Iron Ore Company of Canada (IOC), of which Hanna is the managing agent, sales agent and largest single shareholder. Anderson (who became president of Hanna two years later, while remaining chairman of IOC) was in his office in Cleveland and wanted to fly up to Montreal and have lunch. Mulroney agreed, and the two men met to discuss the problems of Iron Ore.

Anderson repeated William Bennett's job offer of the previous year: executive vice-president of Iron Ore, and president upon Bennett's retirement. Mulroney considered the offer and discussed it with his friends and his superiors in the law firm, who, while making it clear that they would be sorry to lose him, were in no position to make him as attractive an offer as had Iron Ore. With political considerations no longer pressing, Mulroney accepted the offer. A few months later, Mulroney was signed on as IOC executive vice-president. The following year Bennett retired, and Mulroney accepted a five-year contract to become president of the giant mining company.

Mulroney was familiar with IOC before he became an executive of the company, having acted for it as a lawyer in the area of its historically troubled labour relations. He knew the company had troubles, but he really had no idea how serious and wide-ranging these troubles were, or would become. Nor did he have any idea what the full implication of the troubles would be, not only for IOC, but also for the parent multinational, Hanna Mining. With characteristic intensity and energy, he threw himself into the job.

If there was something strange about a man who had never been elected to anything asking to be considered seriously as a candidate for the leadership of the Progressive Conservative party on the basis that he was a sure winner, it also appears odd that a major mining company would choose as its president a man with no administrative experience whose career had been spent as a labour lawyer and politician. To understand why Brian Mulroney would have been considered a valuable addition to the ranks of the Iron Ore Company of Canada in 1976, we need only look at the nature of the company he joined.

The Iron Ore Company of Canada was formed in 1949 out of a convergence of several economic and political factors. For nearly three-quarters of a century, the American steel industry had been based on bringing together iron ore from the upper Great Lakes — especially the great Mesabi Range in Minnesota, initially developed by John D. Rockefeller in the 1890s — and coking coal from the Appalachians. In the 1940s, however, it became clear to American planners that the Mesabi Range was becoming mined out and domestic reserves of iron ore were being dangerously depleted, particularly with the heavy demand for steel occasioned by the Second World War. Fortunately, however, there were highly promising deposits of iron ore in neighbouring Canada.

The initiative for the development of Canadian iron ore came from Cleveland. Although only a secondary centre of steel production, Cleveland occupied a strategic position on Lake Erie and was the major transshipment point for Upper Lakes iron ore. A rail link with Pittsburgh was opened in 1853. The first major Canadian iron ore venture was the work of Cyrus Eaton, a native of Pugwash, Nova Scotia, who had become one of Cleveland's leading industrialists. Among his accomplishments was the development of a major Canadian mine at Steep Rock Lake in northern Ontario, where he not only overcame serious technical obstacles to bring the mine to production but also fought off a challenge to his control of the company by a rival group backed by the powerful federal cabinet minister C. D. Howe. And meanwhile, he approached Quebec Premier Maurice Duplessis with an even more ambitious scheme.

It had been known since the 1890s that the Labrador Trough, straddling the contentious Quebec-Newfoundland border on the Ungava Peninsula, contained vast reserves of iron ore. There the land was so rich in iron that it was rust-coloured. The problem was to get the iron ore out of the isolated northern wilderness, and this was a challenge that was beyond the resources of all but the most potent industrial groups. Eaton's proposal was to organize a consortium of steel companies to mine Ungava iron ore and construct an integrated steel mill in the province. Other industries with huge energy appetites would be attracted to Quebec too — if the province could take over the private electricity companies. Although committed to opening up northern Quebec and developing the province's bountiful resources, Duplessis was deeply skeptical of the idea of provincial ownership of the electricity companies, and nothing ever came of the Eaton scheme.

Part of the scheme, however, was picked up by another Cleveland group, headed by George Humphrey of the Hanna Mining/National Steel empire. The Hanna company was built up in the nineteenth century by Mark Hanna, friend of Joseph Medill, high-school classmate of John D. Rockefeller, and one of the most powerful Americans of his time: his influence in the Republican party was such that he was able to have his protégé, William McKinley, elected president. (Interestingly, Hanna took McKinley under his wing after he was impressed by the young lawyer's defence of a group of striking workers.) Hanna developed business interests inherited from both his father and his father-in-law into a large Great Lakes shipping, mining, steel-making and shipbuilding firm. The Great Lakes trade took him to Canadian as well as American ports, the beginning of a long association with Canada by his company.

Hanna's Canadian interests gave him a lively appreciation of the merits of his country's northern neighbour, and at one Washington gathering just before the Spanish-American War, Hanna, now a senator, brought Roosevelt down from a flight of jingoistic fervour in which Teddy expressed his hope of seeing "the Spanish flag and the English flag gone from the map of North America before I'm sixty!" "You're crazy, Roosevelt!" Hanna replied. "What's wrong with Canada?" When the assassination of McKinley elevated Roosevelt to the presidency, Hanna is reported to have referred to him as a "damned cowboy," but the two men, the leading Republicans of their day, maintained an uneasy alliance, and as noted earlier, Roosevelt was in the wedding party when Hanna's daughter married Medill McCormick in 1903. This did not still the rumours of a possible Hanna challenge to Roosevelt at the next year's Republican convention; however, Hanna died early in 1904.

The company's dominant figure in the twentieth century was George Humphrey, a lawyer from Michigan who joined Hanna in 1918. Humphrey reorganized the company and greatly expanded its reach by going into partnership with two steel producers to form National Steel in 1929. The Humphrey and Hanna families — linked by the marriage of George Humphrey's daughter to Mark Hanna's grandnephew — continued to control the Hanna company right up to the 1980s, while its board of directors included representatives of the Mellon, Grace, Bechtel and other prominent American financial and industrial dynasties.

The development of Ungava iron ore was another major step forward for the Hanna interests, and George Humphrey would later regard this as his greatest achievement. Hanna and National Steel became the two largest shareholders in the corporate vehicle formed to exploit the iron ore deposits, the Iron Ore Company of Canada. The other shareholders were four other American steel companies — Armco, Republic, Wheeling, and Youngstown Sheet and Tube — and a Canadian company, Hollinger Consolidated Gold Mines, owned by the Timmins family of Montreal (Hollinger held the claims in the Labrador Trough through two subsidiaries in which Hanna was a minority shareholder). Another steel company, Bethlehem, joined the group later.

Construction began in 1950, and by the middle of the decade IOC had built a mine and company town, Schefferville, on the Quebec-Newfoundland border, a terminal at what had until then been the sleepy village of Sept-Îles on the Gulf of St. Lawrence, and an almost six hundred-kilometre inland railway linking the two sites. The total investment involved ran to $356 million, making it one of the largest construction projects of the early postwar era. Unlike his Cleveland rival Cyrus Eaton, George Humphrey was on good terms with C. D. Howe, who gave the Iron Ore Company a financial break by granting it accelerated depreciation and making sure it got the steel it needed to build its railway (Howe's long-time assistant, William Bennett, later became president of IOC).

The iron ore deal had political fallout in both Quebec and the United States. In Quebec the financial arrangements between the company and the province became a major issue in the 1952 election campaign, with the Liberal opposition leader, Georges-Émile Lapalme, claiming that IOC's payments to the province represented "one cent a ton" of iron ore extracted. This claim was inaccurate, and Duplessis's admiring biographer, Conrad Black, makes much of this misrepresentation, condemning "the gross calumnies of an irresponsible Opposition," and goes on to argue that the company's payments constituted an adequate return to the province. The post-Duplessis government of Premier Jean Lesage thought otherwise, however, and more than doubled the duties levied on mining companies in 1965. But in 1952 Duplessis, defending the iron ore deal, was re-elected with a comfortable majority, although the Liberals did make gains.

In Washington, Ungava iron ore introduced a new element into the longstanding debate over whether or not to cooperate with Canada in building a St. Lawrence Seaway. Citing America's need for the iron ore, George Humphrey testified in favour of the Seaway before a House of Representatives committee in 1950, but despite his influence, the proposal was rejected on this occasion. In 1952, however, Dwight D. Eisenhower was elected president, and he appointed Humphrey to his cabinet as secretary of the treasury. Although Eisenhower was initially cool to the Seaway, he was brought around by Humphrey, who became one of his closest advisers, and other cabinet members. With the administration working actively for the project, Congress finally approved the Seaway in 1954, and it was completed five years later at a cost to the two countries of almost half a billion dollars.

This was far from being the end of iron ore developments in

Ungava. The largest American steel producer, U.S. Steel, which had initially been skeptical of the IOC scheme, eventually set up its own North Shore mining subsidiary. In addition, a Chicago-born mining promoter named John C. Doyle persuaded the highly suggestible premier of Newfoundland, Joey Smallwood, to help him develop a facility to mine and pelletize low-grade iron ore in western Labrador; Smallwood made a loan of staggering proportions (for a province of Newfoundland's size) to Doyle to build a spur railway from the main Schefferville/Sept-Îles line to his mine at Wabush. Once the Wabush project had demonstrated the feasibility of Labrador iron ore development, IOC built its own, much larger, mine, concentrator and pelletizing plant in the area, along with the new company town of Labrador City. In the late 1960s, the Labrador City concentrator and pelletizing plant were expanded, and in the early 1970s IOC built another concentrator and pelletizing plant in Sept-Îles to upgrade ore from Schefferville. Yet another North Shore iron mining operation, Sidbec-Normines, was established by the Quebec government in the 1970s.

Thus, iron ore development, and primarily IOC, brought wealth and economic activity to an area where virtually the only means of livelihood had previously been hunting and fishing. The opening up of Labrador and the North Shore was a great engineering and organizational achievement. Sept-Îles, in particular, became a boom town, regularly making Statistics Canada's list of the wealthiest Canadian communities based on per capita income, and at one point in the early Seventies actually topping that list.

In the process, the resources of the North Shore and Labrador had been placed at the service of a formidable nexus of economic and political power, and the region's destiny had been inextricably tied to the fortunes of the American steel industry. While two of the smaller North Shore mining companies — Sidbec-Normines and Wabush Mines Limited — had Canadian markets, the area did not become a primary source of supply for Canadian steel producers, which got most of their iron ore from northern Ontario. The other North Shore suppliers, Quebec Cartier Mining (the U.S. Steel subsidiary) and the Iron Ore Company of Canada, were oriented towards American markets. IOC, the largest of the North Shore producers, sold some iron ore to Europe and Japan, but sales to its American shareholders always represented well over half its business.

At the time the great iron ore developments were undertaken, there was no reason to doubt that the steel industry in the United States would ever be anything other than a bedrock sector in the world's strongest economy. If the American steel industry should falter, however, or if it should find more attractive sources of iron ore elsewhere, the North Shore and Labrador would be in trouble.

This relationship was reflected in IOC's corporate structure. It was not a firm operating on its own account but a creature of its foreign shareholders. Since these shareholders were also its major customers, it was at least partially insulated from the play of market forces. The contracting of IOC's management and sales to its largest shareholder, Hanna, lifted the burden of self-support even further from the company's shoulders. IOC's small Montreal office became essentially an intermediary between the company's shareholders and the local population, concerned with such things as relations with the IOC labour force, negotiating with the various governments involved, and maintaining a good corporate image.

If the iron ore communities ranked among the wealthiest in the provinces of Quebec and Newfoundland, they were also among the most volatile. Labour troubles were common — IOC underwent fifty-nine work stoppages, including two major strikes, in the nine years before Brian Mulroney became president of the company. In addition, Sept-Îles early on developed into a bastion of support for the proposition that Quebec should become an independent country, and in the 1966 provincial election it became the first Quebec community to give a majority of its votes to the candidate of a party favouring that proposition, in this case the Rassemblement pour l'Indépendance Nationale (this was before René Lévesque left the Liberal party and founded the Parti Québécois). And in the spirit of insurrection that surrounded the

Common Front strike of 1972, the most dramatic revolt in the province was staged in Sept-Îles, where the unions took over the town, sealed it off and held it for a day before the provincial police began to move in.

The uneasy relationship between the two provinces in whose territory the iron ore deposits are located created another set of irritants. This situation was complicated by Quebec's irredentist claims to Labrador and exacerbated by the sniping over the Churchill Falls power deal that began when the deal was being negotiated in the 1960s and never really abated. Because of the development of Sept-Îles as a service centre for the whole region and IOC's policy of contracting out services for its Labrador City facilities to Sept-Îles–based firms, Newfoundlanders argued that Quebecers, and especially residents of Sept-Îles, were reaping the benefits from the exploitation of Labrador iron ore. The Bartlett Commission, appointed by the Newfoundland government in 1977 to study a number of grievances in Labrador City and the neighbouring town of Wabush (site of the smaller Wabush Mines Limited), backed this view.

> It is this thriving townsite of Sept-Îles that appears to have benefited the most from the exploitation of the iron ore deposits in Labrador. With no ore body of its own, Sept-Îles is known ironically, as "the mining capital of the North."
>
> In the opinion of this Commission, the ever growing list of unemployed workers in Labrador City–Wabush may, in large measure, be attributed to the absence in Labrador, of the many spin-off industries normally associated with major industrial complexes.

The commission also criticized the mining companies for their practice of allowing contracting firms to base their operations on company property "and escape for example, such an elementary obligation as the payment of municipal taxes." And because the companies' purchasing departments were located in Sept-Îles rather than Labrador City–Wabush, virtually no purchasing was done within Newfoundland.

Complaints that IOC was denying Newfoundland the benefits of its own iron ore resources went beyond the Labrador City situation, since more than half of the iron ore shipped from Schefferville was actually mined in Newfoundland territory, even though Schefferville was a wholly Quebec town and the ore was transformed into pellets in Sept-Îles. And even Quebec workers resented the company's contracting-out policy, feeling that the jobs these services represented should be kept within the company itself.

Specific grievances were compounded by the conditions of northern company-town life — the long winters, the isolation, the limited range of recreational facilities. And IOC had developed a reputation for being unresponsive to the needs of its workers and the communities its operations supported. For many people, working in the iron ore communities was considered a way of accumulating some money before returning to the more-settled parts of Quebec or Newfoundland (although they rarely accumulated money as quickly as they had anticipated). Nevertheless, as time went on, an increasing number of people considered Sept-Îles, Labrador City or Schefferville to be home, and a new generation, born in these communities, began to reach adulthood. Schefferville was also home to two Indian bands, who lived in sometimes strained coexistence with the white community.

As its president then, the Iron Ore Company of Canada needed someone who could improve its labour situation, knew the ins and outs of dealing with governments, and had a talent for public relations. In 1976 Brian Mulroney appeared to fulfil all of these conditions handsomely. In addition, he came from a North Shore working-class background and had grown up in a company town not wholly unlike Schefferville or Sept-Îles.

In 1978, the year after Mulroney assumed the presidency, the company underwent a four-month strike. While Mulroney and other company officials placed the blame on "Marxist-Leninists" (a reference to a small band of militants who had infiltrated the United Steelworkers of America local in Sept-Îles), there were serious grievances involved, notably the contracting-out issue. The two sides finally agreed on a contract, and a committee was appointed to study the question of contracting out. After the strike, Mulroney called a meeting of the company's top officials, saying that management was going to "go the extra mile" in an effort to improve labour relations. Mulroney issued directives to middle management urging cooperation on the job: "I will personally fire anybody in this company who thinks I'm impressed by booting the unions around, or being rude or kicking people in the ass. . . . They're going to be kicked out, not the unions. We want sensible, reasonable, enlightened management."

Mulroney's plan to improve the labour climate at Iron Ore emphasized communications. He later described the program to an interviewer:

> You name anything that any enlightened employer in North America has done or will do, and we've done it. That meant dealing with the men. That meant me being there on Christmas Eve; going around and seeing people at regular times during the year — not to talk business, but to find out what the hell they thought. It meant me talking to the unions. It meant making sure that, on all the social occasions, there would be a joint union-management presence. We set up joint human relations committees, separate from our bargaining committees. We set up brown-bag programs where the ordinary guys have lunch with the superintendents and managers on a regular basis.

An outside public relations firm was engaged to handle some of the details of the communications effort, but one of the most important elements in the program was Mulroney himself. He was everywhere. He presented the gold watches at retirement parties and poured the beer at company socials. He was in Sept-

Îles, Labrador City and Schefferville at regular and close intervals, pressing the flesh with the workers and getting photographed. He was one of the boys, but he let everybody know just who was boss. In the view of the Steelworkers, he did everything except actually deal with the workers' grievances. This view was supported by another commission appointed by the Newfoundland government to investigate the contracting-out issue in 1979, a year after the strike that contracting out had helped precipitate. This commission, the Easton industrial inquiry, was highly critical of IOC and compared its response to the Bartlett report unfavourably to that of Wabush Mines. "The Iron Ore Company of Canada," it concluded, "appears to have paid little attention to the recommendations of Judge Bartlett. This Commission found IOCC to be largely unco-operative. Moral suasion does not appear effective in dealing with this company."

All of the major grievances reported by the Bartlett Commission remained unresolved. Work was still contracted out of the province, on-site contractors were still escaping municipal taxes by basing themselves on IOC's property, and even though IOC had appointed a purchasing agent in Labrador City, "this seems to have made little difference to the policies of that company." A new industrial park in Wabush, which the Bartlett Commission had hoped would attract contractors to the area, was not having the desired effect, and the Easton Commission reported pessimistically that "it appears that few of these companies will move into the Industrial Park in Wabush unless they are compelled to do so." The commission also reached the conclusion that "the Iron Ore Company of Canada would do little voluntarily to help" make sure that subcontracted work went to companies resident in Labrador. And it found that IOC's contribution to the operating budget of Labrador City had declined from $1.5 million in 1975 to $900,000 in 1978, while municipal taxes had been "increased dramatically" and were among the highest in Newfoundland. IOC's contribution to Labrador City was approximately one-fifth the amount that the International Nickel Company contributed to the town of Thompson, Manitoba, where Inco maintained an operation of comparable size.

Mulroney's personal style of leadership and his tendency to bypass bargaining procedures were also resented in some quarters, and especially by the United Steelworkers. On one occasion, he unilaterally decided to double the widow's pension. Mulroney says he recalled his father's premature death and the fact that his mother was left without a pension, and decided that the widows of Iron Ore workers should not face that hardship. Union spokesmen say that they had been negotiating an increase in pensions and had always been refused by management. In any case, Mulroney did raise the pension and left the union to explain to its membership why it was angry about the move. Yet for all Mulroney's labour-relations expertise, the chief Steelworkers representative on the North Shore, Lawrence MacBrearty, says he never saw the IOC president across a negotiating table. "There's been a lot of PR but a lot of problems remain," said one Steelworkers official in an interview. "Mulroney is no better or no worse than the others. He's a politician."

IOC's labour climate did improve after 1978. There were some small work stoppages in 1979 — Labrador City workers went off the job for a few days in protest against some work that was being sent outside the plant, while workers in Sept-Îles walked out for a morning over a safety issue — but there were no more major strikes. Mulroney would make much of this improvement during his subsequent campaign for the Conservative leadership. He portrayed his regime as one of sweetness and light, blaming the 1978 strike on factors he inherited from his predecessors and conveniently ignoring the 1979 stoppages, and attributed the change to enlightened management and negotiating skill. According to union officials, however, the new climate had more to do with the vastly different set of economic conditions under which the industry was operating, which began to become apparent about 1979. The boom was over, and the threat of layoffs hung over everyone's head; under these circumstances, some of the effervescence went out of union militancy. As Clément Godbout, Quebec director of the Steelworkers, later explained:

> In the area of labour relations, between the Steelworkers' union and the Iron Ore Company, it's no better and no worse than anywhere else. I won't say there haven't been attempts to improve things, but the Iron Ore Company and the Steelworkers have not become what you would call a mutual admiration society. . . . There are certainly more discussions and overtures now than there were before. But during the good years, when there were markets for iron and the company was operating — I'm talking about from 1970 to about 1975 or 1976 — the Steelworkers, through their negotiating committees, did their job of negotiating, and made heavy demands, but at the same time responsible ones. There were conflicts and strikes, and during that time we were called troublemakers. . . .
>
> Now we're all in this situation, we're all so deep in the ditch that we can barely keep our noses out of the water, so we've become partners.

Meanwhile, the presidency of Iron Ore transported Brian Mulroney into the political stratosphere in both Canada and the United States. In Canada he was constantly involved in negotiations with Ottawa, Quebec and Newfoundland. And through IOC he travelled around the country, "touching base" with Premier Lougheed and the Alberta "oil patch."

But he travelled in even higher economic and political circles on his trips to Cleveland and New York. Mulroney was appointed to the board of Hanna Mining, where he rubbed shoulders with some of the top members of the American corporate elite. Mulroney's colleagues on the Hanna board included Nathan W. Pearson, financial adviser to the Mellon family (whose interests include Alcoa and Gulf Oil); R. L. Ireland III, a partner in the private Wall Street banking firm of Brown Brothers Harriman; William

W. Boeschenstein, chairman of the Owens-Corning Fiberglass Corporation; and William H. Moore, former chairman of Banker's Trust New York Corporation (Ireland and Moore are also members of the Humphrey-Hanna extended family). Mulroney would also meet at times with Henry Kissinger and other American movers and shakers, and return to Montreal and drop little tidbits into conversations with his friends. One friend claims that Mulroney's experience at Iron Ore gave him a more global view of politics and also gave his politics a more discernible right-wing tinge: "He came back from one trip or other to the States, talking about the Shah. 'Imagine the treatment Carter is giving the Shah,' he would say. 'He's our most trusted ally in the world.' Now, what the hell did Brian know about the Shah and how good a friend he was?"

His five-year contract paid him well, and there were plenty of perks. A private airplane was at his disposal, and a lovely house in Westmount. Some people who had gotten to know him earlier found him inaccessible now that he was president of Iron Ore, but he kept his political network intact. His job gave him entrée to people who could help him in the future, while providing an excuse to avoid running in by-elections. And as it turned out, his contract would expire during the very week that it would become appropriate for him to announce that he was again a candidate for the Conservative leadership.

In the early 1970s, a report published by the International Iron and Steel Institute forecast significant growth in North American steel consumption through 1985. In the latter part of the decade, however, it was becoming apparent that the American steel industry was in serious trouble. The industry was hard hit in the recession of 1974–75, but appeared to recover. Then in 1977 some major steel companies, including IOC shareholders Bethlehem, Armco, and Youngstown Sheet and Tube, announced plant closings and cutbacks. A new round of plant closings was touched off in late 1979 by a shock announcement by the industry leader, U.S. Steel. At one stroke, U.S. Steel closed fifteen plants in eight states from Connecticut to California, eliminating thirteen thousand jobs. Within the next year, National, Armco and other companies also cut back operations. Some companies tried to survive by merging: first Jones & Laughlin with Youngstown Sheet and Tube, and then (had it not been for anti-trust authorities) the result of that merger, with Republic. Early in 1984, a planned takeover of National Steel by U.S. Steel was announced. In 1982 the eight largest American steel producers reported losses to-talling more than $3 billion, and in October, 1983, the industry as a whole was operating at 56 per cent of capacity.

In part, this situation was a product of the most recent reces-sion, but the industry's problems were primarily structural rather than cyclical. It was faced with aging facilities (no new steel plant has been built in the United States since the early 1960s), high labour costs, growing foreign competition and declining markets. (By contrast, the Canadian steel industry, which had not expanded as rapidly as the American industry before the 1960s, was not faced with the same problem of overcapacity and was able to continue upgrading its facilities.) Fewer American cars were being produced, and those that were made, were smaller and contained less steel. Aluminum was replacing steel in bev-erage cans. Import penetration of the American market rose from an average of 9 per cent in the 1960s to 22 per cent in 1982. All in all, American steel shipments declined from more than 100 million tons in 1973 to about 60 million tons in 1982. Iron ore consumption declined even more steeply as a result of new steel-making technologies that used less iron ore. At the same time, cheap, high-grade iron ore from Brazil was increasingly available to North American customers.

All these changes were bound to affect Hanna Mining and its affiliated company, the Iron Ore Company of Canada. Hanna had been involved in Brazilian iron ore since the early 1970s, and this operation remained profitable, while its North American iron mines went into the red. But the crux of Hanna's strategy was to diversify into other minerals, and the proportion of its assets devoted to iron ore decreased from 54 per cent at the end of 1978 to 32 per cent four years later. This option was open to

IOC only in a limited way (it has talked about mining strategic metals such as yttrium and zirconium of which deposits have been found in Ungava); for the most part, it could only keep things running as smoothly as possible, maintain a brave front, and close down parts of its operation as markets declined. As early as 1978, IOC executive vice-president Richard Geren wrote to a Schefferville businessman:

> The deterioration of business in Schefferville parallels the decrease in the quantity of Schefferville ore which can be sold and the profit which can be realized for such sales. This has dwindled as has the demand for the ore to the point where it is now a very marginal operation. I, personally, can see nothing in the near future which would change this picture significantly. . . . In closing, I would personally recommend to you that you do not suffer any unnecessary financial loss by hanging on to the slim hope that conditions will somehow improve in the near future.

Of the company's two mine sites, Labrador City was the more profitable one and the one IOC was more committed to maintaining. The company had a larger ore body at Labrador City, a concentrator and pelletizing plant on site, and the ability to make year-round shipments (no shipments could be made from Schefferville in the four coldest winter months), and these factors more than compensated for the lower grade of Labrador City ore. In 1979 there were rumours in Schefferville that the mine might close in two years; they were denied by Mulroney. Nonetheless, mine manager Claude Falardeau told a reporter that "there is no doubt that developments in markets are putting the town's future in danger. It's true that our profit margin on our Schefferville operations is very slim."

The brave front was kept up through 1981. In 1980 the company took the unusual step of declaring a dividend. In 1981 the company achieved a target Mulroney had set of a $100 million profit, representing a 10 per cent return on investment. A dividend was again declared, and Mulroney handed out a $250 bonus to each of the company's employees. This was, however, also the year IOC closed its Sept-Îles concentrator and pelletizing plant, opened only eight years before in more optimistic times. Mulroney would later testify that without the plant closing the company would have lost $77 million. He also said that if IOC's American customers had paid the world price for its iron ore instead of the so-called ''lower Lake Erie price,'' its $100 million profit would have been transformed into a $12 million loss — a good illustration of the perils of taking at face value any transaction between a parent corporation and its subsidiary. The IOC dividends also had something of the character of taking money from one pocket and putting it in another. Since the steel companies are interested in IOC primarily for its supplies of iron ore, Hanna buys large amounts of iron ore from its ''associated company'' and considers its share of IOC's profits part of its own income whether a dividend is paid or not, and Hollinger gets most of its income from the company in the form of royalties on its original claims.

The profits, dividends and bonuses were, however, all good for the image of the company, and especially of its president. For among the side-effects of the good news from Iron Ore was the boost it gave to Brian Mulroney's undeclared but nonetheless very real campaign to succeed Joe Clark as leader of the Progressive Conservative Party of Canada. A number of articles appeared in the press portraying Mulroney as the saviour of the Iron Ore Company of Canada. A September, 1982, article in *Canadian Business* was headed, ''The Tories' turnaround artist,'' and the subhead read: ''Could closet Tory candidate Brian Mulroney run the country like he runs Iron Ore Co.? The country should be so lucky.'' When Mulroney actually became a candidate for the Tory leadership, his Iron Ore achievements would be one of the elements of his standard speech. And while it went down well with his audiences, by that time the picture at Iron Ore did not appear so bright.

In 1982 several events shook Mulroney's tenure at Iron Ore.

The first of these did not involve Mulroney directly, but it raised the possibility of legal complications that could have caused him some damage, or at least embarrassment.

Early in the year, Conrad Black — by now chairman of Argus Corporation as a result of his spectacular 1978 coup — launched an attempt to take over the Hanna Mining Company. In 1960 Argus had acquired a block of shares in Hollinger Mines to prevent the block from falling into the hands of Hanna; after his takeover, Black had added to Argus's holdings in Hollinger so that he was now securely in control of the mining company. Thus, Black's empire included a significant number of shares in the Iron Ore Company of Canada. He was also a long-time friend of Brian Mulroney's. Robert Anderson, the president of Hanna Mining who wanted to stop Black from taking over Hanna, was Mulroney's boss. Brian Mulroney was, according to his own description, "the jam in the sandwich." Mulroney's position was made even more delicate as the battle moved out of the boardrooms into the courts.

Two factors aroused Black's interest in Hanna. One was the company's vulnerability as a result of the weakened state of the iron and steel industry. In addition, Black learned from conversations with members of the Humphrey family that as relations between the family and current Hanna management were strained, at least one family member would be agreeable to a purchase of some shares. Through his recently acquired Norcen Energy Resources, Black began to buy shares in Hanna. Norcen president Ed Battle arranged a massive and secret loan and Black began wooing the Humphrey family.

There ensued a long and complicated corporate battle, much of which was fought in a Cleveland court. By this time, the differences between the Humphreys and Hanna management had been patched up, and they presented a united front in trying to resist the takeover attempt. It looked as if Black had bitten off too much as the full weight of the Hanna board descended upon him. Peter C. Newman quoted Black as saying, "For years I wondered what the difference between Canada and the United

States really was — apart from Quebec and the monarchy. Now I know. This is a very gentle place, and that's a real hardball league down there.''

Hardball or not, as the battle developed, Black proved that he had access to substantial amounts of money and was just as tough and smart as the Hanna management. The struggle spilled over into Canada as the possibility that Norcen had misled its shareholders was investigated by the Toronto police. In Canada the controversy revolved around conflicting interpretations of the minutes of a Norcen executive committee meeting on September 9, 1981. According to these minutes, Norcen president Edward Battle said that his company ''had initiated through stock market transactions the acquisition of a 4.9-per-cent stock interest in a U.S. company listed on the New York Stock Exchange with the ultimate purpose of acquiring a 51-per-cent interest at a later date.'' However, a document filed with the U.S. Securities and Exchange Commission two months later stated only that Norcen wished to ''acquire an investment position in Hanna,'' and a Norcen shareholder circular indicated no major changes were planned. Executives of the American mining company interpreted these documents as meaning that Norcen had deliberately misrepresented its intentions in buying into Hanna, in possible violation of American law; Black denied that the documents meant any such thing. Although a Cleveland judge granted a preliminary injunction against Norcen, an expedited appeal of this decision was later granted, and the Norcen-Hanna feud was settled out of court. No charges were ever laid against Norcen in Canada or the U.S.

The Norcen-Hanna compromise gave Norcen 20 per cent of the giant multinational and three seats on the board, along with Hanna's share of the two Hollinger subsidiaries that receive royalty income from IOC. The battle was over. Mulroney had not been directly involved, though had charges been laid against Norcen, he might well have been called as a witness, as a director of Hanna and president of a major associated company, right in the middle of his leadership campaign.

While Mulroney steered clear of that storm, another one was gathering that he would have to face head on. As the fortunes of the U.S. steel industry declined, Quebec's North Shore, the province's "Klondike" only a few years earlier, became an economic disaster area. Welfare and unemployment insurance offices were the only places where business was booming. The pulp mill at Port-Cartier (the former Shelter Bay, the town from which Colonel McCormick had organized his pulpwood supply early in the century), built with millions of dollars in federal and provincial subsidies in the early 1970s, closed in 1980. In the iron-mining enterprises, there were cutbacks and layoffs everywhere. There was talk of shutting down Sidbec-Normines, the Quebec government's iron-mining venture. Unemployment insurance ran out for hundreds of IOC workers laid off with the closure of the Sept-Îles concentrator and pelletizing plant in 1981, and for most of them welfare was the only choice. The population of Sept-Îles, 38,000 at its peak, was down to 27,000, while Port-Cartier (headquarters for U.S. Steel's Quebec Cartier Mining as well as the ITT mill) had declined from 12,000 to 6,500. Virtually the only good word anybody had to say about the situation came from a laid-off IOC worker in Sept-Îles, Lynn Anctil: "The depression has had the effect of strengthening our little community and bringing it closer together. When everything was going well, we didn't talk to each other. We were too busy working overtime to make some cash. Now, people are rediscovering their families, and traditional activities like cooking and sewing. We don't want to depend on big mining companies any more. We're trying to develop independently."

In Schefferville, the rumours of an impending shutdown were more widespread than ever, although the company was still denying them as late as October, 1982. When IOC finally announced publicly on November 2 that the Schefferville mine was closing for good, it was the first formal notice that anyone in the town had received, but no one was really very surprised. The circumstances surrounding the Schefferville shutdown were far beyond Brian Mulroney's power to affect, but he did have a very important role in the affair. The impact of the shutdown had to be softened and it had to be placed in as favourable a light as possible for the people of Schefferville and of Quebec as a whole, for whom Ungava iron ore had once been the very symbol of the province's economic future. It was a difficult assignment for anybody, but perhaps no one was more qualified to fulfil it than the tough kid from the North Shore who had become a corporate smoothie without losing the common touch.

On November 3, Mulroney was in Schefferville to tell the town's businessmen, for whom the closure of the mine was an economic death sentence, how very sorry he was that he hadn't been able to inform them of the shutdown earlier and couldn't really do much to alleviate its impact on them. He later maintained that the company's responsibility did not extend to the businessmen, who after all took risks as did businessmen anywhere else, and cited Richard Geren's 1978 letter as evidence that the company had done its best to warn entrepreneurs of the gravity of the situation. Meanwhile, town manager Jean-Yves Trucheon was trying to figure out how to maintain essential services without the one-third of the town budget contributed directly by IOC.

In January the company announced what it described as a "fair and generous" compensation and relocation program for its Schefferville employees. Under the program, employees received separation pay, moving assistance (or, for those who chose to remain in Schefferville, a company house for the nominal price of $1), and other benefits. The Steelworkers were informed in advance of the program and their opinion solicited on specific questions, although union spokesmen later described a company claim that they were "consulted" on it as somewhat exaggerated. The company also made much of a favourable initial reaction to the program by Steelworkers Quebec director Clément Godbout.

Subsequently, Steelworkers spokesmen criticized a number of elements in the settlement, pointing out that the company did not extend severance pay to some seventy-five workers eligible for early retirement and did not compensate workers on the Sept-

Îles loading dock or the Sept-Îles/Schefferville railway whose jobs were directly affected by the shutdown. They also argued that the plan should have been negotiated with the union. From one vantage point, however, the Schefferville settlement appeared very generous indeed. In Labrador City, about nine hundred workers were laid off in another part of IOC's continuing cutback program. But because they were laid off rather than terminated, they were not eligible for severance pay, even though the chances that they would ever be rehired were slim. "Up in Schefferville those guys got a good break," Clive Hamilton, one of the laid-off workers, told *Maclean's* magazine in 1983. "But there is nothing for us."

The most important forum in which Mulroney would defend the company's action would be a meeting of a Quebec National Assembly committee discussing "the situation of Schefferville and possible solutions." In an unprecedented move, the committee would hold its hearings not in the National Assembly building in Quebec City but in Schefferville itself, on February 10 and 11, 1983. Mulroney withdrew to Florida to prepare his presentation to the committee. By the time the committee met, IOC had announced its 1982 results, and the $100 million profit of the year before had given way to a $38 million loss. For the turnaround artist, things had turned again.

It was not only the Iron Ore Company of Canada's reputation as a corporate citizen that would be on the line in Schefferville. In late January, a dramatic development occurred on another front. A Progressive Conservative party meeting in Winnipeg gave Joe Clark a vote of confidence that was judged to be insufficient, and Clark resigned as the party's leader, precipitating a leadership convention. The leading undeclared candidate was Brian Mulroney, and the Schefferville committee meeting, Mulroney's first public appearance following Clark's resignation, would be the launching pad for his campaign.

CHAPTER SEVEN

Waiting in the Wings

It now seems conventional wisdom that Canadian politics is in a state of transition between a closed party system and the kind of open primary system that exists in much of the United States. This transition within the political parties reflects a more basic shift in government: the leader of the governing party, the prime minister, stands more and more above the party, the caucus and even the cabinet, and has almost presidential powers in the American sense. Some would argue that a prime minister's powers are even greater than a president's in that he can control the executive, the legislature and, if he is in power long enough, the judiciary.

However, the transition from a closed party system to a public primary system is much more apparent than real. The appearance of change is based on the fact that Canadian political parties choose their leaders in party conventions that increasingly resemble those of the United States. Of course, Canadian parties don't hold a convention before each election the way American ones do, but in the case of the Conservative party, given its recent problems, this difference is becoming marginal. And each time it happens, the actual process of electing a leader is not only more protracted than a general election but is given media attention as if it were one.

Leadership conventions have become media events with all the trappings of a sports spectacular. The glare of publicity has opened the leadership process up somewhat, and the party rank and file has gained a larger role at the expense of the caucus and the party bosses. The Progressive Conservative party in convention is no longer a meeting between the federal caucus and the Warwicks and kingmakers from Ontario and Quebec, as it was once described by John Diefenbaker. Nevertheless, the actual cast remains quite small.

Of the 3,137 potential voting delegates to the Progressive Conservative leadership convention of 1983, only 1,128 were elected adult constituency delegates. Every constituency organization also elects two youth delegates, and every campus club can select three delegates. A campus club can exist anywhere from the University of Toronto to a small secretarial school, and new campus clubs generally sprout like weeds when a leadership race is announced or expected. At the 1983 convention, about four hundred campus clubs were recognized. In addition, all Tory MPs, all candidates defeated in the most recent election, all provincial representatives and all members of the Senate and the Privy Council are delegates. The PC Canada Fund, the Policy Advisory Committee, various national executive bodies and all the provincial leaders can choose some delegates as well. Furthermore, 750 of the delegates to the 1983 convention came from Quebec — a number second only to Ontario's 893 — even though the party in Quebec appears to hibernate between leadership conventions.

Anybody who seriously entertains the hope of becoming leader of the Conservative party must, in the first place, have support — or, in the final analysis, acceptance — within the party establishment. Second, a candidate has to have a strong enough machine to move into the party vacuum in Quebec and in the youth and student groups.

Unlike the office of prime minister, the office of leader of the opposition has been weakened by the apparent change to an open primary system. The leader of the opposition is elected as the potential leader of the government. His basic function is to win an election and thus become prime minister. If he loses an election, then his job becomes open. This may not be written in any constitution or party regulation, but his job is up for grabs nevertheless. This is not to say that he cannot try again (although it should be said in passing that Brian Mulroney was elected leader of the Progressive Conservative party in 1983 on the clear understanding, which Mulroney fully shares, that he must win the next election). Nor does it mean that there are no powers of incumbency in the office of leader of the minority party. The leader can still have control over the party apparatus, and if he holds on to his own constituency, he can make use of his position in Parliament as leader of Her Majesty's Loyal Opposition.

Before 1983, the powers inherent in the leadership of a major party had never been fully tested. Except for John Diefenbaker's futile last-minute decision to place his name in nomination in 1967, there had never been a convention in which the leader campaigned to keep his position. It appears clear, however, that in such a situation, given the methods by which the delegates are chosen and the narrow electorate to which the candidates are appealing, the advantage should rest with the incumbent. In fact, unless his hold on the party is extremely weak, the incumbent should be in an unassailable position. It is a matter not of political science but of arithmetic.

Joe Clark's hold on the party was extremely weak.

Things began to go sour for Clark soon after his surprise victory at the 1976 leadership convention. The Tories' exhilaration at having captured the imagination of Mr. and Mrs. T.V. Canada on a blustery February weekend with a political spectacular that read like a script from a Frank Capra movie (young hero rides into town from nowhere, rescues the party from the bosses and pols) gave way to second thoughts.

The script calls for the obscure young backbencher to turn the tables on the pros and win it all, and the script was followed. But out of the Hollywood fantasy, and back in the political workaday world, it turned out that the man the Tories had elected leader really was precisely that — an obscure young backbencher.

1. Baie-Comeau as it looked when Brian Mulroney was growing up. The roof of the Mulroney house is visible at the bottom of this postcard.

2. The town was still being cut out of the wilderness when this baby photo of Brian was taken.

3. Brian at age three.

4. With mother Irene and sisters
(left to right) Peggy, Doreen
and Olive.

5. With father Ben and younger
brother Gary.

6. The back of this family snapshot reads: "Tough Guy (so
he thinks)."

7. Heading off to university—
with a plaid suitcase.

8. This photo with John Diefenbaker, taken while Brian was a student at St. Francis Xavier University, turned out to be useful in later years. Prints bear the caption: "Cette photographie m'est très précieuse [This photo is very precious to me]."

9. On the phone for the Chief at St. Francis Xavier. Mulroney was vice-chairman of the National Youth for Diefenbaker Committee.

10. Mulroney's St. Francis Xavier graduation picture.

Direction du Premier Congrès des Affaires Canadiennes

Exécutif

MICHEL COGGER,
Vice-Président

PETER G. WHITE,
Président

MICHAEL MEIGHEN
Vice-Président

BRIAN MULRONEY,
Vice-Président

NICOLE SENECAL
Secrétaire

DENIS LETOURNEAU,
Trésorier

11. A page from the program of the 1961 Laval University conference organized by Mulroney and his friends, "Le Canada, expérience ratée ou réussie? [The Canadian Experiment, Success or Failure?]."

12. Irene and Ben Mulroney at the Laval graduation ball in 1964.

13. Brian Mulroney, Davie Fulton and Peter White confer at a meeting during Fulton's 1968 leadership campaign.

14. At James Bay during the Cliche Commission hearings. With Mulroney are fellow commissioners Guy Chevrette and Robert Cliche.

15. In May, 1975, the commissioners submitted their report to Quebec Premier Robert Bourassa (seated).

16. Mulroney wound up 100,000 miles of campaigning for the Conservative leadership in 1976 with a speech at Trois-Rivières one week before the convention. Mila Mulroney campaigned alongside her husband.

17. At a convention breakfast with outgoing leader Robert Stanfield.

18. Claude Wagner, whom Mulroney had helped bring into the party in time for the 1972 election, turned out to be Mulroney's nemesis in 1976. Wagner is flanked by supporters, including MPs Otto Jelinek (second from left) and Eldon Wooliams (far right).

19. Mulroney delegates escort their candidate across the convention floor to the podium. Mulroney's speech failed to set the Ottawa Civic Centre afire.

20. The Mulroney family on the day of Mark Mulroney's christening in 1980. The older children are Benedict and Caroline.

21. The Mulroneys' Westmount home.

22. Mulroney is fond of organizing fishing trips for members of his inner circle. Joining him on a trip to northern Quebec by private jet are, from left to right, John Lynch-Staunton, Michel Cogger, Richard Holden and Ken Morris. Mulroney's book is *Gorky Park*.

23. The catch.

24. With long-time friend Conrad Black at the 1979 annual meeting of Standard Broadcasting.

25. Mulroney pledges his support for Joe Clark at a Montreal fund-raising dinner in December, 1981. Clark had survived his first post-election leadership vote earlier in the year.

26. As president of the Iron Ore Company of Canada, Mulroney had
to handle the company's shutdown of its Schefferville mine early
in 1983. Above, he makes the company's case at a Montreal press
conference; below, before a Quebec government committee in
a Schefferville gym.

27.

28. Brian and Mila Mulroney acknowledge supporters at the leadership convention in Ottawa, June, 1983.

29. Peter Pocklington and Michael Wilson throw their support to Mulroney after the first ballot — resulting in few additional votes, but much momentum.

30. The results on the fourth ballot are announced: Clark, 1,325; Mulroney, 1,584.

31. Acceptance.

32. The Mulroneys back in Montreal after the leadership victory. The children, from left to right, are Caroline (9), Benedict (7) and Mark (4).

33. Initially Mulroney led the caucus from the House of Commons gallery. Here Clark and Mulroney acknowledge each other's presence shortly after the convention.

34. The summer by-election campaign to get Mulroney in the House was an informal one. Elmer MacKay, who gave up his seat for Mulroney, took the candidate around the riding — in this case to a tea party in New Glasgow. Mulroney won handily.

35. MP George Hees and interim leader Eric Nielsen escort Mulroney into the House on September 13, 1983 under the watchful eye of Prime Minister Pierre Trudeau.

36. At the meeting of the PC Executive Committee, October, 1983.
    With Mulroney are Janis Johnson and Peter Elzinga, the party's
    national director and president, respectively.

37. In the
    House.

Clark spent most of his first months as leader outside of Ottawa, and when he was in the capital he appeared to spend most of his time setting up study groups and task forces. The ostensible purpose of these bodies was to formulate policy, but a more important function was to take the heat off the leader, who, of course, didn't have to say anything while policy was being formulated. It seemed like a good strategy at the time, but it had its weaknesses.

The idea was to let the Liberal government wallow in its own problems — by the summer, the Liberals were down to an almost unprecedented low in the Gallup Poll (29 per cent) — and allow time for the previously unknown MP to be seen as a potential prime minister, all the while keeping out of harm's way.

Unfortunately, however, history has an uncomfortable habit of repeating itself in the Progressive Conservative party.

On the level of media and public perception, the strategy appeared to work for a time. But Clark was never able to control his own caucus, still bitterly divided over the leadership convention. He either couldn't or wouldn't establish a relationship with Claude Wagner, and he couldn't get near his prickly fellow Albertan Jack Horner, who had run a strong leadership campaign (finishing fourth on the first ballot, some forty votes behind Clark) and now made no secret of the contempt in which he held "his leader." And there were others taking shots at him, both inside and outside the caucus.

When House of Commons constituencies were redistributed in 1976, Clark opted to seek the nomination in the new riding of Bow River, which contains his home town of High River. Bow River was important to Clark because, as his biographer David Humphreys explained, he "thought his High Riverness was an important dimension of his national image." (Brian Mulroney regards his Baie-Comeauness in much the same way.) Or, as Clark himself wrote in a letter to the Lethbridge *Herald*, "to be known as 'the man from High River' is a source of personal pride for me and is of very real importance to our party's chances of forming the national government because of the general affinity it gives me for the smaller communities across Canada which remain the bedrock of this country.'' However, a backbencher named Stanley Schumacher, who was about as obscure as Clark had been a year earlier and was an unreconstructed Diefenbaker loyalist, also wanted the Bow River nomination. Schumacher was deaf to his new leader's pleas, and succeeded in bumping him out of his chosen riding. A humiliated Clark was forced to find a nomination in the neighbouring constituency of Yellowhead. Being ''the man from Yellowhead'' didn't have the same ring as being ''the man from High River,'' and one Tory said that ''Joe Clark's big problem is that his wife won't call herself Clark, he lost Bow River and he has to go into the House to prove his manhood.''

The pressure was on Clark to get up front and lead the party. Leading the party meant mixing it up in the Commons with the Liberals. Throughout the first months of his leadership, Clark wasn't ready or willing to do this, and the suspicion grew that he wasn't able to.

Meanwhile, politics in Canada were becoming even more complex, and despite Trudeau's vulnerability this young awkward kid appeared to be no match for the hated Liberal leader. This was especially so after René Lévesque was elected premier of Quebec in November, 1976. The conventional wisdom at first was that Lévesque's victory was primarily due to the unpopularity of the Bourassa Liberal government in Quebec and was an indication of the serious difficulties the Liberals were in everywhere in Canada. However, that soon changed as the Conservatives remained out of the political equation in Quebec, and nothing Clark did appeared to have any effect on the situation.

There were rumours of war within the Quebec Tories. Clark tried to move in and replace Wagner people with his own, and Wagner liked this not one bit. Wagner was supposed to relinquish control of his own base, such as it was, to the new leader, while remaining the loyal lieutenant — a role he had, as we have seen, shown himself singularly incapable of playing in his previous incarnation as a Quebec Liberal. Clark was willing to give Wagner the chairmanship of the shadow cabinet and the honorific title of external affairs critic, and even took him on a visit to Europe, but he was determined to run his own show in Quebec. Almost from the beginning of their fights for control of the Quebec party, Wagner wanted out.

The suspicion that Clark was not up to the job continued to grow, and after a series of bad judgment calls and quixotic ventures into Quebec he was so labelled. Within a year the Get Joe Clark campaign had begun. Clark worked hard in a series of Quebec by-elections in 1977, but in the suburban Montreal riding of Verdun one prospective candidate withdrew, charging, "I've never seen such a corrupt convention." In Quebec that is an impressive charge. But Clark suffered even more damage in Terrebonne riding northwest of Montreal, where one Roger Delorme was nominated. Delorme was a popular local radio host. He was also an outspoken anti-Semite. While he disavowed Delorme's views, Clark didn't have the courage to disavow Delorme. Claude Wagner refused to participate in the by-election campaigns in Quebec and by implication blamed the embarrassment on Clark. While Clark put his prestige on the line by campaigning fruitlessly in the five Quebec by-elections, he ignored a sixth one in a Prince Edward Island constituency the Tories had held for two decades. They lost that one too.

For Clark, disaster was becoming routine. The media began referring to his "faltering career." The Gallup showed a decline in Tory popularity, and by the summer of 1977 Clark was showing the same low numbers that Stanfield had some six years earlier. Jacques Lavoie, who in 1975 had upset Liberal parachute Pierre Juneau in the east-end Montreal riding of Hochelaga, now crossed the floor to the Liberals, as did Jack Horner to become a cabinet minister. John Reynolds resigned to become a hot-line host, Sean O'Sullivan quit to become a priest, and Gordon Fairweather left to become chairman of the Canadian Human Rights Commission. (It was around this time too that approaches were made to Brian Mulroney to join the Liberals.)

In November, 1977, Clark had to face a national meeting of

the party in Quebec City. It was here that the first move against the leader was supposed to be made.

The instrument of revolt was to be a resolution that would make it possible for the party to vote non-confidence in its leader while avoiding a leadership convention. The terms of the resolution provided that in the event of a non-confidence vote, leadership would be assumed by the runner-up at the last convention — in this instance, Claude Wagner — until a convention could be held at an appropriate time. While this manoeuvre was shrouded in extraordinary secrecy (the resolutions were not distributed to the press until a few hours before they came up on the floor), there was a palpable undercurrent at the meeting surrounding Resolution 47, as the proposal was known. As near as an outsider could tell, the resolution came from Metro Toronto and from a section of the party that was particularly hostile to Premier William Davis, whose Big Blue Machine at this time was genuinely supporting Clark. However, it is difficult to pin the resolution on any particular ideological wing of the party. Joe Clark was simply being perceived as a loser, and winnability cuts across ideologies like a knife through butter.

That the undercurrent of revolt was not stronger was primarily the result of two factors. One was that by the time the meeting took place, Wagner was ill and pretty much out of the picture, and the anti-Clark forces within the party had nobody around whom to coalesce. The other was that a consensus had been reached that if the differences in the party couldn't be resolved, they should at least be papered over for the moment, and for public consumption the Quebec City meeting would be a celebration of party unity. When Joe Clark's leadership was submitted to the convention for approval, it was endorsed by what one Ontario Tory described as a higher percentage than Christ received from his disciples. By the time Resolution 47 came up, most of the delegates had drifted off to a party and only a few diehards were prepared to speak in its favour. (It is an indication of the general fluidity of federal Tory politics that one of these diehards would be spotted during the 1983 leadership campaign sporting a huge Joe Clark button — when, incidentally, the ardour between the Big Blue Machine and Clark had noticeably cooled.)

Part of the papering over at the Quebec City meeting consisted of the acceptance by the Clark forces of Diefenbaker loyalist Robert Coates as party president. Coates had written a book called *The Night of the Knives*, in which the gory details of the plot to destroy John Diefenbaker were laid out in overwrought prose. Nevertheless, Coates was challenged only from the right, by John Gamble. Although there was no serious contest for the presidency, two slates of candidates appeared for almost all the minor party offices, and the results of the elections in which these slates met head-on could be interpreted as an indication of the relative strength of Joe Clark in the party in 1977. According to this measure, it was roughly a sixty-forty split.

Mulroney was the invisible man in Quebec City, although he did play a role in working out a compromise in the party's Quebec leadership. This compromise saw Mulroney's friend Michel Cogger become national vice-president (Quebec). The deal was endorsed by the Quebec caucus and held when it came to be ratified by the meeting as a whole, although there was an abortive attempt by a few of Clark's Quebec supporters to double-cross Cogger. Throughout this whole period, Mulroney maintained that he was not attempting to undermine Clark, and that he (along with just about everyone else) considered himself out of leadership contention. His actions in Quebec City were a demonstration of the good faith of these assertions. They also indicated that he wanted to keep his hand in Tory backroom politics in Quebec.

He also had his hand in a variety of other activities. He was extremely busy learning the ropes at IOC, and he picked up a number of corporate directorships, including a coveted position on the board of one of Canada's major banks, the Canadian Imperial Bank of Commerce. He also kept up an active pace in community work. At one time or another, he was a director of St. Mary's Hospital in Montreal, the Montreal Heart Institute,

the Robert Cliche Foundation, the Jean Lesage Foundation, the
National Association of Christians and Jews, and Big Brothers
of Canada, as well as a trustee of the Canadian Football League's
Schenley Awards. He headed the United Way Campaign in Montreal and fund-raising drives for the Quebec Association for the
Mentally Retarded, St. Patrick's Home for the Aged, the Canadian Liver Foundation, St. Mary's Hospital, the Salvation Army,
and a number of universities: the universities of Quebec, Montreal, Moncton and Waterloo and Memorial University of Newfoundland. He has also provided continuing support for his own
universities, serving as a governor of St. Francis Xavier and
Honorary Chairman of the Laval alumni association.

While Mulroney made little secret of his lack of enthusiasm
for Clark and his leadership, for the most part their relations were
proper. Mulroney did some work in the name of the party in
Quebec — he was chairman of a fund-raising dinner, and he
spoke on behalf of the party on occasion. He mostly kept his own
counsel (and the counsel of his friends) on party matters. There
is a story of one fund-raising dinner in Montreal that was turning
into a disaster. Louise Leduc, a long-time Conservative party
worker in Quebec, recalls phoning one of Clark's key advisers,
Finlay MacDonald, three weeks before the dinner: "We've got a
terrible problem. There are three weeks to go and we have only
sold eighty-seven tickets." They decided to ask Mulroney to lend
a hand to help salvage the dinner. "Monday morning," Leduc
says, "Brian walked into our office, took off his jacket and tie,
pulled up a chair to my desk and went to work on the phone. I
saw him there for three straight days and in that period he sold
eight hundred tickets."

The first public indication that Mulroney was not entirely happy
with the leadership of the Progressive Conservative party came
in June, 1978. After remaining virtually silent and refusing for
two years to get into the debate swirling about Joe Clark's leadership capacity, Mulroney unburdened himself to reporter Stephen Kimber, and an article entitled "After Joe Who?" appeared
in the *Financial Post Magazine*.

Mulroney, of course, had nothing to do with the title or its publication date, almost a year before Clark was to face his first general election campaign. In fact, Mulroney had asked the reporter not to publish the article until after the election because he didn't want to make things worse for Clark during a campaign, and he disputed elements of what Kimber wrote. However, he did say that he felt Clark could not possibly win an election because he could not possibly win in Quebec. And while he denied any thought of running for the leadership again — "I can't conceive of any circumstances that would change my mind" — he must also have known that if Clark were to lose the coming election, the Tory leadership would, to put it mildly, be in doubt.

Clark also understood that the party had to make inroads in Quebec if it was to win a secure national mandate. In fact, at this stage the only real difference between Clark and Mulroney was that Clark believed he could do it and Mulroney believed he couldn't. In spite of Clark's early blundering in his gestures towards Quebec, as typified by his ineffectual campaigning during the 1977 by-elections, he did do some solid organizational work. And Mulroney and his friends cooperated with him, at least for a time. It was one of the ironies of Clark's leadership that it was he who insisted the party pour money for organization into Quebec and during his term as leader spent more time in Quebec than Pierre Trudeau. And Clark did build a base within the party that remained remarkably loyal to him. But there was not time enough for him to translate this grass-roots organizational work into public support. Perhaps he never would have been able to overcome the perception of him as an outsider, at least not as long as the Liberals were led by Pierre Trudeau.

If there was to be a Quebec challenge to Clark, it would not come from Claude Wagner, who after 1977 was no longer a force in the party. The nature of Wagner's illness was never officially disclosed, but it was generally thought to be a form of leukemia. In 1978 Pierre Trudeau appointed him to the Senate, and in his maiden speech in the Senate (which was also one of his last) he praised Trudeau's policy towards Quebec, and criticized those who "have found it expedient to deliberately downplay the truly perilous nature of the unity crisis, and devote their full attention to convince Canadians that the real and exclusive issue is the economy" — an apt description of the policy then being followed by the Conservative party. At the end, Wagner sounded once more like a Liberal. He died in the summer of 1979, shortly after Joe Clark was sworn in as prime minister.

In a very real sense, Clark's efforts in Quebec and his failure to reap any electoral returns from them substantiated both halves of Brian Mulroney's argument. First, the Tories can't win without support in Quebec. And second, Joe Clark will never be able to deliver francophone seats. Therefore, the argument concluded, the only potential leader who could preside over a lasting Tory victory was Brian Mulroney.

It wasn't simply a matter of speaking the language. It was the recognition of a more complex skein of relationships that Brian Mulroney was seen to have with the body politic in Quebec. While Clark would always, even at best, be considered the sympathetic outsider, Mulroney could claim to be part of the fabric of Quebec politics. Moreover, the political nature of Clark's support within the party in Quebec, coming as it did from the nationalist remnants of the Union Nationale machine, was to cause some severe strains in whatever cooperation did develop, for a time, between Mulroney (whose backers were more clearly identified as federalists) and the leader. And this too would be reflected later in the campaigns both would wage for delegate support in 1983.

Despite their inability to make any headway in Quebec, Clark and the Tories managed to form a minority government in 1979. And they almost immediately began to put that in jeopardy by refusing to call Parliament. After the Tories had been in the political wilderness for so long, for Clark to get elected with only a minority government and then to squander that was unforgivable.

There was so very little to squander. Elected with only 36 per cent of the popular vote, Clark resolved to rule as if he had a majority. He pressed ahead with his determination to sell Petro-Canada even after ministers such as John Crosbie opposed the plan, and made fools of both himself and Robert Stanfield on the question of moving the embassy in Israel. Even the 36 per cent the Tories had at election time in May did not hold; by November, polls showed they had the support of 28 per cent. And then Clark blundered into an election with an unpopular budget.

Clark in power seemed to misjudge everything. On one level, there were many real and perceived personal slights resulting from Clark's seeming aloofness towards his workers. Says Michel Cogger:

> Joe Clark didn't keep in touch. I was on his transition team, and I haven't been on the phone with him since '79. I was on the national executive when we lost in 1980, and I can tell you that if politics is people's business, then they are really poor businessmen. . . . Your duty as leader is to phone every candidate, especially the ones that lose, even if it means half an hour on the phone listening to sob stories about a mortgage or marriage break-up. Even if the guy's a jerk he is entitled to a call now and again.

Of more significance, believing that he could act as if his minority government was a majority, Clark felt he was free to ignore the interests of the Ontario government. The core of his problem was manifest in his policy in the area of provincial rights. Clark's concept of Canada as a community of communities appeared to amount in Quebec to a policy of giving comfort to nationalist forces including the Parti Québécois, while in Ontario it was translated as meaning a weakening of the role and influence of Canada's central province.

With Clark in power, Ontario was the odd man out at federal-provincial discussions. The ill-fated budget was seen as a slap in the face to Ontario, while it enriched the oil-producing provinces. William Davis, presiding over a minority government, attacked both the budget and the confusion in the Clark government about the future of Petro-Canada. Davis told the Ontario

Legislature that "our government believes the present national responsibilities of Petro-Canada should be retained and that the federal government should retain ownership of Petro-Canada." Poor Joe Clark, stubbornly clinging to the notion that he should fulfil at least one of his election promises, wanted to be able to say at some point during the life of his government that Petro-Canada no longer existed. Most of his cabinet wanted to back away. This in itself would not have been enough to stop Clark from forcing the issue, but he couldn't get past William Davis.

On the budget, and the prospect it raised of rapidly rising oil prices, Davis was equally vocal in his objections: "The only thing we know is that a massive increase in the price of oil can stall economic activity and slash economic growth. I will oppose this course so long as I am charged to serve this province. Ontario is not a 'have not' province, but it is not about to be bled white either." Clark really didn't listen to Ontario's objections. It was political talk by a minority government which, he thought, faced an election before he did. Clark's main economic adviser, James Gillies (himself a former chairman of the Ontario Economic Council), thought Ontario had poor economists. As Jeffrey Simpson wrote, Ontario thought Gillies was a dangerous economist.

In 1980 Davis was even featured in Liberal election propaganda. Clark's victory in 1979, such as it was, was made in southern Ontario, and it was there that his 1980 defeat was fashioned.

There is a widespread impression that Joe Clark is a more moderate politician than the serious candidates who were to oppose him in 1983 — notably Brian Mulroney. An examination of Clark's record during his brief tenure as prime minister — his inflexible position on "privatizing" crown corporations, his willingness to meet the demands of the oil lobby — does not give credence to this impression. The Tories in office pursued some foolish and unpopular policies.

And added to these policy difficulties was the disappointment of deserving Conservatives everywhere at not getting their just share of the rewards of belonging to the party in power. This led to a widespread disgust with Clark in the party after his govern-ment was blown away. Few of the great hopes of patronage were fulfilled, few of the promised appointments made. And even fewer Liberals were unmade. One Tory recalls having a few drinks with a friend who had benefited from Liberal political largesse for a number of years: "It was a day or two after the '79 elections, and I said 'You're gone now — the telegram is in the mail.' He agreed; he was just a straight political appointee. He was still there when the [1980] election was called. Trudeau finally had to fire him."

Thus, by the time Joe Clark was back in opposition, his actions and non-actions while in office had added considerably to the ranks of his enemies within the party.

The February federal election was only the first of the political shocks of 1980. In the spring, René Lévesque called his long-awaited Quebec referendum on what was now called "a mandate to negotiate sovereignty-association." While Trudeau's justice minister, Jean Chrétien, took the low road, raising the horrible spectre of what "la tanque de gaz" would cost in an independent Quebec, the resuscitated prime minister himself took the high road, maintaining that a vote against Lévesque's proposal was a vote for constitutional reform within Confederation. The partic-ipation of high-profile Quebecers in the federal government was a key element in the "no" campaign, but the campaign was by no means limited to the federal Liberals; among those who worked hard for the "no" cause was the prominent Montreal businessman and Conservative activist Brian Mulroney. In the May referen-dum, more than 60 per cent of the Quebec electorate voted "no," and a few months later Trudeau delivered on his promise of constitutional reform. It was not, however, constitutional reform in the direction sought by Lévesque — and even by some of his federalist opponents such as provincial Liberal leader Claude Ryan — but rather in the direction of increased federal power and reduced provincial autonomy.

Joe Clark, the champion of provincial rights, challenged Trudeau's proposed constitution. This position entailed renewed differences between Clark and the government of Ontario, which sided with Trudeau on the constitution, the only provincial government to do so wholeheartedly. It also opened up serious policy disagreements between Clark and Brian Mulroney, who also supported Trudeau on the constitution and made no secret of his position. At a meeting in Montreal after Clark had announced he would fight Trudeau's constitutional proposals, Mulroney confronted Clark and said he would not support him. In September, 1980, Mulroney gave a speech in Montreal demanding a new approach to Quebec from the Conservative party. The speech is interesting for some of the points it raised and, in retrospect, perhaps for its timing. Delivered a few days before a meeting of the Quebec wing of the party, the speech in a sense officially opened Mulroney's proto-campaign for the leadership. In it, Mulroney established his distance both from the notion of Canada as a binational state contained in the unfortunate Tory formulations of the late 1960s and from the devolution of federal powers envisaged by Joe Clark with his concept of Canada as a "community of communities." Mulroney's federalism is both consistent and long-standing, and in many respects is at the core of his political persona. He defined its basis in his Montreal speech in the following terms:

> In any discussion of constitutional reform, I start from the premise of an indivisible Canada. The word is clear. It means the same in English as it does in French. I do not believe in the theory of two nations, five nations, or ten nations. Surely we have learned that these *jeux de mots* merely obscure reality and inhibit effective dialogue.

However, Mulroney's "One Canada" position, unlike Diefenbaker's, was not to be a code for perpetuating French Canada's second-class status within Confederation:

Quebec is different, very different. It is not strange or weird, it is just different. And the difference is rooted in language and culture. That is why the preservation and enhancement of these two instruments are so vital. That is why they must be protected and nurtured with a constancy and vigilance that can never be slackened. For English Canadians, comfortably ensconced in the protective linguistic cocoon that envelops all of North America, measures to ensure protection of the French language may sometimes seem silly and vexatious. But they are not. Such concerns are a deadly serious business.

Mulroney also spelled out what these considerations implied for the Progressive Conservative party:

The Conservative party has been consigned to the Opposition benches for one reason alone — its failure to win seats in the French-speaking areas of the nation. From northern and eastern Ontario through Quebec and into northern New Brunswick, the electorate has rejected the Conservative party with a consistency that is at once staggering and overwhelming.

The reasons? Well, take your pick — Louis Riel, conscription, poor organization, Quebec lieutenants, no provincial party, poor policy, unilingual leaders, two-nation theories — take your pick, but make it soon because we are running out of excuses. We may have none to offer if we hesitate too long.

And he went on to criticize the attitude of the rest of the party towards Quebec:

I particularly grieve for that small contingent of courageous Quebecers who have stood firmly for the party over the years, silently suffering the friendly jeers of their neighbours and the unalloyed scorn of their political adversaries. . . . They have received . . . the unenthusiastic tolerance reserved by the party hierarchy for those hapless ne'er-do-wells whose only role of substance is to visibly perpetuate the myth that the Conservative party is truly national in scope, authority and representation.

Mulroney continued in this vein and proposed a series of organizational steps, including the establishment of a Quebec provincial party and a membership campaign ''which would provide the party with 30,000 new card-carrying members when the next writ is issued, which is about 25,000 more than we have at present.'' Demanding that francophones be brought into the decision-making bodies of the party, he insisted that the traditional roles ''of 'assistant to,' 'deputy of' and 'second vice-president' no longer suffice. The era of *Le Roi Nègre* [the Negro King] . . . is over.''

There was a large segment of the Conservative party that believed the Tories could take power in two stages. In the first stage, the party would win a minority government without significant support in Quebec. The second stage would be a snap election in which Quebec would jump on the Tory bandwagon and help give the party a majority. This scheme, in its various forms, was known as the Churchill Formula, after the Diefenbaker confidant and cabinet minister Gordon Churchill, and was based on the party's experience in 1957–58. In his initial, narrow victory, Diefenbaker had won only nine Quebec seats. Nine months later, Quebec had given the Chief fifty seats, contributing to his overwhelming majority. By arguing that the Tories had to change their approach to Quebec before taking power, Mulroney was telling the party to forget 1957–58. The Churchill Formula, he was saying, would not work.

In fact, whatever small base in reality the Churchill Formula had ever enjoyed, had been destroyed by the events of 1979–80. In 1979 Joe Clark ran very strongly in English Canada but was denied a majority by Quebec. According to the Churchill Formula, this should have been Stage One. There were, however, several significant differences between where the Tories stood in

Quebec in 1979 and their situation in 1957. First of all, the party's nine Quebec seats in 1957 represented a gain over the previous election, as did its more than 30 per cent of the popular vote; in 1979 the Tories lost ground, being reduced from three seats to one and winning only 13 per cent of the popular vote. Second, the Tory victory in 1979, unlike the election of John Diefenbaker in 1957, was widely expected; so Quebecers who wanted to vote to have a say in a Tory government could do so in the first round. Third, the fifty Conservative seats in 1958 were, to a large extent, delivered to Diefenbaker by the premier of Quebec, Maurice Duplessis — a favour René Lévesque, however relieved he might be to be rid of the formidable figure of Pierre Trudeau in Ottawa, was not likely to match. And finally, the Liberal party in 1958 was led by an English Canadian, Lester Pearson, who had recently been elected in a convention that included some not so subtle anti-French overtones in the manner in which his Franco-Ontarian opponent Paul Martin, was shuffled aside. The Churchill Formula should have been banished for all time by the time of the 1980 election, in which the Tories did even more poorly in Quebec than they had in 1979 and the province contributed mightily not to a Conservative majority but to a Liberal one.

Nevertheless, the truth that Brian Mulroney spoke in his Montreal address was still not widely recognized in the Conservative party. During the 1976 leadership campaign, the Conservatives had barely concealed their hostility, or at best apathy, towards Quebec. At the time, the Tories seemed to accept the notion that French Canada was hated in English Canada, and conveniently blamed it on the Liberals. John Diefenbaker allowed that he had solved the problem of French-English relations in Canada by introducing simultaneous translation and bilingual cheques. Jack Horner made no apologies for his record of opposition to the Official Languages Act. Sinclair Stevens announced that bilingualism was a problem for Berlitz to solve — he was talking leadership. Patrick Nowlan, returning to English after the few obligatory French phrases during his convention speech, said, "Now back to business," and got a round of applause. Even

Claude Wagner told the convention that a government he would lead would heal the legacy of hatred generated by the Liberals' policy. How he would do this, he did not say.

In a large section of the party, the familiar anti-Quebec code words and phrases had persisted through the intervening years. Thus, it appeared as no small act of courage for Mulroney to launch his unofficial leadership campaign on the note that the party could not win a federal election without support in Quebec — which he and only he could deliver — and that to win such support it had to adopt the essence of the federalist position of the hated Pierre Elliot Trudeau. The party, according to Mulroney, had to be seen to provide a federalist option to the voters of Quebec. There should be no attempt to win an election in English Canada alone, and no flirtation with either the Parti Québécois or with traditional Quebec nationalism.

The official opening of the leadership campaign was still more than two years away, but by late 1980 Brian Mulroney was "ready to go again" and everybody knew it — especially Joe Clark. Mulroney followed his Montreal speech with an appearance at the Albany Club in Toronto, used the occasion to engage in some other political chit-chat around town, and then headed west to test the water. Mulroney's decision to run for the leadership in 1980 was still problematical. The job wasn't open, and the possibility that Clark would be ousted in a leadership review or forced to call a convention was a long-shot bet. But politically, Mulroney had broken with Clark on the constitution, and in an energetic series of public speeches around the country, he began to elaborate his positions on economic development and social policy, including the ritualistic attacks on government spending. Mulroney's friend Sam Wakim regularly distributed the texts of the speeches to a mailing list of Conservatives with little notations such as "read what our next leader had to say." And some of the speeches were later packaged into a book, *Where I Stand*, in time for the 1983 campaign. (During the campaign, Mulroney often became irritated with charges that he was vague or noncommittal on policy issues, and would say, "I'm the only candidate to write a book setting out my ideas.")

The interesting element in these speeches, given the rhetorical excesses that would later dominate the leadership campaign, was their moderate, often even constructive tone. On issues other than the constitution, there was nothing in any of them that could be construed as an attack on the leader. Nevertheless, Mulroney's one crucial political difference with Clark lost none of its clarity as the constitutional debate dragged out over a year and a half.

Eight provincial premiers (five of them Tories) opposed Trudeau's constitutional proposal. Clark made common cause with them. Eventually, seven of the eight premiers came to an agreement with Trudeau, leaving Quebec's René Lévesque (and, to a lesser extent, Joe Clark) out in the cold and making it inevitable that Trudeau's constitution would pass. Clark continued to try to bring Quebec into the constitutional accord, notably by suggesting that Ottawa should agree to Quebec's demand for a provision allowing provinces to opt out of constitutional amendments with financial compensation. This provision had initially been advocated by the common front of eight provincial governments, and the decision of the seven English-speaking provinces to agree to opting-out without compensation was one of the reasons for Quebec's rejection of the accord. Brian Mulroney was strongly opposed to opting-out with compensation, arguing that it amounted to Ottawa's giving away its bargaining power. This division between Mulroney and Clark was still very much alive when the existence of a leadership campaign became official in 1983. (Other leadership candidates, evidently embarrassed by the fact that Clark's position was also the position of the Tory caucus, said they hadn't been paying attention when the position was developed.)

Mulroney's stand on the constitutional issue was far from being the only challenge to Joe Clark's leadership. In 1981 he had to face another leadership review vote at a party meeting in Ottawa, and his main strength at that point was that there were so many credible candidates to succeed him that the party could not agree on a replacement. At the Ottawa meeting, only two-thirds of the delegates voted against holding a leadership convention — nowhere near the proportion that had evoked comparisons with Jesus Christ three and a half years earlier, but comfortably above the 50 per cent plus one that Clark technically needed to stay in office. The Ottawa meeting did not resolve the issue of Joe Clark's leadership, but only postponed it. Nor was the anti-Clark activity in the party much affected by the progress the Tories were making in the Gallup Poll, which brought them ahead of the Liberals in early 1982. Far from ending the struggle, the likelihood that whoever held the leadership of the Conservative party would be the next prime minister merely raised the stakes.

Clark's display of political weakness in Ottawa forced him to promise the caucus that he would call a leadership convention himself if he didn't do appreciably better at the next party meeting. This promise brought into the open a group within the caucus that was determined to make sure he didn't. Although organized by Mulroney's most vociferous caucus ally, Elmer MacKay, and including a number of early Mulroney backers, the group was neither homogeneous ideologically nor in agreement as to who should replace Clark. David Crombie's man Chris Speyer belonged, as did John Crosbie's supporter Bob Wenman.

There were a number of living, breathing candidates about. John Crosbie signalled early, as did David Crombie and Michael Wilson. Clark had time to take a measure of these potential rivals. He could also estimate that neither Peter Lougheed nor William Davis would openly challenge his continued leadership unless forced into it by a power vacuum at the centre. So far, no such vacuum existed.

Of most importance, none of these actual and potential rivals was actually organizing against Clark. A potential candidate who is taking soundings and putting together a campaign team in the expectation of an eventual leadership race is one thing. A potential candidate who is organizing to bring one about — and organizing in such a way as to take control of a crucial base of support in Quebec while appearing as an option to the anti-Clark factions in English Canada — is quite another.

Brian Mulroney was Joe Clark's problem. And putting all other considerations aside, there had to be a test of strength between Mulroney and Clark. It had to take place in Quebec and it had to come soon.

The seriousness of Clark's situation was signalled by the fact that he was losing control of the party organization in Quebec. Mulroney's old friends Michel Cogger, Jean Bazin and Rodrigue Pageau had after 1976 gone to work for Clark; but they had long since given up on him, and after the 1980 election defeat they were openly organizing a Mulroney comeback. Gradually they were joined by others, mostly former Wagner organizers who for a variety of reasons — almost none of them having to do with substantive politics — had either rejected Clark or been rejected by him. Jean-Yves Lortie, who in 1976 had worked against Mulroney on behalf of Wagner, was now doing the same thing to Clark on behalf of Mulroney. By February, 1982, Mulroney supporters were ready to take control of the party executive in Quebec. This involved a compromise worked out between Pageau and Clark's main man in Quebec, Marcel Danis. Pageau and Danis had worked together in Mulroney's 1976 leadership campaign. In Quebec Conservative politics, the sides often change but the players remain the same.

The deal called for a neutral president, with most of the other offices split between Clark and Mulroney people. As such agreements so often do, this deal fell apart at the convention itself, and Mulroney's friends took over amid cries of anguish and foul. National party president Peter Blaikie accused Mulroney's people of "playing politics" at the convention — a strange charge considering the cast of players and the arena in which the game was played. In the meantime, Clark and his organizers were also "playing politics" in Quebec. After the 1981 meeting, where the vast majority of pro-review votes came from Quebec, Clark resolved to hit back. Organizers were hired in Quebec using national party funds, and under the direction of Danis these organizers were instructed to establish pro-Clark organizations throughout the province in preparation for another national party meeting scheduled for January, 1983, in Winnipeg.

The loss of the Quebec executive, which controlled thirty-eight appointed delegates and had the power to recognize delegate credentials, was a blow to Clark, but with his well-financed machine he was able to fight back quite effectively. Well over a year before the campaign was officially under way, the fight in Quebec was well past the hair-pulling stage.

And then, just prior to the Winnipeg meeting, Brian Mulroney endorsed Clark. But the message didn't reach all of his supporters who were working for a review vote, some so zealously that they provoked Dalton Camp into muttering about offshore money financing people to come to Winnipeg to vote for review. Mulroney's position caused some confusion, and there would be doubt among potential supporters when his campaign began to get into gear again. "Is he for real this time," people asked, "or is he going to back out again?" But to read Mulroney's support for Clark before Winnipeg as a failure of nerve was to miss the subtlety of his position.

Mulroney's public support of Clark also caused problems in the Clark camp. Mulroney's last-minute endorsement angered many Clark supporters because they knew that the pro-review movement in Quebec had a momentum and life of its own, regardless of what Mulroney said, did or didn't do in Winnipeg.

Marcel Danis, who though having supported Mulroney in 1976 then went to work for Clark and "just stuck it out until the end," recalls that "Finlay MacDonald was responsible for the *rapprochement* between Brian and Joe. He was convinced that Brian was being straight, but he wasn't actually aware of what was going on in Quebec." In fact, it was never a question of being straight or not. Mulroney's support of Clark was a tactical move. Dalton Camp and Finlay MacDonald, friends of both Clark and Mulroney, convinced Mulroney that it would not do his long-term prospects of becoming leader any good if he were the one to knock over the first domino at Winnipeg.

In any event, it was by no means sure before the Winnipeg meeting that Mulroney had the numbers in Quebec to overturn Clark. Moreover, outside Quebec — and especially in Ontario — the party establishment was not looking forward to a leadership convention, or more precisely was not looking forward to the internal party bloodbath that was likely to precede a leadership convention. Robert Stanfield and William Davis both pronounced against a leadership fight. Most observers felt that Clark would be strong enough in Winnipeg to turn back a leadership review and that a better occasion to force a leadership convention would arise in the future. Mulroney didn't need to force Clark's hand at Winnipeg. He had the one thing going for him that Clark lacked — time.

"Look, we always figured we had a shot at it," said Mulroney adviser Tom McPhail, "but we knew that it was going to be an uphill fight to defeat an incumbent. . . . And we had some other things going against us: his [Mulroney's] lack of a seat in Parliament . . . and we didn't know who all the players were." Mulroney also had other problems that could make an early leadership convention inconvenient and potentially dangerous. As president of the Iron Ore Company of Canada, Mulroney was about to face a difficult public hearing on the closure of operations in Schefferville. At the same time, the investigation of Conrad Black and his takeover bid for Hanna Mining was still going on and the possibility that Mulroney might be dragged into the affair as an innocent bystander, could not be discounted. Thus, if a leadership convention were to follow directly from the Winnipeg meeting, its timing would not likely be to Mulroney's advantage.

At the Winnipeg meeting, Clark received the support of 66.9 per cent of the delegates — up a scant two-tenths of a percentage point from his vote in Ottawa two years earlier. After the vote, he resigned, forcing a leadership convention. He also announced that he would be a candidate to succeed himself.

A great deal has been said about the wisdom or otherwise of

Clark's decision. In retrospect, it is clear that another strategy was called for. "All the guy had to do in Winnipeg," said one Mulroney campaigner (who incidentally didn't bother attending the Winnipeg meeting "because those guys who thought they were going to knock Clark off were dreaming"), "was to stand up after the vote and say, 'Okay, we'll continue the discussion after the next election.' We could have bitched and shouted, but there wasn't a damn thing we could do."

However, it wasn't quite as simple as that. Clark's weakness was displayed in Winnipeg. If he tried to hang on and had to face another leadership review before the next general election, the split in the party might merely grow to unmanageable proportions. Or worse still, if while the Tories were in disarray the Liberals held a leadership convention of their own and with a new leader called a snap election, the result could be disastrous.

So Joe went for it.

His decision to resign and force a leadership convention was something of a pre-emptive strike. It was a desperate gamble stemming from the knowledge that his position was weak — and that it would never be any stronger. It almost worked, because politics is as much perception as it is fact. In Winnipeg, 66.9 per cent of the vote made Clark a lame duck, while 50 per cent plus one of essentially the same people in Ottawa five months later would have made him the undisputed leader.

Clark was prepared, he had an efficient organization — which would come as an unpleasant surprise to a number of leadership candidates — and he had the powers of incumbency. This last entailed control of the party's machinery, including the multi-million-dollar P.C. Canada Fund, which he had used to great advantage over the seven years in which he was leader — especially in Quebec. The strategy of calling for a leadership convention also forced his phantom rivals out in the open, in many cases before they were ready.

With Winnipeg past and the leadership campaign beginning, the problem for Mulroney was to get out in front, but without moving too fast. He could afford to wait while some other candidates announced; yet the signals that he would eventually declare had to be clear, and he couldn't wait too long. He had to be in the race and campaigning before the delegate selection process began. He also had to tread pretty softly in Ontario while William Davis considered the possibilities.

And meanwhile, he had to face a committee of the Quebec National Assembly in a high-school gymnasium in Schefferville.

Mulroney returned from Florida with a sixty-page brief to present to the committee, and large graphs and charts to illustrate his presentation. In a number of areas, he was on fairly safe ground. He could speak of IOC's compensation program ("our responsibilities towards our employees must exceed by far any legal and union contract requirements") and be challenged only by the expected carping from Steelworkers representative Clément Godbout. He could bring along executive vice-president Richard Geren to talk about the possibility of strategic metal mining in nearby Strange Lake, which, even though it was only a possibility, at least provided the people of Schefferville with a basis for hope that their community would not become a ghost town.

A much more delicate area, however, was the financial status of the Iron Ore Company of Canada. Much of Mulroney's presentation was devoted to persuading the ministers that IOC had always been a responsible company and that its shareholders' returns had not been excessive. Among the obstacles he had to overcome were the company's results for the years 1979, 1980 and 1981, three of the best years in its history. IOC declared profits of $96 million in 1979, $81 million in 1980 and $105 million in 1981. In 1980 it distributed dividends of $82 million to its corporate shareholders, and increased that to $92 million the next year. As we have seen, income and dividend figures for a corporation that is owned by its principal customers are somewhat arbitrary. But it was not the figures themselves that were at issue so much as the interpretation of the figures. It was, after all, these results that had allowed Mulroney to be portrayed as the man who turned the Iron Ore Company around. Now, however, these very same results had to be made to justify the company's decision to shut down a significant part of its operations, and to allow it to portray a $10 million compensation program as generous. IOC's 1982 losses made it clear that the company's situation was not as rosy as the earlier figures had indicated, but a corporation does not make a major long-term decision such as the Schefferville shutdown on the basis of one bad year. Thus, Mulroney had to perform a difficult balancing act, and some of the members of the committee, notably PQ cabinet ministers Yves Duhaime and Pierre Marois, suspected that Mulroney's figures didn't quite add up.

Duhaime allowed that the company's profits for the years in question, representing a return on investment of between 9 and 12 per cent, were not excessive. Nevertheless, they did not fit in well with the picture Mulroney had painted of deteriorating markets and declining production. Could the president please explain what happened? Mulroney avoided answering this part of Duhaime's question. And when Marois asked a similar question later in the session, Mulroney again failed to respond. The next day, Marois was still bothered by this point:

> We don't think we got a precise answer about what actually happened since, in a certain sense, when you look at the figures that were presented to us by IOC itself, when you look at the profit figures for the years 1979, 1980 and 1981, in the very tables that were presented to us, the question is still there: "Why?" . . . In 1979, 1980 and 1981, at a time when production in tons was declining, the rate of return on investment reached 10 per cent — which still gives a low average return for the whole period [of IOC's operation]. The question is still there; there's something that's not clear.

Few such doubts, however, were noticeable in the press coverage of Mulroney's performance. In an article headed "Brian Mulroney steals the show" in the Quebec City daily *Le Soleil*, Jean-Didier Fessou quoted Yves Duhaime's remark about IOC's profits not being excessive but not his main point that they still didn't look like the financial results of a corporation facing a major shutdown. And in the Vancouver *Sun*, Jamie Lamb described Mulroney as having emerged from the "Schefferville abattoir" not only smelling like a rose but "as lush as a tropical greenhouse." Lamb called Mulroney a "wild and wonderful prospect" for the Tories, and said the Schefferville appearance was "a political springboard that has flung Mr. Mulroney into a high, graceful orbit over lesser candidates for the Progressive Conservative leadership."

It was, perhaps, uncomfortably reminiscent of the coverage of the early part of Mulroney's 1976 leadership bid. Nevertheless, the fact remained that Mulroney had come to the first hurdle of his still undeclared campaign to succeed Joe Clark as leader, and he had crossed it without a serious misstep.

CHAPTER EIGHT

This Time No Mistakes

The first test of strength between Joe Clark and his most formidable challenger, Brian Mulroney, came in Quebec. Mulroney had to win the majority of elected delegates and control the appointment of delegates-at-large or he was, to all intents and purposes, finished before his campaign moved out of the province. Clark, on the other hand, had to deprive Mulroney of his base. According to one Clark campaign adviser, it was a problem of shifting gears, of changing the "anti-review" committees into Clark re-election committees and of moving fast. Clark was under pressure from his people in Ontario and the West to demonstrate his strength in Quebec quickly.

The first matter that had to be settled was to have the convention called as soon as possible — in the event, on the June 11 weekend in Ottawa's Civic Centre. This done, the problem for Clark was, as Ronald Reagan's people used to say, "to hit the ground running." At a strategy meeting held at Stornoway, Marcel Danis proposed that delegate selection meetings be organized as soon as possible. It was a risk. If these early meetings didn't turn out well for Clark, he would be greatly weakened everywhere at the outset of the campaign. However, they reasoned, if they were to fail now, it would only mean that they would have an even worse failure if they waited. On the first weekend after the campaign officially opened, twenty-eight delegate selection meetings were held in Quebec. At seventeen of these meetings, the Clark slate was selected. Mulroney was caught off balance. That weekend was the high point of Clark's campaign in Quebec.

Mulroney roared back, and what followed was one of the more colourful donnybrooks in Quebec Tory history. When it was over, Mulroney had won a majority, but nowhere near the 85 per cent his organizers were talking about in March. In the course of this bruising fight, both Mulroney and Clark generated a lot of bad publicity for themselves, for the party and for the whole untidy business of selecting delegates for leadership conventions. Dalton Camp captured the spirit of the competition when he referred to the main protagonists as the anti-Clark and the anti-Mulroney forces. Outside of Quebec, where the issue of packed meetings also became an embarrassment to the party, it began to appear that Clark and Mulroney could well kill each other off in the whole unseemly process. But in Quebec there were just too many delegate votes at stake to let niceties stand in the way of getting the numbers.

The Progressive Conservative party has one sitting member from Quebec. In the last general election, it received less than 13 per cent of the popular vote, and in 1982 it had about 5,000 members. Before the Winnipeg meeting there were almost 14,000 members. By the time the delegate selection process for the leadership convention was finished, the party had more than 30,000 members. There is thus meaning to the term "instant Tories."

New members of the PCs were recruited everywhere. Campus clubs blossomed at hairdressing and sailing schools. Media attention was focused on busloads of transients living in places such as the Old Brewery Mission and voting delegates up much past their bedtime falling asleep in their mothers' arms. Comparatively little attention, however, was given to the slates of Clark or Mulroney delegates presented to meetings (in which other possibilities were not even mentioned) and voted on as a group. Nor was much said about the amount of money such tactics required, or the promises that must have been made to the people who were able to get the required number of bodies to the proper place to vote for the correct slate. Tories in Quebec are more than a little defensive about the whole delegate selection procedure. They maintain that the number of packed meetings was exaggerated in the press and that they were victimized by a set of rules that could not be applied in their circumstances. But nobody, at least in Quebec, took the criticism too seriously. As one Clark organizer said, "We proved in Quebec that our thugs were as good as Mulroney's." And when it was over, instead of weakening either Clark or Mulroney, the head-to-head battle in Quebec had squeezed every other candidate, announced or un-announced, out of contention.

The unseemly battle for delegate votes obscured a much more important political division in the party in Quebec, which did not really touch upon any division between old and new Tories or between mission transients and Westmount matrons. For while all the attention was on the "dirty tricks" in Quebec, it somehow escaped notice that the battle between Clark and Mulroney also reflected a deep political cleavage that has implications beyond any intraparty organizational struggle. Mulroney's appeal was to more federally inclined Quebecers, while Clark's was to the nationalists. It would be an exaggeration to suggest that the battle for delegates in Quebec amounted to a rerun of the Quebec referendum, but there were a surprising number of PQ organizers around Clark, and more than a few people generally associated with the Liberals around Mulroney. Mulroney's eventual victory provides a federalist alternative to the Liberals, assuming anyone is looking for one.

The few times the Tories have demonstrated strength in Quebec came when they appealed to the traditional rural nationalist vote. The election of a thoroughgoing federalist such as Mulroney is thus a break with a traditional Tory pattern in Quebec. It is also significant that Mulroney was strong on Montreal Island, and especially its western (and more English) half, while Clark did better in the rural areas. The rural nationalist vote could well be the constituency towards which René Lévesque looked with his apparently reluctant endorsement of a PQ federal front. In any case, the repercussions of the Tory leadership battle will be felt in the next federal election in Quebec.

While attention in Quebec was focused on the delegate wars, in the rest of the country the political right, or rather what was perceived as the political right by the media, appeared to hold the platform. All the candidates trimmed their sails to this prevailing wind, and they all addressed the code issues such as capital punishment and abortion. Abolitionists — Mulroney, Clark and Crosbie — promised a free vote on capital punishment. Even David Crombie, the "red tory" personified, thought capital punishment all right in certain instances. Capital punishment is, naturally enough, the code phrase for a tougher criminal code and more and harsher penalties for criminals. And within the whole complex of emotions, religious values and ethical judgments that the issue of abortion entails, there is an element of protest against a perceived breakdown of the traditional society in which people knew their place and did their duty. There also came an assault on social spending, an issue all the candidates addressed in varying degrees of vagueness. And there was a relentless attack on crown corporations and government institutions in general.

Outside of Quebec, the campaign took on the coloration of an ideological crusade, with all the candidates going with the flow. Peter Regenstreif, ex-pollster and since June 11 ex-campaign manager for Peter Pocklington, claimed there was "a blossoming of the right-wing views within the party." Dalton Camp, while complaining of the "cashew coalition" of right-wingers within the party, agreed that not only the party but also the entire country was more to the right in 1983 than it had been in 1976.

The issue of a "right wing" versus a "left wing" existed in 1976, even if it was never coherently defined. Brian Mulroney and Flora MacDonald — along with the obscure Joe Clark — were defined as the "red tory" candidates. Their credentials as red tories existed in the eyes of the beholder. In general, they were seen to be opposed to John Diefenbaker, friends of Dalton

Camp, perhaps connected with the Ontario Big Blue Machine. Maybe they also seemed to be associated with Robert Stanfield — whatever. It was never really fully worked out. And with Joe Clark's victory, it was assumed that the "red tories," now re-named "moderates," had won the field.

The internecine fighting never really stopped during the Clark leadership, and when the government was defeated in 1980, the war was in the open. By the time the party got to Winnipeg, a resurgent right wing was ready to settle accounts. Moreover, it seemed to be in a position to do it. Several months prior to the Winnipeg meeting, a group of right-wing Conservatives met with a conservative strategist from the United States to discuss whether or not to break from the party to form a new political organization. They decided not to, one of the reasons being that they felt they had a shot at taking over the Conservative party.

Even when it appeared that the Winnipeg meeting would re-confirm Joe Clark as leader, Allan Fotheringham wrote a with-ering column on the Tory right wing. Commenting on a survey taken among delegates to a Conservative meeting, Fotheringham wrote:

> Tory Incarnate, according to the survey, wants Ottawa to cut spending on daycare, unemployment insurance, family allowances and job creation programs. It fits. He wants the government, naturally, to reduce taxes on companies. It is no great surprise that there has been a recent influx of Amway distributors into southern Ontario ridings as Con-servative constituencies select delegates. . . . There are 100,000 Amway distributors in Canada, a "reservoir," as Conservative MP Scott Fennell, chairman of the credentials committee for the Ides of January, so felicitously put it.

The spectre of an Amway conspiracy to push the party to the right ultimately turned out to have as much substance as a soap bubble. The company that brings an evangelical zeal to free enterprise denied dispatching its foot soldiers to flood delegate meetings. As we've seen, the door to delegate meetings is wide open, and many in the party were alarmed by the prospect of delegate-packing from *outside* the party.

Brian Mulroney, however, said nothing. Perhaps he feared that a statement on his part about outsiders taking over constituency organizations would be regarded as being in poor taste. But there was also another reason for Mulroney to stay out of it. He knew he would be the ultimate beneficiary of a resurgent right wing in the party. And he courted this constituency very early, very carefully and very successfully, somehow transforming himself from being a "red tory" in 1976 to being the hero to the right wing in 1983.

That Mulroney was able to do this is a function of his personality, his position as president of the Iron Ore Company of Canada, and his convincing self-portrayal as the personification of the ideal of "success" with which the "free enterprise" system rewards those who have the ability and drive to reach the top. The parliamentary inexperience that had worked against him in 1976 was a clear advantage to him in 1983 in sections of the party, and especially among the younger members — or "Space Cadets" as they became known. While the other candidates were political hacks from the Ottawa talk shop and the bureaucratic maze, Mulroney came from the business community, the "real world." While government was leading Canada to unemployment, high interest rates and galloping inflation, destroying the conditions that allowed the honest entrepreneur to reap the rewards of his own hard work, Mulroney was on the front lines, successfully running a large corporation (including a railway), meeting a payroll and producing a return on investment for his shareholders.

Mulroney fed this impression of himself with a fund of quotable throwaway lines: "Governments have no money; they create no wealth," "A businessman goes up to Ottawa to meet some bureaucrat, and he is sitting behind a huge desk in an office larger than the floor area of your plant," or "[Some of the tax provisions in the National Energy Policy] are like holding up a gas station at 3 a.m." Handsome, well-spoken and well turned out, Mulroney basked in and radiated the glamour of success. With his warm smile, his tough no-nonsense image and his self-assured gait — ''nothing stuffy about this man'' — he had the air of a winner, the same air he had tried and failed to project in 1976. Brian Mulroney was a winner, the party he would lead would be a winner, and the government he would head would bring back the days when people who wished and worked for success could have it. Everybody could be like Brian.

Mulroney's campaign was able to back up this image with clever and well-financed organization. But the Mulroney campaign of 1983, like the campaign of 1976, was not primarily based on organization. It was based on the appeal of the man himself. And it was because of this appeal, the appeal of a winner, that Mulroney was able to remain attractive to the party's right wing as all the leading candidates blurred the political distinctions they laid out at the beginning. Mulroney's own speeches and pronouncements during the campaign were well crafted and cautious, and if it is hard to find anything in Mulroney's utterances in 1976 that made him a ''red,'' it is equally hard to find anything that defined him in 1983 as a ''right.'' The truth is that he is neither — or, more precisely, that he is both.

In any case, Mulroney has never shown much interest in ideological crusades or labels. He said that ''we cannot practise exclusionary politics in the Conservative party,'' adding that if the party divides itself with ''misleading labels, it will help only the Liberals. . . . I have been an active member of this party for twenty-eight years and have learned that categorizing people by hard and fast philosophical labels is both inaccurate and divisive.'' Meanwhile, he continued to capture votes where he could. Since, if David Crombie is discounted, Clark was the main victim of the right thrust in the party, Mulroney could merely shrug it all off, secure in the notion that my enemy's enemy is my friend.

The right-wing thrust in the party was a major factor in the most highly publicized non-campaign of the 1983 leadership contest, that of Ontario Premier William Davis. The notion took hold in Toronto that only Davis could prevent the party from being captured by the right. Davis's stalling and putting the Big Blue Machine on hold made it necessary for Brian Mulroney to tread very carefully in Ontario, and in the end weakened Joe Clark's effort to solidify a base in Ontario — perhaps even forcing on him the rather dubious strategy of packing delegate selection meetings under the guise of broadening the party's appeal to "ethnics."

While the idea of being national leader must certainly have appealed to Davis, the flaming rhetoric of the campaign discouraged his candidacy. The calls for a return to basic "free enterprise," straight up and hold the vermouth, were a source of discomfort to a government that loves its own crown corporations every bit as much as the Liberals love theirs. It is generally recognized that the longevity of the Tory government in Ontario comes from its pragmatism and its capacity for changing and renewing itself. Another source of the Ontario Tories' strength is their ability to get along with and do mutually advantageous deals with the even longer-lived Liberal government in Ottawa. (The Tory interruptions to Liberal rule federally have come mainly when the Ontario Tories got behind their federal brethren, and the end of Tory federal government is generally announced by the silent withdrawal of Ontario's support.)

In Ontario, the fear was not so much that the party's new leader would move the party to the right, but that he would move it right out of Ontario. To Edmonton to be exact. Camp associate Hugh Segal, a strong advocate of Davis's candidacy, suggested that Davis had to get into the race to stop the party from being delivered into the hands of someone farther to the right along the political spectrum, such as Mulroney or Lougheed. This came to the attention of the Alberta premier, who is reported to have telephoned Brian Mulroney to complain about this political stereotyping.

The Davis proto-campaign rubbed up against Mulroney's drive for the leadership from another direction as well. Among those encouraging the Ontario premier to run was a delegation from Quebec that had been part of Peter Blaikie's "network" until the former party president dropped out of the running.

Like Mulroney, Blaikie is a small-town Quebec Anglo who had the drive to make himself fluently bilingual, push himself through law school and make his breaks as a lawyer and toiler (and federal candidate) in the Tory vineyards.

The Blaikie campaign was never really a factor in Quebec, as far as the Mulroney people were concerned. Yet Mulroney did make an effort in February, immediately after the Winnipeg meeting, to keep Blaikie out of the race. In Florida to work out his presentation to the Schefferville committee hearing and get himself together for the leadership campaign, Mulroney kept the long-distance lines between Florida and points north burning with both business and political calls. One such call was placed between Mulroney and a friend of his who is also a friend of Blaikie's: "Tell Peter how much I admire him. Tell him what a gifted and intelligent man I think he is. Tell him that I will offer him the main economic portfolio in my government — minister of economic development or trade and commerce or something." When the message was passed on to Blaikie, the recipient of Mulroney's largesse replied that he wasn't interested.

This exchange may or may not have had a bearing on subsequent events, but Blaikie did throw his hat — and almost his head — into the ring. The campaign sputtered, and when Blaikie recognized his position, he quit.

It was no particular secret that Davis and most of his associates thought Joe Clark to be at best a weak and ineffectual leader, and at worst a conscious opponent of Ontario's aspirations within Confederation. Clark's notion of Canada as a community of communities has no place in William Davis's universe. During the Clark government's brief term — its brevity at least partly the result of Ontario's opposition — there was no love lost between the two governments on either a personal or a political level. After working hard on Clark's behalf in 1979, Davis found himself elsewhere in 1980, and when the call to arms went out in

January, 1983, he reluctantly appeared in Winnipeg with a cor-
poral's guard of his caucus, seeming to do the right thing by his
leader but in fact doing nothing at all.

On the other hand, Brian Mulroney, whose position on many
questions — especially the constitution — most clearly paralleled
that of William Davis, was simply not trusted by many powerful
people in the eastern Tory establishment. He has more than an
image problem in the Ontario party, although he has that also.
The lack of trust could be ascribed to a number of things. He
did not make a good impression during the 1976 campaign when
he came out of nowhere (Ontario Tories know better perhaps
than others farther away from Quebec that a Tory lawyer from
Montreal comes from nowhere), slick, prepackaged and with
what appeared to be plenty of money on lavish display; his flashy
self-assurance grated; and above all, his promise to win seats in
Quebec was suspect for perhaps no other reason than that the
line had been played before.

Marcel Faribault was supposed to ensure Tory gains in Quebec
in 1968 and didn't. And in 1973 Brian Mulroney, then co-chairman
of the federal party in Quebec, came armed with a poll showing
Claude Wagner to be more popular in Quebec than Pierre Trudeau, selling the party on the high-profile Liberal judge. Mulroney
knew that Wagner's drawing power was weaker than the poll
indicated (although he didn't realize that Wagner was as weak as
he turned out to be in the subsequent election), but he justified
the efforts made to recruit Wagner because it gave the whole
party credibility outside Quebec. "Wagner helped us a lot in the
West," he said, "because no one knew how weak we really were
here until the votes were counted. He scared shit out of the
Liberals for the first four weeks." Many Conservatives in Ontario,
while realizing the truth in Mulroney's claim that the party could
not expect to win power without strength in Quebec, did not
necessarily believe Mulroney was capable of delivering. The
stories of the packed meetings and rigged votes merely confirmed
their suspicions.

The Ontario Tories also didn't much like many of Mulroney's

friends and political associates in western Canada, and thought very little of what appeared to be an alliance between him and Peter Lougheed. (Much speculation surrounded the decision of St. Francis Xavier University, Mulroney's alma mater for which he has done so much in the way of fund-raising, to award an honorary degree to Lougheed just when the Alberta premier needed some stroking during the leadership campaign. Actually, the decision to honour Lougheed had been made two or three years earlier, and the timing of the acceptance was in Lougheed's hands.) Another source of misgivings was found among those who didn't like Mulroney's new-found acceptability to the party's rambunctious right wing.

In addition, there was a substantial constituency in Ontario that rejected Mulroney for another reason. This constituency was larger than the Royal Purple and Orange Lodge types, who, in any case, have tended to be unduly overlooked in Tory demographics of late. Without getting into any ethnic or religious overtones — people just don't like to talk about these things, at least not in Ontario where everyone knows that all the bigots come from Alberta — it is one thing to have a "Quebec lieutenant," but quite another to have a Quebec leader. And it was not only Mulroney's ethnic background that made many Tories uneasy but his social background as well. Americans may be most comfortable with the leader who comes from nowhere and pulls himself up by his bootstraps, and who neither tries to disguise his overweening ambition nor apologizes for his determination, but it's all too republican for Canadians, and especially Tory Canadians. Proper Tories should come to power with a sense of public duty, and an appearance, however frayed, of reluctance. This was an amorphous sentiment, but nonetheless a real one. Other people should be self-made men; Tory leaders should be born to it. This class-jumping son of an electrician somehow did not belong. Mulroney himself wryly acknowledged this. "Not only am I the poor kid from the wrong side of the tracks," he said, and nudged Mila, "but then I married this young immigrant just off the boat."

A consensus emerged that John Crosbie stood the most to gain from Davis's decision not to contest the leadership. Despite his forced plebeian manner, Crosbie, the former Liberal from the Newfoundland feudal aristocracy, seemed to be the most proper Tory among the major candidates. In many Ontario Tories' eyes, Crosbie became a serious candidate when he gave a turgid, humourless speech at an all-candidates' debate in Toronto and stopped calling that thing he'd saddled Joe Clark with a boojit, speaking instead of a budget. And besides, delegates from Ontario who didn't think a lack of French disqualified Davis would not likely insist that the Newfoundlander become bilingual either.

Crosbie was running a slick, well-organized and well-financed campaign and was getting plenty of media attention. "Insiders" and people "in the know" were beginning to tout Crosbie as the man on the move. With Davis out and Crosbie running smooth, the word was "Watch John." But the fact was that by deciding to be a non-candidate, Davis had also made himself a non-kingmaker. There was just no agreed-upon alternative.

In the 1983 campaign the fabled Big Blue Machine showed a surprising weakness and vulnerability. Davis confessed that he and the Ontario party were unable to stamp their will upon the party — something that has rarely, if ever, happened before. By the time the campaign reached Ottawa in June, the Big Blue Machine would look like little blue bumper cars wildly careening about the Civic Centre smashing one another into the boards.

In the words of one friendly reporter, Brian Mulroney rode up to the 1976 convention with "nothing more going for him than bilingual charisma and the guts of a bandit." In 1976 he ran a high-profile, expensive media campaign. His friends argue that at the time he had no choice. He was an unknown, his problem was to become known, and he did do that.

This argument is somewhat questionable. Joe Clark was an unknown too. Moreover, Mulroney's 1976 strategy seemed to be not only one that searched out the media but also one that avoided the delegates. It appeared as if he was trying to orchestrate the convention so that, in the words of one commentator at the time, the media would actually choose the leader for the delegates to ratify. And this was a prospect that alienated many delegates.

All this would be moot if another opportunity to run for leader had not arisen. For whatever else one may say about Brian Mulroney, he is a quick study. He rarely makes the same mistake twice. He learned from his experience in 1976 that a leadership campaign is not fought in the media. The media were essentially the battleground for the pollsters, pundits, "people in the know" and scenario writers. Bandwagons could be seen to start in the press, but in the end they would have little effect on the outcome.

Brian Mulroney's strategy in the 1983 campaign was threefold. First he had to secure his base in Quebec, from there he had to curry the favour of caucus dissidents, and then he had to get out and meet the delegates in their homes. All these elements were perfectly suited to the candidate's personality and the strength of his organization. But each of them also involved risks.

The muscle Mulroney's people demonstrated in Quebec created an image of ruthlessness that alienated the gentler souls in the party. It also demonstrated the instability and weakness of the party in Quebec, even as it expressed Mulroney's organizational strength.

Mulroney's stroking and eventual winning of many of the oddments of the Tory federal caucus, including some of the more ultra-right-wing MPs, gave his image a tinge of opportunism, at least among the section of the party that knew him from the 1960s as a "progressive." When the Stanfield loyalist emerged reborn in the 1980s as a candidate ultimately acceptable to the Otto Jelineks of the party, the alarm bells sounded and even lukewarm Clark supporters in the caucus mainstream rallied closer behind the embattled leader.

But the element of Mulroney's campaign that was fraught with the most danger was the effort to reach out to delegates across the country or, as it became known, the "Boonie Strategy."

The winter, 1979, issue of the *Canadian Journal of Communications* contained an article entitled "The Mass Media and Convention Voting Behaviour." Recalling the experience of 1976, it stated: "It would appear that the media certainly did not create a bandwagon effect in favour of one or two leading candidates. It is even possible that direct media support and coverage may have had a negative effect on candidate support." In a survey of delegates to determine the basis for their commitment or preference, 2 per cent cited media coverage, while 25 per cent cited "meeting with the candidate." The article continued: "This suggests that not only is the media's role in transmitting policy reduced by suspicion in the minds of delegates, but also by delegates' relative lack of emphasis on policy as a basis for voting decision."

The authors of the article were Allan Frizzell and Tom McPhail. Frizzell is a Carleton University journalism professor and pollster whose polls were to play a large role in the 1983 leadership campaign, and McPhail was — and remains — a communications adviser to Brian Mulroney. McPhail sent the article to Mulroney along with a detailed memo in early January, 1983. The memo elaborated on the conclusions of the article and outlined suggestions for the campaign. This all reinforced opinions Mulroney already held, and the campaign moved along the lines suggested.

However, if personal meetings with the delegates are the key, the unspoken problems involve finding all the delegates, meeting them and convincing them to vote for you. Meeting the delegates was a gruelling task for Mulroney. In all, he visited 268 federal ridings and pressed the flesh, proving himself to be an indefatigable campaigner.

And then there was The Speech, endlessly repeated. When he is in form, and his resonant baritone voice has had a bit of rest, Brian Mulroney can deliver a speech with such a rich mixture of blarney and glucose that it has been known to knock listeners into a diabetic coma. Much has been said about Mulroney's walking into meetings and singling out future judges and senators in the crowd. There was also his oft-repeated promise to hand out some federal appointments to deserving Liberals a decade or two down the road when all the Conservatives have been taken care of. It was all good fun, and Tories were reminded that they have been missing out on something that Liberals take for granted.

But the essence of the Mulroney speech spoke of other things, and stirred other emotions among the less jaded in the crowd. Its standard elements were the line about gift-wrapping and delivering the francophone seats to the Liberals the moment the writs are served; his experience at Iron Ore; his work for the party; yes, the fact that he never served in Parliament was a disadvantage, but then all the other candidates had disadvantages; and then The Vision. As he developed it in his campaign speeches, Mulroney's vision centred on home, family and community. It harked back to a quiet, civil and orderly country where there was a spirit of generosity and the community helped the individual to get ahead, while supporting the "less fortunate." Economically, his vision was of a Canada like the one of the 1950s and 1960s, where investment flowed and private enterprise flourished. We had this once, he would say, and we can have it again. Only in the 1980s government must reorder its priorities, and use its taxation policies and other levers to regain our lost productivity so that the country may not necessarily work harder but "work smarter."

All this was in public meetings, but the key to what was called the "Boonie Strategy" was the small, informal gatherings without the press, where Tories could talk Tory problems. That was where the convincing took place, delegate by delegate, vote by vote. The Mulroney campaign was well organized, it had lots of money — at least until the very end — and it had all the sophisticated computers it needed. But finally it was Mulroney himself who carried the message to endless numbers of plywood-veneered rec rooms, through gallons of coffee, hours of kitchen-table talk, and innumerable warm handshakes in windowless Holiday Inn meeting rooms.

The message consisted of variations on the theme that he and only he could win, because he and only he could carry seats in

Quebec and francophone constituencies in the other provinces. Sometimes in the West he would regale his listeners by imitating Knowlton Nash and Barbara Frum on a typical election-night telecast: "Things were going well for the Tories until the votes started being counted in Quebec. . . ." And when he was at his sonorous best, he would summon up "John A. Macdonald's Grand Alliance of East and West, French and English" that would keep the Tories in power for the rest of the century: "If one of the components is missing, you are doomed to opposition."

Generally, Mulroney steered clear of any direct criticism of the other candidates. Only at the end did he lash back, when Joe Clark mentioned the "extraordinary risk" the party would take in electing an inexperienced leader. Mulroney retorted that the experienced Clark and Crosbie had let their nine-month government get "blown out of the water. . . . If that's experience, I'll stick with my North Shore common sense."

Mila Mulroney was as tireless as her husband on the campaign trail. Mila had always known of and supported Brian's political ambitions. Since the time they met while she was a campaign worker for Michael Meighen, their political attitudes have meshed. Even after the bruising defeat in 1976 and through the secure and prosperous years while he was president of Iron Ore and they lived in a Westmount mansion, she had been sympathetic to his desire to get back into active politics. And when the opportunity to have another shot at it appeared to present itself, Mila encouraged him to run. "I always knew," she said, "that politics was his mistress." She told him from the outset — even before he was sure himself — that if he wanted to try again he should.

But Mila initially decided that she would stay home with the kids in Montreal while her husband was campaigning. "I told her she was crazy," says Janis Johnson, a close personal friend of the couple whom Mulroney appointed national director of the party. Johnson, who was married to former Newfoundland Premier Frank Moores, told an interviewer: "In politics a wife either throws herself into it or she doesn't. There are no half measures. If you don't, you may jeopardize your marriage. It's easy to lose touch.''

For whatever reason, Mila threw herself into the campaign, and soon emerged as one of Mulroney's major political assets. In the inevitable comparisons with another young woman who had combined the roles of student, mother and political wife, Mila was regarded (quite unfairly) as more traditional than the intense Maureen McTeer — whom Mila admires.

Comfortable in crowds, Mila smiled and chatted, remembered names and faces, talked easily with strangers and comforted old pols with stories of the great reunion of Tory MPs to be held in Ottawa after the next election. On many occasions she seemed to provide a nice balance to the brash and sometimes bellicose candidate. As the campaign developed, so did Mila's role. When she was not with Brian at a meeting, she was generally back at the hotel monitoring coverage of the campaign in the media — especially television. While she never let anybody get away with knocking Brian in her earshot, her attitude towards the transgressions of the media did not have as hard an edge as that of her husband. ''It's a free country, people can voice their opinions,'' she would tell Brian. ''That's why my father moved the family here from Yugoslavia.''

Mila also added an element of human vulnerability that the practised and self-assured Brian often fails to convey. At one point in the campaign someone asked her what would happen if Brian lost. She said they would be very disappointed, of course, but they have family and responsibilities, and they would go back to Montreal, go back to work and start their lives again. ''I was told that that wasn't a very good answer,'' she recalls. ''I should have said something like 'We have no intention of losing,' that we hadn't even thought of the possibility of losing — upbeat stuff. But that's really stupid, I think. You can always lose, but life goes on.''

Mila's steadying influence on Brian was also evident. She tempered her husband's tendency towards verbal embellishment, and friends of the family say she greatly influenced his decision to quit drinking about a year and a half before the leadership campaign (he remains an abstainer). According to friends, Mulroney never had a "drinking problem" but a few drinks would slow him down. Mulroney says he had to stop temporarily while on medication; afterward he simply decided not to start again.

During the campaign, Mulroney didn't slow down for a moment. He lost twenty pounds, living, as he said, "on cheese sandwiches and humility." And he proved to be a great campaigner. He was, as they say in the business, one terrific Closer.

The risk in the Boonie Strategy was this: more small private meetings means fewer media events, and lack of media exposure creates the perception of problems. Mulroney tended to disappear in the media; as the campaign wore on, he seemed to fade and stories that he was in trouble began to circulate. And worse, that magic word of all political campaigns, "momentum," began to be attached to others — to John Crosbie, to Joe Clark. While it is difficult to recall whether the famous Richard Nixon lament about "peaking too soon" was ever associated with Mulroney's campaign, there was the word that Brian was blowing it again.

With Mulroney off the front pages, the Crosbie Scenario for the convention voting, the latest of several theories to arise, began to be heard. It was based on the generally accepted hypothesis that Crosbie was running third. Given Joe Clark's experience in 1976, a strong third was considered to be the magic spot. The idea was that the two front-runners, Clark and Mulroney, would kill each other off, and their supporters in an outpouring of mutual antipathy would move to the least hated candidate who had a chance to win. Crosbie, many thought, fit the bill. There were a number of problems here, not the least being that Clark's first ballot placing in 1976 was important not only because of the deadlock between Mulroney and Wagner but also because of the relatively low vote obtained by Paul Hellyer and Flora MacDonald. Clark's victory also owed much to Sinc Stevens's sudden shift from deep right to shallow left. Stevens's move to Clark came as a surprise — for those who couldn't see past the ideologue to a politician making a simple practical decision. Stevens helped Clark immeasurably, and helped himself as well.

Oddly, the most bullish pushers of the Crosbie Scenario were Joe Clark campaigners. One Clark operative confided, in that intimate tone one saves for the greatest of political lies, that Clark was really worried Crosbie was going to run second on the first ballot. Obviously there is some question whether the Clark forces were really that concerned about Crosbie or whether they were merely trying to feed the rumours then making the rounds about the imminent collapse of the Mulroney campaign.

In the midst of all this idle speculation, the first Carleton Poll was published on May 16. It was a chilly morning in Montreal. In Mulroney's headquarters, a nondescript two-storey building designed for a frugal campaign, things were rather subdued. Most of the heavies were out of town, and the functionaries in the office either hadn't read the newspaper that morning or didn't believe the poll.

Not only did the poll not show Mulroney to be in the lead, but it showed him running a poor second to Clark, with Crosbie in third place breathing down his neck. The Mulroney staff disputed the poll. Wall charts in the headquarters showed Mulroney running well ahead of Clark in Quebec, something like 455 to 290, while the poll indicated Mulroney and Clark almost head-to-head in Quebec, with a slight advantage to Clark. In this sense, the poll gave credence to the claims of the Clark people. Even more ominous for Mulroney, the poll indicated that Crosbie, although third, was running far better than had been thought. He could even catch Mulroney. And worse, in what were then considered the crucial second- and third-ballot choices, Crosbie had the most potential for growth.

The veracity of polls is questionable, but polls are believed. Even someone who tells you that polls are nonsense will take another poll out of his pocket just to prove his point. The trick with polls is not what they say but how they are read and what scenarios are made of them. Even though the poll showed that Clark had only 35 per cent of the first-ballot support — slightly less than half of what the same poll said he would receive in Winnipeg and slightly more than half of what he actually received in that cold city — most headlines on the poll hit on Clark's big lead. "Clark far ahead in leadership, poll finds," said the *Toronto Star*. Clark campaign people used the poll to drop hints that they expected to win on the first ballot. Clark himself tried to dampen the confidence by suggesting that it might take two or three. But some of his workers eagerly accepted the results as a tool to be used on Mulroney supporters.

John Crosbie thought he could draw the most comfort from the poll inasmuch as it indicated that there were more non-Clark votes out there than Clark votes and that he and not Brian Mulroney appeared to be in the best position to get them. There were enough Mulroney and Crosbie supporters with a foot in both camps to make a move to the power both quick and easy, and these delegates could dance either way. The poll had altered, in Crosbie's favour, the perception of who would come to whom on the second ballot.

As for the other candidates, the poll indicated that the also-rans weren't even also-running. The poll also helped the great lather over the influx of Amway soap salesmen disappear, made the militant right suddenly seem less militant, and sent David Crombie off to rescue Dulcinea instead of the Conservative party.

And then Robert Jackson, head of the political science department at Carleton University, took issue with the pollsters' methodology and reinterpreted their results to show that Clark had somewhere between 30 and 40 per cent, Mulroney between 26 and 30 per cent, and Crosbie between 18 and 20 per cent. This turned out to be pretty well how things developed. But at the time, the scenario writers weren't paying much attention.

Thus, the various interpretations of one innocent poll changed the direction of several campaigns, ignited several dreams and torched several others. The one common thread running through all the reactions to the poll was that Brian Mulroney was everyone's designated victim. Given the situation, the Mulroney people kept very cool. They disputed the Quebec figures, but not very loudly. They said there would be other polls, and they made sure that there were. Tom McPhail even claimed the poll helped: "The poll just forced us to go a little harder and look for help. We opened lines of communication with everyone. Clark, on the other hand, was lulled into a sense of security which didn't evaporate until he got to Ottawa."

Above all, the candidate himself had to keep cool and stay the course. And Brian Mulroney tried. But, he wasn't about to let any Crosbie media boom develop unchallenged. "We're winning," he blasted in Kitchener on May 27. "Everyone's writing about Crosbie. Crosbie's going nowhere — it's all hype. It's all media hype." Mulroney's anger over the new attention given Crosbie could have been in part responsible for one of the sillier missteps he took in the campaign — his threat to sue CBC reporter Mike Duffy for suggesting that he and Crosbie had a deal.

But the Mulroney campaign stayed with its game plan and Brian kept stroking the delegates. On March 15, Mulroney campaign strategists calculated that they had 875 first-ballot votes. By June 11, they would lose only one of these votes.

By the weekend before the convention, it was apparent that most of the delegates had already made up their minds, at least as far as their first-ballot choices were concerned. It was also apparent that the various campaigns had a fair idea of who was voting for whom and who was susceptible to being pried away on subsequent ballots. And so, as the crowd gathered at Ottawa's worn-out convention facility on a warm and sunny Wednesday in June, it all seemed a little anti-climactic.

But as the delegates arrived and mingled, everyone seemed determined to make the best of it, and the fun began. Bands played, banners waved, strategists strategized, and the candidates were, as they say, seeking exposure. Joe Clark and John Crosbie arrived to register at about the same time. Each was surrounded by supporters, and the issue quickly became who could muster the largest group for the television cameras. The Crosbie people claimed to have the edge, but the Clark supporters gained the initiative by starting to shout anti-Liberal slogans. This forced

the Crosbie people to join in, giving the impression that everybody was cheering Joe and Maureen. While each side tried to
claim victory, they were both doing better than poor old Brian
Mulroney, who was out at the airport to meet a plane that had
already arrived.

The delegates mingled and seemed genuinely happy to be in
one another's company again — the Tories have a lot of conventions, and since many of the same faces show up at each,
such events take on the air of a reunion. Considering the manner
in which they had battered one another over the past few months
and would continue to batter one another over the next few days,
it seemed a festive truce. Watching the crowd, Mordecai Richler
claimed to know why the Tories throw such good conventions:
"Nobody invites them to parties."

The convention went through its motions at its own pace,
wrapped within its own universe, isolated from outside influences
as if it were a luxury liner in mid-Atlantic. In the universe of
the convention, the driving force was gossip and speculation.
And most of the talk was about Brian Mulroney and the terrible
troubles he was having. Michel Cogger was reported to be running about trying to raise $50,000, Bell was threatening to cut
off Mulroney's phones (apparently when Mulroney first set up
his headquarters in Montreal, Bell first demanded payment of
the balance of his 1976 bill, and this time they weren't about to
wait), a printer was also demanding money, and the tent-rental
company was about to take down the big blue and white tent
across the street from the Civic Centre.

There were also rumours of war within the Mulroney organization. In fact, there were questions about whether there was
a Mulroney organization. (In the end, Mulroney's campaign strategy worked, his polling was bang-on, and his logistics got him
where he had to be, meeting the people he was supposed to meet;
any criticism of his organization should have been silenced by
the final ballot.) A member of Mulroney's staff dismissed the
stories of fights among his main men: "Look, we start off small,
just a group of close friends, then the campaign gains momentum,

more and more people join, everybody wants to get his two cents worth in, and things get unwieldy, that's all.''

His answer had enough truth in it to be serviceable. For despite the obvious seriousness of Mulroney and his friends, there is a quality to the network that differentiates it from the cooler, more professional, more practical and more temporary campaign teams that are generally put together. Friends of Mulroney see similarities with the Kennedys and their cronies. In a sense it is almost a perfect political package. There are buzz words about an ''Irish Mafia,'' and variations on the ''in crowd'' invited to football games in Hyannis Port come to mind — people are now counting the times they were included in the fishing trips Mulroney likes to organize. But perhaps before this linking of Mulroney with the Kennedy mystique all goes too far, a more ''Canadian'' comparison should be applied to Mulroney and his friends — the old beer commercial, for example (for years now Brian, Peter, Michel, Jean and the boys have been getting together over a few beers while planning to take over the Progressive Conservative party. . .). With its middle-aged macho style, it is a tight group, but as the campaign grew, the network also grew and broadened. And the very success of the Mulroney network in this campaign may also have marked the beginning of its end. For there is a two-way process: the new leader takes over the party, but the party also takes over the new leader. (One of Mulroney's first key appointments after he was elected leader went outside his circle of cronies: Janis Johnson was named national director. And the slick Ontario campaign strategist Norman Atkins came on board for the next federal election campaign.)

Throughout the campaign, Brian Mulroney had been attacked, teased and taunted for being ''fuzzy on the issues.'' He was criticized for not only refusing to disguise his own personal ambitions, but also for tempting the personal ambitions of others by talking patronage, making promises and recognizing a very important interest that resides in everybody — self-interest. But in Mulroney's view, the only issue was leadership. His campaign pitch boiled down to two simple contentions: the party had to change leaders to be assured of defeating the Liberals in the next election, and the only way to change leaders was to vote for Brian Mulroney.

Once the convention opened, it became clear that Mulroney's definition of what was at stake had been right all along. It was as if all the speeches, the great thrust to the right, and the heroic defence of the twentieth century by the embattled "red tories" had never taken place. It was not only Mulroney who was appealing to self-interest; now everybody was doing it. Even David Crombie, who had defiantly, almost poetically, rediscovered his "red toryism" and denounced all the tough talk of cutbacks in social spending, selling off crown corporations and new economic links with the United States, was not immune. He had attacked John Crosbie, Michael Wilson and "all those who would lead the party along a path Canadians would not follow" — which would presumably include Peter Pocklington, who along with John Gamble stood furthest to the right of all the candidates. And now he was fiddling around with Crosbie, Wilson and Pocklington in an effort to defeat Joe Clark who stood for a "modern and moderate" party, and at the same time stop Brian Mulroney who supposedly stood for nothing at all.

Getting to the delegates at a convention is hard and requires a large army. All the candidates had loyalists assigned to delegates in other camps. The most complete "buddy system" was the one developed by Joe Clark. With a rather complete profile of every delegate, Clark would attempt to match up delegates with something in common.

Mulroney also had a buddy system of sorts, although a much more limited and direct one. While it courted defections wherever it could find them, its immediate interest was in wavering supporters of the other candidates. It was especially designed to stay attuned to the mood of Clark's Quebec supporters. The message was also more basic: 'We didn't come all this way to elect Joe Clark. It's time to get on board.''

The first-ballot totals would be important not only in themselves but also as an indication of the validity of Mulroney's contention that he and only he could defeat Joe Clark. Despite a Carleton Poll released on the eve of the convention showing that a two-way race between Mulroney and Clark was too close to call, Mulroney's people were confident that their candidate could beat Clark in a showdown. But if Clark's vote were weaker than expected, or if it were to crumble rapidly, the whole race could open up again. Thus, for the Mulroney strategy to work, Clark had to be in the lead on all ballots except the final one.

A Gallup Poll commissioned by the Mulroney campaign indicated that Mulroney had 28 per cent of the first-ballot vote — a brighter and in the event a more accurate estimate than others circulating about. The Mulroney people liked this poll so much that they leaked it to the *Globe and Mail*. ''I know we pissed off Gallup leaking this poll,'' said Tom McPhail. ''But we needed a bit of a boost.'' The poll showed that Mulroney would finish a strong second on the first ballot and had good second- and third-ballot potential. But it also showed that in spite of all the campaigning, all the meetings, all the speeches, more than 70 per cent of the delegates wanted someone other than Brian Mulroney as leader. While Mulroney was always confident that he could make the party love him, the courtship had been long, arduous and mostly one-sided. Much publicity had surrounded the Anybody But Clark movement in the party. But there was also a latent Anybody But Mulroney movement that could not coalesce so long as Joe Clark was the issue. If Clark were to disappear, however, anything could happen.

A cross-check of Mulroney's internal surveys indicated that Clark's solid support was between 1,000 and 1,050 votes. The Mulroney camp also estimated, contrary to widely held opinion, that very little erosion would take place in Clark's vote if the gap between Clark and Mulroney on the first ballot was in the neighbourhood of the expected figure of 200 votes. Clark's support would be less solid if the Clark-Mulroney gap was under 100 votes, but this was unlikely. Mulroney's people also expected Crosbie's vote to have a ceiling of 650, with the other candidates splitting the remaining 350 to 400. It followed from this analysis that if Mulroney was about 200 votes behind Clark and more than 200 votes ahead of Crosbie on the first ballot, he would be unstoppable. On the other hand, if the gap between Mulroney and Crosbie were to be under 200 votes, an unfavourable split in the also-ran vote could put Crosbie in contention.

In the event, Clark's first-ballot vote of 1,091, 217 ahead of Mulroney's 874, placed him out of reach on the second ballot but vulnerable on subsequent ones. Crosbie's 639 was not enough to stop Mulroney. Now the moves were made. Peter Pocklington had come to an earlier understanding with Mulroney, and says he phoned Michael Wilson and convinced him to move as well. Crombie was also called, but he was under the impression that an understanding had been reached among Wilson, Pocklington and himself to go to Crosbie. It has also been reported that Crombie decided to remain on the ballot because he is stubborn and had vowed he was staying on until he was forced out. Whatever his motivation, Crombie's decision to stay on the second ballot gave Crosbie one final shot at Mulroney.

There was some tension, and a brief moment of fear, as Wilson and Pocklington made their way to the Mulroney seats. Mila Mulroney, who in 1976 had watched Heward Grafftey, Jim Gillies, Sinclair Stevens and Flora MacDonald walk right on past their section to sit with Joe Clark, now saw Pocklington and Wilson hesitating in front of the seats. "My God," she muttered, "they're going to Crosbie!" Actually they were merely searching for the gate. "When I saw Michael the next day," she said, "I told him I was never so happy to see anybody in my life."

The move of Pocklington and Wilson to Mulroney was a morale booster, but it had little practical effect. Of more importance were the efforts being made by Mulroney supporters to bring in the strays. The people who had been parked waiting to see where the power was, were now buttonholed. Sam Wakim seemed to catch every waverer: "Now is the time. We need you now." It was both a promise and a threat. "Sam was on to everybody around me," a delegate said. "If he could work as hard and effectively in his own interests as he did for Brian

Mulroney, he could get anything he wanted.'' Many other friends of Mulroney had also been waiting for this moment and went to work for him. The enemies of Brian Mulroney were also working, mostly on behalf of the embattled Clark. As far as Mulroney was concerned, this was the safest place for them to be. Some Mulroney strategists even briefly considered giving some votes to Clark to shore up his position. While this was soon discounted as being too risky, the Mulroney camp did, for a time, discourage any Clark defections. In the words of Michel Cogger, ''They should stay with their chicken until it was cooked.''

Despite the endorsement of Wilson and Pocklington, Mulroney picked up only five more votes than Crosbie on the second ballot, but it was enough. It was now clear that Crosbie could not gain on Mulroney. Of equal significance, Clark lost a mere six votes. The Mulroney scenario was being played out. The first ballot demonstrated that the party wanted a new leader, and the second ballot demonstrated that Mulroney was the only alternative to Clark.

Nevertheless, there was still time for some last-minute wheeling and dealing. Clark was urged to move to Crosbie. This was an impractical idea for a number of reasons. First of all, Clark led Crosbie by more than 300 votes. And if he were to drop out, there was no assurance that he could deliver his vote to another candidate. In fact, there was every indication that his Quebec vote would stay with him to the end, but if the end came before the final ballot it would move to Mulroney — and that would be enough for Mulroney to win. Besides, if Crosbie were to be eliminated on the third ballot, there was still a wan hope that one last bit of life could be breathed into the Anybody But Mulroney movement, maybe enough for Clark to squeak by.

Clark had waged a tough and courageous campaign, an emotional battle in which he gave as good as he got. But if he was going to lose, the way in which he lost was still important to him. And the way he chose was to stand his ground and keep his dignity. Clark disagreed with Brian Mulroney on many questions, but they had both fought for the concept that the Progressive

Conservative party had to gain a foothold in Quebec if it was not to stay forever in opposition. A showdown between John Crosbie and Brian Mulroney, with Crosbie conceivably winning, would set the party back to square one. And perhaps most important of all, Clark owed Crosbie not one single thing.

Clark stayed in for the third ballot and lost fewer than 30 votes. Brian Mulroney only picked up about 15. But the essential outcome of the ballot was the elimination of John Crosbie. And so the campaign was to end as it began, in the words of Dalton Camp, the anti-Clark forces against the anti-Mulroney. Sixty-three voting delegates didn't bother to stay around for the showdown, and another 19 spoiled their ballots, but in the end there were 269 more anti-Clark votes than there were anti-Mulroney. A safe enough margin, about the size Mulroney figured it would be.

Brian Mulroney's organization, which had adroitly picked a campaign strategy, accurately defined the issues, got the numbers right and displayed the muscle to get it all done, had forgotten one thing. It had forgotten to book space for a victory party. There was a wedding scheduled in the ballroom of the Chateau Laurier, and Clark had booked the hotel's second largest facility. But the Mulroney celebrants didn't seem to mind. They were happy enough as they coursed through the lobby and corridors, squeezed between a wedding and a wake.

CHAPTER NINE

The Great Negotiator

I f the essence of winning a leadership convention is convincing the delegates and getting their votes, then the natural emphasis of a leadership campaign is on the mechanics of organization. However, winning the support of the delegates means speaking to them and telling them what they want to hear, or at least leading them to believe that you have told them what they want to hear.

The problem is that they don't all want to hear the same message.

The Progressive Conservative party is divided on many philosophical and ideological matters. The essence of this division is the fact that the party is out of power federally. All parties out of office tend to divide, simply because the question "Why did we lose?" does not elicit the same answer from everybody concerned. The curiosity of winners is generally muted by the thought that "whatever we did, we should continue to do." There are, therefore, solid grounds to argue that the party will unite if and when it wins a federal election.

In the meantime, a candidate running for the Conservative leadership must criss-cross the country meeting delegates, and every inch of the terrain is mined. Moreover, what is said to influence the delegates is overheard by the electorate at large.

Thus, not only must the man who would be Tory leader cross a minefield, but some of the mines have delayed-action devices, set to explode later, during a federal election campaign for example.

The politics of any leadership hopeful must therefore out of necessity run on two tracks. No one appears to understand this better than Brian Mulroney. To situate him within the politics of the Conservative party as they came to be manifested during the leadership campaign is one thing; how his politics will be expressed within the larger context of the electorate as a whole is quite another. In other words, the things a politician says and the image he creates in addressing that small and highly unrepresentative group of Canadians who act as the delegates to a Progressive Conservative convention are somewhat different from the way in which he addresses the much larger group that votes in federal elections. In Mulroney's case, given the peculiarities of the 1983 leadership campaign, this is not merely a matter of emphasis.

Mulroney's problem was to build a coalition around himself out of many disparate elements in his party who were united only in their belief that the party needed a new leader. Mulroney was not drafted by anyone, nor was he a spokesman for any wing of the party. Joe Clark simply had the job that Brian Mulroney wanted. Mulroney's solution was to be as vague and general as possible. He was not about to move any embassies or dismantle any crown corporations. The extent to which this strategy succeeded can be seen in some of the reasons people who supported him gave when they declared for Mulroney during the leadership campaign.

George Hees, when he announced his support for Mulroney, said: "We have to improve our production in order to make our goods attractive to others. . . . Brian is the man who knows how to do that."

When Sinclair Stevens announced his support, he said Mulroney would take measures to slash Canada's deficit: "That's what this country needs, and Brian can do it."

Walter McLean, the Tory MP for Waterloo and an opponent of

testing the Cruise missile, linked his support for Mulroney with a vague reference to an even vaguer position on the Cruise enunciated by Mulroney early in the campaign. (Mulroney later came out in favour of the test.)

Alvin Hamilton switched support from Joe Clark to Brian Mulroney in 1983 for the simple reason that he felt Clark had had his chance and was not up to the job.

In general, Mulroney's caucus support was one of the curiosities of the campaign. The majority and "mainstream" of the caucus supported Clark, while Mulroney attracted the outsiders and those credited with the most extreme right-wing views, such as Otto Jelinek and Robert Coates. In the end, however, it was not an ideological affinity with Mulroney that attracted this support — one MP, Gordon Gilchrist, supported Mulroney at the same time as he elaborated his idea that English should be the only official language in all of Canada. Mulroney built his support among caucus dissidents not essentially because of what he stood for but because he was seen as an attractive alternative to Clark. There was thus an element of good fortune for Mulroney in the fact that he was somewhat of an unknown quantity and was not part of the fractious caucus of the Clark period.

Yet Mulroney does not accept the notion that luck has had anything to do with his fortunes in the party. "They said I couldn't get elected leader. Then they said my election would divide the party. Then I couldn't win in Nova Scotia. Then I couldn't get a larger plurality than Elmer MacKay. Then I wouldn't be able to handle myself in the House. . . ."

"They" are the Liberals and important sections of the national media. And to the extent that "they" have underestimated the abilities of the new Tory leader in his first months in office, they have been proved wrong.

After the leadership campaign, although handicapped by being forced almost immediately into another campaign to give him a seat in the House of Commons, Mulroney moved with relative ease and precision. The construction of his shadow cabinet was a case in point. He paid off political debts in some quarters, and established himself in a net creditor position in others. But the essential thing was that he pre-empted the possibility of a base for a rival power centre within the caucus. He demonstrated both tact and power with Clark and his main supporters in the House. He made Sinclair Stevens external affairs critic, but only after Stevens agreed not to repeat certain of his own previous statements on foreign policy. He was very generous with John Crosbie, making him finance critic, and magnanimously gave David Crombie a profile. He rewarded Michael Wilson, not only by giving him a senior economic portfolio (industry and trade) but also and perhaps more significantly by making him the potential political minister for Ontario.

Since Wilson is the man most acceptable to the Ontario party, this helps in building a relationship with the Tory dynasty, another area where Mulroney has moved deftly. The new leader also took Ontario's interests into account in the distribution of minor shadow cabinet positions and either embraced the Big Blue Machine or allowed the machine to embrace him. There were a few muffled cries in the new leader's personal entourage, but as far as the caucus and party were concerned, Mulroney was the man of consensus. Yet everyone knows that whatever else the Progressive Conservative party may have, it does not have a consensus. There is a thin line between being a man of consensus and being a man of obfuscation, and treading that line is something that Mulroney has raised to an art form.

Stated simply, Brian Mulroney believes that precise policy positions have been the bane of the party. Outlining his campaign strategy early in the 1976 leadership race, Mulroney said that one of the criteria for a successful leader was to avoid being specific on policy. The Liberals, Mulroney said at the time, won the 1974 election because they forced the Tories to defend their specific position on wage and price controls, instead of being forced by the Tories to defend their own record. What the Tories needed in 1976, Mulroney believed, was a winner, not a policy debate.

He carried the same message in 1983. But if the message was the same, the candidate himself had changed. In 1976 Mulroney was criticized for lacking political substance. As one associate who refused to support him at the time said, Mulroney had never even addressed national politics or issues. He was a slick, successful Montreal lawyer, adept at the nuts and bolts of backroom politics, but his political experience was limited to the infighting of that rather little band of mostly unsuccessful politicians connected with the federal Conservative party in Quebec.

However, between 1977 and 1983, Mulroney was the president of a company that is, in effect, the Canadian arm of a large and politically sophisticated multinational corporation, and also served as a director of the parent firm. He had the opportunity to broaden his political horizon, to get into the game at the highest levels, and to learn at first hand how the mesh of economic, political and social forces operates. As president of the Iron Ore Company of Canada, he had extensive experience in a role that is also one of the most important functions performed by North American political leaders — mediating between powerful economic interests and the people who are affected by their activities.

Those who read him in 1976 as little more than a charming facade are unlikely to dismiss him in the same way now. Mulroney still has all the political qualities he had in 1976, plus one or two new and significant ones. Having added his tenure at Iron Ore to his previous participation in complex labour negotiations and his position on the Cliche Commission, he came to the Tory leadership with more specialized training and experience in the management of relations among business, labour, government and the public than any other leader of a major Canadian political party since Mackenzie King.

The second difference between 1976 and 1983 was that in 1983 Mulroney succeeded in convincing the delegates of the validity of his twofold political message: that power comes before policy, and that he, Brian Mulroney, was the man with whom the party could achieve power. Because Mulroney's message was ''power first,'' and because he is basically a pragmatic politician who sees the running of government as a matter of problem-solving and not as an ideological crusade, it is tempting to characterize his politics, in the sense of a set of clear objectives, principles or views, as the absence of same.

Yet Mulroney does have a set of definite social, economic and political views, which he has expressed sometimes in vague generalities and sometimes very forcefully. One important question is the extent to which the drive to win the leadership forced Mulroney into alliances that may compromise some of these views. For now, Mulroney's strength within the party, his grip on the caucus, and his abilities as a negotiator have kept almost everybody in line, but as the Liberals develop their strategy of painting him into a narrowly defined rightist corner — a corner, incidentally, where a large body of his caucus wants to be — intracaucus disputes can be expected to develop.

The question of universal access to medical care is an issue that might have provoked such a dispute, but Mulroney apparently had little trouble convincing the whole caucus to go along with Health and Welfare Minister Monique Bégin's new health legislation, even though all the provinces with Tory provincial governments opposed the bill. Alberta MPs even faced down the very vociferous opposition of the Alberta government. "All he had to do with that," said one Tory, "was to wave the polls [on medicare] in front of his caucus."

A larger and more difficult problem for Mulroney will be to develop an energy policy that will satisfy both William Davis and Peter Lougheed, and to do it without either generating a split in Tory ranks or providing the Liberals with an election issue that will play in central Canada. It seems clear at this point that Mulroney intends to gut the National Energy Policy. In a rousing speech in Calgary in November, 1983, he got a standing ovation when he told the audience that "you've seen the last of Marc Lalonde and his socialist allies who have inflicted such overwhelming damage on the economy of western Canada." He also promised to establish a "constant dialogue with the producing provinces and with the industry" without saying anything about establishing a dialogue with the consuming provinces — Ontario and Quebec.

Lalonde and his "socialist allies" are easy targets for Mulroney, but it is a measure of the difficulty of his task that some of the western members of his caucus would consider William Davis to be in the same camp as Lalonde. For it is, after all, the Davis government that has done perhaps more than anything else to make the NEP a credible policy with its large purchase into Suncor. Thus, the original text of Mulroney's Calgary speech read: "With a majority Progressive Conservative government you've seen the last of the NEP." By the time the speech was delivered it read: "You've seen the last of the confiscatory and punitive provisions of the NEP." The story is that party officials, fearing the wrath of Davis, convinced the leader to make the changes. And when Mulroney spoke again in Edmonton the following night, the speech was toned down even further.

Peter Lougheed appears to believe that Brian Mulroney agrees with him on energy, and he has said that he will not make any demands until the Conservatives are in power in Ottawa. Mulroney would also like the whole issue to go away until then. On the other hand, the Liberals — and especially the current energy minister, Jean Chrétien, who has leadership aspirations of his own — are unlikely to let any such thing happen.

Intracaucus disputes will be all the more likely if the polls begin to indicate that the Conservatives may be headed for an election rather than a coronation. If Mulroney's status as the man who can lead the Tories to power is challenged, then other assumptions will be challenged as well.

Beyond the drive for power, two core principles define the politics of Brian Mulroney. The first is that the Canadian state is indivisible, and regional interests within the country are to be melded together by a strong central government. And the second is that the free-enterprise system, with all that it entails, including Canada's firm adherence to the Western Alliance, is sacrosanct.

The first principle is, in itself, not unanimously agreed upon within the Conservative party (to say the least). While the second can be more plausibly regarded as common Tory property, the way in which it works itself out in Mulroney's mind differs in several important respects from the approach taken by many within the party — including many who supported him for the leadership.

His answer to all questions, problems or differences flowing from these principles is: "We'll negotiate."

Translated into political tactics, Mulroney's pragmatism means that the Tories will attempt to reach out beyond the minority they have traditionally represented and appeal to the mainstream of the electorate in Canada as a whole while also becoming an alternative to voters in Quebec (and preferably appear to be united while doing it). In other words, the party has all the Conservative votes it is ever going to get, and what it needs now is a large chunk of Liberal votes.

When pressed by a reporter to name some political figures he admired, Mulroney, interestingly, singled out two liberal American Democrats — the late Hubert Humphrey and current New York Governor Mario Cuomo:

"About Humphrey, I always felt: now there's a guy who understands people. He may not have been a great administrator but I had a great empathy with that side of him, his understanding of people. That's what a country is all about." And about Cuomo: "I like his approach, I like his populism, I like his feeling for people, his roots, I admire the way he overcame the odds he had to overcome. He seems a pretty level-headed guy."

However, in observing Mulroney operate, one sees a resemblance to another American politician.

There is a lot of Lyndon Johnson in the make-up of Brian Mulroney. Connections between the two can be made not only in the skein of their political and social beliefs but also in their approach to the game or art of politics itself. Like the late American president, Mulroney believes one gets what one wants by demonstrating power, then doing deals and making trade-offs. In her book *Lyndon Johnson and The American Dream*, Doris Kearns described Johnson's style: "He would persuade everyone — businessmen, union chiefs, bankers, politicians — that his goals were in their interest, an interest that he thought, perhaps naively, was buried somewhere in everyman — the desire to contribute, to leave behind a mark of which he can be proud.''

Mulroney's approach to politics was reflected in his approach to the constitutional impasse, and will be reflected again in his approach to future federal-provincial discussions. While his federalism is similar in conception to Pierre Trudeau's, he has said he differs from Trudeau in that he would not be as rigid or as confrontational. Deals, he feels, can be struck with just about anyone, provided all parties agree upon the fundamental tenet of the integrity of the Canadian state. Almost immediately after his election as leader, in a speech in Joliette, Mulroney promised to work for Quebec's support of the constitution. Both Senator Arthur Tremblay, the Quebec constitutional expert appointed to the Upper House by Joe Clark, and Perrin Beatty, Tory constitutional reform critic in the House of Commons, interpreted this pledge as a willingness on Mulroney's part to consider a compromise package with Quebec. Tremblay, who still supports the original party position of opting out with full financial compensation, was given the impression ''that the dialogue is open and he will consider all aspects.'' Beatty also said the ''dialogue is open,'' although he qualified it by saying that Mulroney is ''quite adamant'' about giving anything away to a ''separatist government.'' While Mulroney thus maintained his rock-hard position towards the PQ, his signal was received by the once, and in all likelihood the future, premier of Quebec, Robert Bourassa.

In his 1978 interview with Stephen Kimber, Mulroney ruminated upon the possible course of political events had he instead of Joe Clark become Tory leader: ''The PQ wouldn't have won that election if I was the leader. It's true. The Quebec people were looking for an alternative to a profoundly unpopular provincial government. I would have given that alternative. It's all in my platform. . . . You know who would have been the Tory provincial leader if I had been elected? — Claude Ryan, that's who. . . . he would have taken the job . . . I'm sure of it.''

The interesting element in this quote is not the implausible what-might-have-been scenario but the notion that he could not

only negotiate with Claude Ryan on the latter's decentralist constitutional position and viewpoint about the reorganization of
English Canada, but also persuade the rest of the Tory party to
accept Ryan and his views.

Mulroney's pragmatism and position as a negotiator are often
expressed in gambling metaphors. He talks about "not tipping
your hand" or of "keeping your high cards." And he justifies
his policy generalities as part of the tools of a skilful negotiator.
During the leadership campaign, he criticized Clark's position on
opting-out formulas as giving away one's bargaining power: "I'm
not prepared to sit down with René Lévesque and offer him one
plugged nickel until he tells me what he will offer Canada." In
much the same tone, he made fun of Lévesque after the so-called
provincial common front broke down and the Quebec premier
was left out in the cold at the final constitutional conference:

> I have the impression that the brilliance of the tactics of a
> Marcel Pépin or the engaging personality of a Louis La-
> berge, which hides the talent of a first-rate negotiator, might
> have better served Quebec than an army of theologically-
> minded civil servants of the PQ who, it would appear, have
> not learned that the human and acceptable answers to com-
> plex questions are not always found in the tranquillity of
> our best universities.

When pressed for details of his policies, Mulroney always goes
back to his experience as a negotiator:

> I've been involved in negotiations for twenty years in the
> labour field and in the financial field — very successfully,
> very successfully — because I know how to bargain. . . .
> The key to bargaining is that you never give anything away
> until you sit down at the table. . . . You create a climate of
> confidence beforehand . . . and then you sit down and play
> poker. . . . You don't get very far by giving anything away
> in advance or by indicating to anyone reading the newspa-

pers today, what you are going to be doing in a year and a half. They'll find out at the bargaining table.

To a certain extent, Mulroney's vagueness on — and indeed impatience with — most issues can be traced to the fact that he believes that there is really only one important issue in Canada, and that is the preservation of the country as he sees it. The corollary of this for the Progressive Conservative party is that it must accept the political reality of Canada, and during the leadership campaign he had some tough talk for English Canadian Tory ears. He scarcely made one speech that didn't include the litany of Tory impotence among French-speaking Canadians in general and in Quebec in particular. Mulroney's promise to the Tories was not only that he could win but also that he could deliver strength in Quebec. In convincing the party to take up this challenge, he also forced it to make one of the most significant policy changes it has ever made in its history.

Mulroney's bitterness over his defeat in 1976 was based not only on his belief that the candidates from the federal caucus — "the club" — ganged up on him but also on his firm conviction that Joe Clark could not defeat Trudeau because he could not, however extensive his efforts, make any inroads in Quebec. By electing him in 1983, Mulroney suggested, the party could reverse the historic error that it had perpetuated in 1976. In his comment on Mulroney's official announcement of his leadership candidacy in 1983, Dalton Camp provided perhaps the clearest explanation of what Brian Mulroney stands for and what he has promised the party:

> During his presentation, Mr. Mulroney made a devastating analysis of the historic weakness of his party in the province of Quebec. . . .
>
> "Someone must address this fundamental electoral problem on behalf of the Conservative party," Mr. Mulroney said. "I propose to do just that and in the process, bring

French Canada into the fullness and magnificence of Canadian life.''

Brian Mulroney is a compelling man — articulate, resonant, serious, utterly composed and attractive in the bargain. Perhaps he is so beguiling in his person that no one truly understands what he is saying. But the import of all he has just said, for me at least, is that no Conservative leadership candidate in memory has ever promised to deliver so much to his party and to the country if only his ambition is realized.

If in 1976 the issue for the Tories was expressed as ''Can we elect a bilingual Quebecer as leader?'' in 1983 Mulroney was able to force the party to rephrase it as ''How can we not?''

Mulroney's potential support in Quebec is based less on any specific constitutional position than on the feeling that as a Quebecer with deep roots in French Canadian society he will be able to represent the interests of the province. This is the same message that Pierre Trudeau so effectively conveyed to Quebecers, including those who supported the Parti Québécois provincially. The wild card in all this is the presence of the Parti Nationaliste, the PQ's entry on the federal scene. While as a party with no chance of forming the government (''Créditistes of the left,'' in *La Presse* columnist Lysiane Gagnon's description) the PN's appeal is limited, it does offer a place to go for Quebecers who want to vote against the Liberals' constitutional position — which is, after all, Brian Mulroney's position as well. And if the PN manages to attract even a relatively small number of anti-Liberal votes, that could be enough to blunt any possible Tory thrust.

A more serious problem for Mulroney, and for the party he leads, is that the promise of making the Tories a serious political force in Quebec may not be entirely consistent with other commitments, explicit or implicit, that he made during the leadership campaign.

For one can discount the strange business of the Amway dealers, assume also that the right-wing zealots of the Tory youth groups will grow up, and still understand that the wash into Canada of right-wing Republicanism would naturally buttress a traditional, indigenous conservatism that has always been a potent force within the party and among the Canadian electorate as a whole. What is perceived as the right wing of the Conservative party is a very difficult constituency to define because traditional right-wing orthodoxy has become associated and mixed with a regional populism that cuts to the core of the nature of the modern Canadian state. In Canada, natural right-wing politics is affected in a peculiar but nonetheless direct way by the fundamental issue of regional disparity and the contradiction between the centre and the regions, made even more complicated by the position of Quebec, which is seen as both part of central Canada and isolated at the same time.

The debate between the right and the centre in the Conservative party has become epitomized by the question of whether or not to dismantle Canada's crown corporations. For the free enterprisers of the Conservative right, crown corporations stand for all that is most objectionable in Liberal interventionism, while for the upholders of Tory Tradition, crown corporations are an integral part of that tradition. In a list of the eighteen largest federal crown corporations (as of 1975) compiled by sociologist Jorge Niosi, fourteen were established by Liberal governments while four were Tory creations. These numbers are roughly proportional to the amount of time spent in office by Liberal and Tory governments since the first of these corporations, the Canadian National Railways, was established in 1919. All the evidence suggests that the great government initiatives, whether in the form of crown corporations (the CNR, the CBC, Air Canada) or otherwise (the Post Office, the building of the CPR, even today's National Energy Policy), did not come from a government of any particular ideological stripe. When the need arose, whatever government was in office did the job.

The underlying rationale for all these initiatives was to unite the country — to create and protect a national market. Government intervention into the Canadian economy — or as Richard

Gwyn put it, politicization of our economy — began shortly after Confederation. An early manifestation of it was Sir John A. Macdonald's National Policy, which favoured Ontario manufacturers at the expense of consumers by sheltering them behind high tariff walls. Gwyn echoed earlier observers of the Canadian reality when he wrote: "As a country, we exist in defiance of economics as well as geography. To create an east-west axis where no natural one existed, it was politically necessary to create the Canadian Pacific Railway, Air Canada and the CBC."

The point is, however, that these great national projects were designed to create a country for Ontario, and as the West grew and a continent-wide westward shift of economic power became obvious, the great projects — symbolized by the crown corporations — appeared to be instruments through which power was held artificially in central Canada at the expense of the West. The West saw these projects as obstacles to its initiative, and in the context of the politics of North America, it was the smallest of leaps to consider them also to be examples of growing government interference or creeping socialism.

Quebec has also traditionally seen these great national projects as irrelevant if not inimical to its interests. And while it would be a vulgarization of Quebec politics to see the federalists as trying to provide a means for Quebecers to get in on the action in Ottawa and the Parti Québécois as arguing that the Canadian Confederation at best offers Quebec nothing that cannot be gotten in a North American common market, such an equation is certainly part of the political background.

These regional differences, which are often masked by right-wing rhetoric from western Canadian Tories, put Brian Mulroney in a particular bind.

On the one hand, Mulroney's appeal in Quebec has been described by Quebec journalist Dominique Clift in the following terms:

He sounds like a Trudeau Liberal when he discusses the Constitution, bilingualism, the economy and the role of federal government. His basic message is that under his leadership the Conservative party will achieve exactly what the Liberals are no longer able to do: provide the French with an access to power and ensure a good working relationship with the English-speaking population in the rest of the country.

On the other hand, Mulroney's criticism of the civil service and his cheerful endorsement of the entrepreneurial spirit as opposed to the dry hand of government is read in western Canada as a diminution of the same power he has promised Quebecers access to. He has promised Quebec to do what Trudeau is no longer able to do, and he has promised the West to undo all the things Trudeau ever did. Moreover, he has promised to do all these things in a spirit of civility and negotiation.

But if Mulroney's free-enterprise rhetoric is examined a little more closely, it turns out to have some subtleties that are lacking in the positions of some of the more ideologically inclined Conservatives.

Brian Mulroney's conception of the free-enterprise system has been expressed in the following terms:

> I am a Conservative, but one does not need to wear a label to believe that governments should balance budgets; that industry, being the motor of the country, must be kept turning; that initiative should be rewarded; that relations between labour and management should be civil; that research and development are the keys to our national well-being; that the essense of federalism, or any system of administration, is cooperation and consensus.
>
> Neither does one need to belong to a political party to believe that men and women will stand on their own two feet when given half a chance; that government must show concern — even tenderness — in dealing with the less fortunate among us; that only free men and women are able to sever the knots tied by government bureaucrats.

Mulroney believes, to paraphrase Calvin Coolidge, that the business of government is business. The role of government, in his view, is to provide a good business environment in which investment, including foreign investment, will be encouraged so as to expand the economy and create jobs. "What concerns me," he said during the leadership campaign, "is not who owns the factory; I want to be able to convince the guy with the cash to build the factory in the first place. . . . We must encourage small and middle-sized businesses to come here — and we will, because 1.6 million jobless Canadians say we have to."

The encouragement of foreign investment capital has been the cornerstone of the economic policy of Canadian governments — all governments — since at least the Abbott Plan, which laid out the strategy of economic development through foreign-financed resource projects (such as iron ore mining in northern Quebec) in the early 1950s. If quibbles have emerged from time to time, if attempts have been made to impose restrictions on the terms of investment or even assert some measure of control over various sectors of the economy, these have always been tangential to the main thrust of policy. This policy has always been coupled with an understanding that the main pool of foreign investment capital is the United States.

Mulroney's policy, and even his negotiating strategy, appears little different from those of the current Liberal government. In early September, 1983, a Department of External Affairs discussion paper entitled "Canadian Trade Policy for the 1980s" was released. While the paper finessed the question of a policy of full free trade with the United States, it did project a series of incremental moves in that direction. "The attraction of greater cooperation" with the U.S., the paper argued, "is that it recognizes the realities of geography and economics. The respective private sectors are already largely integrated; trade runs more easily north-south than east-west; and the U.S. market is not greatly different from the Canadian market."

Mulroney's criticism of the government rests on the assumption that the reason foreign and especially American capital is not flowing into Canada at the same rate as it used to has to do mainly with Canadian attitudes rather than with larger economic problems. His own experience at the Iron Ore Company of Canada would seem to indicate otherwise. And the chief obstacle to greater economic integration with the United States is that the Americans have not expressed any interest. With the growing mood of protectionism in the United States, there is little chance that the American market will be opened to the Canadian steel or transportation industries or any pretensions Canada might have in the area of high technology. In fact, Canada-U.S. conflict over the past few years has been based on the Americans' determination to protect their own industries — lumber, fish, potatoes, cattle or anything else — from Canadian encroachment.

Mulroney's concept of friendly negotiations with the U.S. on economic matters is further removed from the proposal for a Canada-U.S. common market advanced by his own finance critic, John Crosbie, than it is from the policies of the minister of finance across the floor. It also has to face up to the reality that it takes two sides to negotiate, and the other, senior, party does not appear to "give" as well as "take."

Even when he engaged in the ritual attack on the Foreign Investment Review Agency during the leadership campaign, Mulroney stopped short of saying that it should be abolished but only argued that "it should be placed on the back burner." Without putting too fine a point on it, it would be difficult for Mulroney to put FIRA any farther back on the stove than the Liberals have.

Mulroney claims to envision a government that would protect Canadians and provide them with the basic social amenities, encourage private initiative and social responsibility within the business community, and create an atmosphere of civility and negotiation within and among the various interest groups that make up Canada.

To do the things Mulroney says a federal government must do requires a strong, well-oiled, interventionist government mainery. Mulroney, in view of the circumstances of the leadership campaign, did not like to think about — or at least did not dwell upon — the implications of the various economic propositions he advanced.

A few days before Marc Lalonde brought down his 1983 budget, Brian Mulroney addressed a delegates' meeting in Dorval, Quebec, and issued the most comprehensive economic statement of his leadership campaign. His statement is interesting in several respects, not least of all in the fact that it expressed no real philosophical difference with the subsequent Lalonde budget. Moreover, Mulroney made several suggestions that indicated he in effect envisaged more and not less direct government intervention in the economy.

> I believe Mr. Lalonde should look very seriously at discouraging unproductive takeovers of Canadian industry by disallowing the interest costs involved in such activity. I am talking here about . . . the kind of "corporate monopoly game" we have witnessed in recent years where assets are bought and sold in transactions that tie up vast amounts of scarce investment capital with no apparent gain or benefit to our national economy.

This proposal elicited a "harrumph" from the Toronto *Globe and Mail*: "Does Mr. Mulroney know what he is getting into here? Are we to expect a domestic version of the Foreign Investment Review Agency, arbitrarily drawing the line between good and bad takeovers?"

Most of Mulroney's suggestions involved changing taxation policies to encourage high-tech investment and the like, and taking various measures to tighten federal spending. He was reluctant to accept a higher federal deficit but felt that it might be necessary. He said that "a firm commitment should be to bring the budget for current expenditures into balance over the next five years on a full-employment basis. This means that in conditions of full employment there would be no deficit and probably a small surplus." While he qualified this by saying that "full employment does not mean zero unemployment," the important

point he made was that the main priority for the federal government should be to encourage economic growth rather than to
slash spending in an attempt to balance a budget.

His most innovative proposals were in the field of govern-
ment/labour/management relations and in the need to direct attention to the problems of productivity and research and
development: ''The government must proceed immediately to
the creation of a National Tripartite Productivity Commission,
composed of labour, management and Government. The principal
immediate objectives should be an agreement on a fair manner
in which productivity increases can be measured, according to
industry sector.''

In another section of his statement, Mulroney said: ''Many
industries hard hit by the recession will look very different as
they adapt to the changing requirements when the recovery takes
hold. Many of the unemployed will find their existing skills
obsolete.'' He went on to propose incentives for industry to
develop training programs. He also suggested that the expansion
of research and development in Canada be encouraged through
tax changes that would allow 100 per cent write-offs. Taken
separately, all these economic proposals involve establishing a
consultative process and tinkering with the tax system. But taken
as a whole, they constitute a more sweeping approach to economic planning by government.

Opposition Leader Mulroney has yet to spell out the nature or
form of the consultations that Prime Minister Mulroney would
try to establish. He wants labour to be part of the process, and
he has already opened communications with the president of the
Canadian Labour Congress, Dennis McDermott. ''The workers
in the factories know what the problems of productivity are,''
he has said. ''One thing is, we will never get anywhere trying
to kick the trade unions in the ass. My friends in B.C. are finding
that out.'' Mulroney believes that labour and management can
come together under the aegis of government to find victimless
solutions. His experience at Iron Ore and his involvement in the
affairs of the troubled American steel industry through his po-

sition on the board of Hanna Mining must have given him some indication of how difficult this is going to be.

Willy-nilly, Brian Mulroney has entered what has been widely characterized as the post-Reagan economic debate on industrial policy. The parameters of this debate, which is now under way in the United States, have been set out by Harvard economist Robert Reich, and the basic argument is over what new forms of government intervention in the American economy are necessary to reverse what has been termed the deindustrialization of America. Tax breaks for industrial research and development are one thing, but research and development is a sterile concept without a technological and industrial base to make it possible to apply this research. As Mulroney often said during the campaign, increasing productivity is not necessarily working harder but working smarter. But to do either, people have to be working in the first place.

How far a Mulroney government would go with the approach outlined in the Dorval economic statement is anybody's guess. In any event, on some rather basic questions of economic strategy, Brian Mulroney has distanced himself from much of the Tory rhetoric advanced during the leadership campaign.

To be sure, during the months of the official Tory leadership race and over the two or three years of the unofficial campaign, Brian Mulroney was extremely active on the speakers' circuit as he travelled from coast to coast establishing his turf as an unreconstructed "free enterpriser." Slashing government spending was a main component of his speeches.

Under the general charge that "governments have no money, they can only spend the money we give them," he made good yardage recounting atrocities involving government blunders, fiscal irresponsibility, and bureaucratic arrogance and incompetence. Thus: "You go up to Ottawa to see one of them in their offices which are usually larger than your factory, and you don't know if they will talk to you, or send you out for coffee." Or: "Central Mortgage and Housing Corporation bought the Quai d'Orsay Hotel in Ottawa for $3 million and resold it for $1 million. It bought the Howard Johnson Hotel in Montreal for $19 million and sold it for $6 million. . . . It embarked on a land-banking program, lost $775 million in six years and then abandoned the program.'' Or again: ''The Canadian International Development Agency spent $1.4 million on a fisheries training vessel that was supposed to cost $308,000 to purchase and refit. The government of Colombia refused to accept the ship because it would not float.''

He made great sport of Pierre Trudeau's former NDP connections, and often accused him of ''Swedenizing Canada,'' an unconscious slur not so much on Trudeau as on Sweden. Mulroney's pointed criticism of the public sector bureaucracy gave him credentials in a section of the party that saw Joe Clark as not only unelectable but also too far to the left. But when the verbal attacks were over, Mulroney seemed to be saying not less government but better government — smarter, nicer, more efficient government.

If Mulroney's lack of parliamentary experience and apparent disdain of electoral politics constituted an overall handicap in his campaigns for leadership, in 1983 the image of him as an outsider, and specifically an outsider from the world of big business, in a sense served him well, especially with elements of the party distrustful of politicians in general. Clark was seen as part of the ''club'' and thus was somehow tainted. But Mulroney came from ''the real world.'' He ''knows what it's like to meet a payroll.'' The president of the Iron Ore Company of Canada was somehow seen as being at one with the hardware merchant trying to get a loan extension to keep inventory and going crazy filling out various forms that all came from one government agency or another in Ottawa, all the while waiting for accounts receivable in the mail, which, of course, was either late, lost or struck.

However, when Mulroney got down to cases about what he would do, given the chance, he skated away. While other candidates talked about selling off crown corporations, Mulroney talked about ''sunset laws'' and bringing government agencies and corporations under control. Always the negotiator, he would say that there is no sense tying your hand until you get to the game. But the impression was given that Mulroney would ruthlessly slash government to the bone while reordering priorities: "What would I do? I'd cut consultants, outside lawyers and accountants, advertising, public service compensation, waste, unproductive subsidies, travel, indexed pensions and fringe benefits, capital construction programs, capital overruns and just plain bureaucratic excess."

But in today's Tory parlance, slashing government spending means more than just efficiency. It is a buzzword for cutting social services. Indeed, any savings brought about by the efficiencies Mulroney would introduce into government would not make up for the revenue losses his proposed tax incentives would entail along with the cost of his other promises, including increased spending on the military. There is only one area of the budget where the needed money can be obtained. But when pushed, Mulroney would only go into his poker player mode.

The only concrete measure he has advanced in the area of social spending is to have a parliamentary committee study the universality of some government programs:

> The concept is such that what was good for Mackenzie King is not necessarily good for Canada today, to coin a phrase. . . .
> Maybe we can do a better job for the taxpayer and for the needy people [Mulroney apparently doesn't appear to realize that they are usually one and the same] than by issuing an automatic cheque to someone who is making $200,000 a year, and then hire a couple more civil servants to make sure he adds that to his income which then jumps him into a higher tax bracket already.

Thus, it may be best to write about the politics of Brian Mulroney in terms of what is missing — missing, that is, in terms of Tory rhetoric. When he talks about government spending, he talks about efficiency, not "slashing." When he talks about crown corporations, he again talks about efficiency and value, not "privatizing." When he talks about Canada-U.S. economic relations, he talks about negotiations, not "free trade and a common market."

In international affairs, to the degree he has ever considered them, Mulroney sees Canada in a firm lockstep with the United States. It is not making light of the simplicity of his position to suggest that he accepts the Yalta theory of spheres of influence as it applies to Canada. While he always refers to the U.S. as our closest ally and partner, his view of the nature of this alliance and the subordinate role that Canada plays within it is unsentimental. Criticizing Prime Minister Trudeau's international initiatives, Mulroney stated: "Our pride in Canada should not obscure the hard realities of superpower existence. Nor should that pride give rise to illusions of influence, beyond legitimate bounds, that can only disappoint and confuse." The best we can expect is to be able to turn our recognition of the nature of our relationship with the United States to our advantage. Once again, this involves doing a deal:

> Good relations . . . superb relations with the United States will be the cornerstone of our foreign policy. That doesn't mean dependency, that means good, good relations. . . . There's a price to be paid for good relations on both sides. . . . The Americans have to pay a price for having such a tremendous country and people such as Canada as their neighbour. . . . Things like auto pacts and fishing treaties . . . [are] a small price to have such a wonderful country like Canada sitting on your doorstep.

Brian Mulroney sometimes has a problem of merely seeming cheerfully vacuous when he is attempting to sound cheerfully vague. But maybe that too is part of what he considers the art of the political negotiator.

A typical Mulroney speech is a marvel of political flatulence. But his speeches do always seem to make one point. Mulroney is no hard-faced Tory ideologue. He is no clone of Margaret Thatcher or Ronald Reagan.

A typical Mulroney speech also usually contains something else — the view from Baie-Comeau: "Here one may find a sense of regional solidarity, a spirit of mutual aid . . . all the more important today because it assists us in supporting those among us who, through a quirk of nature or by accident, find themselves less than well-equipped to face the necessities of everyday life." And this view from Baie-Comeau relates to his concept of government as one that "must show concern — even tenderness — in dealing with the less fortunate among us." It has a paternalistic, almost Victorian charity-ward ring to it, but he is quite sincere. In private life, Mulroney has involved himself in any number of fund-raising activities for hospitals, universities and organized charities. This public work has been buttressed by personal generosity to friends — including, in many instances, political adversaries.

There is, naturally enough, an element in this charity work that can be seen as public relations, both for Mulroney personally and, during his years at Iron Ore, for the company. But there is much more to it than that. While there is no evidence to suggest that he believes the role of government in funding social services should be cut back (his support of the government's health services legislation is an example of his doing what he said he would do), he does feel that corporations should also play a role on a more informal level, particularly in the area of higher education and research funding, as should individuals in community works.

As we have seen, much of the basis of Brian Mulroney's political philosophy was formed in Baie-Comeau. The conditions that brought the paper mill — and later the iron mine and pelletizing plant — to the North Shore were resources, a labour force, social stability, and governments at both the provincial and the federal level that saw the need for economic development and created the conditions in which huge pools of private capital could be tapped and put to work. Deals had to be struck and concessions given, but the work was done and, for people of Brian Mulroney's generation, for the most part the good times did roll.

Baie-Comeau was, in some ways, a perfect little microcosm of Brian Mulroney's best of all possible worlds. But Baie-Comeau was not a complete world in itself. There were the mill managers, the guys in charge, the people who "made things happen," but they were powerful only in a limited sphere. The important decisions were made elsewhere, and most of them were made outside the country. The town owed its very existence to the vision of an entrepreneur from Chicago, and its growth was fuelled by decisions made in Minneapolis, London and elsewhere. There is no evidence that Mulroney ever saw anything wrong with this scheme of things. He grew up to become the chief Canadian spokesman and mediator for another American group that had brought economic development to another part of the North Shore, and it is entirely consistent that now, as a politician, he should stand for "good, good relations" between Canada and the United States.

It is perhaps not unfair to Mulroney to suggest that he sees Canada as one large company town. And within that context, if the Gallup Poll is any indication, he is about to achieve his ambition of becoming the guy in charge, the man who makes things happen.

Baum, Gregory. *Catholics and Canadian Socialism: Political Thought in the Thirties and Forties.* Toronto: James Lorimer & Co., 1980.

Beer, Thomas. *Hanna.* New York: Alfred A. Knopf, 1928.

Black, Conrad. *Duplessis.* Toronto: McClelland and Stewart, 1977.

Bothwell, Robert, and Kilbourn, William. *C. D. Howe: A Biography.* Toronto: McClelland and Stewart, 1979.

Bothwell, Robert; Drummond, Ian; English, John. *Canada Since 1945: Power, Politics and Provincialism.* Toronto: University of Toronto Press, 1981.

Brown, Patrick; Chodos, Robert; and Murphy, Rae. *Winners, Losers: The 1976 Tory Leadership Convention.* Toronto: James Lorimer & Co., 1976.

Caulfield, Jon. *The Tiny Perfect Mayor.* Toronto: James Lorimer & Co., 1974.

Clement, Wallace. *Continental Corporate Power.* Toronto: McClelland and Stewart, 1977.

Coady, M.M. *The Man from Margaree.* Edited by Alexander F. Laidlaw. Toronto: McClelland and Stewart, 1971.

Coates, Robert. *The Night of the Knives.* Fredericton, Brunswick Press, 1969.

Collier, Peter, and Horowitz, David. *The Rockefellers: An American Dynasty.* New York: Holt, Rinehart and Winston, 1976.

215

Conn, Charles. *The Possible Dream*. New York: Berkley Books, 1977.

Diefenbaker, John G. *One Canada*. 2 vols. Toronto: Macmillan of Canada, 1975–76.

Ferns, Henry, and Ostry, Bernard. *The Age of Mackenzie King*. Toronto: James Lorimer & Co., 1976.

Fotheringham, Allan. *Look Ma . . . No Hands: An Affectionate Look at Our Wonderful Tories*. Toronto: Key Porter Books, 1983.

Gies, Joseph. *The Colonel of Chicago*. New York: E. P. Dutton, 1979.

Granatstein, J. L., and Hitsman, J. M. *Broken Promises: A History of Conscription in Canada*. Toronto: Oxford University Press, 1977.

Hogan, William T., S.J. *Economic History of the Iron and Steel Industry in the United States*. 4 vols. Lexington, Mass.: D. C. Heath & Co., 1971.

Humphreys, David L. *Joe Clark: A Portrait*. Ottawa: Deneau & Greenberg, 1978.

Kearny, Doris. *Lyndon Johnson and The American Dream*. New York: Harper and Row, 1976.

Linteau, Paul-André; Durocher, René; and Robert, Jean-Claude. *Quebec: A History 1867–1929*. Translated by Robert Chodos. Toronto: James Lorimer & Co., 1983.

Martin, Patrick; Gregg, Allan; and Perlin, George. *Contenders*. Scarborough, Ont.: Prentice-Hall, 1983.

Mulroney, Brian. *Where I Stand*. Toronto: McClelland and Stewart, 1983.

Newman, Peter C. *The Canadian Establishment*. Toronto: McClelland and Stewart, 1975.

Newman, Peter C. *Distemper of Our Times*. Toronto: McClelland and Stewart, 1968.

Newman, Peter C. *The Establishment Man: A Portrait of Power*. Toronto: McClelland and Stewart, 1982.

Newman, Peter C. *Renegade in Power*. Toronto: McClelland and Stewart, 1964.

Niosi, Jorge. *Canadian Capitalism: A Study of Power in the Canadian Business Establishment*. Translated by Robert Chodos. Toronto: James Lorimer & Co., 1981.

Nurgitz, Nathan, and Segal, Hugh. *No Small Measure*. Ottawa: Deneau, 1983.

Persico, Joseph. *The Imperial Rockefeller*. New York: Simon and Schuster, 1982.

Pickersgill, Jack. *My Years with Louis St. Laurent*. Toronto: University of Toronto Press, 1975.

Quebec. *Commission d'enquête sur l'exercice de la liberté syndicale dans l'industrie de la construction. Rapport*. Quebec: Editeur Officiel du Québec, 1975.

Radwanski, George. *Trudeau*. Toronto: Macmillan of Canada, 1978.

Siegel, Arthur. *Politics and the Media in Canada*. Toronto: McGraw-Hill Ryerson, 1983.

Simpson, Jeffrey. *Discipline of Power*. Toronto: Personal Library, 1980.

Stevens, Geoffrey. *Stanfield*. Toronto: McClelland and Stewart, 1973.

Stewart, Walter. *Divide and Con*. Toronto: New Press, 1973.

Taylor, A. J. P. *Beaverbrook*. London: Hamish Hamilton, 1972.

Taylor, Charles. *Radical Tories*. Toronto: Anansi, 1982.

Tees, Douglas H. *Chronicles of Ogilvy, Renault 1879–1979*. Montreal, 1979.

Wade, Mason. *The French Canadians 1760–1967*. 2 vols. Rev. ed. Toronto: Macmillan of Canada, 1968.

Waldrop, Frank. *McCormick of Chicago*. Englewood Cliffs, N.J.: Prentice-Hall, 1966.

Wiegman, Carl. *Trees to News: A Chronicle of the Ontario Paper Company's Origin and Development*. Toronto: McClelland and Stewart, 1953.

Willoughby, William R. *The St. Lawrence Waterway: A Study in Politics and Diplomacy*. Madison, Wis.: University of Wisconsin Press, 1961.

Abortion: as issue in 1983 election campaign, 165
Agricultural Rehabilitation and Development Act (ARDA), 56
Aitken, Max (Lord Beaverbrook), 25, 53, 59
Amway Corporation, 166, 181, 201
Anderson, Robert, 112, 129
"Antigonish movement," 29-30
Argus Corporation, 53
Atkins, Norman, 184

Baie-Comeau, 2, 6, 25, 55, 65, 213-14
  description of, 11, 12, 13
  development of, 8-9, 10-11, 15, 16, 22-23
  politics in, 19
  "view from," 2, 22-23, 27, 28-29, 32, 61, 213-14
Balcer, Léon, 38, 39, 87
Barrette, Antonio, 43
Bartlett Commission, 119, 122
Bazin, Jean, 46, 51, 52, 55, 56, 155

Beatty, Perrin, 198
Bennett, R.B., 35
Bennett, William, 61, 82, 112, 116
Bergeron, Gérard, 43
Bertrand, Jean-Jacques, 95
Black, Conrad, 53, 104
  attempted takeover of Hanna Mining, 129-30, 157
  biography of Duplessis, 15, 18, 53, 116
Blaikie, Peter, 155, 170
"Boonie Strategy," 174-77, 179
Borden, Robert, 34
Bourassa, Henri, 33
Bourassa, Robert, 76, 78, 79, 82, 95, 198
Brown, Albert, 59, 60, 61

Camp, Dalton, 92, 156, 163, 165, 189, 200-201
  and replacement of Diefenbaker as PC leader, 87, 89, 104, 105, 107
Canadian Union of Students (CUS), 55, 56

Capital punishment, as issue in
1983 leadership campaign, 165
Carleton University Poll, 180-82,
186
Cashin, Richard, 31, 36
Catholic church, 18, 29, 30, 44
anti-Liberalism of, 32-33
Chapleau, Joseph-Adolphe, 58
Chaput, Marcel, 49-50
Charbonneau, Joseph (archbishop
of Montreal), 17, 18
Chartrand, Michel, 80-81
Chevrette, Guy, 79
Chrétien, Jean, 147, 196
Churchill Formula, 150, 151
Clark, Joe, 52, 92, 100, 110
challenges to leadership,
137-40, 142-43, 144, 148-50,
152, 153-54, 155, 156, 166
on constitution, 148, 153
leadership campaign, 1975-'76,
99, 106-107, 108-109, 173,
179
leadership campaign, 1983,
162-64, 165, 169, 177, 180,
181, 210
and Ontario, 145-46, 148,
170-71
at Ottawa convention (1983),
182-83, 185, 186, 187,
188-89
as prime minister, 144-47
as "progressive," 85, 105, 146,
165, 166, 185
and Quebec, 143, 144, 150,
153, 155-56, 164, 188-89
at Quebec City meeting (1977),
139-41
relationship with Mulroney,
142-43, 148, 152, 153, 155,

156, 188-89, 193, 200
and right wing of PCs, 165, 168
at Winnipeg meeting (Jan. '83),
133, 156-58
Cliche, Robert, 78-79, 80, 100
Cliche Commission, 78-82, 102
Coady, Rev. Dr. Moses, 29-30,
31
Coates, Robert, 141, 192
Cogger, Michel:
at Laval, 46, 48, 50, 51, 52,
54, 55
lawyer and backroom
politician, 56, 74, 75-76, 88,
91, 92, 94, 96-97, 141, 145
and Mulroney's leadership
campaigns, 99-100, 111, 155,
183, 188
Conscription crises, 34, 35
Constitutional reform, 147-48,
153, 198, 199
Conventions, political, 134-35
1976, 107-109, 179, 187
1983, 135, 182-83, 185-89
Courtois, Jacques, 106
Créditistes, 93
Crombie, David, 154, 165, 168,
181, 185, 187, 193
Crosbie, John, 145, 154, 193, 206
1983 leadership campaign, 165,
173, 179, 180, 181, 182, 186,
187, 188, 189
Crown corporations, 202, 203,
211

Dalhousie University, 42
Danis, Marcel, 155, 156, 162
Davis, William, 88, 140, 145-46,
154, 157, 159, 168-69, 170-71,
173, 195, 196

Delegate selection:
  1975-76, 103-104
  1983, 162-64
Deschênes, Réal, 25
Desmarais, Paul, 60, 72, 73, 74, 97, 106
"Deux nations" concept, 88, 91
Diefenbaker, John, 19, 37, 90, 91, 105, 135, 136, 150, 151
  attitude toward Quebec, 38-39, 148
  relationship with Mulroney, 37-40, 46, 86, 104, 107-108
  replacement as leader, 84-88, 89
Doucet, Gerald, 41
Drapeau, Jean, 17, 73
Drew, George, 37
Duffy, Mike, 182
Duhaime, Yves, 160
Duplessis, Maurice, 15-19, 33, 43, 47, 113, 114, 116, 151
  defender of Quebec's autonomy, 18
  labour policies, 17
  treatment of political opponents, 17-18
Dupras, Claude, 103

Easton industrial inquiry, 122
Eaton, Cyrus, 113, 114, 116
Eisenhower, Dwight D., 116
Election campaigns, federal:
  1957, 150, 151
  1958, 150, 151
  1968, 91
  1972, 96-97
  1974, 97-98
  1979, 144, 150, 151
  1980, 145, 147, 151
Elliott, Dick, 26, 27, 28, 29

Energy policy, 195-96

Faribault, Marcel, 90-91, 96, 171
Federalism, Mulroney on, 148-49, 152, 153, 164, 196, 198
Fisher, Douglas, 49
Foreign investment, 205-206
Foreign Investment Review Agency, 206
Fotheringham, Allan, 166
Fox, Francis, 58
Fraser, John, 99
Free-enterprise system, Mulroney's views on, 196-97, 204-205
French Canadians, see Quebec.
Frizzell, Allan, 175
Fulton, Davie, 38, 49, 56, 86, 88-89
Fulton-Favreau formula, 49

Gamble, John, 141, 185
Geren, Richard, 127, 132, 159
Gérin-Lajoie, Paul, 43
Gilchrist, Gordon, 192
Gillies, Jim, 99, 108, 146, 187
Godbout, Clément, 124, 132, 159
Gold, Judge Allan, 68, 69
Goodman, Eddie, 96
Government intervention in the economy, 202-203, 205, 206-207, 208, 209
Government spending, Mulroney on, 209-210, 211
Grafftey, Heward, 97, 108, 187
Gwyn, Richard (quoted), 203

Hamilton, Alvin, 54-55, 56, 57, 192
Hanna, Mark, 7, 15, 114, 115

Hanna Mining Company, 15, 112, 114, 115, 118, 124, 126, 128, 129, 130, 157
Hartt, Stanley, 61-62, 67, 70
Health services, Mulroney's position on, 195, 213
Hees, George, 37, 191
Higgins, Robert, 42
Hollinger Mines, 53
Horner, Jack, 137, 139, 151
Howard, Cate, Ogilvy, Bishop, Cope, Porteous & Hansard, 55, 58-61, 64
Howe, C.D., 36-37, 61, 113, 116
Hudon, Guy, 45, 48
Humphrey, George, 114, 115, 116

International affairs, Mulroney's views on, 212, 214
International Longshoremen's Association (ILA), 65, 67
Iron Ore Company of Canada, 43, 61, 194, 206
  background of company, 15, 113-20
  "contracting out" policy, 119, 120, 121, 122
  effects of industry changes on, 126-28, 131
  hearings into Schefferville shutdown by, 159-61
  labour relations in, 118-19, 120-21, 122, 123-24
  Mulroney offered position at, 82, 99, 101-102, 112
  settlement for Schefferville employees, 132-33

Jackson, Robert, 181
James Bay hydroelectric project, 76-77, 78, 82

Jelinek, Otto, 174, 192
Johnson, Janis, 177, 184
Johnson, Lyndon B., 197-98
Johnston, James, 86

Kimber, Stephen, 142, 143, 198
King, Mackenzie, 34, 35, 69, 194

Laberge, Louis, 72, 74
Labour relations:
  in the iron ore communities, 118-19, 120-21, 122, 123-24
  on the Montreal waterfront, 65-69, 74, 82, 97
Labrador City, Labrador, 117, 119, 120, 122, 127, 133
Labrador Mining and Exploration Company, 53
Lalonde, Marc, 195, 196, 207
Lapointe, Ernest, 34
La Presse affair, 71-73, 97
LaSalle, Roch, 98, 109
Laurier, Wilfrid, 33, 34
Laval Congress on Canadian Affairs (1961), 47, 48-51, 86
Laval University (Quebec City), 42, 45-46, 142
Leader of the opposition, function and powers of, 135-36
Leadership campaigns, Progressive Conservative:
  1967, 88-89, 101
  1975-'76, 99-109, 111, 151
  1983, 109, 133, 152, 153, 158, 162-89
  conventions: (1976), 107-109, 179, 187
  (1983), 135, 182-83, 185-89
Leduc, Louise, 142

Lesage, Jean, 43, 46, 47, 94, 95, 116
Lévesque, Father Georges-Henri, 17, 18, 45
Lévesque, René, 17, 19, 43, 49, 118
  as premier of Quebec, 138, 147, 151, 153, 164-65, 199
Liberal party, federal, 32, 33-34, 35, 36-37, 93, 97, 98. *See also* Trudeau, Pierre Elliott.
Liberal party, Quebec provincial, 32, 33, 43-44, 47, 95, 116
Lortie, Jean-Yves, 103, 155
Lougheed, Peter, 99, 124, 154, 169, 172, 195, 196

McCormick, Robert, 7-8, 9, 10, 14, 15-16
MacDonald, Finlay, 96, 142, 156
MacDonald, Flora, 99, 105, 165, 187
MacDougall, Don, 99
Mackasey, Bryce, 66, 68, 95
MacKay, Elmer, 154
McKenzie, Robert (quoted), 31, 53-54, 73, 104
McKinley, William, 114
McLean, Walter, 191-92
McMichael, Robert, 59, 60
McPhail, Tom, 74, 105, 157, 175, 182, 186
McTeer, Maureen, 178
Malouf, Albert, 76-77
Marchand, Jean, 17, 45, 95
Maritime Employers' Association (MEA), 68, 69
Marois, Pierre, 160
Martin, Paul, 151
Masters, Arnie, 66, 68, 70

Media, *see also* Television, and political conventions.
  and convention voting behaviour, 175
  and Mulroney, 105-106, 173-74, 179, 182
Medill, Joseph, 6, 7, 114
Meighen, Arthur, 35, 46
Meighen, Michael, 46, 51, 52, 56, 62, 86, 100
Mercier, Honoré, 33
Montgomery, George, 59, 60
Montmorency Falls thinkers' conference, 88, 91
Morrow, Robert, 62
Mount Royal Tennis Club, 71, 75
Mulroney, Benedict (father), 5, 10, 11, 12-13, 21-22, 23, 55, 63
Mulroney, Brian:
  EARLY LIFE:
  childhood, 11, 12, 13-15, 19-22, 24-27
  at Laval University, 42, 45-51
  at St. Francis Xavier University, 25, 29-31, 35-42
  LAWYER AND EXECUTIVE:
  on Cliche Commission, 79, 80-81
  as labour relations lawyer, 61-62, 64-70, 71, 73, 97, 101-102
  as president of Iron Ore Company of Canada, 112-13, 120-57, 159, 194, 206, 210
  PERSONAL:
  ancestry and birth, 4-6
  family life, 11, 12-13, 21-22, 23, 24, 26, 63-64
  girl friends, 27, 42, 62
  marriage, 75-76, 97

religious convictions, 32
POLITICAL CAREER:
assistant to Alvin Hamilton,
54-55
early political interests, 19-20,
27, 28, 30-31, 35-41, 46
further involvement in politics,
70, 74-75, 82-83, 85-86,
88-89, 91, 92-94, 95-96, 97,
141
1975-'76 leadership campaign,
99-109, 173-74, 187
1983 leadership campaign, 109,
158-59, 161, 162-89
"campaign pitch," 184-85
delegate selection, 162-64
organization, 168, 183-84,
189
right-wing influence, 165-69
strategy, 174-77, 179
voting, 186-89
post-election actions, 192-93
QUALITIES:
ambition, 27, 28, 29, 32, 37,
64, 82, 94, 110
attachment to family, 63-64
bilingualism, 12, 66-67
as debater and public speaker,
21, 42, 70, 175, 176, 212-13
experience in business-labour-
government relations, 194
negotiating skills, 69-70, 191,
197, 199, 208
popularity, 41, 61. *See also*
RELATIONSHIPS: with friends.
pragmatism, 194, 197, 199
quick temper, 80-81, 182
thoughtfulness, 62, 213
RELATIONSHIPS:
with caucus, 192, 193, 195, 196

with Clark, 142-43, 148, 152,
153, 155, 156, 188-89, 193,
200
with Diefenbaker, 37-40, 46,
86, 104, 107-108
with friends, 20-21, 24, 25, 41,
42, 46, 48, 51-54, 55-57,
62, 63, 74, 92, 111, 125, 184
with media, 105-106, 173-74,
179, 182
with Ontario PCs, 171-72, 193
with right wing of PC party,
165, 167, 168, 169, 172, 174,
210
VIEWS:
conservatism, 31-32, 85, 86,
94, 125, 196-97, 200-201,
204-205, 209-212
on economic policies, 205-208,
209, 211
on energy policies, 195-96
on federalism, 148-49, 152,
153, 164, 196, 198, 200
on free enterprise, 196-97,
204-205
on international affairs, 212,
214
on government intervention in
the economy, 205, 206, 207,
209
on government-labour-manage-
ment relations, 208-209
on Quebec, 1, 2, 28-29, 50-51,
102, 103, 144, 147, 148-49,
151-53, 164, 171, 174, 177,
198, 200-201, 203-204
on social services, 195, 211,
213
"view from Baie-Comeau," 2,

22, 23, 27, 28-29, 32, 61,
213-14
Mulroney, Doreen (sister), 11, 24
Mulroney, Irene (mother), 5, 21,
23, 26
Mulroney, Mila (wife), 75, 76,
99, 107, 110-11, 172, 177-78,
187
Mulroney, Olive (sister), 5, 13,
20, 21, 24, 26
Mulroney, Peggy (sister), 5, 24,
26, 28
Murray, Lowell, 92, 100

National Energy Policy (NEP),
195, 196
Newman, Peter C. (quoted), 39,
86-87, 129-130
Norcen Energy Resources, 129,
130
Nowlan, Patrick, 151

Ogilvy, Angus, 61
Ontario PCs, 145-46, 169, 170-73,
193
"Opting-out" of constitutional
amendments, 153, 198, 199

Padlock Law, 17
Pageau, Rodrigue, 155
Parti Nationaliste, 201
Parti Québécois, 82, 93, 118, 198,
201, 203
Pathy, Alex, 68, 70
Patronage:
and Clark government, 146-47
Mulroney's promises and use
of, 175-76, 192-93
under Union Nationale, 18
Patterson, Joe, 7, 8

P.C. Canada Fund, 135, 158
Pearson, Lester, 87, 89-90, 151
Pelletier, Gérard, 17, 95
Petro-Canada, 145, 146
Picard Commission, 66, 67
Pipeline Debate, 37
Pocklington, Peter, 185, 187, 188
Political conventions, see
Conventions, political.
Polls, 96, 137, 139, 145, 154
Carleton University Poll,
180-82, 186
Porteous, Jack, 60, 106
Porteous, Timothy, 60
Power Corporation of Canada, 72,
102, 106
Pratte, Yves, 45
Progressive Conservative party.
See also Clark, Joe;
Diefenbaker, John.
caucus, 90, 92, 98, 107, 137,
154, 174, 192
divisions in, 190. See also "red
tories" and right wing,
below.
in election campaign, see
Election campaigns, federal.
leadership conventions, see
Leadership campaigns,
Progressive Conservative.
minority government (1979),
144-46
in Nova Scotia, 36
and Quebec, 32-35, 70, 85, 86,
90-91, 92-93, 96-98,
102-103, 135, 138-39, 143,
144, 148-52, 155, 163-65,
174, 189, 200
Quebec City meeting (1977),
139-41

"red tories," 165-66, 185
replacement of Diefenbaker
   as leader, 84-88, 89
right wing of, 165-69, 172, 181,
   202
Winnipeg meeting (1983), 156-
   58, 166

Quebec. *See also* Duplessis,
   Maurice; Parti Québécois;
   Union Nationale.
   federal Liberals and, 32-33,
      34-35, 37, 93, 98
   federal PC party and, 32-35, 70,
      85, 86, 87-88, 90-92, 93,
      96-98, 102-103, 135, 138-39,
      143, 144, 148-52, 155,
      163-65, 174, 189, 200
   Mulroney and, 1, 2, 28-29,
      50-51, 86, 102, 103, 144,
      147, 148-49, 151-53, 164,
      171, 174, 177, 198, 200, 201,
      203-204
   nationalism, 18, 19, 47, 118.
      See also Parti Québécois.
   provincial Liberals in 32, 33,
      43-44, 47, 95, 116
   "Quiet Revolution" in, 19, 43,
      44, 84
   referendum (1980), 147
   trade union movement in, 17,
      71-72, 73-74, 77-78
Quebec North Shore Paper
   Company, 23, 25, 48

Rasminsky, Louis, 90
Rassemblement pour l'Indépen-
   dance Nationale, 47, 118
"Red tories," 165-66, 185
Regenstreif, Peter, 165

Regional differences in Canada,
   203. *See also* Quebec.
Renault, Paul-F., 64, 65, 66
"Resolution 47," 140
Richler, Mordecai, 179, 183
Right-wing views in PC party,
   165-69, 172, 181, 202
Roblin, Duff, 87
Rocque, Pierre, 19-20
Roosevelt, Theodore, 114, 115
Rosa Rita, Sister, 20, 21
Ryan, Claude, 198, 199

Sainte-Catherine-de-Portneuf, 4-5
St. Francis Xavier University
   (Antigonish, N.S.), 25, 29-31,
   35-36, 38, 41, 42, 142, 172
Saint-Laurent, Louis, 34, 37
St. Lawrence Seaway, 116
St. Thomas High School
   (Chatham, N.B.), 24, 25
Sauvé, Maurice, 56
Sauvé, Paul, 43
Schefferville, Quebec, 43, 115,
   117, 120, 127
   closing of mine at, 131-33
   hearings of Quebec National
      Assembly committee
      concerning, 133, 159-61, 170
Schmon, Arthur, 10, 15, 16-17, 23
Schmon, Robert M., 16, 48
Schumacher, Stanley, 138
Scott, Graham, 94, 100
Segal, Hugh, 169
Sept-Îles, Quebec, 43, 115, 117,
   118, 119, 120, 131
7-Up bottling plant strike, 74
Smallwood, Joey, 117
Social services, 211, 213

Stanfield, Robert, 36, 75, 82, 96, 99, 101, 145, 157
chosen PC leader, 38, 87-88, 89
problems as leader, 90-91, 92, 94, 95, 98
Steel industry, problems of, 125-26
Stevens, Sinclair, 99, 108, 151, 179-80, 187, 191, 193

Television, and political conventions, 89, 101
Tompkins, Father Jimmy, 29, 30
Trade union movement, Quebec, 17, 71-72, 77-78, 121
and Cliche Commission investigations, 79-81
Common Front strike (1972), 73-74, 119
Tremblay, Senator Arthur, 198
Trudeau, Pierre Elliott, 17, 18, 60, 70, 95, 96, 98, 110, 111, 138, 143, 151, 204, 210, 212
federalist position of, 91, 147, 152, 153, 198, 201
Turner, John, 111

Union Générale des Étudiants du Québec, 56
Union Nationale, 15, 16, 17, 19, 32, 93, 95, 144. See also Duplessis, Maurice.
Caisse Electorale, 18
United States – Canada relations, 205-206, 212, 214
United Steelworkers of America, 121, 123, 124, 132

Vanier, Georges, 58

Wabush, Labrador, 117, 119, 120, 122
Wade, Mason, 29, 45, 48
Wage and price controls, 98
Wagner, Claude, 94-95, 137, 138-39, 140, 143-44, 152, 171
campaign for PC leadership, 103-104, 108, 109
and Mulroney, 74-75, 82, 95-96, 97, 99, 104
Wakim, Sam, 41, 42, 152, 187-88
Where I Stand, 152-53
White, Peter, 46, 48, 51, 52-53, 56, 59, 86, 97, 104
Wilson, Michael, 154, 187, 188, 193

Also from James Lorimer & Company

Winners, Losers
The 1976 Tory Leadership Convention
Patrick Brown, Robert Chodos and Rae Murphy

The behind-the-scenes story of Brian Mulroney's first bid for the leadership and Joe Clark's surprise victory at the 1976 Conservative leadership convention.

"I recommend the book highly. . . . Jam-packed with excellent perceptions of clear-eyed observers." — Douglas Fisher, syndicated columnist.

Trust
The Greymac Affair
Terrence Belford

The most incredible story ever in Canadian business — the "flip" of 11,000 apartment units by trust company owner Lenny Rosenberg — has been expertly pieced together by Terrence Belford. As a friend of many of the major players, and a long-time observer of the world of real estate at the Toronto *Star* and the *Globe and Mail*, Belford was able to unravel the byzantine workings of a deal that led to the dramatic takeover of Greymac Trust, Seaway Trust and related companies by the Ontario government early in 1983.

"It's a great yarn, and Belford tells it well . . . in cogent, fast-moving style." — Kitchener-Waterloo *Record*.
"A fascinating and disturbing look at the issues raised by the trust company affair." — Ottawa *Citizen*.

The Arrow
James Dow

The Arrow was a supersonic Canadian supersonic fighter that, in the 1950s, promised to fly faster than anything had before. When it was scrapped by the Diefenbaker government in 1959, many saw it as an end both to Canadian efforts to emerge from the shadows of the U.K. and U.S. as an industrialized nation, and to the possibility of an independent Canadian defence policy. Working from a wide range of sources, James Dow reconstructs this remarkable chapter in Canadian history.

The Developers
James Lorimer

A controversial bestseller, *The Developers* is a revealing account of the men and the companies that have radically changed the shape and size of Canadian cities since the Second World War. Portraits of developers like Ottawa's Robert Campeau and Toronto's Bruce McLaughlin are coupled with an in-depth look at the huge development corporations like Genstar and Cadillac Fairview.

"Brilliantly written." — *Financial Post*

"An impressive look at the Canadian city. . . . It's an important book." — *Globe and Mail*

Bassett
Maggie Siggins

This telling biography of John Bassett provides a fascinating behind-the-scenes look at the worlds of politics, publishing, business and sports in which Bassett has wheeled and dealed for over four decades. Maggie Siggins interviewed more than 200 of Bassett's friends, family, business associates, critics and enemies to piece together a public career that includes masterminding the rise and fall of the Toronto *Telegram* and the building of a media empire.

"*Bassett's* information on the sports-newspaper-and-TV business world is first-rate, indeed excellent." — Larry Zolf, *Montreal Gazette*.

"This is an important book because it documents the cynicism and opportunism which too often prevail among our publishing and broadcasting moguls." — *Globe and Mail*

Voyage of the Iceberg
The Story of the Iceberg that Sank the Titanic
Richard Brown

This book has established Richard Brown in the ranks of Canada's distinguished nature writers. It is the story of the *Titanic*, and of history's most infamous iceberg. But there is much more in *Voyage of the Iceberg*. As the iceberg makes its way from Baffin Bay to the fateful meeting in the North Atlantic, it passes through many other lives — of Inuit, whales, whalers and sealers — that Brown portrays in quiet, compelling prose. The acclaim this richly illustrated book has received in Canada has been echoed by its success in American and British editions.

"Lilting, lyrical and loving . . . a smashing little book." — Vancouver *Province*.

"Eminently worthwhile reading." — Frank Rasky, *Books in Canada*.

Willie: A Romance
Heather Robertson

Heather Robertson's historical novel about Mackenzie King and Ottawa during the national trauma of the Great War has been welcomed with accolades from all corners. It has been described as "brilliant" (*Maclean's*), "totally charming, funny and real" (*Chatelaine*), "a triumph" (William French, *Globe and Mail*) and "a Canadian *Gone with the Wind*" (Montreal *Gazette*).

"The most extraordinary Canadian book of this fall season. . . rich, detailed and vivid." — Peter Gzowski, CBC *Morningside*.

"A fascinating, entertaining, and important book that carries the unmistakable stamp of a true writer's passion." — *Books in Canada*.

Printed in Canada